Early Modern Philosophy

Blackwell Readings in the History of Philosophy

Series Editors: Fritz Allhoff and Anand Jayprakash Vaidya

The volumes in this series provide concise and representative selections of key texts from the history of philosophy. Expertly edited and introduced by established scholars, each volume represents a particular philosophical era, replete with important selections of the most influential work in metaphysics, epistemology, moral and political philosophy, and the philosophy of science and religion.

1. *Ancient Philosophy: Essential Readings with Commentary*
Edited by Nicholas Smith with Fritz Allhoff and Anand Jayprakash Vaidya

2. *Medieval Philosophy: Essential Readings with Commentary*
Edited by Gyula Klima with Fritz Allhoff and Anand Jayprakash Vaidya

3. *Early Modern Philosophy: Essential Readings with Commentary*
Edited by A. P. Martinich with Fritz Allhoff and Anand Jayprakash Vaidya

4. *Late Modern Philosophy: Essential Readings with Commentary*
Edited by Elizabeth S. Radcliffe and Richard McCarty with Fritz Allhoff and Anand Jayprakash Vaidya

Early Modern Philosophy

Essential Readings with Commentary

Edited by

A. P. Martinich

with Fritz Allhoff and Anand Jayprakash Vaidya

Blackwell
Publishing

BLACKWELL PUBLISHING
350 Main Street, Malden, MA 02148-5020, USA
9600 Garsington Road, Oxford OX4 2DQ, UK
550 Swanston Street, Carlton, Victoria 3053, Australia

First published 2007 by Blackwell Publishing Ltd

1 2007

Library of Congress Cataloging-in-Publication Data

Early modern philosophy : essential readings with commentary / edited by A. P. Martinich; with Fritz Allhoff and Anand Jayprakash Vaidya. – 1st ed.
p. cm. — (Blackwell readings in the history of philosophy)
Includes bibliographical references and index.
ISBN-13: 978-1-4051-3566-5 (hardcover : alk. paper)
ISBN-10: 1-4051-3566-2 (hardcover : alk. paper)
ISBN-13: 978-1-4051-3567-2 (pbk. : alk. paper)
ISBN-10: 1-4051-3567-0 (pbk.: alk. paper) 1. Philosophy, Modern. I. Martinich, Aloysius. II. Allhoff, Fritz. III. Vaidya, Anand. IV. Series.

B791.E28 2006
190—dc22

2006016981

A catalogue record for this title is available from the British Library.

Set in 10/12.5pt Dante
by Graphicraft Limited, Hong Kong
Printed and bound in Great Britain
by TJ International Ltd, Padstow, Cornwall

The publisher's policy is to use permanent paper from mills that operate a sustainable forestry policy, and which has been manufactured from pulp processed using acid-free and elementary chlorine-free practices. Furthermore, the publisher ensures that the text paper and cover board used have met acceptable environmental accreditation standards.

For further information on
Blackwell Publishing, visit our website:
www.blackwellpublishing.com

To the Memory of Richard H. Popkin
Philosopher, Historian, Teacher, Friend

Contents

Preface

This anthology can be used either in a historically oriented introduction to Western philosophy or in a course on early modern philosophy, especially one that concentrates on the rationalists. When feasible, complete works have been included. There is more than enough material for use in either a quarter or semester course.

Because of its length, it is likely that few people will read all of this book; even fewer will read it from front to back, and certainly no one will read it all in one sitting. With these things in mind, some redundancy has been built in to my commentaries. For example, skepticism is discussed in several places. But each discussion differs in certain respects. This practice has the advantage that a reader who does not understand what a concept means from one explanation of it may be able to understand it by reading another one.

Modern philosophy was one of my first loves in philosophy. I hope readers of this book will find the philosophers represented here as intriguing and exhilarating as I did.

I would want to thank Max Rosenkrantz, Long Beach State University, and Jo Ann Carson, Texas State University, for their comments on the introductions. My editors Jeff Dean and Danielle Descoteaux have been helpful throughout the process. I also want to thank Janet Moth for her careful and thorough editing of the introductions and selections.

A.P.M.

Acknowledgments

Text Credits

The editors and publisher gratefully acknowledge the permission granted to reproduce the copyright material in this book:

1: Michel de Montaigne, "Apology for Raymond Sebond," pp. 320–7, 330–1, 333, 361–2, 364, 370–5, 404–6, 420–1, 428, 430, 443–6, 452–7 from *The Complete Essays of Montaigne* (Stanford: Stanford University Press, 1958). © 1943 by Donald M. Frame, 1957, 1958 by the Board of Trustees of the Leland Stanford Junior University. Renewed 1971, 1976. All rights reserved. Reprinted by permission of Stanford University Press, <www.sup.org>.

2: Francis Bacon, "The New Organon and Related Writings," preface and excerpts from aphorisms: pp. iii, xiv, xv, xix, xxxviii, xxxix, xl, xli, xlii, xliii, xliv, xlv, xlvi, xlvii, xlviii, l, li, lii, liii, liv, lv, lviii, lix, lx, lxi, lxii, lxiv, lxv, lxvii, lxviii, lxx from *The New Organon and Related Writings* (Indianapolis: Bobbs Merrill Co., 1960).

3: Galileo Galilei, "Galileo Galilei to the Most Serene Grand Duchess Mother," pp. 177, 179–86, 273–8 from Stillman Drake, *Discoveries and Opinions of Galileo* (New York: Doubleday Anchor Books, 1957). © 1957 by Stillman Drake. Reprinted by permission of Doubleday, a division of Random House, Inc.

4: René Descartes, "Discourse on the Method of Rightly Conducting the Reason and Seeking for Truth in the Sciences," excerpts from Parts 1–3 of *Discourse On the Method of Rightly Conducting the Reason and Seeking for Truth in the Sciences* (Cambridge: Cambridge University Press, 1911). © 1911 by Cambridge University Press. Reprinted by permission of the publisher.

5: Thomas Hobbes, "Introduction, Chapters 1, 2, 6," pp. 9, 13, 14–17, 40–9 from Thomas Hobbes *Leviathan*, ed. A. P. Martinich (Peterborough, Ont.: Broadview Press, 2002). © 2002 by Broadview Press. Reprinted by permission of the editor and Broadview Press.

6: Isaac Newton, "Definitions; Axioms, or Laws of Motion; Rules of Reasoning in Philosophy," pp. 2–3, 13–14, 398–400 from Florian Cajori, *Sir Isaac Newton's Mathematical Principles of Natural Philosophy and His History of the World, vols I and II* (Berkeley: University of California Press, 1962).

7: René Descartes, "The Meditations," pp. 133–99 from *The Meditations* (Cambridge: Cambridge University Press, 1911). © 1911 by Cambridge University Press. Reprinted by permission of the publisher.

8: René Descartes, "Reply to Objections II," pp. 38–9, 42, and "Arguments Demonstrating the Existence of God . . . ," pp. 52–9 from *The Philosophical Works of Descartes, vols I and II* (Cambridge: Cambridge University Press, 1911). © 1911 by Cambridge University Press. Reprinted by permission of the publisher.

9: Thomas Hobbes, "The Third Set of Objections with the Author's Reply," pp. 61, 66–8 from *The Philosophical Works of Descartes, vols I and II* (Cambridge: Cambridge University Press, 1911). Copyright © 1911 by Cambridge University Press. Reprinted by permission of the publisher.

10: Antoine Arnauld, "Fourth Set of Objections and Replies," pp. 92 (+1) from *The Philosophical Works of Descartes, vols I and II* (Cambridge: Cambridge University Press, 1911). © 1911 by Cambridge University Press. Reprinted by permission of the publisher.

11: Pierre Gassendi, "Fifth Set of Objections and Replies," pp. 185–6, 228–9 from *The Philosophical Works of Descartes, vols I and II* (Dover: Dover Publications [public domain], 1961). © 1911 by Cambridge University Press. Reprinted by permission of the publisher.

12: René Descartes, "Letters to and from Princess Elizabeth de Bohemia," pp. 274–82 from Elizabeth Anscombe and Peter T. Geach, *Descartes: Philosophical Writings*, 1e (Indianapolis: Bobbs-Merrill Educational Publishing, 1954). © 1971. Reprinted by permission of Pearson Education, Inc., Upper Saddle River, NJ.

13: Blaise Pascal, pp. 23, 64–9, 79 (+2) from *Pascal's Pensées* (New York: E. P. Dutton & Co., Inc. 1958). © 1958. Reprinted by permission of Everyman's Library, Northburgh House, 10 Northburgh Street, London, EC1V 0AT.

14: Benedict Spinoza, "The Ethics," pp. 85–152, 603–17 from *The Collected Works of Spinoza*, 1e (Princeton: Princeton University Press, 1985). © 1985 by Princeton University Press. Reprinted by permission of the publisher.

15: Nicolas Malebranche, "Book III, Part II: The Pure Understanding. The Nature of Ideas. Chapter One, Two, Three, Four, Six and Seven," pp. 217–27, 230–4, 236–9 from Thomas M. Lennon and Paul J. Olscamp, *The Search After Truth* (Columbus: Ohio State University Press, 1980). © 1980 by Thomas M. Lennon and Paul J. Olscamp. Reprinted by permission of the authors.

16: G. W. F. Leibniz, "Discourse on Metaphysics," pp. 3–63 from Baron Gottfried Wilhelm von Leibniz, *Basic Writings*, trans. George R. Montgomery (La Salle, ILL: The Open Court Publishing Company, 1902).

17: G. W. F. Leibniz, "The Theodicy: Abridgment of the Argument," pp. 509–20 from *Leibniz: Selections*, ed. Philip P. Wiener (New York: Charles Scribner's Sons, 1951). © 1951 by Marjorie Wiener and Leonard S. Wiener. Reprinted by permission of Pearson Education, Inc, Upper Saddle River, NJ.

18: G. W. F. Leibniz, "The Monadology," pp. 251–72 from Baron Gottfried Wilhelm von Leibniz, *Basic Writings*, trans. George R. Montgomery (La Salle, ILL: The Open Court Publishing Company, 1902).

19: Niccolò Machiavelli, "The Prince," pp. 44, 53–4, 56–67, 91–4 from *The Prince and The Discourses* (New York: The Modern Library, 1950).

20: Thomas Hobbes, pp. 93–123, 125–9, 130–5, 149–50 from Thomas Hobbes, *Leviathan*, ed. A. P. Martinich (Peterborough, Ont.: Broadview Press, 2002). © 2002 by Broadview Press. Reprinted by permission of the editor and Broadview Press.

21: Samuel Pufendorf, "Book I and II," pp. 17, 27–31, 33–5, 115–18, 132–4, 136–9 from James Tully, *On the Duty of Man and Citizen According to Natural Law* (Cambridge: Cambridge University Press, 1991). © 1991 by Cambridge University Press. Reprinted by permission of the publisher.

Every effort has been made to trace copyright holders and to obtain their permission for the use of copyright material. The publisher apologizes for any errors or omissions in the above list and would be grateful if notified of any corrections that should be incorporated in future reprints or editions of this book.

General Introduction

Studying early modern European philosophy is both a good way to discover what philosophy is and a good way to broaden and deepen one's knowledge of philosophy because early modern philosophers usually explain the meanings of their technical terms relatively clearly and deal with a broad range of the basic issues in philosophy. This anthology is designed to serve as a textbook for either an introductory course in philosophy or a survey of early modern European philosophy. It contains most of the best philosophy written during that period, roughly from the sixteenth century to the first quarter of the eighteenth century. It may seem odd that people and events more than 300 years old could count as modern, but in philosophy, a century ago is like yesterday.

Western philosophy for the most part consists of insightful remarks about the nature of reality or human beings ("Everything changes" or "The unexamined life is not worth living," or "No decision is a decision"), analyses of fundamental concepts ("Knowledge is justified true belief"), and systematic treatments of the basic structure of reality ("Everything is a body" or "Only minds and ideas exist").

Systematic treatments of reality predominate among the great rationalist philosophers of the early modern period, the philosophers on whom this volume focuses. Rationalism is the most important of the three focuses of this volume (parts II and III). René Descartes, Benedict Spinoza, Nicolas Malebranche, and Gottfried Leibniz are paradigmatic rationalists and systematizers. Rationalists are contrasted with empiricists, who are the focus of volume 4 of this series. The contrast between rationalism and empiricism will be discussed in section 1 below.

The second focus of this volume is philosophical and scientific method. This topic was extremely important to early modern philosophers because their rejection of scholastic philosophy, the dominant philosophy of the Middle Ages, was accompanied by ideas of new ways of doing philosophy and science. Many of these new ways are discussed in part I. Michel de Montaigne (1533–92) uses skeptical arguments to show that human knowledge is impossible. Francis Bacon advocates an empirical method of gathering data but warns against various prejudices endemic to human beings, prejudices which interfere with reasoning. Galileo argues that the scientific view of things shows that qualitative properties, such as being colored, do not exist. Descartes advises that complex problems be broken down into their simplest components, and these components should then be solved individually. Hobbes recommends breaking down complex concepts into simple concepts that mention only the movement of bodies toward or away from something. Finally, the basic laws and axioms of Isaac Newton's physics are presented because of the importance of his results for philosophy as much as science.

The third focus is on political philosophy. This volume contains selections from Niccolò Machiavelli (1469–1527), Thomas Hobbes (1588–1679), and Samuel Pufendorf (1632–94). Although Machiavelli is part of the Italian Renaissance world, his thought is modern because he concentrated on how to ensure "the actualization of the right [political] order," in contrast, say, with Plato or Aristotle, who thought that it was worthwhile to describe what an ideal city or state would be like (see Strauss in Tarcov and Pangle 1987: 917). Also, Machiavelli's political views are neither part of nor supported by any theological system, as most medieval theories were. His advice to rulers in *The Prince* is motivated completely by expediency. He answers the question, "What is the best way for a ruler to retain power?" Hobbes very likely read Machiavelli, as did other seventeenth-century theorists. Hobbes is important because of the genius displayed in his political philosophy, which he claimed was scientific, in the same sense that physics is scientific. According to Hobbes, the natural condition of human beings is dreadful. This view was too harsh for Samuel Pufendorf and others. Pufendorf tried to extract what was scientific in Hobbes's philosophy from what was offensive to conventional opinion. For example, Pufendorf begins his political philosophy in *The Whole Duty of Man* with a definition of "duty," followed by a definition of law and an assertion of the free will of human beings, while the natural condition of human beings, which is an undesirable condition, is not formally introduced until Book II .

In this introduction I will say something about what rationalism is in order to orient the reader conceptually, but also in order to introduce the reader to a few basic philosophical concepts that are relevant to understanding the selections (section 4). Before doing that, I will devote sections 1–3 to discussing the cultural and intellectual influences on early modern philosophy.

My approach is historical for four reasons. First, all concepts and values arise from a person's experience, and this experience consists of things either (a) occurring during a person's life or (b) handed down from the past. Since all the philosophers in this book are long dead, they are part of (b) for us; moreover, what was (a) for them is also part of (b) for us. So in order to understand their concepts and values, we need to know something about their experiences. To know what they experienced, we need to know some history.

Second, to understand what a philosopher (or any author) meant is to know what that philosopher believed or intended you to believe. What the philosopher believed or intended you to believe is conveyed by his words, and the words he used have a specific sense and reference. To take a very simple example, if an author wrote, "Lee went to the bank," then a complete understanding of what he meant must include knowing whether the word "bank" has the sense "financial institution" or "edge of a river," and, on the supposition that it is the former, knowing which particular financial institution is being referred to, say, the bank on the southeast corner of Guadalupe and 22nd St.[1] Knowing these things depends upon

1 It's worth mentioning that one may figure out what sense "bank" has by first figuring out what the speaker is referring to, for example, if the speaker was standing in front of a financial institution.

knowing about the culture within which the author lived. We usually don't think about these facts because so much of what most of us read is about our own time and culture. But in any investigation of a long gone culture, this information is essential.

Also, what a philosopher (or any author) writes about is going to be influenced by the most important events in his culture. No twenty-first-century Western philosopher is trying to *refute* the theory of absolute sovereignty or the hylomorphic theory of Aristotle, because those are not important issues today. If a philosopher is writing about political philosophy or the philosophy of science, he or she will very probably be thinking specifically about the governments and the actual scientific theories that are familiar to him or her. Neither Machiavelli, Hobbes, Locke, nor Pufendorf were thinking about the kind of popular democracies that exist in North America or western Europe today. Such things were not even imagined by them. Descartes, Gassendi, Spinoza, and Leibniz were not thinking about contemporary atomic theory, even though Gassendi believed in atoms and Leibniz had monads, entities so tiny they lacked mass. Nor were they thinking about relativity theory even though Leibniz thought that space was relative. (Newton thought that it was absolute.) So in order to understand what things early modern philosophers were thinking about, we need to know something about what was important to them. Context matters. The large array of readings from major and minor philosophers in this anthology is intended to give the reader a better sense of the context of early modern philosophy. My general point is that what a philosopher might mean by a text is made more or less probable by what his experience has been. So, in order to arrive at a more or less probably correct understanding of what the philosopher meant, we need to know something about his experience.

The third reason to treat early modern philosophy historically is that part of being educated (or cultured, in contrast with being part of a culture) is to know something about the great events and thoughts of the past. Fourth, the history of this period is fascinating. Few eras contain greater events and thoughts or more colorful figures than the early modern period.

1 The Beginning and End of Modern Philosophy

Although the beginnings and endings of all historical periods are to some extent arbitrary, identifying certain events as initiating and terminating an epoch often helps one to understand and organize the events within that span of time. If an epoch always begins with some great event, then the publication of Descartes's *Meditations on First Philosophy* in 1641 by general consensus begins modern philosophy. But it would be a mistake to give an important event too much importance. Two major aspects of Descartes's philosophy, namely, skepticism and the supposed discovery of an adequate response to skepticism, can be found in his predecessors.[2] Desiderius Erasmus (ca. 1466–1536), a great scholar and an important opponent of Martin Luther (1483–1546), pointed out the skeptical implications of Luther's view and recommended submission to the authority of the Roman Catholic Church as its solution. Erasmus also defended free will, as Descartes did.

Because this volume treats only early modern philosophy, it is not necessary to say when modern philosophy ends. This is fortunate because there is no work comparable to Descartes's *Meditations* to mark either the end of modern philosophy or the beginning of a new era for European philosophy (contemporary philosophy). The distinction between early and later

2 Skepticism is explained in more detail in section 3 below. For the time being, skepticism may be understood as doubt that reason is able to lead people to knowledge.

modern philosophy is even more artificial than the distinction between ancient and medieval or medieval and modern. It is dictated more by what can be covered in an academic quarter or semester than it is by some dramatic and philosophical turn of events. For us, the last great early modern philosopher is simply stipulated as being Gottfried Leibniz (1646–1716).

Let's now consider the intellectual and cultural background to early modern philosophy.

2 Influences on Modern Philosophy: Science, Religion, and Politics

Science

Modern science can be said to begin with the heliocentric theory of the Polish cleric Nicolaus Copernicus (1473–1543). According to Copernicus, who propounded the theory around 1512, the earth goes around the sun, rather than the sun going around the earth, as the Ptolemaic theory asserted. Copernicus published his view in *De revolutionibus orbium coelestium* (1543). His view was condemned by the Church in due time, because it contradicted the biblical view of the cosmos. So powerful was confidence in the Bible and one's own senses, not to mention the virtues of the Ptolemaic system, that many educated people refused to believe the heliocentric theory even a century later. However, the truth has a way of prevailing, and other astronomers accepted Copernicus's view and then refined it. One of the most important of these was Johannes Kepler (1571–1630), who proved that the orbits of planets are elliptical. Copernicus had thought that they were circular.

The science of astronomy was greatly enhanced by the discovery of the telescope. Galileo Galilei (1564–1642) made his own and used it to discover that there were mountains on the moon. This undercut one of the principal claims of pre-modern science, namely, that astronomical bodies were made of a kind of substance different from those on earth. The four earthly substances were fire, air, water, and earth. The fifth thing or essence was hence the "quintessence." He also discovered that bodies do not fall at a speed proportional to their weight, and devised equations that described the motion of various moving objects. His mathematical treatment of physical phenomena began to spell the end of Aristotelian physics. Because much of his research was sponsored by military leaders, his discovery that the path of a projectile is a parabola came from experimenting with firing cannon balls. His *Dialogue Concerning the Two Chief World Systems* (1632) defended the Copernican system and eventually led him to be imprisoned by the Inquisition.

In addition to physics and astronomy, other sciences were making progress. William Harvey (1578–1657) was the first to discover how blood is pumped through the arteries and returned to the heart through the veins. This included his discovery that arteries contain small flaps of skin which allow the pumping blood to flow away from the heart and inhibits it from flowing backward toward the heart. Harvey also performed dissections on various animals, such as deer. Hobbes, a friend of Harvey, was present at some of these dissections. Completeness also requires me to mention that some experiments involved vivisection of dogs, and other practices now understood to be cruel. One concerns some experiments by Robert Boyle (1627–91) to create a vacuum in a jar. The general strategy was to rig a pump on a glass globe and pump the air out of it. Sometimes a small dog was placed in the jar. As the air was removed the dog first became listless, then unconscious, and then died. Sometimes when the dog became unconscious, air was allowed to re-enter the globe and the dog regained consciousness. Out of these experiments, Boyle came to discover what was later called Boyle's gas law, namely, that the pressure of a gas is inversely related to its volume.

Boyle was part of the Royal Society, begun in 1661, which was dedicated to the advancement of science. Because it was not clear what was scientific and what was not, how to conduct experiments and how to collect data that would be scientifically fruitful, the early records of the society include all sorts of bizarre, false, and trivial information and speculation. It's important to note how internationally oriented the Royal Society was. Its first secretary, Henry Oldenburg, corresponded with many Continental intellectuals, such as Spinoza.

The last scientist to be mentioned as important to early modern philosophy is Isaac Newton (1642–1727), Lucasian Professor of Natural Philosophy at Cambridge University. His *Philosophiae naturalis principia mathematica* (*Mathematical Principles of Natural Philosophy*, 1687) was one of the two or three greatest works of physics in human history. It showed how universal gravitation could explain both the motion of objects close to the earth, including the tides, and the motion of heavenly bodies, planets, moons, and comets. His particle theory of light was the standard one until the nineteenth century. Along with Leibniz, he was a co-discoverer of the infinitesimal calculus, and formulated his famous three laws of motion, which had been anticipated by Galileo. Galileo, Descartes, Gassendi, Christian Huygens, and Hobbes all had stated some law of inertia before Newton.

Religion

The second great influence on modern philosophy was religion. Martin Luther, who has already been mentioned, was far from being the first person to challenge the doctrine and practices of the Roman Catholic Church. Various heretics and reformers were active in western European countries in the Middle Ages and the Renaissance. What distinguishes Luther from the others is that his challenge to the Church had more obvious, lasting, widespread consequences for politics, philosophy, and, of course, religion.

After Luther posted his 95 theses on the cathedral door of Wittenberg in 1517, the Church responded by calling in one of its best polemicists, Jon von Eck, to suppress Luther's ideas by defeating him in debate. The attempt failed. So did the attempt of other champions of the Church. One of the most notable was Erasmus, as mentioned above. He debated Luther on the issue of free will. Erasmus was for it and Luther against it. Luther was promoting the ideas that those who are saved are saved by grace alone (*sola gratia*) and that God inscrutably decides who they will be. "Grace" means gift. So salvation is a gift from God, and not the result of any merit that may accrue to a person by doing good works. It is not always easy in early modern philosophy to distinguish sharply between theological and philosophical disputes. For example, when Hobbes debated with Bishop John Bramhall about free will, he often appealed to the teaching of Luther and denied that the will was free, while Bramhall championed the same position as Erasmus. Because Luther and Hobbes denied that the will was free, they thought that people were predestined. Leibniz tried to combine free will with predestination by arguing that people have free will but, given that God creates a particular possible world, how the people in that world act is predetermined by that creation.

The general religious turmoil of the seventeenth century contributed to a decline in religious belief. Francis Bacon has astutely observed in his essay "Of Atheism" that religious divisions contribute to atheism. If many different people believe in many different religions, religion begins to appear to be an ungrounded opinion, not something known. An alternative to this unhappy choice between maintaining that religious belief is either opinion or knowledge, is the view that the foundation of religion is faith, as both Luther and Hobbes said.

Religious belief was also challenged by a growing awareness of non-Christian religions. The Ottoman empire, which captured Hungary and a large part of the Balkan peninsula in the sixteenth century, and continued to threaten western Europe in the seventeenth century, was Muslim. So European intellectuals paid some attention to the existence of Islam, according to which Christianity had been superseded. Historical studies revealed that Judaism and Christianity were indebted to and in many ways not very different from some pagan religions. These facts led intellectuals to wonder whether a rational case could be made for any revealed religion.

Also important was the fact that some Christians and Jews were confident that the coming of the messiah was imminent. They downplayed their disagreement about whether it would be the messiah's first or second arrival. Although it is conventional to think of scientists as rational agents free of all religious mystery, the truth is quite different. John Napier (1550–1617) invented the logarithm as part of his project of calculating the date of the impending end of the world. He explained his views in *Plaine Discovery of the whole Revelation of Saint John . . .* (1593). Isaac Newton devoted a large part of his life to interpreting the biblical books of Daniel and Revelation with the intention of predicting the second coming of the messiah. He eventually placed it in the middle of the nineteenth century.[3]

Religious divisions were also one of the causes of the Thirty Years War (1618–48), often called the last religious war in Europe. The fighting between Protestants and Roman Catholics in Northern Ireland and other relatively localized conflicts do not count as wars to those at a safe distance. The Thirty Years War ended with the Peace of Westphalia (1648), according to which the religion of the people would be the same as the religion of the prince (*cujus regio ejus religio*). Frenchmen are Catholics, Swedes are Lutherans, and so on. Religion became more regional and more closely associated with a nation. It also provided an additional rationalization for going to war. Roman Catholic France might use religion to justify going to war against the Protestant United Provinces (the Netherlands), and vice versa. Of course, if France and the United Provinces allied to fight Roman Catholic Spain, the religious issue would not be raised. For all of its faults, one benefit of the Roman Catholic Church prior to the Reformation was that it was an international organization that could counteract aggressive actions taken by one state against another. Although it did not have great armies, it did have the use of interdicts and other ecclesiastical penalties, which had some effect as long as people believed they had efficacy.

Politics

The effect of politics on political philosophy, almost nonexistent in the case of Anglo-American philosophy during the last century, was substantial during the early modern period.

Spinoza was politically engaged in Holland. He was a friend of Jan de Witt, a leader of the republican[4] party and an opponent of the House of Orange. When William of Orange, the future William III of England, became *stadtholder*, de Witt resigned his position. He, along

3 James E. Force, "Newton's God of Dominion," in James E. Force and Richard H. Popkin, *Essays on the Context, Nature, and Influence of Isaac Newton's Theology* (Dordrecht: Kluwer Academic Publishers, 1990), p. 82.

4 There are two aspects of republicanism. One is that political power is distributed to a large number of citizens in various offices, in order to avoid tyranny. The other is that participation in public affairs is considered the greatest virtue. The idea originated in ancient Greece and Rome but was renewed in the Renaissance and early modern period, notably by Machiavelli.

with his brother, was later killed by a mob. So disgusted was Spinoza with the mob that he wanted to place a placard at the site of the crime with the words *ultimi barbarorum*, "the greatest of barbarians."

Spinoza's *Tractatus Theologico-Politicus* (1670) was motivated by the various conflicts between political factions and religious authorities, proponents and opponents of freedom. Spinoza favored freedom. The title page of the *Tractatus* includes the declaration that "perfect liberty" is compatible with "the peace of the state" and that "to take away such liberty is to destroy the public peace and even piety itself." Spinoza argued explicitly for freedom of speech and religion. His main enemies were the Calvinist clergy, who appealed to the Bible to defend their intolerance.

Gottfried Wilhelm von Leibniz engaged in many political activities. Early in his career, he wrote a 360-page dissertation which demonstrated in mathematico-deductive form that the Poles should choose Count Philipp Wilhelm von Neuberg as their next king. They didn't. Leibniz served as a diplomat for the elector of Mainz, and was later employed by the duke of Brunswick. He also tried to convince Louis XIV to invade Egypt. His purpose was less to vanquish the Muslims and more to relieve French pressure on Germany. He worked hard to reunite Protestants and Roman Catholics, but to no avail. His goal was to ease political tensions among the Christian nations of Europe.

One of Leibniz's triumphs was to persuade the elector of Brandenburg to establish a scientific academy in Berlin. He became its first president in 1700. Leibniz was a workaholic, writing hundreds of articles and thousands of letters. Many of his friends and correspondents were women. Sophie Charlotte, who became queen of Prussia in 1701, helped him clarify his thoughts, and his *Theodicy* was in effect written for her. All of this being said, it is not clear how these political activities influenced the content of his philosophy.

The two clearest cases of political influence on philosophical content involve the two greatest English philosophers of the seventeenth century, Thomas Hobbes and John Locke. In 1640, trouble was brewing in England. Hobbes, who was a candidate for a seat in the Short Parliament but was not selected, circulated the manuscript of his first major political work, *Elements of Philosophy, Natural and Politic*, about the time that the Short Parliament was breaking up.[5] Because it was a defense of the king, it earned him enemies in parliament. Consequently, when the Long Parliament began in late 1640 Hobbes fled to France, where he lived for a decade, and where he published his second major work, *De Cive* (*On the Citizen*) in 1642, with a second, expanded, edition appearing in 1647. The English Civil War raged from 1642 until 1649, when a remnant of the Long Parliament tried and executed Charles I. This last event was probably a partial motive for Hobbes to write his greatest work, *Leviathan* (1651). In it, Hobbes argues for absolute sovereignty, the kind of sovereignty that Charles had claimed for himself. After the execution of the king and the formation of a new government, the Commonwealth, the most pressing questions for Englishmen were "What constitutes a legitimate government?" "Is any entity that has the power to enforce laws and provide protection to people legitimate, or do people have to agree to accept that power as government?" Hobbes answered those questions in *Leviathan*.

5 The Short Parliament lasted from April 13 to May 5, 1640. Charles II called it in order to get support for his war against Scotland. He dissolved it because of the fierce criticisms of his policies that emanated from it. Because he needed money for his war, he called another parliament, which began in November 3, 1640 and was not finally dissolved until 1660. In between were the English Civil War (1642–9) and the Commonwealth (1649–60).

In 1660 the monarchy was restored in England because the Commonwealth had proven to be ineffective. Charles II was a nominal member of the Church of England, not to mention its head, but he was quite sympathetic to Roman Catholics. His brother James, duke of York, and next in line to become king, was an ardent Roman Catholic, but the large majority of English people did not want a Roman Catholic monarch. In the late 1670s and early 1680s, there were several attempts, both parliamentary and extra-parliamentary – planned assassinations – to get rid of James, who became king in 1685. His reign was as bad as the Protestants had feared, and he fled the country in 1688 (the year of the Glorious Revolution) when William of Orange invaded England. William, now King William III, had the support of John Locke, who said in the preface to his *Two Treatises of Government* that he wrote it "to establish the Throne of our Great Restorer, Our present King William; to make good his Title, in the Consent of the People, which . . . [is] the only one of all lawful Governments." In fact, most of that book had been written between 1679 and 1683 as a series of political tracts supporting the efforts of the earl of Shaftesbury and others to prevent James II from becoming king. Because of the themes and tone of *The Two Treatises*, some scholars do not even consider it a work of political philosophy. But the philosophical scholarship on that book shows that it is.

Much more could be said about the influence of politics on philosophy. For example, Niccolò Machiavelli served as defense secretary to the Florentine republic and was imprisoned by the Medicis for his political affiliations; and Samuel Pufendorf wrote *De statu imperii germanici, liber unus* (*On the State of the German Empire, Book One*, 1667) to attack the Holy Roman Empire, and *De habitu religionis christianae ad vitam civilem* (*On the Character of the Christian Religion for Civil Life*, 1687) to clarify the relationship between Church and state. In the latter, he distinguishes between the supreme jurisdiction that the civil state has over the Church and the ecclesiastical power within the Church, a distinction that Prussia used to justify its authority over the Church. These examples amply illustrate the interconnections between philosophy and politics in the early modern period.

3 Some Consequences for Early Modern Philosophy of Scientific and Religious Events

Two of the most conspicuous consequences for philosophy of the scientific and religious events described above are (1) a desire on the part of philosophers to be scientific, and (2) a worry about skepticism. Concerning (1), Hobbes devised a plan to describe all of reality scientifically. The project, called Elementa Philosophiae, had three parts: *De Corpore* (1655), which discussed logic, scientific method, geometry, and physics, *De Homine* (1658), which treated human beings scientifically, and *De Cive* (1642, 1647), which discussed moral and political philosophy. For Hobbes geometry was the science par excellence, and he met or knew many of the greatest scientists of his age, including Galileo, Harvey, and Boyle. Descartes was an excellent mathematician, the originator of the Cartesian coordinate system; he worked on geometry and optics, wrote *Discourse on the Method of Rightly Conducting One's Reason and Seeking the Truth in the Sciences* (1637), and laid out his physics in *The World*. Blaise Pascal (1623–62) also did impressive work in mathematics and physics on the equilibrium in fluids. Leibniz was a co-founder of the infinitesimal calculus. Leibniz and Newton were rivals, and the rivalry was played out in a long debate between Leibniz and Clarke, who was Newton's representative, about whether space was relative (Leibniz's position) or absolute (Newton's position). Leibniz and Newton also disagreed about the existence of vacuums: while Newton thought they existed, Leibniz thought there was no good evidence for them. Concerning the experiments with air pumps, Leibniz observed that, since light and magnetism can pass through glass, why shouldn't small bits of air? A nice point, even though factually mistaken.

Concerning (2), there is a definite irony in the fact that one of the periods of greatest scientific progress was also one in which skepticism exercised philosophers most. (Something similar could be said about the last century of philosophy.) The problem of skepticism is the problem of figuring out whether human beings know anything, and if they do, how and what they know. There are basically two kinds of skeptics, Academic and Pyrrhonist (see the introduction to part I for the origin of these terms). The Academic skeptic asserts that nothing can be known. Academic skepticism is also known as dogmatic skepticism because, by asserting that nothing is known, the skeptic has a dogma, a teaching. Academic skepticism appears to be easy to refute. By asserting that nothing is known the Academic skeptic is claiming to know something. But if he knows something, then it is false that nothing is known. An Academic skeptic could revise his position by asserting that he knows nothing except that he knows nothing. But even this revision puts his view at risk. How does he know that he knows nothing except that he knows nothing? If he says that he infers it from the fact that philosophers disagree about almost everything, that a round tower viewed from afar looks square, that a hot hand placed in tepid water has the sensation of coolness and a cold hand placed in the same water has the sensation of warmness, that morals differ from society to society, the critic can point out that the Academic skeptic is relying on logic or the justifiability of induction, and thus claims to know more than he has admitted to.

The Pyrrhonist is not so easy to defeat. He asserts nothing. The Pyrrhonist simply raises possibilities that contradict any assertion that anyone else makes. If someone says, "I know that I have a hand because I see it," the Pyrrhonist may say, "Perhaps you have a brain tumor or perhaps what looks like a hand is an artificial limb attached to your wrist during a coma." The Pyrrhonist is not saying that these are in fact true. The Pyrrhonist is asserting nothing, merely getting his opponents to see that they are not justified in thinking that they know anything. In its original ancient form, Pyrrhonism had an ethical purpose. The regimen of questioning everything was supposed to induce a state of emotional tranquility (*ataraxia*), which would lead one to follow the conventions of one's society. Although there seems to be no good reason to follow the conventions of one's society simply because one is tranquil, that was the Pyrrhonist position.

Three modern religious responses to skepticism may be mentioned. Luther and other Protestants thought that the inability of people to discover truth through reason should lead Christians to truth by listening to their conscience. The Holy Spirit would enlighten them. Many Roman Catholic theologians urged that, because people cannot themselves know by reason what the truth is, they should trust in what the Church tells them, for the Church is guided by the Holy Spirit. Montaigne advocated a Christian Pyrrhonist solution to the problem. People should believe what is taught by the religion into which they were born.

No one was convinced by these responses who did not want to be convinced. Descartes, a better philosopher than the people mentioned in the preceding paragraph, came up with a more sophisticated solution. His strategy was to give the skeptic enough rope to hang himself. After enumerating all the classes of propositions that may be doubted, Descartes called attention to the following fact. In the very experience of doubting, it is indisputable that the person doubting exists. So skepticism itself gives rise to a certain knowledge. If one considers that to doubt is to think, and to think is to exist, one can see how Descartes can hold, "I think; therefore, I am." (For more about Descartes and skepticism, see part II.) Since Descartes is not a genuine skeptic, but someone who uses skepticism as a way of proving that knowledge exists, his practice is called methodological skepticism.

As brilliant as Descartes's strategy was, it too was rejected by most philosophers. One of the other alternatives to Pyrrhonism was mitigated skepticism. Marin Mersenne and Pierre Gassendi in France and John Locke in England in effect conceded much to the skeptic. They thought that the skeptic had undermined dogmatic metaphysics and the pretension of science to uncover the essence of things, but that empirical science was able to frame hypotheses on the basis of empirical evidence. These hypotheses organized appearances and were inherently revisable, and hence non-dogmatic.

To the two conspicuous consequences of scientific and religious events for philosophers described above, I want to add some more general kinds of disorientation connected to science and religion. One is that people lost their belief that they occupied a privileged position in the universe. If the earth is not the center of the universe, then humans certainly are not at the center, and this leads to the thought that they are not the center of creation. (Let's extrapolate. If the solar system is not the center of the universe, there's a good chance that people do not know much about where they are at all. If the location of the Big Bang is the center, we know where we are, but it's not a reassuring fact.) Another consequence of accepting the Copernican system is that it no longer makes sense to say that heaven is up and hell is down. Anyone who does not know up from down is radically disoriented.

With specific reference to religious beliefs, the Copernican system proved that the Bible does not give a literally true or scientific description of the universe. So, either the Bible needed to be given up or it needed to be thought of in a very different way. Galileo endorsed the view of Cardinal Baronius that the Bible does not teach us how the heavens go, but how to go to heaven. Other discoveries in the seventeenth century – such as that the world is much older than the Bible says it is and that there was never enough water to flood the entire land as the story about Noah says it did – further undermined belief in the Bible as a book of general information. If it was to be saved at all, it had to be understood as only a religious book.

Another kind of disorientation involved politics. Various changes in the type of government people were under – changes from monarchies to republics, from commonwealths to monarchies, from republics to aristocracies – inspired political philosophers to explain what the justification for government is. Some widely accepted beliefs, such as the divine right of kings and patriarchalism, were harshly treated, and new ones had to be devised, notably, the social contract theories of Hobbes, Locke, and Pufendorf.

4 Rationalism[6]

Since rationalist theories predominate in this book, it makes sense to try to say something about what makes an early modern philosopher a rationalist. Rationalists are contrasted with

6 You may find this material difficult. Keep in mind that most philosophical texts need to be read slowly and often more than once in order to be understood; also, you can always return to this section after you have read some of the selections in this volume and have more motivation for understanding what is special about rationalism and what some philosophical concepts mean.

The definition of rationalism eventually adopted is this:

(R′) Rationalism is the view that (a) there are nontrivial propositions, (b′) that are not known by sensation, (c) from which a general description of reality can be deduced.

empiricists. Hence, to understand rationalism is to some extent to understand the difference or distinction between it and empiricism. So we will be exploring two questions simultaneously in this section: what is rationalism, and what is a distinction? The latter question is important because it is impossible to do philosophy without making distinctions. We will be as interested in illuminating the practice of making distinctions as in coming up with an airtight understanding of rationalism.

Let's begin with some comments about ways to make a distinction. One of these is simply to choose a couple of words or terms (words that designate a group or category of things) to form a nomenclature for the distinction and then to specify which individuals belong to each.

This is what is typically done with rationalism and empiricism. Rationalists include Descartes, Spinoza, Malebranche, and Leibniz. Empiricists include John Locke, George Berkeley, and David Hume. Making a distinction in this way can hardly be wrong, because it simply stipulates what objects are assigned to which term. However, such a distinction is also of limited usefulness because no idea or description is attached to the terms of the distinction; that is, if no idea or description is given to one or both terms, it is not clear what makes a person or thing belong to one term or category and another person or thing belong to the other. As regards rationalism, what important feature do the philosophies of Descartes, Spinoza, Malebranche, and Leibniz have that the philosophies of Locke, Berkeley, and Hume, do not have? To associate an idea or description with the term "rationalist" (or to both terms "rationalist" and "empiricist") is to make the distinction informative. But it also opens up the possibility that the distinction is defective or mistaken. For example, if a rationalist is defined as a seventeenth-century philosopher who lived most of his life in France or the Netherlands, then Descartes, Spinoza, and Malebranche are rationalists, but Leibniz is not. So this description of a rationalist is *too strong*, because it excludes someone who ought to be included among the rationalists.

One way to get Leibniz into the class of rationalists would be to weaken the description, say, to this: a rationalist is a seventeenth-century philosopher who lived most of his life in western Europe. But this description is *too weak*. Dozens, if not hundreds, of seventeenth-century philosophers – for example, Aristotelian scholastic philosophers – lived most of their lives in western Europe but were not rationalists.

Even if we could get a description of rationalism that included all and only Descartes, Spinoza, Malebranche, and Leibniz (and whoever else should be included), there would be something unsatisfying about it if it identified them solely on the basis of time and place. Merely giving the century and place of residence of a philosopher is insufficiently informative. It does not say anything about what doctrines they taught or why.

We have just seen that two of the requirements for a good way of distinguishing philosophers are (1) that the idea or description attached to a term should apply to or be true of the philosophers categorized as such, and (2) that the idea or description should be philosophically informative. There are other requirements on distinctions, which will emerge later. For now, let's consider a more fruitful way of describing rationalism.

What we need to find is a way of describing rationalism that is philosophically informative. The term "rationalism" itself provides a hint. Rationalists must emphasize reason in some way, apparently in contrast with empiricists. This is a start, but unless we have more information about what the rationalists actually taught, we are hardly in a position to judge how good this start is.

Here are some of the main propositions defended by Descartes, Spinoza, and Leibniz.

Descartes (*Meditations*):

1 Ideas of substances have more objective reality than ideas of modes or accidents.
2 Now it is manifest by the natural light that there must be at least as much reality in the efficient and total cause as in its effect.
3 Something cannot proceed from nothing.
4 What is more perfect – what has more reality within itself – cannot proceed from what is less perfect.
5 In order that an idea should contain some one certain objective reality rather than another, it must without doubt derive it from some cause in which there is at least as much formal reality as this idea contains of objective reality.
6 Just as the mode of objective existence pertains to ideas by their proper nature, so does the mode of formal existence pertain to the causes of those ideas – this is at least true of the first and principal ideas – by the nature peculiar to them.
7 The light of nature causes me to know clearly that the ideas in me are like images which can, in truth, easily fall short of the perfection of the objects from which they have been derived.

Spinoza (*Ethics*):

D1 By cause of itself I understand that whose essence involves existence, or that whose nature cannot be conceived except as existing.
D2 That thing is said to be finite in its own kind that can be limited by another of the same nature.
D3 By substance I understand what is in itself and is conceived through itself, that is, that whose concept does not require the concept of another thing, from which it must be formed.
D4 By attribute I understand what the intellect perceives of a substance as constituting its essence.

D1–D4 are definitions. No one before Spinoza defined these words or concepts in just the way he did, although there is a relationship between his definitions and those of his philosophical predecessors. I'll give just three of the many remarkable consequences he derives from them:

P1 A substance is prior in nature to its affections.
P3 If things have nothing in common with one another, one of them cannot be the cause of the other. . . .
P5 In Nature there cannot be two or more substances of the same nature or attribute.

Malebranche (*The Search After Truth* and *Dialogues on Metaphysics*):

1 God is the cause of everything.
2 Finite beings cause nothing.
3 Body and soul are different things.
4 Ideas are different from perceptions.

5 There is no necessary connection between movements in the brain and sensations in the soul.
6 Certain motions of bodies are the occasions for certain cognitions in human beings.
7 Human beings see all things in God.

Leibniz (*Monadology*):

1 A monad is a simple substance, which goes to make up composites.
2 A simple substance is one that has no parts.
3 If something has no constituent parts, it cannot have extension or form and it cannot be divisible.
4 What has no extension or form and cannot be divisible is an atom.
5 Atoms cannot be dissolved or destroyed because they are not divisible and hence do not have parts.
6 Atoms come into and go out of existence only through creation and annihilation, respectively.

The propositions from Spinoza, Malebranche, and Leibniz are either definitions or supposedly follow from definitions of terms that seem to be quite general. Apropos of Spinoza everything is either a substance or attribute; apropos of Malebranche everything other than God is a creature, either material or spiritual; and apropos of Leibniz (at least during the last period of his life), everything is or is reducible to entities that are immaterial and indivisible. Descartes's propositions do not seem to be definitions, but do seem to be quite general. What all the propositions from these philosophers seem to have in common is that they are propositions about concepts, not individual things existing in the world. Now concepts seem to be closely connected with reason and rationality. It's plausible that if something (or somebody) has reason, then it has concepts, and if something has concepts, then it can reason; and if something has reason, then it is rational. So we seem to be on the track of describing rationalism.

Our list of propositions from Descartes, Spinoza, and Leibniz also seems to be nontrivial. They are not the kinds of propositions that are just obvious, as, say, "A white horse is white" and "1 = 1," are obvious. Finally, it seems that, in addition to being nontrivial conceptual propositions, they seem, taken as a whole, to be able to describe or explain all or almost all of reality. For example, everything is either a substance or an attribute of a substance. Using these features of the numbered propositions above suggests that rationalism may be described as follows:

(R) Rationalism is the view that (a) there are nontrivial propositions, (b) about concepts, (c) from which a general description of reality can be deduced.

By (a) a nontrivial proposition, I mean one that is informative, whether it is a definition or not. By (b), I mean that the proposition is about something that is general and understood by the mind. By (c) I mean that enough propositions will be deduced to give a complete, general picture of the nature of reality.

No doubt (R) could be criticized. Condition (c) is vague because it is not clear how much information is required for the system to be complete. Even worse, the most distinctive claim of Descartes's philosophy, "I think; therefore, I am," was not included in the propositions describing his philosophy; and if it were to be added, then not all of the resulting set of propositions would be conceptual. Perhaps the most remarkable thing about Descartes's philosophy is that it begins with a particular proposition, not a general conceptual one, that does not depend upon sensation in order to be known. Descartes does not say, "I see or hear or smell or touch or taste myself; therefore, I am." He has an experience of himself that is not a sense experience.

Far from interfering with our attempt to describe rationalism, this fact about Descartes's philosophy may inspire a better description of rationalism. Although (R) is inadequate, it provides the basis for a better description of rationalism, and the counterexample[7] provided by Descartes's philosophy provides a hint about how to improve (R):

(R′) Rationalism is the view that (a) there are nontrivial propositions, (b′) that are not known by sensation, (c) from which a general description of reality can be deduced.

There's another way of expressing what clause (b′) says. Philosophers call knowledge that does not depend on sensation "*a priori* knowledge" because it is knowledge that is supposedly prior to[8] sense knowledge. The propositions, "A triangle has three sides" and "A bachelor is an unmarried, adult male" are not known through sense experience, even though a person would need to have some sense experience to know what many of the words of those propositions mean. If one has the idea or the concept of a triangle, then one knows that it has three sides; and if one has the idea or concept of a bachelor, then one knows that it is an unmarried, adult male. *A priori* knowledge is contrasted with *a posteriori* knowledge, which is the knowledge that comes from or after sense experience, for example, the propositions, "Socrates is human," and "This paper is white with black type on it." *A priori* knowledge depends only on ideas or concepts, which brings us back to the intuition that led to (R).

The purpose of (R′) is to state conditions that pick out all and only rationalist philosophers. Does it succeed? There are two ways for a description like (R′) to fail. It can be too strong in the sense that the conditions are so stringent that some things that we want to satisfy the conditions and be included within a category do not satisfy them and hence are excluded from the category. (R′) does not seem to fail in this way because the key rationalists, Descartes, Spinoza, Malebranche, and Leibniz, all seem to satisfy the conditions set down by (R′).

The other way in which a description like (R′) can fail is to be too weak in the sense that the conditions are so loose that philosophers we do not want to be included as rationalists nonetheless do satisfy the conditions and hence must be counted as rationalists. The alternative is to change the description in such a way that the unwanted philosophers get excluded. This means that one makes the conditions of the description stronger, without making them so strong as to exclude some of the philosophers we want to count as rationalists. The key empiricist philosophers are Locke, Berkeley, and Hume. Unfortunately, we cannot sensibly judge whether they are included or excluded by (R′) because this volume does not contain their texts. (But fortunately they are in volume 4 of this series, which I urge you to read.)

7 A counterexample is an example that shows that some general claim is false. A counterexample to the claim that humans are the only humans that communicate is the existence of chimpanzees, who are able to use signs and tokens to communicate.

8 The term "*a priori* knowledge" also suggests that it has a priority over sense knowledge. This is a prejudice of some philosophers.

We do, however, have some basis for judging whether Montaigne, Bacon, Hobbes, and Newton are rationalists or not, because this volume contains some of their texts. I won't make a judgment about this issue but leave it to the reader to ponder.

Without judging the ultimate cogency of (R′), we can learn something more about making distinctions from it. Rationalism, recall, is contrasted with empiricism. How should we describe empiricism in order to distinguish it from rationalism?

Before answering that question, we need to know whether the distinction is supposed to be a proper one or not. A proper distinction is one in which the terms[9] are contradictory. Two terms are contradictory exactly when:[10]

1 one or the other term is true of each object that is being talk about (the universe of discourse),[11] and
2 it is not the case that both terms are true of any object.

So, a distinction is a proper one exactly when the terms are (1) exhaustive and (2) mutually exclusive. Red/nonred, green/nongreen, canine/noncanine, feline/nonfeline, mammal/nonmammal are proper distinctions, because the terms are contradictory.

Contradictory terms should not be confused with contrary terms. Two terms are contrary exactly when not more than one term is true of an object in the universe of discourse or domain and possibly neither is true. "Red" and "green" are contrary terms for a universe of discourse that includes blue objects.[12] "Canine" and "feline" are contrary terms for most universes of discourse, say, one that includes things that include horses or humans. The terms "canine" and "mammalian" are neither contradictory nor contrary terms because although there is a difference between being canine and being mammalian, whatever is canine is mammalian.

So there are at least two ways in which a distinction may be improper. The terms of the distinction may not apply to all the members of the universe of discourse (the distinction between red and green for a universe of discourse that includes things that are blue) or both terms may apply to some members of the universe of discourse (the distinction between cats and mammals). Occasionally, two terms that are supposed to mark a distinction have the same meaning ("eye doctor" and "oculist") and thus constitute *a distinction without a difference*. Such terms do not really constitute a distinction.

The best way to guarantee that a distinction is a proper one is to choose one term *T* to be the one that gets an informative description attached to it, and then to call the second

9 "Term" is being used ambiguously to indicate either a word or phrase or the concept denoted by a word or phrase.

10 I am using the phrase "exactly when" to mean "precisely under the following conditions": it means the same as "if and only if" and "just in case."

11 When people make distinctions, they are usually talking about some restricted set of objects, such as the natural numbers or human beings or colored objects, rather than talking about absolutely everything. The things being talked about are the universe of discourse, sometimes called the "domain." One reason to specify the universe of discourse is to make clear what is being talked about. Another reason is that paradoxes can result from not restricting the universe of discourse. For example, some sets are members of other sets. Is the set that contains as members only sets that are not members of themselves a member of itself?

12 Suppose the universe of discourse consists of things that are only red or green. Relative to this universe of discourse, are red and green contradictory terms?

term "non*T*" and to describe or define it as "whatever is not *T*." So, given that being human is being a rational animal, the term "nonhuman" is described or defined as not being human. As regards rationalism, the best way to make sure one ends up with a proper distinction is to define a term "nonrationalism" as "what is not rationalism." People who are not philosophers often think that this way of drawing a distinction is fishy. They want the term *T* to have as its contradictory some term *U*, where *U* is then given its own description in terms different from the ones used to describe *T*. But the philosophical style of making a proper distinction, far from being fishy, is ingenious. It guarantees that each member of the universe of discourse will be either *T* or non*T*. In contrast, if T and U are not defined in exactly the right way, you end up with one of three results: (1) *U* means exactly the same as *T* and so everything is both *T* and *U*; (2) *U* means something other than *T*, and some things in the universe of discourse are neither *T* nor *U*; or (3) the meanings of *T* and *U* overlap, so some things are both *T* and *U*. (In order to have a good grasp of this idea, you should try to think of examples of each of these possibilities, examples not already given.) These three possibilities can be described as follows: (1) a distinction without a difference; (2) a distinction consisting of contrary terms; and (3) a distinction consisting of neither contradictory nor contrary terms.

Is the distinction between rationalism and empiricism a proper one? Typically, the distinction happens to turn out to be a proper one because usually only six philosophers constitute the domain or universe of discourse; each one is assigned to one term or the other; and no precise description is given for either category. Here is the standard distinction: rationalists: Descartes, Spinoza, and Leibniz; empiricists: Locke, Berkeley, and Hume.

If the universe of discourse is expanded to include, say, Montaigne, Bacon, Hobbes, and Newton, it will not be obvious to which term or category each should be assigned, unless we commit ourselves to some description that constitutes a criterion for being a rationalist or empiricist. Suppose we want the distinction to be a proper one, accept (R′) for rationalism, and describe empiricism as anything that satisfies (E):

(E) An empiricist is a philosopher who believes that all knowledge begins with sense experience.

I leave it to the reader to decide for each of them whether Montaigne, Bacon, Hobbes, and Newton are rationalists, empiricists, both, or neither.

Suppose that the distinction between rationalism and empiricism is not a proper one. Does it need to be? Whether it is objectionable that a distinction is not a proper one or not depends upon the purpose that the distinction is supposed to have. Goodness and badness are often relative to a purpose. Perhaps it is just as illuminating if the terms for them are not contradictory.

(R) and (R′) are not the only descriptions that one might choose to describe rationalism. After reading parts I–III, the reader may want to return to this part of the general introduction and consider two other candidate descriptions of rationalism:

(I) A rationalist is a philosopher who believes that humans have some innate knowledge.

Knowledge is innate if a person is born with that knowledge. Descartes and Leibniz believe in innate knowledge. Do Spinoza and Malebranche? If they do, what does this say about how strong or weak (I) is? If at least one of them does not, what does this say about the strength of (I)?

The other candidate is:

(N) A rationalist is a philosopher who believes that genuine knowledge or scientific knowledge is necessary.

Do Descartes, Spinoza, Malebranche, Leibniz, Montaigne, Bacon, Hobbes, and Newton fit this description? What are the implications of your answer?

Many historians of philosophy will be unhappy that so much attention has been devoted to trying to understand rationalism as if it were a movement or specific philosophy. They would rightly observe that the actual historical relations between the philosophers described as rationalists and those described as empiricists, and the actual doctrines taught by each, are so intertwined as to make the distinction between rationalism and empiricism misleading at best, and probably downright false. Every non-scholastic European philosopher writing after Descartes's *Meditations* had to contend with his philosophy, Locke and Berkeley as much as Spinoza and Leibniz. Spinoza borrowed heavily from Hobbes. Malebranche influenced both Berkeley and Hume. Spinoza corresponded with the head of the Royal Society, Henry Oldenberg, as mentioned before. Leibniz tried to correspond with Hobbes and Locke. Descartes, Spinoza, and Leibniz knew the new empirical science and saw themselves as part of that intellectual movement.

In exploring the distinction between rationalism and empiricism, I have not been assuming that being a rationalist excludes a person from being influenced by empiricists or for sharing some of the doctrines. My main goal was to explore the viability of that familiar concept and to use it to introduce some philosophical methods and vocabulary.

Part I

Science, Skepticism, and Method

Introduction

The three topics mentioned in the title of this part are interrelated. As described in the general introduction, one of the most distinctive features of early modern western Europe was the rise of modern science, the science of Nicolaus Copernicus, Johannes Kepler, Galileo, William Harvey, Robert Boyle, and Isaac Newton. Yet the progress in modern science was accompanied by a renewed interest in, and often a fear of, skepticism. There is something ironic in this combination, especially since science and skepticism were connected.

Some of the great scientific discoveries justified skepticism about human beliefs in general. Consider Copernicus's theory that the earth goes around the sun. This challenged one of the most firmly held beliefs that people have: that the sun goes around the earth. We see (or seem to see) the sun rising in the morning, moving higher across the sky until it begins to descend, and then finally setting in the evening. The sun is (or seems to be) moving, not the earth. (Perhaps a majority of the people on earth continue to believe that the sun goes around the earth, and this is only partly due to the absence of science education.)

Now consider Galileo's discovery that the moon has craters. If a person looks at the moon, it seems to be fairly obvious that the moon does not have craters. But if one looks at the moon with a telescope, it seems to have craters. Looking through a telescope does not in itself undermine the belief in a craterless moon. Why should a person believe what he seems to see through a long tube that has curved glass inside? Also, the image seen through the telescope shakes very easily, and easily goes out of focus. Why not believe that the telescope distorts the appearance of the moon? In order to take the telescopic image to be more reliable than the naked eye many additional beliefs are needed to support its accuracy. Alternatively, why not be skeptical about the possibility of knowledge in general?

Next, consider the scientific theory that the physical world in itself consists only of quantitative features. The qualities of color, sound, and taste seem to exist only in the perceiver and not in the world itself. The selections from Galileo, Bacon, and Hobbes state the case. Examples from science could be multiplied. It seems impossible that people and other objects, not firmly attached, could exist on the other side of the world. Wouldn't they have to fall off, since they are (or seem to be) upside down?

Given that these beliefs, seemingly so certain to our senses, are false – moving sun, craterless moon, no antipodal objects – what other beliefs might be false? To put the point paradoxically, our skepticism is justified by our scientific knowledge. Science contributes not just to a pragmatic, everyday skepticism, but to philosophical skepticism. How do I know what I think I know? Perhaps I don't know anything. Science seems both to undermine my belief in sensation and itself to depend upon sensation. Copernicus constructed his counterintuitive theory on the basis of his *observation* of motions, and Galileo constructed his on the basis of *seeing* images in his telescope.

In addition to scientific discoveries, skepticism was fueled by religious controversies. The Roman Catholic Church claimed that it was infallible. Martin Luther contested that point on the grounds that the Church taught doctrines that were inconsistent with the Bible. His argument had great force because everyone at the time, that is, sixteenth-century European Christian theologians, agreed that the Bible contained the revelation of God. Since the Church based its claim to infallibility in part on the authority of the Bible – "Upon this rock, I will build my Church" (Matthew 16:18) – the Bible seemed to enjoy some priority relative to the Church. So, if the Church's teaching contradicted the Bible's teaching, it would seem that the Church was fallible.

When he posted his Ninety-Five Theses in 1517, Luther accepted the same criterion for religious truth that the Church accepted: the Bible, tradition, church councils, and papal decrees. It was only later, when he reflected on the full consequences of his challenge to papal authority, that he realized that popes and councils are just men and subject to the failings of other men.

Unfortunately for naive belief in religious authority, Luther's challenge to the Church made philosophers and theologians aware of a much deeper problem. If a criterion for knowledge can be changed or even reasonably disputed, then the criterion itself cannot provide the certainty required for knowledge. In order to be sure that the accepted criterion C_1 is the right one, some other criterion C_2 is needed to identify or warrant C_1. But if C_1 needs some criterion to identify or warrant it, then it seems that C_2 also needs some criterion to identify or warrant it. So some third criterion C_3 is needed; and so on *ad infinitum*. This logic did not get played out immediately. When Luther proposed the Bible or the individual conscience as the criterion for religious truth, the Church was able to show that the Bible itself sometimes seemed to be contradictory and obscure. So a naive trust in the self-interpretation of the Bible did not seem tenable. Also, even if the Bible were self-interpreting, too many people are too ignorant for most theologians to be comfortable saying that each person could reliably interpret the Bible.

It seemed that something or someone more educated and objective was needed to interpret the Bible. The Church had volunteered for the job many centuries earlier, but in the sixteenth century first Luther, then thousands, then millions de-volunteered the Church.

Much of the skepticism just described is also connected with the rediscovery of the writings of Sextus Empiricus (third century A.D.). Sextus, for example, showed in his *Outlines of Pyrrhonism* (book 2, chapter 4) that the need for a criterion of knowledge generates an infinite regress. Montaigne read Sextus and used his arguments in *Apology for Raymond Sebond*, selections from which appear in this part. Sextus was a follower of the skeptic Pyrrho of Elis. Before Pyrrho, the principal kind of skepticism was Academic, named after the skepticism taught in the Academy after Plato's death. The Academics argued that no one knows anything. This is also called dogmatic skepticism because it commits itself to a truth: people know nothing. The Pyrrhonists were more radical. Not only did they not know whether they or anyone else knew anything, they asserted nothing. Rather, they simply raised possible problems for any proposition that their opponents asserted. For the most part, these problems clustered around a few considerations that came to be called tropes. Sextus's collection of these tropes came to be the standard collection.

What was Montaigne's purpose in raising skeptical objections to knowledge? He did not accept skepticism for its own sake, and Montaigne was not worried about modern science. He was worried about religion, and this worry became serious in the wake of Luther's attempt to reform the Roman Catholic Church. For Montaigne, the solution to the skeptical problem was to put one's faith in the Church. Thus, he has been called a "fideist."[1] Unfortunately, there's no logical requirement to accept Montaigne's solution and have faith in the Church. Moreover, many scholars think that Montaigne's recommendation to trust in the Church was not sincere, but a strategy to cast doubt on revealed religion in general.

By the middle of the seventeenth century, a large part of the religious crisis caused by skepticism had been settled in the minds of ordinary people. The Peace of Westphalia, which ended the economically devastating Thirty Years War, dictated roughly that the religion of the people should be the same as the religion of their prince. This political solution was not a philosophical solution.

In this part of the book are selections from several philosophers who more or less explicitly proposed scientific and philosophical method as the solution. Each of them believed that if people followed the right method, the discombobulating contradictions and paradoxes of past doctrines would be avoided.

Skepticism was not the only obstacle to knowledge. After criticizing the syllogistic method of the scholastics, Francis Bacon admonished his readers to guard against "four classes of idols which beset men's minds." The first is the Idols of the Tribe, the tendency of individual people to believe whatever their senses tell them. But, Bacon says, the measure of man is not "the measure of the universe." The second is the Idols of the Cave. These are the prejudices of individual human beings that result from their own peculiar experience or education. The third are the Idols of the Marketplace, those prejudices that result from conversations with other people. The words of common discourse are often vague or otherwise defective. Often the words take on a life of their own and "overrule the understanding." The fourth is the Idols of the Theater, those false beliefs that come from philosophical and scientific theories.

Bacon's critique is especially relevant today because of the emphasis of current epistemologists on the fact that human knowledge consists of a large, complicated network of beliefs. The network includes basic beliefs such as that the world is very old, and trivial, passing beliefs, like the belief that a pigeon just flew past my window. While this network of beliefs makes the increase of knowledge possible, the kinds of false belief that Bacon describes interfere with it.

In addition to his eloquent admonitions against intellectual "idols," Bacon had a view about the proper method of science: to form "ideas and axioms by true induction" from specific instances of things. It is because of this doctrine that Bacon is considered an empiricist. Bacon's

1 Fideism comes in various forms. Fideism in a weak sense is the view that religious faith does not depend on reason. It leaves open whether propositions of faith are consistent with reason or not. Fideism in a strong sense is the view that human reason is unreliable and hence that one must put one's faith in something. Thinkers who are fideists in the strong sense, as Montaigne was, believe that one's faith must be religious. Typically, they think that a person should put his or her faith in the accepted religion even though there is no logical justification for this. Strong fideism is the religious counterpart of the Pyrrhonic skeptic who chooses to follow the accepted beliefs of his community.

suggestion was brought to fruition by the great physicist Isaac Newton. In addition to his three laws of motion, he formulated some "Rules of Reasoning in Philosophy." One is essentially Ockham's razor: "We are to admit no more causes of natural things than such as are both true and sufficient to explain their appearances." Another, "Therefore to the same natural effects we must, as far as possible, assign the same cause," is tantamount to urging scientists to generalize as much as the phenomena allow. A third rule advises scientists to accept a hypothesis that explains phenomena as long as there are no other phenomena that falsify or refute it. That is, it recommends the method of hypothesis and experimentation.

While Bacon's method is to begin with the evidence of the senses, corrected by reason, Descartes's method was radically different. In his *Meditations on First Philosophy*, he employed the method of doubt, which will be described in part II, "Descartes and his Critics." In an earlier work, *Discourse on the Method of Rightly Conducting the Reason and Seeking for Truth in the Sciences*, he gives such homey advice as to "accept nothing as true" except what is clearly true, to "divide up each of the difficulties" in a problem "into as many parts as possible," and so on. The obvious problem with this "method" is that it is not a method; it does not give the kind of "how-to" information needed for the directions to be carried out.

Whenever Thomas Hobbes wrote about an area of philosophy, he shocked the reader. His scientistic attitude is expressed in the introduction to *Leviathan*. Its first clause ("Nature, the art by which God hath made and governs the world") is in effect a new Genesis ("In the beginning, God created the heavens and the earth"). Notice that Hobbes's passage promotes Nature above God, at least rhetorically, by being mentioned first. It then sets about to destroy traditional categories and beliefs. Nature is art; humans are machines, and machines are alive. If these ideas are nowhere near as shocking today as they were in the seventeenth century, it is in large part because of Hobbes's influence.

Hobbes tried to give substance to the claim that everything consists of matter in motion, including mental and emotional phenomena. Sensation is a motion in the brain and heart, and thinking is computation, the movement of words or numbers according to some rules. Even goodness and evil are understood in terms of motion. What is good is what an animal desires or moves toward, while what is evil is what an animal is averse to or moves away from. His analyses of things like appetite, aversion, joy, hope, and fear are examples of classic conceptual analysis, the mode of reasoning that one finds in Locke, Hume, and many Anglo-American philosophers of the twentieth century.

Hobbes's pattern of analysis was followed by Spinoza, who defines "inclination" (*propensio*) as "joy with the accompanying idea of some object of being accidentally the cause of joy"; "aversion" as "sorrow with the accompanying idea of some object which is accidentally the cause of the sorrow"; and "hope" as "joy not constant, arising from the idea of something future or past, about the issue of which we sometimes doubt."[2]

But, according to his own program for philosophy, he should have been doing something else. In *Leviathan*, Hobbes defined philosophy as *"the knowledge acquired by reasoning, from the manner of generation of anything, to the properties; or from the properties to some possible way of generation of the same."*[3] So, he should have been saying how certain bodies move and thereby cause some other motion, usually involving other bodies. In the twenty-first century, most of the physical sciences from physics to physiology do this.

2 *Ethics*, part III, "The Affects," propositions viii, ix, xii; cf. Hobbes's analyses of "appetite," "aversion," and "hope."

3 *Leviathan* 46.1, Hobbes's italics.

While Hobbes equated philosophy with science, natural science had fairly well divorced itself from philosophy by the end of the seventeenth century. Early modern philosophy was the beginning of something new in part because it was reacting against something old. What was new was modern science; what was old was authority. What made the new science new was its search for a new understanding of nature without the presuppositions of traditional Aristotelian science and philosophy. If one wants to know whether a body dropped from a height falls at a uniform rate, one does not read a book to find the answer, one drops bodies from various heights and times their descent. Of course, this requires some mathematics, and instruments to measure time. So mathematics developed and technical equipment began to be developed.

The embodiment of the old authority was the Roman Catholic Church. When it resisted the changes required by the new science and new political ideas, many left the Church. This solved a large part of the problem for many intellectuals. But it did not solve all of it, and it did not solve any of it for those who remained within the Church. It is very difficult to simply give up beliefs that are as central to human life and human aspirations as those taught by the Church. These beliefs are tenacious. So what many philosophers did, in one way or another, including Descartes, Hobbes, Pierre Gassendi, Antoine Arnauld, Blaise Pascal, Nicolas Malebranche, and Gottfried Leibniz, all of whom are represented in the readings in this book, was to reinterpret the traditional beliefs rather than to reject them outright.

1

Michel de Montaigne, *The Apology for Raymond Sebond*

Michel Eyquem, seigneur de Montaigne (1533–92), born at the chateau of Montaigne, was the son of a rich Catholic landowner and a mother of Jewish descent. He is probably the greatest French essayist. He published three books of essays, two in 1580, and one in 1586. He was magistrate of Bordeaux (1557) and then mayor (1581–5). Many of his early essays were about himself, very different from the impersonal writing of the Middle Ages. These early essays often talk of pain and death. His later essays indicate an acceptance of life as it is. In his middle period, he was greatly influenced by skepticism. His motto was "Que sais-je?" ("What do I know?").

The greatest of these skeptical essays is *Apology for Raymond Sebond*, a large part of which was written in 1575–6. Raymond Sebond, a fifteenth-century Roman Catholic theologian, wrote *Theologia naturalis* (*Natural Theology*), which purported to prove all the propositions of the Christian religion by reason. Montaigne's father asked him to translate it. Later, when some readers objected to some of the arguments or confessed to not understanding them, Montaigne wrote his defense, which consisted of defending fideism by arguing that, since all human reasoning is fallible, Sebond's reasoning is no worse than any other theologian's. Montaigne in effect destroyed Sebond's reasoning in order to save it.

Now some days before his death, my father, having by chance come across this book under a pile of other abandoned papers, commanded me to put it into French for him. It is nice to translate authors like this one, where there is hardly anything but the matter to reproduce; but those who have given much care to grace and elegance of language are dangerous to undertake, especially to render them into a weaker idiom. It was a very strange and a new occupation for me; but being by chance at leisure at the time, and being unable to disobey any command of the best father there ever was, I got through it as best I could; at which he was singularly pleased, and ordered it to be printed; and this was done after his death.

I found the ideas of this author fine, the arrangement and sequence of his work good, and his plan full of piety. Because many people are busy reading it, and especially the ladies, to whom we owe additional help, I have often found myself in a position to help them by clearing their book of two principal objections that are made against it. His purpose is bold and courageous, for he undertakes by human and natural reasons to establish and prove against the atheists all the articles of the Christian religion; wherein, to tell the truth, I find him so firm and felicitous that I do not think it is possible to do better in that argument, and I think that no one has equaled him.

[. . .]

[First Objection to Sebond: Defense]

The first criticism that they make of his work is that Christians do themselves harm in trying to support their belief by human reasons, since it is conceived only by faith and by a particular inspiration of divine grace. In this objection there seems to be a certain pious zeal, and for this reason we must try with all the more mildness and respect to satisfy those who advance it. This would be rather the task for a man versed in theology than for myself, who know nothing about it.

However, I think thus, that in a thing so divine and so lofty, and so far surpassing human intelligence, as is this truth with which it has pleased the goodness of God to enlighten us, it is very necessary that he still lend us his help, by extraordinary and privileged favor. [. . .] And I do not think that purely human means are at all capable of this; if they were, so many rare and excellent souls, so abundantly furnished with natural powers, in ancient times, would not have failed to arrive at this knowledge through their reason. It is faith alone that embraces vividly and surely the high mysteries of our religion.

But this is not to say that it is not a very fine and very laudable enterprise to accommodate also to the service of our faith the natural and human tools that God has given us. There can be no doubt that this is the most honorable use that we could put them to, and that there is no occupation or design more worthy of a Christian man than to aim, by all his studies and thoughts, to embellish, extend, and amplify the truth of his belief. [. . .] We must do the same here, and accompany our faith with all the reason that is in us, but always with this reservation, not to think that it is on us that faith depends, or that our efforts and arguments can attain a knowledge so supernatural and divine.

[. . .]

If this ray of divinity touched us at all, it would appear all over: not only our words, but also our works would bear its light and luster. [. . .]

Do you want to see this? Compare our morals with a Mohammedan's, or a pagan's; we always fall short of them. Whereas, in view of the advantage of our religion, we should shine with excellence at an extreme and incomparable distance, and people ought to say: "Are they so just, so charitable, so good? Then they are Christians."

All other signs are common to all religions: hope, trust, events, ceremonies, penitence, martyrs. The peculiar mark of our truth should be our virtue, as it is also the most heavenly and difficult mark, and the worthiest product of truth.

[. . .]

See the horrible impudence with which we bandy divine reasons about, and how irreligiously we have both rejected them and taken them again, according as fortune has changed our place in these public storms. This proposition, so solemn, whether it is lawful for a subject to rebel and take arms against his prince in defense of religion – remember in whose mouths, this year just past, the affirmative of this was the buttress of one party, the negative was the buttress of what other party; and hear now from what quarter comes the voice and the instruction of both sides, and whether the weapons make less din for this cause than for that. And we burn the people who say that truth must be made to endure the yoke of our need. And how much worse France does than say it!

Let us confess the truth: if anyone should sift out of the army, even the average loyalist army, those who march in it from the pure zeal of affection for religion, and also those who consider only the protection of the laws of their country or the service of their prince, he could not make up one complete company of men-at-arms out of them. [. . .]

Our religion is made to extirpate vices; it covers them, fosters them, incites them.

[. . .]

We are Christians by the same title that we are Perigordians or Germans.

[. . .]

Sebond has labored at this worthy study, and shows us how there is no part of the world that belies its maker. It would be doing a wrong to divine goodness if the universe did not assent to our belief. The sky, the earth, the elements, our body and our soul, all things conspire in this; we have only to find the way to use them. They instruct us, if we are capable of understanding.

[. . .]

Now our human reasons and arguments are as it were the heavy and barren matter; the grace of God is their form; it is that which gives them shape and value. [. . .]

These men [Sebond's opponents] have some prepossession in judgment that makes their taste jaded for Sebond's reasons. Furthermore, it seems to them that they are given an easy game when set at liberty to combat our religion by purely human weapons, which they would not dare attack in its authoritative and commanding majesty.

The means I take to beat down this frenzy, and which seems fittest to me, is to crush and trample underfoot human arrogance and pride; to make them feel the inanity, the vanity and nothingness, of man; to wrest from their hands the puny weapons of their reason; to make them bow their heads and bite the ground beneath the authority and reverence of divine majesty.

[. . .]

[Man Is No Better Than the Animals]

Presumption is our natural and original malady. The most vulnerable and frail of all creatures is man, and at the same time the most arrogant. He feels and sees himself lodged here, amid the mire and dung of the world, nailed and riveted to the worst, the deadest, and the most stagnant part of the universe, on the lowest story of the house and the farthest from the vault of heaven, with the animals of the worst condition of the three; and in his imagination he goes planting himself above the circle of the moon, and bringing the sky down beneath his feet. It is by the vanity of this same imagination that he equals himself to God, attributes to himself divine characteristics, picks himself out and separates himself from the horde of other creatures, carves out their shares to his fellows and companions the animals, and distributes among them such portions of faculties and powers as he sees fit. How does he know, by the force of his intelligence, the secret internal stirrings of animals? By what comparison between them and us does he infer the stupidity that he attributes to them?

[. . .]

We recognize easily enough, in most of their works, how much superiority the animals have over us and how feeble is our skill to imitate them. We see, however, in our cruder works, the faculties that we use, and that our soul applies itself with all its power; why do we not think the same thing of them? Why do we attribute to some sort of natural and servile inclination these works which surpass all that we can do by nature and by art? Wherein, without realizing it, we grant them a very great advantage over us, by making Nature, with maternal tenderness, accompany them and guide them as by the hand in all the actions and comforts of their life; while us she abandons to chance and to fortune, and to seek by art the things necessary for our preservation, and denies us at the same time the power to attain, by any education and mental straining, the natural resourcefulness of the animals: so that their brutish stupidity surpasses in all conveniences all that our divine intelligence can do.

Truly, by this reckoning, we should be quite right to call her a very unjust stepmother. But this is not so; our organization is not so deformed and disorderly. Nature has universally embraced all her creatures; and there is none that she has not very amply furnished with all powers necessary for the preservation of its being.

[. . .]

The philosopher Pyrrho, incurring the peril of a great storm at sea, offered those who were with him nothing better to imitate than the assurance of a pig that was traveling with them, and that was looking at this tempest without fear. Philosophy, at the end of her precepts, sends us back to the examples of an athlete or a muleteer, in whom we ordinarily see much less feeling of death, pain, and other discomforts, and more firmness than knowledge ever supplied to any man who had not been born and prepared for it on his own by natural habit.

[. . .]

Our well-being is but the privation of being ill. That is why the sect of philosophy that set the greatest value on voluptuousness still ranked it with mere freedom from pain. To have no ill is to have the most good that man can hope for; as Ennius said: "Who has no ill has only too much good."

[. . .]

Evil is in its turn a good to man. Neither is pain always something for him to flee, nor pleasure always for him to pursue.

[. . .]

[Man Has No Knowledge]

Yet must I see at last whether it is in the power of man to find what he seeks, and whether that quest that he has been making for so many centuries has enriched him with any new power and any solid truth.

I think he will confess to me, if he speaks in all conscience, that all the profit he has gained from so long a pursuit is to have learned to acknowledge his weakness. The ignorance that was naturally in us we have by long study confirmed and verified.

[. . .]

The wisest man that ever was, when they asked him what he knew, answered that he knew this much, that he knew nothing. He was verifying what they say, that the greatest part of what we know is the least of those parts that we do not know; that is to say that the very thing we think we know is a part, and a very small part, of our ignorance.

We know things in a dream, says Plato, and we are ignorant of them in reality.

[. . .]

The Peripatetics, Epicureans, Stoics, and others thought they had found it. These established the sciences that we have, and treated them as certain knowledge.

Clitomachus, Carneades, and the Academics despaired of their quest, and judged that truth could not be conceived by our powers. The conclusion of these men was man's weakness and ignorance. This school had the greatest following and the noblest adherents.

Pyrrho and other Skeptics or Epechists [. . .] say that they are still in search of the truth. These men judge that those who think they have found it are infinitely mistaken; and that there is also an overbold vanity in that second class that assures us that human powers are not capable of attaining it. For this matter of establishing the measure of our power, of knowing and judging the difficulty of things, is a great and supreme knowledge, of which they doubt that man is capable:

> Whoever thinks that we know nothing does not know
> Whether we know enough to say that this is so.
>
> LUCRETIUS

Ignorance that knows itself, that judges itself and condemns itself, is not complete ignorance: to be that, it must be ignorant of itself. So that the profession of the Pyrrhonians is to waver, doubt, and inquire, to be sure of nothing, to answer for nothing. Of the three functions of the soul, the imaginative, the appetitive, and the consenting, they accept the first two; the last they suspend and keep it ambiguous, without inclination or approbation, however slight, in one direction or the other.

[. . .]

Now this attitude of their judgment, straight and inflexible, taking all things in without adherence or consent, leads them to their Ataraxy, which is a peaceful and sedate condition of life, exempt from the agitations we receive through the impression of the opinion and knowledge we think we have of things. Whence are born fear, avarice, envy, immoderate desires, ambition, pride, superstition, love of novelty, rebellion, disobedience, obstinacy, and most bodily ills. Indeed, they free themselves thereby from jealousy on behalf of their doctrine. For they dispute in a very mild manner. They do not fear contradiction in their discussion. When they say that heavy things go down, they would be very sorry to have anyone take their word for it; and they seek to be contradicted, so as to create doubt and suspension of judgment, which is their goal. They advance their propositions only to combat those they think we believe in.

If you accept their proposition, they will just as gladly take the opposite one to maintain; it is all one to them; they have no preference in the matter. If you postulate that snow is black, they argue on the contrary that it is white. If you say that it is neither one nor the other, it is up to them to maintain that it is both. If you maintain with certain judgment that you know nothing about it, they will maintain that you do. Yes, and if by an affirmative axiom you assure them that you are in doubt about it, they will go and argue that you are not, or that you cannot judge and prove that you are in doubt. And by this extremity of doubt that shakes its own foundations, they separate and divide themselves from many opinions, even from those which in many ways have upheld doubt and ignorance.

Why, they say, since among the dogmatists one is allowed to say green, the other yellow, are they not also allowed to doubt? Is there anything that can be proposed for you to admit or deny, which it is not legitimate to consider ambiguous? And where others are swept – either by the custom of their country, or by their parental upbringing, or by chance – as by a tempest, without judgment or choice, indeed most often before the age of discretion, to such or such an opinion, to the Stoic or Epicurean sect, to which they find themselves pledged, enslaved, and fastened as to a prey they have bitten into and cannot shake loose [. . .] why shall it not be granted similarly to these men to maintain their liberty, and to consider things without obligation and servitude? [. . .]

Is it not an advantage to be freed from the necessity that curbs others? Is it not better to remain in suspense than to entangle yourself in the many errors that the human fancy has produced? Is it not better to suspend your conviction than to get mixed up in these seditious and quarrelsome divisions?

What am I to choose? What you like, provided you choose! There is a stupid answer, to which nevertheless all dogmatism seems to come, by which we are not allowed not to know what we do not know.

Take the most famous theory, it will never be so sure but that in order to defend it you will have to attack and combat hundreds of contrary theories. Is it not better to keep out of this melee? You are permitted to espouse, as you would your honor and your life, Aristotle's belief about the eternity of the soul, and to contradict and give the lie to Plato on the matter; and shall they be forbidden to doubt it?

[. . .]

The Pyrrhonians have kept themselves a wonderful advantage in combat, having rid themselves of the need to cover up. It does not matter to them that they are struck, provided they strike; and they do their work with everything. If they win, your proposition is lame; if you win, theirs is. If they lose, they confirm ignorance; if you lose, you confirm it. If they prove that nothing is known, well and good; if they do not know how to prove it, just as good. *So that, since equal reasons are found on both sides of the same subject, it may be the easier to suspend judgment on each side* [Cicero].

And they set store by the fact that they can find much more easily why a thing is false than that it is true; and what is not than what is; and what they do not believe than what they believe.

Their expressions are: "I establish nothing; it is no more thus than thus, or than neither way; I do not understand it; the appearances are equal on all sides; it is equally legitimate to speak for and against. Nothing seems true, which may not seem false." Their sacramental word is ἐπέχω, that is to say, "I hold back, I do not budge." Those are their refrains, and others of similar substance. Their effect is a pure, complete, and very perfect postponement and suspension of judgment. They use their reason to inquire and debate, but not to conclude and choose. Whoever will imagine a perpetual confession of ignorance, a judgment without leaning or inclination, on any occasion whatever, he has a conception of Pyrrhonism.

[. . .]

People who judge and check their judges never submit to them as they ought. How much more docile and easily led, both by the laws of religion and by political laws, are the simple and incurious minds, than those minds that survey divine and human causes like pedagogues!

There is nothing in man's invention that has so much verisimilitude and usefulness. It presents man naked and empty, acknowledging his natural weakness, fit to receive from above some outside power; stripped of human knowledge, and all the more apt to lodge divine knowledge in himself, annihilating his judgment to make more room for faith; neither disbelieving nor setting up any doctrine against the common observances; humble, obedient, teachable, zealous; a sworn enemy of heresy, and consequently free from the vain and irreligious opinions introduced by the false sects. He is a blank tablet prepared to take from the finger of God such forms as he shall be pleased to engrave on it. The more we cast ourselves back on God and commit ourselves to him, and renounce ourselves, the better we are. [. . .]

That is how, of three general sects of philosophy, two make express profession of doubt and ignorance; and in that of the dogmatists, which is the third, it is easy to discover that most of them have put on the mask of assurance only to look better. They have not thought so much of establishing any certainty for us as of showing us how far they had gone in this pursuit of the truth.

[. . .]

We must know whether fire is hot, whether snow is white, whether there is anything hard or soft within our knowledge. And as for those answers about which ancient stories are made, as when the man who doubted heat was told to throw himself into the fire, and when the one who denied the cold of ice was told to put some into his bosom: they are most unworthy of the philosophical profession. If they had left us in our natural state, receiving external impressions as they present themselves to us through our senses, and had let us follow our simple appetites, regulated by the condition of our birth, they would be right to speak thus. But it is from them that we have learned to make ourselves judges of the world; it is from them that we get this fancy, that human reason is controller-general of all that is outside and inside the heavenly vault, embracing everything, capable of everything, by means of which everything is known and understood.

This answer would be good among the cannibals, who enjoy the happiness of a long, tranquil, and peaceable life without the precepts of Aristotle and without acquaintance with the name of physics. This answer might perhaps be better and stronger than all those that they will borrow from their reason and their invention. Not only we ourselves, but all the animals, and everything over which the domination of natural law is still pure and simple, would be capable of using this answer; but they have renounced it.

They must not tell me: "It is true, for you see it and feel it so." They must tell me whether what I think I feel, I therefore actually do feel; and if I feel it, let them next tell me why I feel it, and how, and what I feel. Let them tell me the name, the origin, the ins and outs of heat and cold, the qualities of him who acts and of him who suffers; or let them abandon their profession, which is to accept or approve nothing except by the way of reason. That is their touchstone for every kind of experiment; but indeed it is a touchstone full of falsity, error, weakness, and impotence.

How do we want to test reason better than by herself? If we are not to believe her speaking of herself, she will hardly be fit to judge of alien things; if she knows anything, at least it will be her being and her domicile. She is in the soul, and a part or effect of it. For true and essential reason, whose name we steal on false pretenses, dwells in the bosom of God; there is her lair and her retreat, it is from there that she issues when God is pleased to let us see some ray of her, as Pallas sallied from the head of her father to communicate herself to the world.

Now let us see what human reason has taught us of herself and the soul. [. . .]

Reason taught Crates and Dicaearchus that there was no soul at all, but that the body stirred thus by a natural movement; Plato, that it was a substance moving by itself; Thales, a nature without rest; Asclepiades, an exercising of the senses; Hesiod and Anaximander, a thing composed of earth and water; Parmenides, of earth and fire; Empedocles, of blood; [. . .] Posidonius, Cleanthes, and Galen, a warmth or warm disposition; [. . .] Hippocrates, a spirit spread throughout the body; Varro, an air received by the mouth, warmed in the lungs, moistened in the heart, and spread throughout the body; Zeno, the quintessence of the four elements; Heraclides Ponticus, the light; Xenocrates and the Egyptians, a mobile number; the Chaldeans, a power without determined form:

> A certain vital habit of the body
> Which the Greeks call a harmony.
>
> LUCRETIUS

Let us not forget Aristotle: what naturally makes the body move is something which he calls entelechy – by as frigid an invention as any other, for he speaks of neither the essence, nor the origin, nor the nature of the soul, but merely notes its effect. Lactantius, Seneca, and the better part of the dogmatists have confessed that it was a thing they did not understand.

[. . .]

[Man Can Have No Knowledge]

Thus the liberty and wantonness of these ancient minds produced, in philosophy and the knowledge of man, many schools of different opinions, each undertaking to decide and choose in order to take sides.

[. . .]

Man is as capable of all things as he is of any. And if he confesses, as Theophrastus says, ignorance of first causes and principles, let him boldly give up all the rest of his knowledge. If his foundation is lacking, his argument is flat on the ground. Discussion and inquiry have no other aim and limit but principles; if this terminus does not stop their course, they fling themselves into infinite irresolution. [. . .]

Now it is likely that if the soul knew anything, it would first of all know itself; and if it knew anything outside of itself, that would be its body and shell before anything else. [. . .] We are nearer to ourselves than the whiteness of snow or the weight of stone are to us. If man does not know himself, how does he know his functions and powers? Not that it is impossible that some true knowledge may dwell in us; but if it does, it does so by accident. And since by the same road, the same manner and process, errors are received into our soul, it has no way to distinguish them or to pick out truth from falsehood.

[. . .]

I attempted at one time to keep myself tensed to withstand it and beat it down: for I am so far from being one of those who invite vices, that I do not even follow them, unless they drag me away. I would feel it come to life, grow, and increase in spite of my resistance, and finally seize me, alive and watching, and possess me, to such an extent that, as from drunkenness, the picture of things began to seem to me other than usual. I would see the advantages of the object of my desire visibly expanding and growing, and increasing and swelling from the breath of my imagination; the difficulties of my undertaking growing easy and smooth, my reason and my conscience withdrawing. But, this fire having vanished all in an instant like a flash of lightning, I would see my soul regain another kind of sight, another state, and another judgment; the difficulties of the retreat would seem to me great and invincible, and the same things would appear in a light and aspect very different from that in which the heat of desire had presented them to me.

Which of these states is the more truthful, Pyrrho does not know. We are never without sickness. Fevers have their heat and their cold; from the effects of a burning passion we fall back into the effects of a shivering passion. [. . .]

Now from the knowledge of this mobility of mine I have accidentally engendered in myself a certain constancy of opinions, and have scarcely altered my original and natural ones. For whatever appearance of truth there may be in novelty, I do not change easily, for fear of losing in the change. And since I am not capable of choosing, I accept other people's choice and stay in the position where God put me. Otherwise I could not keep myself from rolling about incessantly. Thus I have, by the grace of God, kept myself intact, without agitation or disturbance of conscience, in the ancient beliefs of our religion, in the midst of so many sects and divisions that our century has produced.

Now these are things that often clash; and I have been told that in geometry (which thinks it has reached the high point of certainty among the sciences) there are irrefutable demonstrations that controvert the truth of experience. For instance, Jacques Peletier was telling me at my house that he had found two lines traveling toward each other so as to meet, which nevertheless he proved could never come to touch even at infinity. And the Pyrrhonians use their arguments and their reason only to ruin the apparent facts of experience; and it is marvelous how far the suppleness of our reason has followed them in this plan of combating the evidence of the facts. For they demonstrate that we do not move, that we do not speak, that there is no weight or heat, with the same force of arguments with which we prove more likely things.

Ptolemy, who was a great man, had established the limits of our world; all the ancient philosophers thought they had its measure, except for a few remote islands that might escape their knowledge. It would have been Pyrrhonizing, a thousand years ago, to cast in doubt the science of cosmography, and the opinions that were accepted about it by one and all; it was heresy to admit the existence of the Antipodes. Behold in our century an infinite extent of terra firma, not an island or one particular country, but a portion nearly equal in size to the one we know, which has just been discovered. [. . .] The question is, if Ptolemy was once mistaken on the grounds of his reason, whether it would not be stupid for me now to trust to what these people say about it; and whether it is not more likely that this great body that we call the world is something quite different from what we judge.

[. . .]

[The Senses Are Inadequate]

This subject has brought me to the consideration of the senses, in which lies the greatest foundation and proof of our ignorance. All that is known, is doubtless known through the faculty of the knower; for since judgment comes from the operation of him who judges, it stands to reason that he performs this operation by his means and will, not by the constraint of others, as would happen if we knew things through the power and according to the law of their own essence. [. . .] Knowledge begins through them and is resolved into them.

After all, we would know no more than a stone, if we did not know that there is sound, smell, light, taste, measure, weight, softness, hardness, roughness, color, smoothness, breadth, depth. There are the base and the principles of the whole edifice of our knowledge. And according to some, knowledge is nothing else but sensation. Whoever can force me to contradict the senses has me by the throat; he could not make me retreat any further. The senses are the beginning and the end of human knowledge.

[. . .]

We cannot conceive of an absurdity more extreme than to maintain that fire does not heat, that light does not illumine, that there is no weight or hardness in iron; these are items of knowledge brought to us by the senses; and man has no belief or knowledge that can compare with this sort for certainty.

The first consideration that I offer on the subject of the senses is that I have my doubts whether man is provided with all the senses of nature. I see many animals that live a complete and perfect life, some without sight, others without hearing; who knows whether we too do not still lack one, two, three, or many other senses? For if any one is lacking, our reason cannot discover its absence. It is the privilege of the senses to be the extreme limit of our perception. There is nothing beyond them that can help us to discover them; no, nor can one sense discover the other.

[. . .]

It is impossible to make a man who was born blind conceive that he does not see; impossible to make him desire sight and regret its absence. Wherefore we should take no assurance from the fact that our soul is content and satisfied with those senses we have, seeing that it has no means of feeling its malady and imperfection therein, if any there be. It is impossible to say anything to this blind man, by reason, argument, or comparison, that will place in his imagination any apprehension of light, color, and sight. There is nothing further behind that can push that sense into evidence. When we see men blind from birth desire to see, it is not because they understand what they ask: they have learned from us that they lack something, that they have something to desire, which is in us; which they name perfectly well, and its effects and consequences; but nevertheless they do not know what it is, nor do they have a close or distant apprehension of it.

[. . .]

We grasp an apple by almost all our senses; we find in it redness, smoothness, smell, and sweetness; besides these it may have other properties, like drying up or shrinking, to which we have no sense that corresponds. The properties that we call occult in many things, as that of the magnet to attract iron – is it not likely that there are sensory faculties in nature suitable to judge them and perceive them, and that the lack of such faculties causes our ignorance of the true essence of such things? Perhaps it is some particular sense that reveals to cocks the hours of morning and midnight, and moves them to crow; that teaches hens, before any practice and experience, to fear a sparrow hawk, and not a goose or a peacock, which are bigger creatures; which warns chickens of the quality in the cat that is hostile to them, and not to distrust the dog: to beware of mewing, a rather caressing sound, and not of barking, a harsh and quarrelsome sound; that teaches wasps, ants, and rats always to select the best cheese and the best pear, before having tasted them; and that guides the stag, the elephant, the snake, to the knowledge of a certain herb suitable for their cure.

[. . .]

It is likely that the eyes of animals, which we see are of different colors, make bodies appear to them as matching their eyes.

To judge the action of the senses, then, we should first of all be in agreement with the animals, and second, among ourselves. Which we are not in the least; and we get into disputes at every turn because one man hears, sees, or tastes something differently from someone else; and we dispute about the diversity of the images that the senses bring us as much as about anything else. By the ordinary rule of nature, a child hears, sees, and tastes otherwise than a man of thirty, and he otherwise than a sexagenarian.

The senses are in some people more obscure and dim, in others more open and acute. We receive things in one way and another, according to what we are and what they seem to us. Now since our seeming is so uncertain and controversial, it is no longer a miracle if we are told that we can admit that snow appears white to us, but that we cannot be responsible for proving that it is so of its essence and in truth; and, with this starting point shaken, all the knowledge in the world necessarily goes by the board.

What of the fact that our senses interfere with each other? A painting seems to the eye to be in relief, to the touch it seems flat. Shall we say that musk is agreeable or not, which rejoices our sense of smell and offends our taste? There are herbs and unguents suitable for one part of the body which injure another. Honey is pleasant to the taste, unpleasant to the sight. As for those rings which are cut in the form of feathers and are called in heraldry feathers without ends, there is no eye that can discern their width and that can defend itself against this illusion, that on one side they grow wider, and narrower and tapering on the other, even when you roll them around your finger; however, to the touch they seem equal in width and everywhere alike.

[. . .]

Is it our senses, I say, which likewise fashion these objects out of various qualities, or do they really have them so? And in the face of this doubt, what can we decide about their real essence?

Moreover, since the accidents of illnesses, madness, or sleep make things appear to us otherwise than they appear to healthy people, wise men, and waking people, is it not likely that our normal state and our natural disposition can also assign to things an essence corresponding to our condition, and accommodate them to us, as our disordered states do? And that our health is as capable of giving them its own appearance as sickness? Why should the temperate man not have some vision of things related to himself, like the intemperate man, and likewise imprint his own character on them?

The jaded man assigns the insipidity to the wine; the healthy man, the savor; the thirsty man, the relish.

Now, since our condition accommodates things to itself and transforms them according to itself, we no longer know what things are in truth; for nothing comes to us except falsified and altered by our senses. When the compass, the square, and the ruler are off, all the proportions drawn from them, all the buildings erected by their measure, are also necessarily imperfect and defective. The uncertainty of our senses makes everything they produce uncertain. [. . .] Furthermore, who shall be fit to judge these differences? As we say in disputes about religion that we need a judge not attached to either party, free from preference and passion, which is impossible among Christians, so it is in this. For if he is old, he cannot judge the sense perception of old age, being himself a party in this dispute; if he is young, likewise; healthy, likewise; likewise sick, asleep, or awake. We would need someone exempt from all these qualities, so that with an unprejudiced judgment he might judge of these propositions as of things indifferent to him; and by that score we would need a judge that never was.

To judge the appearances that we receive of objects, we would need a judicatory instrument; to verify this instrument, we need a demonstration; to verify the demonstration, an instrument: there we are in a circle.

Since the senses cannot decide our dispute, being themselves full of uncertainty, it must be reason that does so. No reason can be established without another reason: there we go retreating back to infinity.

Our conception is not itself applied to foreign objects, but is conceived through the mediation of the senses; and the senses do not comprehend the foreign object, but only their own impressions. And thus the conception and semblance we form is not of the object, but only of the impression and effect made on the sense; which impression and the object are different things. Wherefore whoever judges by appearances judges by something other than the object.

And as for saying that the impressions of the senses convey to the soul the quality of the foreign objects by resemblance, how can the soul and understanding make sure of this resemblance, having of itself no communication with foreign objects? Just as a man who does not know Socrates, seeing his portrait, cannot say that it resembles him.

Now if anyone should want to judge by appearances anyway, to judge by all appearances is impossible, for they clash with one another by their contradictions and discrepancies, as we see by experience. Shall some selected appearances rule the others? We shall have to verify this selection by another selection, the second by a third; and thus it will never be finished.

[Changing Man Cannot Know Changing Things]

Finally, there is no existence that is constant, either of our being or of that of objects. And we, and our judgment, and all mortal things go on flowing and rolling unceasingly. Thus nothing certain can be established about one thing by another, both the judging and the judged being in continual change and motion.

[Changing Man Cannot Know Unchanging God]

We have no communication with being, because every human nature is always midway between birth and death, offering only a dim semblance and shadow of itself, and an uncertain and feeble opinion. And if by chance you fix your thought on trying to grasp its essence, it will be neither more nor less than if someone tried to grasp water: for the more he squeezes and presses what by its nature flows all over, the more he will lose what he was trying to hold and grasp. Thus, all things being subject to pass from one change to another, reason, seeking a real stability in them, is baffled, being unable to apprehend anything stable and permanent; because everything is either coming into being and not yet fully existent, or beginning to die before it is born.

[. . .]

But then what really is? That which is eternal: that is to say, what never had birth, nor will ever have an end; to which time never brings any change. For time is a mobile thing, which appears as in a shadow, together with matter, which is ever running and flowing, without ever remaining stable or permanent. To which belong the words *before* and *after*, and *has been* or *will be*, which at the very first sight show very evidently that time is not a thing that *is*; for it would be a great stupidity and a perfectly apparent falsehood to say that that *is* which is not yet in being, or which already has ceased to be. And as for these words, *present*, *immediate*, *now*, on which it seems that we chiefly found and support our understanding of time, reason discovering this immediately destroys it; for she at once splits and divides it into future and past, as though wanting to see it necessarily divided in two.

The same thing happens to nature that is measured, as to time that measures it. For there is nothing in it either that abides or is stable; but all things in it are either born, or being born, or dying. For which reason it would be a sin to say of God, who is the only one that *is*, that he *was* or *will be*. For those terms represent declinings, transitions, or vicissitudes of what cannot endure or remain in being. Wherefore we must conclude that God alone *is* – not at all according to any measure of time, but according to an eternity immutable and immobile, not measured by time or subject to any decline; before whom there is nothing, nor will there be after, nor is there anything more new or more recent; but one who really is – who by one single *now* fills the *ever*; and there is nothing that really is but he alone – nor can we say "He has been," or "He will be" – without beginning and without end.

To this most religious conclusion of a pagan I want to add only this remark of a witness of the same condition, for an ending to this long and boring discourse, which would give me material without end: "O what a vile and abject thing is man," he says, "if he does not raise himself above humanity!"

[Conclusion: Man Is Nothing without God]

That is a good statement and a useful desire, but equally absurd. For to make the handful bigger than the hand, the armful bigger than the arm, and to hope to straddle more than the reach of our legs, is impossible and unnatural. Nor can man raise himself above himself and humanity; for he can see only with his own eyes, and seize only with his own grasp.

He will rise, if God by exception lends him a hand; he will rise by abandoning and renouncing his own means, and letting himself be raised and uplifted by purely celestial means.

It is for our Christian faith, not for his Stoical virtue, to aspire to that divine and miraculous metamorphosis.

2

Francis Bacon, *The New Organon*

Francis Bacon (1561–1626) was educated at Trinity College, Cambridge, and Gray's Inn. His father was Sir Nicholas Bacon, Lord Keeper to Queen Elizabeth I. He was a member of parliament in 1584, and later participated in the prosecution of his friend the earl of Essex. He was knighted by James I in 1603 and became Attorney General in 1613, Lord Keeper 1617, and Lord Chancellor in 1618. He was created Baron Verulam in 1621. In the same year he pleaded guilty to accepting bribes. This ended his public life, and he devoted the rest of his life to philosophy and literature. He completed two parts of *Instauratio Magna: The Advancement of Learning* (1623) and *Novum Organum* (1620). His *Essays* appeared in several editions between 1597 and 1625.

In the selection below, Francis Bacon discusses four idols that interfere with acquiring knowledge. The Idols of the Tribe are rooted in human nature, in the belief that sensation is a reliable guide to the nature of the universe. The Idols of the Cave are those beliefs that an individual has acquired in his upbringing that interfere with his ability to judge objectively. The Idols of the Marketplace are those beliefs that result from interaction with other people. Most conspicuously, "the ill or unfit" definitions of words interfere with the acquisition of knowledge. Lastly, the Idols of the Theater are those false beliefs that come from philosophical and scientific theories.

As regards correct scientific methodology, he advocated collecting all the facts relevant to a certain topic and then framing an induction, a hypothesis, to account for those facts. Critics have pointed out that, for most phenomena, it is impossible to collect all the facts.

The New Organon; or, True Directions Concerning the Interpretation of Nature

Preface

[. . .]

Now my method, though hard to practice, is easy to explain; and it is this. I propose to establish progressive stages of certainty. The evidence of the sense, helped and guarded by a certain process of correction, I retain. But the mental operation which follows the act of sense I for the most part reject; and instead of it, I open and lay out a new and certain path for the mind to proceed in, starting directly from the simple sensuous perception. The necessity of this was felt no doubt by those who attributed so much importance to logic; showing thereby that they were in search of helps for the understanding, and had no confidence in the native and spontaneous process of the mind. But this remedy comes too late to do any good, when the mind is already, through the daily intercourse and conversation of life, occupied with unsound doctrines and beset on all sides by vain imaginations. And therefore that art of logic, coming (as I said) too late to the rescue, and no way able to set matters right again, has had the effect of fixing errors rather than disclosing truth. There remains but one course for the recovery of a sound and healthy condition, – namely, that the entire work of the understanding be commenced afresh, and the mind itself be from the very outset not left to take its own course, but guided at every step; and the business be done as if by machinery.

[...]

Aphorisms Concerning the Interpretation of Nature and the Kingdom of Man

[...]

III

Human knowledge and human power meet in one; for where the cause is not known the effect cannot be produced. Nature to be commanded must be obeyed; and that which in contemplation is as the cause is in operation as the rule.

[...]

XIV

The syllogism consists of propositions, propositions consist of words, words are symbols of notions. Therefore if the notions themselves (which is the root of the matter) are confused and overhastily abstracted from the facts, there can be no firmness in the superstructure. Our only hope therefore lies in a true induction.

XV

There is no soundness in our notions whether logical or physical. Substance, Quality, Action, Passion, Essence itself, are not sound notions: much less are Heavy, Light, Dense, Rare, Moist, Dry, Generation, Corruption, Attraction, Repulsion, Element, Matter, Form, and the like; but all are fantastical and ill defined.

[...]

XIX

There are and can be only two ways of searching into and discovering truth. The one flies from the senses and particulars to the most general axioms, and from these principles, the truth of which it takes for settled and immovable, proceeds to judgment and to the discovery of middle axioms. And this way is now in fashion. The other derives axioms from the senses and particulars, rising by a gradual and unbroken ascent, so that it arrives at the most general axioms last of all. This is the true way, but as yet untried.

[. . .]

XXXVIII

The idols and false notions which are now in possession of the human understanding, and have taken deep root therein, not only so beset men's minds that truth can hardly find entrance, but even after entrance obtained, they will again in the very instauration of the sciences meet and trouble us, unless men being forewarned of the danger fortify themselves as far as may be against their assaults.

XXXIX

There are four classes of idols which beset men's minds. To these for distinction's sake I have assigned names, – calling the first class *Idols of the Tribe*; the second, *Idols of the Cave*; the third, *Idols of the Marketplace*; the fourth, *Idols of the Theater.*

XL

The formation of ideas and axioms by true induction is no doubt the proper remedy to be applied for the keeping off and clearing away of idols. To point them out, however, is of great use, for the doctrine of idols is to the interpretation of nature what the doctrine of the refutation of sophisms is to common logic.

XLI

The Idols of the Tribe have their foundation in human nature itself, and in the tribe or race of men. For it is a false assertion that the sense of man is the measure of things. On the contrary, all perceptions, as well of the sense as of the mind, are according to the measure of the individual and not according to the measure of the universe. And the human understanding is like a false mirror, which, receiving rays irregularly, distorts and discolors the nature of things by mingling its own nature with it.

XLII

The Idols of the Cave are the idols of the individual man. For everyone (besides the errors common to human nature in general) has a cave or den of his own, which refracts and discolors the light of nature; owing either to his own proper and peculiar nature or to his education and conversation with others; or to the reading of books, and the authority of those whom he esteems and admires; or to the differences of impressions, accordingly as they take place in a mind preoccupied and predisposed or in a mind indifferent and settled; or the like. So that the spirit of man (according as it is meted out to different individuals) is in fact a thing variable and full of perturbation, and governed as it were by chance. Whence it was well observed by Heraclitus that men look for sciences in their own lesser worlds, and not in the greater or common world.

XLIII

There are also idols formed by the intercourse and association of men with each other, which I call Idols of the Market-place, on account of the commerce and consort of men there. For it is by discourse that men associate; and words are imposed according to the apprehension of the vulgar. And therefore the ill and unfit choice of words wonderfully obstructs the understanding. Nor do the definitions or explanations wherewith in some things learned men are wont to guard and defend themselves, by any means set the matter right. But words plainly force and overrule the understanding, and throw all into confusion, and lead men away into numberless empty controversies and idle fancies.

XLIV

Lastly, there are idols which have immigrated into men's minds from the various dogmas of philosophies, and also from wrong laws of demonstration. These I call Idols of the Theater; because in my judgment all the received systems are but so many stage-plays, representing worlds of their own creation after an unreal and scenic fashion. Nor is it only of the systems now in vogue, or only of the ancient sects and philosophies, that I speak: for many more plays of the same kind may yet be composed and in like artificial manner set forth; seeing that errors the most widely different have nevertheless causes for the most part alike. Neither again do I mean this only of entire systems, but also of many principles and axioms in science, which by tradition, credulity, and negligence have come to be received.

But of these several kinds of idols I must speak more largely and exactly, that the understanding may be duly cautioned.

XLV

The human understanding is of its own nature prone to suppose the existence of more order and regularity in the world than it finds. And though there be many things in nature which are singular and unmatched, yet it devises for them parallels and conjugates and relatives which do not exist. Hence the fiction that all celestial bodies move in perfect circles; spirals and dragons being (except in name) utterly rejected. Hence too the element of fire with its orb is brought in, to make up the square with the other three which the sense perceives. Hence also the ratio of density of the so-called elements is arbitrarily fixed at ten to one. And so on of other dreams. And these fancies affect not dogmas only, but simple notions also.

XLVI

The human understanding when it has once adopted an opinion (either as being the received opinion or as being agreeable to itself) draws all things else to support and agree with it. And though there be a greater number and weight of instances to be found on the other side, yet these it either neglects and despises, or else by some distinction sets aside and rejects; in order that by this great and pernicious predetermination the authority of its former conclusions may remain inviolate. And therefore it was a good answer that was made by one who when they showed him hanging in a temple a picture of those who had paid their vows as having escaped shipwreck, and would have him say whether he did not now acknowledge the power of the gods, – "Aye," asked he again, "but where are they painted that were drowned after their vows?" And such is the way of all superstition, whether in astrology, dreams, omens, divine judgments, or the like; wherein men, having a delight in such vanities, mark the events where they are fulfilled, but where they fail, though this happen much oftener, neglect and pass them by. But with far more subtlety does this mischief insinuate itself into philosophy and the sciences; in which the first conclusion colors and brings into conformity with itself all that come after, though far sounder and better. Besides, independently of that delight and vanity which I have described, it is the peculiar and perpetual error of the human intellect to be more moved and excited by affirmatives than by negatives; whereas it ought properly to hold itself indifferently disposed towards both alike. Indeed in the establishment of any true axiom, the negative instance is the more forcible of the two.

XLVII

The human understanding is moved by those things most which strike and enter the mind simultaneously and suddenly, and so fill the imagination; and then it feigns and supposes all other things to be somehow, though it cannot see how, similar to those few things by which it is surrounded. But for that going to and fro to remote and heterogeneous instances, by which axioms are tried as in the fire, the intellect is altogether slow And unfit, unless it be forced thereto by severe laws and overruling authority.

XLVIII

The human understanding is unquiet; it cannot stop or rest, and still presses onward, but in vain. Therefore it is that we cannot conceive of any end or limit to the world; but always as of necessity it occurs to us that there is something beyond. Neither again can it be conceived how eternity has flowed down to the present day: for that distinction which is commonly received of infinity in time past and in time to come can by no means hold; for it would thence follow that one infinity is greater than another, and that infinity is wasting away and tending to become finite. The like subtlety arises touching the infinite divisibility of lines, from the same inability of thought to stop. But this inability interferes more mischievously in the discovery of causes: for although the most general principles in nature ought to be held merely positive, as they are discovered, and cannot with truth be referred to a cause; nevertheless the human understanding being unable to rest still seeks something prior in the order of nature. And then it is that in struggling towards that which is further off it falls back upon that which is more nigh at hand, – namely, on final causes; which have relation clearly to the nature of man rather than to the nature of the universe, and from this source have strangely defiled philosophy. But he is no less an unskilled and shallow philosopher who seeks causes of that which is most general, than he who in things subordinate and subaltern omits to do so.

[. . .]

L

But by far the greatest hindrance and aberration of the human understanding proceeds from the dullness, incompetency, and deceptions of the senses; in that things which strike the sense outweigh things which do not immediately strike it, though they be more important. Hence it is that speculation commonly ceases where sight ceases, insomuch that of things invisible there is little or no observation. Hence all the working of the spirits inclosed in tangible bodies lies hid and unobserved of men. So also all the more subtle changes of form in the parts of coarser substances (which they commonly call alteration, though it is in truth local motion through exceedingly small spaces) is in like manner unobserved. And yet unless these two things just mentioned be searched out and brought to light, nothing great can be achieved in nature, as far as the production of works is concerned. So again the essential nature of our common air, and of all bodies less dense than air (which are very many), is almost unknown. For the sense by itself is a thing infirm and erring; neither can instruments for enlarging or sharpening the senses do much: but all the truer kind of interpretation of nature is effected by instances and experiments fit and apposite; wherein the sense decides touching the experiment only, and the experiment touching the point in nature and the thing itself.

LI

[. . .] Matter rather than forms should be the object of our attention, its configurations and changes of configuration, and simple action, and law of action or motion; for forms are figments of the human mind, unless you will call those laws of action forms.

LII

Such then are the idols which I call *Idols of the Tribe*; and which take their rise either from the homogeneity of the substance of the human spirit, or from its preoccupation, or from its narrowness, or from its restless motion, or from an infusion of the affections, or from the incompetency of the senses, or from the mode of impression.

LIII

The *Idols of the Cave* take their rise in the peculiar constitution, mental or bodily, of each individual; and also in education, habit, and accident. Of this kind there is a great number and variety; but I will instance those the pointing out of which contains the most important caution, and which have most effect in disturbing the clearness of the understanding.

LIV

Men become attached to certain particular sciences and speculations, either because they fancy themselves the authors and inventors thereof, or because they have bestowed the greatest pains upon them and become most habituated to them. But men of this kind, if they betake themselves to philosophy and contemplations of a general character, distort and color them in obedience to their former fancies; a thing especially to be noticed in Aristotle, who made his natural philosophy a mere bondservant to his logic, thereby rendering it contentious and well nigh useless. The race of chemists again out of a few experiments of the furnace have built up a fantastic philosophy, framed with reference to a few things; and Gilbert also, after he had employed himself most laboriously in the study and observation of the lodestone, proceeded at once to construct an entire system in accordance with his favorite subject.

LV

There is one principal and as it were radical distinction between different minds, in respect of philosophy and the sciences; which is this: that some minds are stronger and apter to mark the differences of things, others to mark their resemblances. The steady and acute mind can fix its contemplations and dwell and fasten on the subtlest distinctions; the lofty and discursive mind recognizes and puts together the finest and most general resemblances. Both kinds however easily err in excess, by catching the one at gradations the other at shadows.

[. . .]

LVIII

Let such then be our provision and contemplative prudence for keeping off and dislodging the Idols of the Cave. [. . .] And generally let every student of nature take this as a rule, – that whatever his mind seizes and dwells upon with peculiar satisfaction is to be held in suspicion, and that so much the more care is to be taken in dealing with such questions to keep the understanding even and clear.

LIX

But the *Idols of the Market-place* are the most troublesome of all: idols which have crept into the understanding through the alliances of words and names. For men believe that their reason governs words; but it is also true that words react on the understanding; and this it is that has rendered philosophy and the sciences sophistical and inactive. Now words, being commonly framed and applied according to the capacity of the vulgar, follow those lines of division which are most obvious to the vulgar understanding. And whenever an understanding of greater acuteness or a more diligent observation would alter those lines to suit the true divisions of nature, words stand in the way and resist the change. Whence it comes to pass that the high and formal discussions of learned men end oftentimes in disputes about words and names; with which (according to the use and wisdom of the mathematicians) it would be more prudent to begin, and so by means of definitions reduce them to order. Yet even definitions cannot cure this evil in dealing with natural and material things; since the definitions themselves consist of words, and those words beget others: so that it is necessary to recur to individual instances, and those in due series and order; as I shall say presently when I come to the method and scheme for the formation of notions and axioms.

LX

The idols imposed by words on the understanding are of two kinds. They are either names of things which do not exist (for as there are things left unnamed through lack of observation, so likewise are there names which result from fantastic suppositions and to which nothing in reality correponds), or they are names of things which exist, but yet confused and ill-defined, and hastily and irregularly derived from realities. Of the former kind are Fortune, the Prime Mover, Planetary Orbits, Elements of Fire, and like fictions which owe their origin to false and idle theories. And this class of idols is more easily expelled, because to get rid of them it is only necessary that all theories should be steadily rejected and dismissed as obsolete.

But the other class, which springs out of a faulty and unskillful abstraction, is intricate and deeply rooted. Let us take for example such a word as *humid*, and see how far the several things which the word is used to signify agree with each other; and we shall find the word *humid* to be nothing else than a mark loosely and confusedly applied to denote a variety of actions which will not bear to be reduced to any constant meaning. For it both signifies that which easily spreads itself round any other body; and that which in itself is indeterminate and cannot solidize; and that which readily yields in every direction; and that which easily divides and scatters itself; and that which easily unites and collects itself; and that which readily flows and is put in motion; and that which readily clings to another body and wets it; and that which is easily reduced to a liquid, or being solid easily melts. Accordingly when you come to apply the word, – if you take it in one sense, flame is humid; if in another, air is not humid; if in another, fine dust is humid; if in another, glass is humid. So that it is easy to see that the notion is taken by abstraction only from water and common and ordinary liquids, without any due verification.

There are however in words certain degrees of distortion and error. One of the least faulty kinds is that of names of substances, especially of lowest species and well-deduced (for the notion of *chalk* and of *mud* is good, of *earth* bad); a more faulty kind is that of actions, as *to generate, to corrupt, to alter*; the most faulty is of qualities (except such as are the immediate objects of the sense) as *heavy, light, rare, dense*, and the like. Yet in all these cases some notions are of necessity a little better than others, in proportion to the greater variety of subjects that fall within the range of the human sense.

LXI

But the *Idols of the Theater* are not innate, nor do they steal into the understanding secretly, but are plainly impressed and received into the mind from the play-books of philosophical systems and the perverted rules of demonstration. To attempt refutations in this case would be merely inconsistent with what I have already said: for since we agree neither upon principles nor upon demonstrations there is no place for argument. And this is so far well, inasmuch as it leaves the honor of the ancients untouched. For they are no wise disparaged – the question between them and me being only as to the way. For as the saying is, the lame man who keeps the right road outstrips the runner who takes a wrong one. Nay it is obvious that when a man runs the wrong way, the more active and swift he is the further he will go astray.

But the course I propose for the discovery of sciences is such as leaves but little to the acuteness and strength of wits, but places all wits and understandings nearly on a level. For as in the drawing of a straight line or a perfect circle, much depends on the steadiness and practice of the hand, if it be done by aim of hand only, but if with the aid of rule or compass, little or nothing; so is it exactly with my plan. But though particular confutations would be of no avail, yet touching the sects and general divisions of such systems I must say something; something also touching the external signs which show that they are unsound; and finally something touching the causes of such great infelicity and of such lasting and general agreement in error; that so the access to truth may be made less difficult, and the human understanding may the more willingly submit to its purgation and dismiss its idols.

LXII

[. . .]

In general however there is taken for the material of philosophy either a great deal out of a few things, or a very little out of many things; so that on both sides philosophy is based on too narrow a foundation of experiment and natural history, and decides on the authority of too few cases. For the rational school of philosophers snatches from experience a variety of common instances, neither duly ascertained nor diligently examined and weighed, and leaves all the rest to meditation and agitation of wit.

There is also another class of philosophers, who having bestowed much diligent and careful labor on a few experiments, have thence made bold to educe and construct systems; wresting all other facts in a strange fashion to conformity therewith.

And there is yet a third class, consisting of those who out of faith and veneration mix their philosophy with theology and traditions; among whom the vanity of some has gone so far aside as to seek the origin of science among spirits and genii. So that this parent stock of errors – this false philosophy – is of three kinds: the *sophistical*, the *empirical*, and the *superstitious*.

[. . .]

LXIV

But the empirical school of philosophy gives birth to dogmas more deformed and monstrous than the sophistical or rational school. For it has its foundations not in the light of common notions [. . .] but in the narrowness and darkness of a few experiments. To those therefore who are daily busied with these experiments, and have infected their imagination with them, such a philosophy seems probable and all but certain; to all men else incredible and vain. [. . .]

LXV

But the corruption of philosophy by superstition and an admixture of theology is far more widely spread, and does the greatest harm, whether to entire systems or to their parts. For the human understanding is obnoxious to the influence of the imagination no less than to the influence of common notions. For the contentious and sophistical kind of philosophy ensnares the understanding; but this kind, being fanciful and tumid and half poetical, misleads it more by flattery. For there is in man an ambition of the understanding, no less than of the will, especially in high and lofty spirits.

[. . .]

LXVII

A caution must also be given to the understanding against the intemperance which systems of philosophy manifest in giving or withholding assent; because intemperance of this kind seems to establish idols and in some sort to perpetuate them, leaving no way open to reach and dislodge them.

This excess is of two kinds: the first being manifest in those who are ready in deciding; and render sciences dogmatic and magisterial; the other in those who deny that we can know anything, and so introduce a wandering kind of inquiry that leads to nothing; of which kinds the former subdues, the latter weakens the understanding.

[. . .]

LXVIII

So much concerning the several classes of idols, and their equipage: all of which must be renounced and put away with a fixed and solemn determination, and the understanding thoroughly freed and cleansed; the entrance into the kingdom of man, founded on the sciences, being not much other than the entrance into the kingdom of heaven, whereinto none may enter except as a little child.

LXX

But the best demonstration by far is experience, if it go not beyond the actual experiment. For if it be transferred to other cases which are deemed similar, unless such transfer be made by a just and orderly process, it is a fallacious thing. But the manner of making experiments which men now use is blind and stupid. And therefore, wandering and straying as they do with no settled course, and taking counsel only from things as they fall out, they fetch a wide circuit and meet with many matters, but make little progress; and sometimes are full of hope, sometimes are distracted; and always find that there is something beyond to be sought. For it generally happens that men make their trials carelessly, and as it were in play; slightly varying experiments already known, and, if the thing does not answer, growing weary and abandoning the attempt. And even if they apply themselves to experiments more seriously and earnestly and laboriously, still they spend their labor in working out some one experiment, as Gilbert with the magnet, and the chemists with gold, – a course of proceeding not less unskillful in the design than small in the attempt. For no one successfully investigates the nature of a thing in the thing itself; the inquiry must be enlarged, so as to become more general.

And even when they seek to educe some science or theory from their experiments, they nevertheless almost always turn aside with overhasty and unseasonable eagerness to practice; not only for the sake of the uses and fruits of the practice, but from impatience to obtain in the shape of some new work an assurance for themselves that it is worth their while to go on; and also to show themselves off to the world, and so raise the credit of the business in which they are engaged. Thus, like Atalanta, they go aside to pick up the golden apple, but meanwhile they interrupt their course, and let the victory escape them. But in the true course of experience, and in carrying it on to the effecting of new works, the divine wisdom and order must be our pattern. [. . .]

3

Galileo Galilei, *Letter to the Grand Duchess Christina* and *The Assayer*

Galileo Galilei (1564–1642) studied medicine at the University of Pisa. At the age of 19 he was working on the physics of the pendulum. He counted the oscillations of a swinging lamp by using his pulse as a timing device. He discovered that the time for each swing remained the same no matter what the amplitude was.[1] As a professor at the University of Pisa, he continued his experiments with motion. In 1592 he became a professor at the University of Padua. Having constructed a telescope – he was not the first to do this – he discovered mountains on the moon, individual stars in the Milky Way, and four of Jupiter's moons. In 1610 he went to Florence to serve as Cosimo II de 'Medici's philosopher and mathematician. In 1632 Roman Catholic officials in Rome warned him not to teach the Copernican system. The publication of his *Dialogues on the Two Chief Systems of the World* (1632) led to troubles with the Inquisition. He spent his last years under house arrest, but he was able to receive visitors, for example, Thomas Hobbes, and to write. His last book, *Dialogues Concerning Two New Sciences* (1638), contained most of the results of his physics.

Galileo begins his letter to the Grand Duchess Christina by noting that Copernicus did not discuss religion or faith and argued solely from "astronomical and geometrical demonstrations, founded primarily upon sense experiences and very exact observations" (p. 50). Thus, given that the Bible is true and that a literal interpretation of it is inconsistent with Copernicus's findings, a different interpretation of the Bible is needed. The key to this new interpretation is implicit in Galileo's comment, derived from Cardinal Baronius, that the Bible teaches people, not how the heavens go, but how to go to heaven (p. 51).

Notice that Galileo takes the truth of the Bible to be given. A century later, some intellectuals gave up that belief, and either argued for its truth or denied that it was true at all. Significant intellectual atheism belongs much more to the eighteenth century than to the seventeenth.

The distinction between primary and secondary qualities is introduced by Galileo in his letter to the Grand Duchess. Heat, he holds, is not "a real phenomenon, or property, or quality." The real properties of material objects are location, size and shape, motion, and

1 The amplitude of a pendulum is the greatest distance between the end points of the arc made by the pendulum.

a few other things. Taste, colors, odors, and other qualitative properties are products of sensation or the mind. These things are caused by the "shapes, numbers, and slow or rapid movements" of bodies. Although heat may seem to belong to bodies themselves, in fact, it is the result of the primary properties of bodies, shapes, and numbers, and so on.

Galileo introduced the distinction between primary and secondary qualities in the course of arguing that heat is not, contrary to how it seems to people, a quality of objects. Rather, it is the subjective experience of a person sensing an object, the molecules of which are moving rapidly.

To The Most Serene Grand Duchess Mother

Some years ago, as Your Serene Highness well knows, I discovered in the heavens many things that had not been seen before our own age. The novelty of these things, as well as some consequences which followed from them in contradiction to the physical notions commonly held among academic philosophers, stirred up against me no small number of professors – as if I had placed these things in the sky with my own hands in order to upset nature and overturn the sciences. They seemed to forget that the increase of known truths stimulates the investigation, establishment, and growth of the arts; not their diminution or destruction.

Showing a greater fondness for their own opinions than for truth, they sought to deny and disprove the new things which, if they had cared to look for themselves, their own senses would have demonstrated to them. To this end they hurled various charges and published numerous writings filled with vain arguments, and they made the grave mistake of sprinkling these with passages taken from places in the Bible which they had failed to understand properly, and which were ill suited to their purposes.

[. . .]

Copernicus never discusses matters of religion or faith, nor does he use arguments that depend in any way upon the authority of sacred writings which he might have interpreted erroneously. He stands always upon physical conclusions pertaining to the celestial motions, and deals with them by astronomical and geometrical demonstrations, founded primarily upon sense experiences and very exact observations. He did not ignore the Bible, but he knew very well that if his doctrine were proved, then it could not contradict the Scriptures when they were rightly understood.

[. . .]

The reason produced for condemning the opinion that the earth moves and the sun stands still is that in many places in the Bible one may read that the sun moves and the earth stands still. Since the Bible cannot err, it follows as a necessary consequence that anyone takes an erroneous and heretical position who maintains that the sun is inherently motionless and the earth movable.

With regard to this argument, I think in the first place that it is very pious to say and prudent to affirm that the holy Bible can never speak untruth – whenever its true meaning is understood. But I believe nobody will deny that it is often very abstruse, and may say things which are quite different from what its bare words signify. Hence in expounding the Bible if one were always to confine oneself to the unadorned grammatical meaning, one might fall into error. Not only contradictions and propositions far from true might thus be made to appear in the Bible, but even grave heresies and follies. Thus it would be necessary to assign to God feet, hands, and eyes, as well as corporeal and human affections, such as anger, repentance, hatred, and sometimes even the forgetting of things past and ignorance of those to come. These propositions uttered by the Holy Ghost were set down in that manner by the sacred scribes in order to accommodate them to the capacities of the common people, who are rude and unlearned. For the sake of those who deserve to be separated from the herd, it is necessary that wise expositors should produce the true senses of such passages, together with the special reasons for which they were set down in these words. This doctrine is so widespread and so definite with all theologians that it would be superfluous to adduce evidence for it. [. . .] [T]he primary purpose of the sacred writings – the service of God and the salvation of souls – matters infinitely beyond the comprehension of the common people.

This being granted, I think that in discussions of physical problems we ought to begin not from the authority of scriptural passages, but from sense-experiences and necessary demonstrations; for the holy Bible and the phenomena of nature proceed alike from the divine World, the former as the dictate of the Holy Ghost and the latter as the observant executrix of God's commands.

[. . .]

But I do not feel obliged to believe that that same God who has endowed us with senses, reason, and intellect has intended to forgo their use and by some other means to give us knowledge which we can attain by them. He would not require us to deny sense and reason in physical matters which are set before our eyes and minds by direct experience or necessary demonstrations. This must be especially true in those sciences of which but the faintest trace (and that consisting of conclusions) is to be found in the Bible. Of astronomy, for instance, so little is found that none of the planets except Venus are so much as mentioned, and this only once or twice under the name of "Lucifer." If the sacred scribes had had any intention of teaching people certain arrangements and motions of the heavenly bodies, or had they wished us to derive such knowledge from the Bible, then in my opinion they would not have spoken of these matters so sparingly in comparison with the infinite number of admirable conclusions which are demonstrated in that science. Far from pretending to teach us the constitution and motions of the heavens and the stars, with their shapes, magnitudes, and distances, the authors of the Bible intentionally forbore to speak of these things, though all were quite well known to them. Such is the opinion of the holiest and most learned Fathers.

[. . .]

From these things it follows as a necessary consequence that, since the Holy Ghost did not intend to teach us whether heaven moves or stands still, whether its shape is spherical or like a discus or extended in a plane, nor whether the earth is located at its center or off to one side, then so much the less was it intended to settle for us any other conclusion of the same kind. [. . .] I would say here something that was heard from an ecclesiastic of the most eminent degree: "That the intention of the Holy Ghost is to teach us how one goes to heaven, not how heaven goes."

[. . .]

[I]n St. Augustine we read: "If anyone shall set the authority of Holy Writ against clear and manifest reason, he who does this knows not what he has undertaken; for he opposes to the truth not the meaning of the Bible, which is beyond his comprehension, but rather his own interpretation; not what is in the Bible, but what he has found in himself and imagines to be there."

This granted, and it being true that two truths cannot contradict one another, it is the function of wise expositors to seek out the true senses of scriptural texts. These will unquestionably accord with the physical conclusions which manifest sense and necessary demonstrations have previously made certain to us.

[. . .]

The Assayer

It now remains for me to tell Your Excellency, as I promised, some thoughts of mine about the proposition "motion is the cause of heat," and to show in what sense this may be true. But first I must consider what it is that we call heat, as I suspect that people in general have a concept of this which is very remote from the truth. For they believe that heat is a real phenomenon, or property, or quality, which actually resides in the material by which we feel ourselves warmed. Now I say that whenever I conceive any material or corporeal substance, I immediately feel the need to think of it as bounded, and as having this or that shape; as being large or small in relation to other things, and in some specific place at any given time; as being in motion or at rest; as touching or not touching some other body; and as being one in number, or few, or many. From these conditions I cannot separate such a substance by any stretch of my imagination. But that it must be white or red, bitter or sweet, noisy or silent, and of sweet or foul odor, my mind does not feel compelled to bring in as necessary accompaniments. Without the senses as our guides, reason or imagination unaided would probably never arrive at qualities like these. Hence I think that tastes, odors, colors, and so on are no more than mere names so far as the object in which we place them is concerned, and that they reside only in the consciousness. Hence if the living creature were removed, all these qualities would be wiped away and annihilated. But since we have imposed upon them special names, distinct from those of the other and real qualities mentioned previously, we wish to believe that they really exist as actually different from those.

I may be able to make my notion clearer by means of some examples. I move my hand first over a marble statue and then over a living man. As to the effect flowing from my hand, this is the same with regard to both objects and my hand; it consists of the primary phenomena of motion and touch, for which we have no further names. But the live body which receives these operations feels different sensations according to the various places touched. When touched upon the soles of the feet, for example, or under the knee or armpit, it feels in addition to the common sensation of touch a sensation on which we have imposed a special name, "tickling." This sensation belongs to us and not to the hand. Anyone would make a serious error if he said that the hand, in addition to the properties of moving and touching, possessed another faculty of "tickling," as if tickling were a phenomenon that resided in the hand that tickled. A piece of paper or a feather drawn lightly over any part of our bodies performs intrinsically the same operations of moving and touching, but by touching the eye, the nose, or the upper lip it excites in us an almost intolerable titillation, even though elsewhere it is scarcely felt. This titillation belongs entirely to us and not to the feather; if the live and sensitive body were removed it would remain no more than a mere word. I believe that no more solid an existence belongs to many qualities which we have come to attribute to physical bodies – tastes, odors, colors, and many more.

A body which is solid and, so to speak, quite material, when moved in contact with any part of my person produces in me the sensation we call touch. This, though it exists over my entire body, seems to reside principally in the palms of the hands and in the finger tips, by whose means we sense the most minute differences in texture that are not easily distinguished by other parts of our bodies. Some of these sensations are more pleasant to us than others. . . . The sense of touch is more material than the other sense; and, as it arises from the solidity of matter, it seems to be related to the earthly element.

Perhaps the origin of two other senses lies in the fact that there are bodies which constantly dissolve into minute particles, some of which are heavier than air and descend, while others are lighter and rise up. The former may strike upon a certain part of our bodies that is much more sensitive than the skin, which does not feel the invasion of such subtle matter. This is the upper surface of the tongue; here the tiny particles are received, and mixing with and penetrating its moisture, they give rise to tastes, which are sweet or unsavory according to the various shapes, numbers, and speeds of the particles. And those minute particles which rise up may enter by our nostrils and strike upon some small protuberances which are the instrument of smelling; here likewise their touch and passage is received to our like or dislike according as they have this or that shape, are fast or slow, and are numerous or few. The tongue and nasal passages are providently arranged for these things, as the one extends from below to receive descending particles, and the other is adapted to those which ascend. Perhaps the excitation of tastes may be given a certain analogy to fluids, which descend through air, and odors to fires, which ascend.

Then there remains the air itself, an element available for sounds, which come to us indifferently from below, above, and all sides – for we reside in the air and its movements displace it equally in all directions. The location of the ear is most fittingly accommodated to all positions in space. Sounds are made and heard by us when the air – without any special property of "sonority" or "transonority" – is ruffled by a rapid tremor into very minute waves and moves certain cartilages of a tympanum in our ear. External means capable of thus ruffling the air are very numerous, but for the most part they may be reduced to the trembling of some body which pushes the air and disturbs it. Waves are propagated very rapidly in this way, and high tones are produced by frequent waves and low tones by sparse ones.

To excite in us tastes, odors, and sounds I believe that nothing is required in external bodies except shapes, numbers, and slow or rapid movements. I think that if ears, tongues, and noses were removed, shapes and numbers and motions would remain, but not odors or tastes or sounds. The latter, I believe, are nothing more than names when separated from living beings, just as tickling and titillation are nothing but names in the absence of such things as noses and armpits. And as these four senses are related to the four elements, so I believe that vision, the sense eminent above all others in the proportion of the finite to the infinite, the temporal to the instantaneous, the quantitative to the indivisible, the illuminated to the obscure – that vision, I say, is related to light itself. But of this sensation and the things pertaining to it I pretend to understand but little; and since even a long time would not suffice to explain that trifle, or even to hint at an explanation, I pass this over in silence.

Having shown that many sensations which are supposed to be qualities residing in external objects have no real existence save in us, and outside ourselves are mere names, I now say that I am inclined to believe heat to be of this character. Those materials which produce heat in us and make us feel warmth, which are known by the general name of "fire," would then be a multitude of minute particles having certain shapes and moving with certain velocities. Meeting with our bodies, they penetrate by means of their extreme subtlety, and their touch as felt by us when they pass through our substance is the sensation we call "heat." This is pleasant or unpleasant according to the greater or smaller speed of these particles as they go pricking and penetrating; pleasant when this assists our necessary transpiration, and obnoxious when it causes too great a separation and dissolution of our substance. The operation of fire by means of its particles is merely that in moving it penetrates all bodies, causing their speedy or slow dissolution in proportion to the number and velocity of the fire-corpuscles and the density or tenuity of the bodies. Many materials are such that in their decomposition the greater part of them passes over into additional tiny corpuscles, and this dissolution continues so long as these continue to meet with further matter capable of being so resolved. I do not believe that in addition to shape, number, motion, penetration, and touch there is any other quality in fire corresponding to "heat"; this belongs so intimately to us that when the live body is taken away, heat becomes no more than a simple name. . . .

Since the presence of fire-corpuscles alone does not suffice to excite heat, but their motion is needed also, it seems to me that one may very reasonably say that motion is the cause of heat. . . .

4

René Descartes, *Discourse on the Method of Rightly Conducting the Reason and Seeking for Truth in the Sciences*

In this selection, Descartes begins by saying, "Good sense is of all things in the world the most equally distributed," and that it is not the case that some men are more rational than others. He is often interpreted as being sarcastic and not meaning what he says. If that is true, then these opening remarks undercut the point of the *Discourse*, namely, that what is most important in the pursuit of knowledge is use of the correct method of inquiry.[1] But he then denies that he is laying down universal prescriptions. He is merely reporting the method that has proved fruitful to himself.

The four maxims that he followed are (1) to accept nothing as true that he did not clearly recognize to be true; (2) to divide each problem into as many parts as possible; (3) to reflect on the simplest parts of the problem before going onto increasingly more difficult parts; and (4) to enumerate everything that he had done in order to be sure that nothing had been left out. The problem with these maxims is that they do not provide any help in carrying them out. What counts as clarity? How does one divide up a problem? How does one know which parts of a problem are simple and which not, prior to solving the parts? What counts as a complete enumeration?

Descartes's project of reconsidering all of his earlier beliefs includes his moral and religious beliefs. How can he live in the world if he doubts these? His recommendation is that of the Pyrrhonian skeptic: "to obey the laws and customs of my country, adhering constantly to the religion in which by God's grace I had been instructed since my childhood." This advice is all very well so long as one does not live in a country that brutalizes a significant part of its citizens and so long as one's religion does not include things like killing people of a different religion.

Part of Descartes's narrative is a brief autobiography, a rare occurrence in a seventeenth-century philosophical work.

For Descartes's life, see the discussion of selection 7 in the introduction to part II.

1 I am not denying that "Some people are smarter than others" and "The most important thing in discovery knowledge is use of the proper method" are logically consistent.

Part I

Good sense is of all things in the world the most equally distributed, for everybody thinks himself so abundantly provided with it, that even those most difficult to please in all other matters do not commonly desire more of it than they already possess. It is unlikely that this is an error on their part; it seems rather to be evidence in support of the view that the power of forming a good judgment and of distinguishing the true from the false, which is properly speaking what is called Good sense or Reason, is by nature equal in all men. Hence too it will show that the diversity of our opinions does not proceed from some men being more rational than others, but solely from the fact that our thoughts pass through diverse channels and the game objects are not considered by all. For to be possessed of good mental powers is not sufficient; the principal matter is to apply them well. The greatest minds are capable of the greatest vices as well as of the greatest virtues, and those who proceed very slowly may, provided they always follow the straight road, ready advance much faster than those who, though they run, forsake it.

For myself I have never ventured to presume that my mind was in any way more perfect than that of the ordinary man.

[. . .]

[M]y design is not here to teach the Method which everyone should follow in order to promote the good conduct of his Reason, but only to show in what manner I have endeavoured to conduct my own.

[. . .]

Part II

I was then in Germany, to which country I had been attracted by the wars which are not yet at an end. And as I was returning from the coronation of the Emperor to join the army, the setting in of winter detained me in a quarter where, since I found no society to divert me, while fortunately I had also no cares or passions to trouble me, I remained the whole day shut up alone in a stove-heated room, where I had complete leisure to occupy myself with my own thoughts. One of the first of the considerations that occurred to me was that there is very often less perfection in works composed of several portions, and carried out by the hands of various masters, than in those on which one individual alone has worked. Thus we see that buildings planned and carried out by one architect alone are usually more beautiful and better proportioned than those which many have tried to put in order and improve, making use of old walls which were built with other ends in view. In the same way also, those ancient cities which, originally mere villages, have become in the process of time great towns, are usually badly constructed in comparison with those which are regularly laid out on a plain by a surveyor who is free to follow his own ideas. Even though, considering their buildings each one apart, there is often as much or more display of skill in the one case than in the other, the former have large buildings and small buildings indiscriminately placed together, thus rendering the streets crooked and irregular, so that it might be said that it was chance rather than the will of men guided by reason that led to such an arrangement. And if we consider that this happens despite the fact that from all time there have been certain officials who have had the special duty of looking after the buildings of private individuals in order that they may be public ornaments, we shall understand how difficult it is to bring about much that is satisfactory in operating only upon the works of others. Thus I imagined that those people who were once half-savage, and who have become civilised only by slow degrees, merely forming their laws as the disagreeable necessities of their crimes and quarrels constrained them, could not succeed in establishing so good a system of government as those who, from the time they first came together as communities, carried into effect the constitution laid down by some prudent legislator. Thus it is quite certain that the constitution of the true Religion whose ordinances are of God alone is incomparably better regulated than any other. And, to come down to human affairs, I believe that if Sparta was very flourishing in former times, this was not because of the excellence of each and every one of its laws, seeing that many were very strange and even contrary to good morals, but because, being drawn up by one individual, they all tended towards the same end. And similarly I thought that the sciences found in books – in those at least whose reasonings are only probable and which have no demonstrations, composed as they are of the gradually accumulated opinions of many different individuals – do not approach so near to the truth as the simple reasoning which a man of common sense can quite naturally carry out respecting the things which come immediately before him. Again I thought that since we have all been children before being men, and since it has for long fallen to us to be governed by our appetites and by our teachers (who often enough contradicted one another, and none of whom perhaps counselled us always for the best), it is almost impossible that our judgments should be so excellent or solid as they should have been had we had complete use of our reason since our birth, and had we been guided by its means alone.

It is true that we do not find that all the houses in a town are razed to the ground for the sole reason that the town is to be rebuilt in another fashion, with streets made more beautiful; but at the same time we see that many people cause their own houses to be knocked down in order to rebuild them, and that sometimes they are forced so to do where there is danger of the houses falling of themselves, and when the foundations are not secure. From such examples I argued to myself that there was no plansibility in the claim of any private individual to reform a state by altering everything, and by overturning it throughout, in order to set it right again. Nor is it likewise probable that the whole body of the Sciences, or the order of teaching established by the Schools, should be reformed. But as regards all the opinions which up to this time I had embraced, I thought I could not do better than endeavour once for all to sweep them completely away, so that they might later on be replaced, either by others which were better, or by the same, when I had made them conform to the uniformity of a rational scheme. And I firmly believed that by this means I should succeed in directing my life much better than if I had only built on old foundations, and relied on principles of which I allowed myself to be in youth persuaded without having inquired into their truth. For although in so doing I recognised various difficulties, these were at the same time not unsurmountable, nor comparable to those which are found in reformation of the most insignificant kind in matters which concern the public. In the case of great bodies it is too difficult a task to raise them again when they are once thrown down, or even to keep them in their places when once thoroughly shaken; and their fall cannot be otherwise than very violent. Then as to any imperfections that they my possess (and the very diversity that is found between them is sufficient to tell us that these in many cases exist) custom has doubtless greatly mitigated them, while it has also helped us to avoid, or insensibly corrected a number against which mere foresight would have found it difficult to guard. And finally the imperfections are almost always more supportable than would be the process of removing them, just as the great roads which wind about amongst the mountains become, because of being frequented, little by little so well-beaten and easy that it is much better to follow them than to try to go more directly by climbing over rocks and descending to the foot of precipices.

[. . .]

Among the different branches of Philosophy, I had in my younger days to a certain extent studied Logic; and in those of Mathematics, Geometrical Analysis and Algebra – three arts or sciences which seemed as though they ought to contribute something to the design I had in view. But in examining them I observed in respect to Logic that the syllogisms and the greater part of the other teaching served better in explaining to others those things that one knows. [. . .] This made me feel that some other Method must be found, which, comprising the advantages of the three, is yet exempt from their faults. And as a multiplicity of laws often furnishes excuses for evil-doing, and as a State is hence much better ruled when, having but very few laws, these are most strictly observed; so, instead of the great number of precepts of which Logic is composed, I believed that I should find the four which I shall state quite sufficient, provided that I adhered to a firm and constant resolve never on any single occasion to fail in their observance.

The first of these was to accept nothing as true which I did not clearly recognise to be so: that is to say, carefully to avoid precipitation and prejudice in judgments, and to accept in them nothing more than what was presented to my mind so clearly and distinctly that I could have no occasion to doubt it.

The second was to divide up each of the difficulties which I examined into as many parts as possible, and as seemed requisite in order that it might be resolved in the best manner possible.

The third was to carry on my reflections in due order, commencing with objects that were the most simple and easy to understand, in order to rise little by little, or by degrees, to knowledge of the most complex, assuming an order, even if a fictitious one, among those which do not follow a natural sequence relatively to one another.

The last was in all cases to make enumerations so complete and reviews so general that I should be certain of having omitted nothing.

Those long chains of reasoning, simple and easy as they are, of which geometricians make use in order to arrive at the most difficult demonstrations, had caused me to imagine that all those things which fall under the cognizance of man might very likely be mutually related in the same fashion; and that, provided only that we abstain from receiving anything as true which is not so, and always retain the order which is necessary in order to deduce the one conclusion from the other, there can be nothing so remote that we cannot reach to it, nor so recondite that we cannot discover it.

[. . .]

Part III

And finally [. . .] in order that I should not remain irresolute in my actions while reason obliged me to be so in my judgments, and that I might not omit to carry on my life as happily as I could, I formed for myself a code of morals for the time being which did not consist of more than three or four maxims, which maxims I should like to enumerate to you.

The first was to obey the laws and customs of my country, adhering constantly to the religion in which by God's grace I had been instructed since my childhood.

[. . .]

My second maxim was that of being as firm and resolute in my actions as I could be, and not to follow less faithfully opinions the most dubious, when my mind was once made up regarding them, than if these had been beyond doubt.

[. . .]

My third maxim was to try always to conquer myself rather than fortune, and to alter my desires rather than change the order of the world, and generally to accustom myself to believe that there is nothing entirely within our power but our own thoughts: so that after we have done our best in regard to the things that are without us, our ill-success cannot possibly be failure on our part.

[. . .]

And last of all, to conclude this moral code, I felt it incumbent on me to make a review of the various occupations of men in this life in order to try to choose out the best; and without wishing to say anything of the employment of others I thought that I could not do better than continue in the one in which I found myself engaged, that is to say, in occupying my whole life in cultivating my Reason, and in advancing myself as much as possible in the knowledge of the truth in accordance with the method which I had prescribed myself.

[. . .]

Having thus assured myself of these maxims, and having set them on one side along with the truths of religion which have always taken the first place in my creed, I judged that as far as the rest of my opinions were concerned, I could safely undertake to rid myself of them. And inasmuch as I hoped to be able to reach my end more successfully in converse with man than in living longer shut up in the warm room where these reflections had come to me, I hardly awaited the end of winter before I once more set myself to travel. And in all the nine following years I did nought but roam hither and thither, trying to be a spectator rather than an actor in all the comedies the world displays. More especially did I reflect in each matter that came before me as to anything which could make it subject to suspicion or doubt, and give occasion for mistake, and I rooted out of my mind all the errors which might have formerly crept in. Not that indeed I imitated the sceptics, who only doubt for the sake of doubting, and pretend to be always uncertain; for, on the contrary, my design was only to provide myself with good ground for assurance, and to reject the quicksand and mud in order to find the rock or clay. In this task it seems to me, I succeeded pretty well, since in trying to discover the error or uncertainty of the propositions which I examined, not by feeble conjectures, but by clear and assured reasonings, I encountered nothing so dubious that I could not draw from it some conclusion that was tolerably secure, if this were no more than the inference that it contained in it nothing that was certain. And just as in pulling down an old house we usually preserve the debris to serve in building up another, so in destroying all those opinions which I considered to be ill-founded, I made various observations and acquired many experiences, which have since been of use to me in establishing those which are more certain. And more than this, I continued to exercise myself in the method which I had laid down for my use; for besides the fact that I was careful as a rule to conduct all my thoughts according to its maxims, I set aside some hours from time to time which I more especially employed in practising myself in the solution of mathematical problems according to the Method, or in the solution of other problems which though pertaining to other sciences, I was able to make almost similar to these of mathematics, by detaching them from all principles of other sciences which I found to be not sufficiently secure. [. . .] And hence, without living to all appearance in any way differently from those who, having no occupation beyond spending their lives in ease and innocence, study to separate pleasure from vice, and who, in order to enjoy their leisure without weariness, make use of all distractions that are innocent and good, I did not cease to prosecute my design, and to profit perhaps even more in my study of Truth than if I had done nothing but read books or associate with literary people.

5

Thomas Hobbes, *Leviathan*

Like Descartes, Thomas Hobbes said that people were roughly equal in intelligence and thought that the key to scientific progress was having the right method of inquiry. He distinguished between synthesis, which consisted of beginning with causes and deducing effects, and analysis, which consisted of beginning with an effect and reasoning to a possible cause for it. In addition to these general ideas about method, Hobbes insisted on a particular metaphysics, mechanistic materialism, according to which, only bodies exist – he thought the phrase "material bodies" pleonastic – and that the only way that things change is by contact of one moving body against another.

In the first several chapters of *Leviathan*, Hobbes tries to make his view plausible by analyzing apparently complex and high-level cognitive and affective states and events into purely material terms. For example, he defines an endeavor as an imperceptibly small motion in a body. Appetite or desire is an endeavor toward the thing that causes the endeavor. An aversion is an endeavor away from the object that causes it. Hope, which seems to be a fairly high-level affective state, is merely an appetite for something and the opinion that one expects to get it ("*x* hopes for *y*" = "*x* has an appetite for *y* and *x* has the opinion that *x* will get *y*"). Since appetites are imperceptibly small motions toward an object, hopes are imperceptibly small motions toward an object.

If one is not already upset by this reduction of hope to motion, one may be upset by his relativistic analysis of goodness. According to Hobbes, something is good exactly when someone desires it. Although he does not say it in the selection printed here, he knows that the relativism of goodness leads to conflict. For him, the only solution to this conflict is to have citizens agree to desire whatever the sovereign desires. The relativism of goodness is thus made tantamount to an objective good because everyone ends up desiring the same thing.

Equally controversial was his treatment of will. Hobbes held that much of human behavior is free because it originates from something inside the person, but that people do not have free will. Will is just the last desire one has before an action. He means that the last desire causes the action. Deliberation is just an alternation of appetites, aversions, hopes, and fears.

Hobbes needed to prepare his readers for his radical views (radical for the seventeenth century) in some way. He does this by arguing in the introduction to *Leviathan* that nature is artificial, that machines are alive, and that humans are machines. It is as if he was saying, "Fasten your philosophical seatbelts; it's going to be a bumpy ride."

For Hobbes's life, see the discussion of selection 20 in the introduction to part IV.

The Introduction

1. Nature (the art whereby God hath made and governs the world) is by the art of man, as in many other things, so in this also imitated, that it can make an artificial animal. For seeing life is but a motion of limbs, the beginning whereof is in some principal part within, why may we not say that all *automata* (engines that move themselves by springs and wheels as doth a watch) have an artificial life? For what is the *heart*, but a *spring*; and the *nerves*, but so many *strings*; and the *joints*, but so many *wheels*, giving motion to the whole body, such as was intended by the Artificer? *Art* goes yet further, imitating that rational and most excellent work of nature, *man*. For by art is created that great LEVIATHAN called a COMMONWEALTH, or STATE (in Latin, CIVITAS), which is but an artificial man, though of greater stature and strength than the natural, for whose protection and defense it was intended; and in which the sovereignty is an artificial *soul*, as giving life and motion to the whole body. The *magistrates* and other *officers* of judicature and execution [are] artificial *joints*. *Reward* and *punishment* (by which fastened to the seat of the sovereignty, every joint and member is moved to perform his duty) are the *nerves* that do the same in the body natural. The *wealth* and *riches* of all the particular members are the *strength*. *Salus populi* (the *people's safety*) [is] its *business*. *Counsellors*, by whom all things needful for it to know are suggested unto it, are the *memory*. *Equity* and laws [are] an artificial *reason* and *will*. *Concord* [is] *health*. *Sedition* [is] *sickness*. And *civil war* [is] *death*. Lastly, the *pacts* and *covenants* by which the parts of this body politic were at first made, set together, and united, resemble that *fiat*, or the *let us make man*, pronounced by God in the Creation.

Part I
Of Man

Chapter I
Of Sense

1. Concerning the thoughts of man, I will consider them first singly and afterwards in train or dependence upon one another. Singly, they are every one a representation or appearance of some quality or other accident of a body without us, which is commonly called an *object*. Which object worketh on the eyes, ears, and other parts of man's body, and by diversity of working, produceth diversity of appearances.

2. The original of them all is that which we call SENSE (for there is no conception in a man's mind which hath not at first, totally or by parts, been begotten upon the organs of sense). The rest are derived from that original.

[. . .]

4. The cause of sense is the external body or object which presseth the organ proper to each sense either immediately, as in the taste and touch, or mediately, as in seeing, hearing, and smelling; which pressure, by the mediation of nerves and other strings and membranes of the body, continued inwards to the brain and heart, causeth there a resistance or counter-pressure or endeavour of the heart to deliver itself, which endeavour, because outward, seemeth to be some matter without. And this seeming or fancy is that which men call *sense* and consisteth, as to the eye in a *light* or *colour figured*; to the ear in a *sound*; to the nostril in an *odour*; to the tongue and palate in a *savour*; and to the rest of the body in *heat*, *cold*, *hardness*, *softness*, and such other qualities as we discern by *feeling*. All which qualities called *sensible* are in the object that causeth them, but so many several motions of the matter, by which it presseth our organs diversely. Neither in us that are pressed are they anything else but divers motions (for motion produceth nothing but motion). But their appearance to us is fancy, the same waking [as] that dreaming. And as pressing, rubbing, or striking the eye makes us fancy a light, and pressing the ear produceth a din, so do the bodies also we see or hear produce the same by their strong, though unobserved action. For if those colours and sounds were in the bodies or objects that cause them, they could not be severed from them, as by glasses, and in echoes by reflection, we see they are where we know the thing we see is in one place, the appearance in another. And though at some certain distance the real and very object seem invested with the fancy it begets in us; yet still the object is one thing, the image or fancy is another. So that sense in all cases is nothing else but original fancy, caused (as I have said) by the pressure, that is, by the motion of external things upon our eyes, ears, and other organs, thereunto ordained.

[. . .]

Chapter II
Of Imagination

1. That when a thing lies still, unless somewhat else stir it, it will lie still for ever is a truth that no man doubts of. But that when a thing is in motion, it will eternally be in motion, unless somewhat else stay it, though the reason be the same (namely, that nothing can change itself), is not so easily assented to. For men measure, not only other men, but all other things, by themselves; and because they find themselves subject after motion to pain and lassitude think everything else grows weary of motion and seeks repose of its own accord, little considering whether it be not some other motion wherein that desire of rest they find in themselves consisteth. From hence it is that the schools say heavy bodies fall downwards out of an appetite to rest and to conserve their nature in that place which is most proper for them ascribing appetite, and knowledge of what is good for their conservation (which is more than man has) to things inanimate, absurdly.

2. When a body is once in motion, it moveth (unless something else hinder it) eternally; and whatsoever hindreth it cannot in an instant but in time and by degrees quite extinguish it. And as we see in the water, though the wind cease, the waves give not over rolling for a long time after, so also it happeneth in that motion which is made in the internal parts of a man, then, when he sees, dreams, etc. For after the object is removed or the eye shut, we still retain an image of the thing seen, though more obscure than when we see it. And this is it the Latins call *imagination*, from the image made in seeing; and [they] apply the same,

though improperly, to all the other senses. But the Greeks call it *fancy*, which signifies *appearance*, and is as proper to one sense as to another. *Imagination*, therefore, is nothing but *decaying sense* and is found in men and many other living creatures, as well sleeping as waking.

3. The decay of sense in men waking is not the decay of the motion made in sense, but an obscuring of it, in such manner as the light of the sun obscureth the light of the stars, which stars do no less exercise their virtue by which they are visible in the day than in the night. But because amongst many strokes which our eyes, ears, and other organs receive from external bodies, the predominant only is sensible; therefore the light of the sun being predominant, we are not affected with the action of the stars.

[. . .]

Chapter VI

Of the Interiour Beginnings of Voluntary Motions, Commonly Called the Passions, and the Speeches by which They are Expressed

1. There be in animals two sorts of *motions* peculiar to them: one called *vital*, begun in generation, and continued without interruption through their whole life, such as are the course of the blood, the pulse, the breathing, the concoction, nutrition, excretion, etc.; to which motions there needs no help of imagination; the other is *animal motion*, otherwise called *voluntary motion*; as to *go*, to *speak*, to *move* any of our limbs, in such manner as is first fancied in our minds. That sense is motion in the organs and interior parts of man's body, caused by the action of the things we see, hear, etc., and that fancy is but the relics of the same motion, remaining after sense, has been already said in the first and second chapters. And because *going, speaking*, and the like voluntary motions depend always upon a precedent thought of *whither, which way*, and *what*, it is evident that the imagination is the first internal beginning of all voluntary motion. And although unstudied men do not conceive any motion at all to be there where the thing moved is invisible or the space it is moved in is (for the shortness of it) insensible; yet that doth not hinder but that such motions are. For let a space be never so little, that which is moved over a greater space, whereof that little one is part, must first be moved over that. These small beginnings of motion within the body of man, before they appear in walking, speaking, striking, and other visible actions, are commonly called Endeavour.

2. This endeavour, when it is toward something which causes it, is called Appetite or Desire, the latter being the general name, and the other oftentimes restrained to signify the desire of food, namely *hunger* and *thirst*. And when the endeavour is fromward something, it is generally called Aversion. These words *appetite* and *aversion* we have from the *Latins*; and they both of them signify the motions, one of approaching, the other of retiring. So also do the Greek words for the same, which are *orme* and *aphorme*. For Nature itself does often press upon men those truths which afterwards, when they look for somewhat beyond Nature, they stumble at. For the Schools find in mere appetite to go or move, no actual motion at all; but because some motion they must acknowledge, they call it metaphorical motion, which is but an absurd speech; for though words may be called metaphorical, bodies and motions cannot.

3. That which men desire they are said to Love, and to Hate those things for which they have aversion. So that desire and love are the same thing, save that by desire, we signify the

absence of the object; by love, most commonly the presence of the same. So also by aversion, we signify the absence; and by hate, the presence of the object.

4. Of appetites and aversions, some are born with men; as appetite of food, appetite of excretion, and exoneration (which may also and more properly be called aversions, from somewhat they feel in their bodies), and some other appetites, not many. The rest, which are appetites of particular things, proceed from experience and trial of their effects upon themselves or other men. For of things we know not at all or believe not to be, we can have no further desire than to taste and try. But aversion we have for things, not only which we know have hurt us, but also that we do not know whether they will hurt us, or not.

5. Those things which we neither desire nor hate, we are said to *contemn*: CONTEMPT being nothing else but an immobility or contumacy of the heart in resisting the action of certain things, and proceeding from that the heart is already moved otherwise by other more potent objects or from want of experience of them.

6. And because the constitution of a man's body is in continual mutation, it is impossible that all the same things should always cause in him the same appetites and aversions; much less can all men consent in the desire of almost any one and the same object.

7. But whatsoever is the object of any man's appetite or desire, that is it which he for his part calleth *good*; and the object of his hate and aversion, *evil*; and of his contempt, *vile* and *inconsiderable*. For these words of *good*, *evil*, and *contemptible* are ever used with relation to the person that useth them, there being nothing simply and absolutely so, nor any common rule of good and evil to be taken from the nature of the objects themselves, but from the person of the man (where there is no commonwealth) or (in a commonwealth) from the person that representeth it, or from an arbitrator or judge whom men disagreeing shall by consent set up and make his sentence the rule thereof.

[. . .]

9. As in sense that which is really within us is (as I have said before) only motion, caused by the action of external objects (but in appearance, to the sight, light and colour; to the ear, sound; to the nostril, odour, etc.); so when the action of the same object is continued from the eyes, ears, and other organs to the heart, the real effect there is nothing but motion or endeavour, which consisteth in appetite or aversion to or from the object moving. But the appearance or sense of that motion is that we either call DELIGHT or TROUBLE OF MIND.

10. This motion, which is called appetite and for the appearance of it *delight* and *pleasure*, seemeth to be a corroboration of vital motion and a help thereunto; and therefore such things as caused delight were not improperly called *jucunda* (*a juvando*, from helping or fortifying); and the contrary, *molesta*, *offensive*, from hindering and troubling the motion vital.

11. *Pleasure* therefore (or delight) is the appearance or sense of good; and *molestation* or *displeasure*, the appearance or sense of evil. And consequently all appetite, desire, and love is accompanied with some delight more or less; and all hatred and aversion with more or less displeasure and offence.

12. Of pleasures or delights, some arise from the sense of an object present; and those may be called *pleasures of sense* (the word *sensual*, as it is used by those only that condemn them, having no place till there be laws). Of this kind are all onerations and exonerations of the body, as also all that is pleasant, in the *sight*, *hearing*, *smell*, *taste*, or *touch*. Others arise from the expectation that proceeds from foresight of the end or consequence of things, whether those things in the sense please or displease; and these are *pleasures of the mind* of him that

draweth in those consequences, and are generally called Joy. In the like manner, displeasures are some in the sense and called Pain; others, in the expectation of consequences and are called Grief.

13. These simple passions called *appetite, desire, love, aversion, hate, joy,* and *grief,* have their names for divers considerations diversified. As first, when they one succeed another, they are diversely called from the opinion men have of the likelihood of attaining what they desire. Secondly, from the object loved or hated. Thirdly, from the consideration of many of them together. Fourthly, from the alteration or succession itself.

14. For *appetite* with an opinion of attaining is called Hope.

15. The same, without such opinion, Despair.

16. *Aversion,* with opinion of *hurt* from the object, Fear.

17. The same, with hope of avoiding that hurt by resistance, Courage.

18. Sudden *courage,* Anger.

19. Constant *hope,* Confidence of ourselves.

20. Constant *despair,* Diffidence of ourselves.

21. *Anger* for great hurt done to another, when we conceive the same to be done by injury, Indignation.

22. *Desire* of good to another, Benevolence, Good will, Charity. If to man generally, Good nature.

23. *Desire* of riches, Covetousness, a name used always in signification of blame, because men contending for them are displeased with one another's attaining them; though the desire in itself be to be blamed, or allowed, according to the means by which those riches are sought.

24. Desire of office or precedence, Ambition, a name used also in the worse sense, for the reason before mentioned.

25. *Desire* of things that conduce but a little to our ends, and fear of things that are but of little hindrance, Pusillanimity.

26. *Contempt* of little helps and hindrances, Magnanimity.

27. *Magnanimity* in danger of death or wounds, Valour, Fortitude.

28. *Magnanimity* in the use of riches, Liberality.

29. *Pusillanimity,* in the same, Wretchedness, Miserableness, or Parsimony, as it is liked or disliked.

30. *Love* of persons for society, Kindness.

31. *Love* of persons for pleasing the sense only, Natural Lust.

32. *Love* of the same, acquired from rumination, that is, imagination of pleasure past, Luxury.

33. *Love* of one singularly, with desire to be singularly beloved, The Passion of Love. The same, with fear that the love is not mutual, Jealousy.

34. *Desire* by doing hurt to another to make him condemn some fact of his own, Revengefulness.

35. *Desire* to know why and how, Curiosity, such as is in no living creature but *man;* so that man is distinguished, not only by his reason, but also by this singular passion from other *animals,* in whom the appetite of food and other pleasures of sense by predominance, take away the care of knowing causes, which is a lust of the mind, that by a perseverance of delight in the continual and indefatigable generation of knowledge, exceedeth the short vehemence of any carnal pleasure.

36. *Fear* of power invisible, feigned by the mind, or imagined from tales publicly allowed, Religion; not allowed, Superstition. And when the power imagined is truly such as we imagine, True Religion.

37. *Fear* without the apprehension of why or what, PANIC TERROR, called so from the fables that make Pan the author of them; whereas in truth there is always in him that so feareth, first, some apprehension of the cause, though the rest run away by example, every one supposing his fellow to know why. And therefore this passion happens to none but in a throng, or multitude of people.

38. *Joy* from apprehension of novelty, ADMIRATION; proper to man because it excites the appetite of knowing the cause.

39. *Joy* arising from imagination of a man's own power and ability is that exultation of the mind which is called GLORYING; which, if grounded upon the experience of his own former actions, is the same with *confidence*; but if grounded on the flattery of others or only supposed by himself for delight in the consequences of it, is called VAIN-GLORY; which name is properly given, because a well-grounded *confidence* begetteth attempt, whereas the supposing of power does not and is therefore rightly called *vain*.

40. *Grief* from opinion of want of power is called DEJECTION of mind.

41. The *vain-glory* which consisteth in the feigning or supposing of abilities in ourselves, which we know are not, is most incident to young men and nourished by the histories or fictions of gallant persons, and is corrected oftentimes by age and employment.

42. *Sudden glory* is the passion which maketh those *grimaces* called LAUGHTER, and is caused either by some sudden act of their own that pleaseth them or by the apprehension of some deformed thing in another by comparison whereof they suddenly applaud themselves. And it is incident most to them that are conscious of the fewest abilities in themselves, who are forced to keep themselves in their own favour by observing the imperfections of other men. And therefore much laughter at the defects of others is a sign of pusillanimity. For of great minds one of the proper works is to help and free others from scorn, and compare themselves only with the most able.

[. . .]

47. *Contempt* or little sense of the calamity of others is that which men call CRUELTY, proceeding from security of their own fortune. For, that any man should take pleasure in other men's great harms, without other end of his own, I do not conceive it possible.

48. *Grief* for the success of a competitor in wealth, honour, or other good, if it be joined with endeavour to enforce our own abilities to equal or exceed him, is called EMULATION; but joined with endeavour to supplant or hinder a competitor, ENVY.

49. When in the mind of man appetites and aversions, hopes and fears concerning one and the same thing arise alternately, and divers good and evil consequences of the doing or omitting the thing propounded come successively into our thoughts, so that sometimes we have an appetite to it, sometimes an aversion from it, sometimes hope to be able to do it, sometimes despair, or fear to attempt it, the whole sum of desires, aversions, hopes and fears, continued till the thing be either done or thought impossible, is that we call DELIBERATION.

50. Therefore of things past there is no *deliberation*, because manifestly impossible to be changed, nor of things known to be impossible, or thought so, because men know or think such deliberation vain. But of things impossible, which we think possible, we may deliberate, not knowing it is in vain. And it is called *deliberation*; because it is a putting an end to the *liberty* we had of doing or omitting, according to our own appetite or aversion.

51. This alternate succession of appetites, aversions, hopes and fears is no less in other living creatures than in man; and therefore beasts also deliberate.

52. Every *deliberation* is then said to *end* when that whereof they deliberate is either done or thought impossible, because till then we retain the liberty of doing or omitting, according to our appetite or aversion.

53. In *deliberation*, the last appetite, or aversion, immediately adhering to the action or to the omission thereof, is that we call the will; the act (not the faculty) of *willing*. And beasts that have *deliberation* must necessarily also have *will*. The definition of the *will*, given commonly by the Schools, that it is a *rational appetite*, is not good. For if it were, then could there be no voluntary act against reason. For a *voluntary act* is that which proceedeth from the *will* and no other. But if instead of a rational appetite, we shall say an appetite resulting from a precedent deliberation, then the definition is the same that I have given here. *Will*, therefore, *is the last appetite in deliberating*. And though we say in common discourse a man had a will once to do a thing that nevertheless he forbore to do; yet that is properly but an inclination, which makes no action voluntary, because the action depends not of it, but of the last inclination or appetite. For if the intervenient appetites make any action voluntary, then by the same reason all intervenient aversions should make the same action involuntary; and so one and the same action should be both voluntary and involuntary.

54. By this it is manifest that not only actions that have their beginning from covetousness, ambition, lust, or other appetites to the thing propounded, but also those that have their beginning from aversion or fear of those consequences that follow the omission are *voluntary actions*.

55. The forms of speech by which the passions are expressed are partly the same and partly different from those by which we express our thoughts. And first generally all passions may be expressed *indicatively*; as, *I love, I fear, I joy, I deliberate, I will, I command*; but some of them have particular expressions by themselves, which nevertheless are not affirmations, unless it be when they serve to make other inferences besides that of the passion they proceed from. Deliberation is expressed *subjunctively*, which is a speech proper to signify suppositions, with their consequences, as, *If this be done, then this will follow*, and differs not from the language of reasoning, save that reasoning is in general words, but deliberation for the most part is of particulars. The language of desire and aversion is *imperative*, as, *Do this, forbear that*; which when the party is obliged to do or forbear is *command*; otherwise *prayer* or else *counsel*. The language of vain-glory, of indignation, pity and revengefulness, *optative*; but of the desire to know, there is a peculiar expression called *interrogative*; as, *what is it, when shall it, how is it done*, and *why so*? Other language of the passions I find none: for cursing, swearing, reviling, and the like do not signify as speech, but as the actions of a tongue accustomed.

56. These forms of speech, I say, are expressions or voluntary significations of our passions; but certain signs they be not, because they may be used arbitrarily, whether they that use them have such passions or not. The best signs of passions present are either in the countenance, motions of the body, actions, and ends, or aims, which we otherwise know the man to have.

57. And because in deliberation the appetites and aversions are raised by foresight of the good and evil consequences and sequels of the action whereof we deliberate, the good or evil effect thereof dependeth on the foresight of a long chain of consequences, of which very seldom any man is able to see to the end. But for so far as a man seeth, if the good in those consequences be greater than the evil, the whole chain is that which writers call *apparent* or *seeming good*. And contrarily, when the evil exceedeth the good, the whole is *apparent* or *seeming evil*; so that he who hath by experience or reason the greatest and surest prospect of consequences deliberates best himself, and is able, when he will, to give the best counsel unto others.

58. *Continual success* in obtaining those things which a man from time to time desireth, that is to say, continual prospering, is that men call FELICITY; I mean the felicity of this life. For there is no such thing as perpetual tranquillity of mind while we live here, because life itself is but motion and can never be without desire, nor without fear no more than without sense. What kind of felicity God hath ordained to them that devoutly honour him a man shall no sooner know than enjoy, being joys that now are as incomprehensible as the word of Schoolmen, *beatifical vision*, is unintelligible.

59. The form of speech whereby men signify their opinion of the goodness of anything is PRAISE. That whereby they signify the power and greatness of anything is MAGNIFYING. And that whereby they signify the opinion they have of a man's felicity is by the Greeks called *makarismos*, for which we have no name in our tongue. And thus much is sufficient for the present purpose to have been said of the PASSIONS.

6

Isaac Newton, *Mathematical Principles of Natural Philosophy*

Isaac Newton (1642–1727) studied at Cambridge and taught there from 1669 until his death. For much of this time, he was Lucasian Professor of Natural Philosophy.

He discovered the law of gravitation, the infinitesimal calculus, and the fact that white light is composed of all the colors of the spectrum. (He had a public argument with Leibniz over who discovered the calculus first. It appears that Newton figured it out first but published it after Leibniz did.) He presented these discoveries in *Philosophiae naturalis principia mathematica* (*Mathematical Principles of Natural Philosophy*, 1687). Newton's discoveries in optics were presented in his *Opticks* (1704), in which he argued that light consisted of corpuscles. This view held sway until the nineteenth century, when it was replaced by wave theory, but it re-emerged in quantum theory, which describes light in terms of corpuscles. He served in parliament in 1689–90 and 1701–2, and was president of the Royal Society from 1703 until 1727.

In large part, the greatness of his discovery of the universal law of gravitation was its application to diverse phenomena: falling terrestrial bodies, the moon, planets, and comets. This includes an explanation of Kepler's three laws of planetary motion.

In the selection below from *Principia mathematica*, Newton begins with definitions of some technical terms, such as *vis insita* or *inertia* and impressed force. Explicit definitions of terms are supposed to preclude vagueness and ambiguity. The definitions are followed by axioms or laws of motion. Like Euclid's axioms, Newton's axioms or laws are not proved, but unlike the former, the latter are not obvious to a non-physicist. It is counterintuitive, but true, that every body in motion remains in motion in a straight line unless acted upon by another body (law 1). Equally counterintuitive, but true, is the quotable third law: for every action, there is an equal and opposite reaction.

Newton's four rules of reasoning may be named or briefly described as: (1) Ockham's razor: do not posit more entities than are necessary to explain the phenomena; (2) the uniformity of nature: if a law is true at one place in nature, it is true at every place; (3) the generalizability of qualities: if bodies known to us by experience have certain qualities, all bodies are assumed to have those qualities; and (4) the tenacity of inductive propositions: accept a proposition or hypothesis unless it is disproved or until it is improved upon by further experience.

Definitions

[. . .]

Definition III

The vis insita, *or innate force of matter, is a power of resisting, by which every body, as much as in it lies, continues in its present state, whether it be of rest, or of moving uniformly forwards in a right line.*

This force is always proportional to the body whose force it is and differs nothing from the inactivity of the mass, but in our manner of conceiving it. A body, from the inert nature of matter, is not without difficulty put out of its state of rest or motion. Upon which account, this *vis insita* may, by a most significant name, be called inertia (*vis inertiœ*) or force of inactivity. But a body only exerts this force when another force, impressed upon it, endeavors to change its condition; and the exercise of this force may be considered as both resistance and impulse; it is resistance so far as the body, for maintaining its present state, opposes the force impressed; it is impulse so far as the body, by not easily giving way to the impressed force of another, endeavors to change the state of that other. Resistance is usually ascribed to bodies at rest, and impulse to those in motion; but motion and rest, as commonly conceived, are only relatively distinguished; nor are those bodies always truly at rest, which commonly are taken to be so.

Definition IV

An impressed force is an action exerted upon a body, in order to change its state, either of rest, or of uniform motion in a right line.

This force consists in the action only, and remains no longer in the body when the action is over. For a body maintains every new state it acquires, by its inertia only. [. . .]

Definition V

A centripetal force is that by which bodies are drawn or impelled, or any way tend, towards a point as to a centre.

Of this sort is gravity, by which bodies tend to the centre of the earth; magnetism, by which iron tends to the loadstone; and that force, whatever it is, by which the planets are continually drawn aside from the rectilinear motions, which otherwise they would pursue, and made to revolve in curvilinear orbits. A stone, whirled about in a sling, endeavors to recede from the hand that turns it; and by that endeavor, distends the sling, and that with so much the greater force, as it is revolved with the greater velocity, and as soon as it is let go, flies away.

[. . .]

Axioms, or Laws of Motion

Law I

Every body continues in its state of rest, or of uniform motion in a right line, unless it is compelled to change that state by forces impressed upon it.

Projectiles continue in their motions, so far as they are not retarded by the resistance of the air, or impelled downwards by the force of gravity. A top, whose parts by their cohesion are continually drawn aside from rectilinear motions, does not cease its rotation, otherwise than as it is retarded by the air. The greater bodies of the planets and comets, meeting with less resistance in freer spaces, preserve their motions both progressive and circular for a much longer time.

Law II

The change of motion is proportional to the motive force impressed; and is made in the direction of the right line in which that force is impressed.

If any force generates a motion, a double force will generate double the motion, a triple force triple the motion, whether that force be impressed altogether and at once, or gradually and successively. And this motion (being always directed the same way with the generating force), if the body moved before, is added to or subtracted from the former motion, according as they directly conspire with or are directly contrary to each other; or obliquely joined, when they are oblique, so as to produce a new motion compounded from the determination of both.

Law III

To every action there is always opposed an equal reaction: or, the mutual actions of two bodies upon each other are always equal, and directed to contrary parts.

Whatever draws or presses another is as much drawn or pressed by that other. If you press a stone with your finger, the finger is also pressed by the stone. If a horse draws a stone tied to a rope, the horse (if I may so say) will be equally drawn back towards the stone; for the distended rope, by the same endeavor to relax or unbend itself, will draw the horse as much towards the stone as it does the stone towards the horse, and will obstruct the progress of the one as much as it advances that of the other. If a body impinge upon another, and by its force change the motion of the other, that body also (because of the equality of the mutual pressure) will undergo an equal change, in its own motion, towards the contrary part. The changes made by these actions are equal, not in the velocities but in the motions of bodies; that is to say, if the bodies are not hindered by any other impediments. For, because the motions are equally changed, the changes of the velocities made towards contrary parts are inversely proportional to the bodies.

[. . .]

Rules of Reasoning in Philosophy

Rule I

We are to admit no more causes of natural things than such as are both true and sufficient to explain their appearances.

To this purpose the philosophers say that Nature does nothing in vain, and more is in vain when less will serve; for Nature is pleased with simplicity, and affects not the pomp of superfluous causes.

Rule II

Therefore to the same natural effects we must, as far as possible, assign the same causes.

As to respiration in a man and in a beast; the descent of stones in *Europe* and in *America*; the light of our culinary fire and of the sun; the reflection of light in the earth, and in the planets.

Rule III

The qualities of bodies, which admit neither intensification nor remission of degrees, and which are found to belong to all bodies within the reach of our experiments, are to be esteemed the universal qualities of all bodies whatsoever.

For since the qualities of bodies are only known to us by experiments, we are to hold for universal all such as universally agree with experiments; and such as are not liable to diminution can never be quite taken away. We are certainly not to relinquish the evidence of experiments for the sake of dreams and vain fictions of our own devising; nor are we to recede from the analogy of Nature, which is wont to be simple, and always consonant to itself. We no other way know the extension of bodies than by our senses, nor do these reach it in all bodies; but because we perceive extension in all that are sensible, therefore we ascribe it universally to all others also. That abundance of bodies are hard, we learn by experience; and because the hardness of the whole arises from the hardness of the parts, we therefore justly infer the hardness of the undivided particles not only of the bodies we feel but of all others. That all bodies are impenetrable, we gather not from reason, but from sensation. The bodies which we handle we find impenetrable, and thence conclude impenetrability to be an universal property of all bodies whatsoever. That all bodies are movable, and endowed with certain powers (which we call the inertia) of persevering in their motion, or in their rest, we only infer from the like properties observed in the bodies which we have seen. The extension, hardness, impenetrability, mobility, and inertia of the whole, result from the extension, hardness, impenetrability, mobility, and inertia of the parts; and hence we conclude the least particles of all bodies to be also all extended, and hard and impenetrable, and movable, and endowed with their proper inertia. And this is the foundation of all philosophy. Moreover, that the divided but contiguous particles of bodies may be separated from one another, is matter of observation; and, in the particles that remain undivided, our minds are able to distinguish yet lesser parts, as is mathematically demonstrated. But whether the parts so distinguished, and not yet divided, may, by the powers of Nature, be actually divided and separated from one another, we cannot certainly determine. Yet, had we the proof of but one experiment that any undivided particle, in breaking a hard and solid body, suffered a division, we might by virtue of this rule conclude that the undivided as well as the divided particles may be divided and actually separated to infinity.

Lastly, if it universally appears, by experiments and astronomical observations, that all bodies about the earth gravitate towards the earth, and that in proportion to the quantity of matter which they severally contain; that the moon likewise, according to the quantity of its matter, gravitates towards the earth; that, on the other hand, our sea gravitates towards the moon; and all the planets one towards another; and the comets in like manner towards the sun; we must, in consequence of this rule, universally allow that all bodies whatsoever are endowed with a principle of mutual gravitation. For the argument from the appearances concludes with more force for the universal gravitation of all bodies than for their impenetrability; of which, among those in the celestial regions, we have no experiments, nor any manner of observation. Not that I affirm gravity to be essential to bodies: by their *vis insita* I mean nothing but their inertia. This is immutable. Their gravity is diminished as they recede from the earth.

Rule IV

In experimental philosophy we are to look upon propositions inferred by general induction from phenomena as accurately or very nearly true, notwithstanding any contrary hypotheses that may be imagined, till such time as other phenomena occur, by which they may either be made more accurate, or liable to exceptions.

This rule we must follow, that the argument of induction may not be evaded by hypotheses.

Part II

Descartes and his Critics

Introduction

The single most important philosophical work in the early modern period is Descartes's *Meditations on First Philosophy*, published in 1641. With the *Meditations* were published six sets of objections by respected intellectuals, along with Descartes's replies to them. The next year, a second edition of the *Meditations* was published with a seventh set of objections, by the Jesuit Pierre Bourdin.

The *Meditations* was written in Latin, the standard academic language of the time, but its structure and content were not standard academic fare. In it, Descartes questions the truth of all previous philosophy; indeed, he questions all of his previous beliefs.

The complete text of Descartes's *Meditations* is the major selection in this part. In the first meditation, he presents the case for skepticism. He begins by reporting that he has discovered that many of the things he once believed are false, and that he has decided to rid himself of all the opinions that he had formerly accepted. I think it is doubtful whether it is possible to doubt everything. Descartes seems to have continued to believe that words had their old meaning, because he used them to express his doubts. So his belief in the meaning of his words precedes his proof that he exists. Also, in the third meditation, he is assuming all sorts of substantive philosophical principles, some of which will be mentioned later.

It is also questionable whether it makes sense to get rid of every belief just because some of them are mistaken. Is it sensible to throw away every apple in a barrel because some of them are rotten? Since Descartes was able to detect the falsity of some of the beliefs he held before he wrote the *Meditations*, there is some evidence that his former beliefs, far from being dogmatic and bankrupt, appear to be self-regulating. In any case, Descartes thinks it is reasonable to withhold assent from each one if he can find some reason to justify rejecting them generally.

The first beliefs to go are those based upon sensation because "the senses sometimes deceive us." Moreover, he observes, he may be dreaming; to quote his famous words, "on many occasions I have in sleep been deceived." For the purposes of the skeptical exercise, he assumes that he is asleep. This assumption runs far ahead of the evidence. A safer bet would have been to assume neither that he was awake nor asleep. His former beliefs in physics, astronomy, medicine "and all other sciences," in effect his beliefs in heaven, earth, and the extended body, are the next to go, followed by his beliefs in the propositions of mathematics. It is possible that God, or "an evil genius," has deceived him about whether two plus three really equals five.

Although Descartes may seem to be promoting radical skepticism, he is not. His skepticism is only methodological. His goal is to use skeptical doubts in order to defeat skepticism and to find firm grounds for knowledge that would be secure from all doubt. According to him, doubting what we believe is the way to discover which truths are certain. The first of these truths will be that he exists as a thinking thing.

In the second meditation, Descartes introduces the *cogito*, the claim that he is thinking. He observes that whether he is being deceived by an evil genius or not, it is indubitable that he exists: "I am, I exist, is necessarily true each time that I pronounce it, or that I mentally conceive it." That is, a presupposition of ignorance as much as knowledge is the existence of the person who is ignorant or knowing. Let's put Descartes's point in the first person, as he does. Given my doubts, which are expressible as "I doubt that I have a body," "I doubt that $2 + 2 = 4$," and so on, something is nonetheless certainly true: I am thinking; and this entails that I exist.

As simple as the move from "thinking" to "existing" sounds, it is unclear in this way. What exactly is the connection between "I think" and "I exist"? Is it the logical relation of entailment? Is Descartes saying this: Necessarily, if "I think" is true, then "I exist" is true? The "therefore" (*ergo*) of "*cogito, ergo sum*" suggests that it is an inference. Alternatively, do I *experience* my existence when I think, or experience myself as thinking? Is that how I know that I exist? Descartes says or implies this latter interpretation in his replies to Mersenne and his *Rules for the Direction of the Mind* (1628): "each individual can mentally have intuition of the fact that he exists, and that he thinks" (Rule 3). Notice that the conclusion that he exists does not depend upon a sensation of himself. It was purely intellectual cognition. This is an important aspect of Descartes's rationalism.

Having established that he exists, Descartes asks what *kind* of thing he is. Philosophers often want to know what kind of thing something is, or what category it belongs to. For example, is a certain thing a body or not, finite or infinite, living or nonliving? Descartes's initial answer is that he is a thinking thing. From this, he draws the invalid conclusion that he is *only* a thinking thing.

Thomas Hobbes, the author of the third set of objections, in effect criticized Descartes for this inference. Hobbes said that "I am thought (or intellect)" no more follows from "I am thinking" than "I am the walk" follows from "I am walking." What followed, said Hobbes, is that something is thinking or walking, and this thing must be a body, "something corporeal." Hobbes was a thoroughgoing materialist.

Descartes completely rejected Hobbes's objection. He said that the comparison between walking and thinking is invalid because "walking" refers only to the action of walking, while "thinking" refers sometimes to the action, sometimes to the faculty of thinking, and sometimes to the substance in which the faculty exists. Descartes's reply has no force, it seems to me. By pointing out the ambiguity in the word "thinking," he may be explaining why he mistakenly inferred that the thing that was thinking was a "thought" or a mind, but it does not justify the inference.

Descartes then purportedly proves that it is easier to know the nature of mind than the nature of body by way of his famous piece of wax. When it is cold, a piece of wax is hard and sweet-smelling. But when it is heated it becomes soft, and loses its aroma. The wax itself remains, even though none of its sensible qualities do. Since the wax is known to persist independently of its sensible qualities, intellectual knowledge is superior to sense knowledge, Descartes concludes. The substance of wax is "a certain extended thing," which "my mind alone . . . perceives." This knowledge, like the knowledge of the *cogito*, is an intuition, direct, unmediated knowledge. Since bodies are known, not by sensation, "but only because they are understood" and since "there is nothing easier" for him to know than his own mind, mental things are easier to know than bodily things. This conclusion is another part of his rationalism. (In the nineteenth century, philosophers, notably Friedrich Nietzsche, would throw doubt on the transparency of the mind. People often do not know their own minds, *pace* Descartes.)

After proving to his own satisfaction that understanding is more certain than sensation, Descartes goes on to prove the existence of God in the third meditation. Although we do not learn this until later, Descartes wants to prove the existence of God in order to prove that clarity and distinctness are the right criteria for certainty. If God is perfect, then he is not a deceiver; and if he is not a deceiver, then he would not give us a criterion for knowledge that is not the right one. The problem with this strategy is that the proof for the existence of God depends upon premises which are declared to be certain because they are clearly and distinctly apprehended. This is problematic because if the argument for the existence of God depends on the correctness of the criteria of clarity and distinctness, the existence of God cannot be used to justify those criteria. To do so is to reason in a circle, as Antoine Arnauld, the author of the fourth set of objections, pointed out.

Let's look at the proof in the third meditation. It appears to Descartes that some of his ideas are innate (native to his mind), some adventitious (coming from outside of himself), and some invented by himself. What, he wonders, is the cause of all of these ideas? He himself could be the cause of most of them, because he has as much formal reality as they. (Formal reality is what we usually think of as actual or real existence; for physical objects, it is having a location in space and time.) One idea seems to elude this confidence, the idea of God. In addition to formal reality, Descartes believes that there is objective reality, which is the reality that an idea presents itself as having, even if it does not exist. In the French translation of the *Meditations*, Descartes explained that to exist objectively in the intellect is to exist representatively in the intellect. The idea of redness represents itself as being a property that must inhere in a finite, material substance. The idea of a finite, material substance represents itself as depending on something else for its being. (A unicorn has the same objective reality as a horse, even though horses exist and have a formal reality unicorns do not have.) Now comes a crucial move. The idea of God, the objective reality of God, is that of an infinite, immaterial, perfect being. This is how God is conceived to be.

Descartes next introduces as an indubitable truth the proposition that "in order that an idea should contain some one certain objective reality rather than another, it must without doubt derive it from some cause in which there is at least as much formal reality as this idea contains of objective reality." Descartes "knows" that he does not have the formal reality adequate to cause the objective idea of God, because if he did have adequate formal reality "I should doubt nothing and I should desire nothing, and finally no perfection would be lacking to me; for I should have bestowed on myself every perfection of which I possessed any idea and should thus be God." So there must be a being who does. The only being who does have the required formal reality is the only being who could have it, God himself. Therefore, God exists. Here is the essence of the proof: "if the objective reality of any one of my ideas is of such a nature as clearly to make me recognize that it is not in me either formally or eminently [i.e., in a higher way], and that consequently I cannot myself be the cause of it, it follows of necessity that I am not alone in the world, but that there is another being which exists, or which is the cause of this idea."

Few philosophers in the seventeenth century accepted Descartes's proof; no one today does, to my knowledge. His principle about the formal cause required by objective reality is too obscure or doubtful to be believed. What is useful for us to observe, however, is that Descartes thought that his principle was indubitably true. Since he uses the principle to prove the existence of God, it is logically prior to the proposition that God exists. And this is not the only proposition that Descartes thought was indubitably true or true by the natural light. In the general introduction to this book, several of these propositions were set out, including these two:

1 Ideas of substances have more objective reality than ideas of modes or accidents.
2 Now it is manifest by the natural light that there must be at least as much reality in the efficient and total cause as in its effect.

Although Descartes wanted to doubt everything, he accepted as true several propositions that are scarcely intelligible today, much less thought to be true. What is obvious to one generation of people is often far from obvious to another.

In the fourth meditation, Descartes explains the origin of human error. Since God is not a deceiver, he would not have given humans any faculty that was defective. Human understanding is finite but that does not make it defective. The human will is infinite because it can make choices about whatever proposition the understanding presents it. It might seem that this makes the will defective because it is paired with the finite understanding of human beings. But that, Descartes thinks, is a mistake. Whether a person chooses error over truth or evil over goodness is within the power of the person himself and not the result of a defect in either the understanding or the will.

In the fifth meditation, Descartes offers a different proof for the existence of God, a proof that is much more intriguing than the previous one. It is a version of what is known as the ontological argument. Descartes begins by observing that his ideas of mathematical objects, such as triangles, do not come from sensation. He has never seen an exact triangle; all physical instances of "triangles" depart to some degree from the requirement that the sides be straight lines. Yet he can prove all sorts of interesting things simply by paying close attention to the contents of the ideas. For example, necessarily the longest side of the triangle is opposite the greatest angle. This relationship between the clear and distinct contents of ideas and clear and distinct conclusions makes him realize that he can demonstrate the existence of God in the same way. By drawing implications from the idea of God, he can prove that God exists. His idea of God is of "a supremely perfect Being." Such a Being is one in whom existence is part of his essence, just like having three angles is part of the essence of a triangle. Then, Descartes worries. The fact that he conceives of God as existing may not mean that God does exist, "for my thought does not impose any necessity on things." But this worry, he sees immediately, is based upon a mistake. Of course his thought does not make God exist. What is crucial is this: the fact that God cannot be conceived without existing means that "existence is inseparable from him, and hence that he really exists." It is not Descartes's thinking that makes it necessary that God exists, it is the idea of God that reveals that God exists. The idea of God necessarily includes existence because God himself must possess existence. At least that is Descartes's claim.

One criticism of this argument comes from Thomas Hobbes, who denied that humans have an idea of God: "we have no image, no idea corresponding to it [the name 'God']." For Hobbes, sensation is the origin of all knowledge. Since God is not something that can be sensed, there can be no idea of him. Hobbes thinks that, with regard to God, humans are like blind people who infer the existence of a fire from the heat they feel. People see the universe and infer the existence of a cause of it, and they name this unperceivable cause "God." Hobbes's error, according to Descartes, is to think that by "idea" he means "image." He does not. By "idea" Descartes means "whatever the mind directly perceives"; and even immaterial things are perceived, such as volitions and fears.

Another criticism of Descartes's argument came from Pierre Gassendi, a friend of Hobbes and Mersenne. Gassendi claimed that existence is not a property. It is a precondition for something's having properties. Gassendi would be willing to grant that omnipotence, omniscience, and omnibenevolence are properties of the idea of God, but not existence. If, as Descartes claimed, existence were a perfection of God, then it is also a perfection of mountains and triangles: "existence is a perfection neither in God nor in anything else; it is rather that in the absence of which there is no perfection."

Descartes replied that existence is as much a property of a thing as anything else is, because a property is "any attribute or anything which can be predicated of a thing." He means that "exists" occupies the predicate position in a sentence, "God exists." Existence is a property of God because it "belongs" to God.

At the end of his ontological proof for the existence of God, Descartes says that the conclusion cannot be doubted because he conceived the argument "clearly and distinctly." Then comes his fatal error. He says that so important is the conclusion that God exists that "the certainty of all other things depends on it so absolutely, that without this knowledge it is impossible ever to know anything perfectly." Even if we exclude the *cogito* and the proposition that God exists from the scope of "know anything perfectly," Descartes has an enormous problem. He seems to be resting the justification of the criteria of clarity and distinctness on his proof of the existence of God. But the proof for the existence of God depends upon the clarity and distinctness of the premises used in that proof. This reasoning is circular, as mentioned earlier. Descartes's reply to this objection seems to be that he relies on the existence of God only to reassure people that if they remember that they once clearly and distinctly perceived something, then they did clearly and distinctly perceive something, because God, as a nondeceiver, would not have it any other way: "it is enough for us to remember that we have perceived something clearly in order to be sure that it is true; but this would not suffice, unless we knew that God existed and that he did not deceive us."

In the sixth meditation, Descartes both asserts that his body belongs to himself in an intimate way and that his body is no part of his essence. Descartes is essentially a mind, something that is immaterial, is not in space, and is indivisible. A body, by contrast, is material, fills up a space, and is divisible. This tension between Descartes's essence and his relation to his body is exacerbated by the fact that he believes that motion occurs by contact. One body moves only when another moving body hits it. But if motion requires contact, how can the mind move the body? And since the mind is unextended, how can the motion in the body cause sensations in the mind?

These problems of mind–body interaction were picked up by Princess Elizabeth of Bohemia. As she trenchantly observes, "the determination of movement always seems to come about from the moving body's being propelled," which involves contact, but "you [Descartes] utterly exclude extension from your notion of soul, and contact seems to me incompatible with a thing's being immaterial." Descartes's reply is that people have an irreducible innate idea of the union of body and soul, and the ideas of what the soul can do and what the body can do independently of the other should not be confused with this idea of the union. The interaction between mind and body is not the same as but is analogous to the action of gravity on bodies.

Princess Elizabeth rightly denied the usefulness of the idea of gravity as an explanation. It would be preferable, she wrote, if the soul had matter and hence extension. Descartes replied that it is easier to understand the idea of union if one does not think about it! One learns of the union from ordinary life. This answer evades the issue, the issue being whether Descartes's dualism of mind and body can account for the unity of a human being.

Notwithstanding substantial objections to his philosophy and violent opposition by various institutional authorities, Cartesianism in various forms became an influential philosophical view in the seventeenth century. In part III, three philosophers who drew inspiration from Descartes's philosophy are presented.

Let me end by mentioning two important medieval elements in Descartes's philosophy. One is the belief that creatures are absolutely dependent on God. This means that they are not only created at one moment in time, but kept in existence by the same creative power at every moment of their existence. If creatures did not require this constant divine causation, then they would not be absolutely dependent on him. In the third meditation, Descartes wrote,

> For all the course of my life may be divided into an infinite number of parts, none of which is in any way dependent on the other; and thus from the fact that I was in existence a short time ago it does not follow that I must be in existence now, unless some cause at this instant, so to speak, produces me anew, that is to say, conserves me. . . . [S]o that the light of nature shows us clearly that the distinction between creation and conservation is solely a distinction of the reason.

The other medieval element is his belief in a hierarchy of being. An infinite, immaterial, and perfect being is better than a finite, immaterial being (an angel or a human mind), and a finite, immaterial being is better than a body, and a body is better than a property (a characteristic or feature of a body). No matter how original philosophers are, they always carry with them some relics of what they wanted to leave behind.

7

René Descartes, *The Meditations on First Philosophy*

René Descartes (1596–1650) was born in a small village between Tours and Poitiers on March 31, 1596. He was educated by the Jesuits at their school La Flèche, France, in traditional Aristotelian scholasticism, and later received a law degree at Potiers. Having independent means, he traveled through Europe. In 1629 he decided to make Holland his home. He lived in the country and adopted as his motto "shun publicity," but this did not preclude him from corresponding with some of the most important intellectuals of the seventeenth century.

At some point, he underwent a skeptical crisis, which led him to doubt everything that he had known. His account of this crisis is in his *Discourse on the Method of Rightly Conducting the Reason and Seeking for Truth in the Sciences* (1637). At some point after the crisis, he decided to create a new philosophy. In 1632 he had completed *Le Monde* (*The World*), which contained his physics and treatise on human beings. His intention to publish it ended when he discovered the problems that Galileo suffered from the Church because of his *Two Dialogues*. Descartes wrote to his friend, Marin Mersenne, that he did not want to assert opinions "against the authority of the Church," and expressed his desire to "live in peace."

Discourse on the Method of Rightly Conducting the Reason and Seeking for Truth in the Sciences, written in French, was theologically uncontroversial and hence safe. The *Discourse* included examples of the method applied to optics, meteorology, and geometry. The importance of method, according to Descartes (and Bacon and Hobbes), cannot be overemphasized. Method was the key to scientific progress. Out of the somewhat confused efforts of Descartes and others, the scientific method eventually emerged.

The *Discourse* also contains proofs for the existence of God and the difference between mind and body. In it, Descartes revealed his *cogito* as the foundation of knowledge. He wrote, "I think; therefore I am" ("Je pense; donc je suis"). The doctrine of the *Discourse* is materialist, with one exception. Thought cannot be explained in materialistic terms.

Attacked by the academic establishment and hoping to get his philosophy taught in universities, Descartes published *Principles of Philosophy* (1644) in Latin. The book contained his metaphysics, physics, and cosmology, among other things. In 1649 he published *The Passions of the Soul* in French, and then accepted an invitation from Queen Christina of Sweden to educate her in philosophy. Her penchant for instruction at 5 a.m. was too much for Descartes's weak constitution, and he died on February 11, 1650, at the age of 53.

In the following selection, *Meditations on First Philosophy*, Descartes tried to place scientific knowledge on a firm footing, so firm that it cannot sensibly be doubted. He does this by beginning with the most extreme doubt of which he could conceive and then showing that this doubt itself must be grounded in the existence of the person doubting. This intuition, according to Descartes, is clear and distinct. This, he believes, must be the proper criterion for certain truth. Because people sometimes prove something and then forget the exact steps in the proof, some general assurance of the knowledge the person has obtained is in order. Descartes believes that he will have this assurance if God exists, because God, as the most perfect being, cannot be a deceiver. Thus Descartes proves the existence of God in the third meditation, and again in the fifth. Hence, something infinite, that is, God, must cause that idea to exist. In the sixth meditation, Descartes goes on to prove that it is easier to know the mind than it is to know the body.

To the Most Wise and Illustrious the Dean and Doctors of the Sacred Faculty of Theology in Paris

The motive which induces me to present to you this Treatise is so excellent, and, when you become acquainted with its design, I am convinced that you will also have so excellent a motive for taking it under your protection, that I feel that I cannot do better, in order to render it in some sort acceptable to you, than in a few words to state what I have set myself to do.

I have always considered that the two questions respecting God and the Soul were the chief of those that ought to be demonstrated by philosophical rather than theological argument. For although it is quite enough for us faithful ones to accept by means of faith the fact that the human soul does not perish with the body, and that God exists, it certainly does not seem possible ever to persuade infidels of any religion, indeed, we may almost say, of any moral virtue, unless, to begin with, we prove these two facts by means of the natural reason. And inasmuch as often in this life greater rewards are offered for vice than for virtue, few people would prefer the right to the useful, were they restrained neither by the fear of God nor the expectation of another life; and although it is absolutely true that we must believe that there is a God, because we are so taught in the Holy Scriptures, and, on the other hand, that we must believe the Holy Scriptures because they come from God (the reason of this is, that, faith being a gift of God, He who gives the grace to cause us to believe other things can likewise give it to cause us to believe that He exists), we nevertheless could not place this argument before infidels, who might accuse us of reasoning in a circle. And, in truth, I have noticed that you, along with all the theologians, did not only affirm that the existence of God may be proved by the natural reason, but also that it may be inferred from the Holy Scriptures, that knowledge about Him is much clearer than that which we have of many created things, and, as a matter of fact, is so easy to acquire, that those who have it not are culpable in their ignorance. This indeed appears from the Wisdom of Solomon, chapter xiii., where it is said *'Howbeit they are not to be excused; for if their understanding was so great that they could discern the world and the creatures, why did they not rather find out the Lord thereof?'* and in Romans, chapter i., it is said that they are *'without excuse'*; and again in the same place, by these words *'that which may be known of God is manifest in them,'* it seems as though we were shown that all that which can be known of God may be made manifest by means which are not derived from anywhere but from ourselves, and from the simple consideration of the nature of our minds. Hence I thought it not beside my purpose to inquire how this is so, and how God may be more easily and certainly known than the things of the world.

And as regards the soul, although many have considered that it is not easy to know its nature, and some have even dared to say that human reasons have convinced us that it would perish with the body, and that faith alone could believe the contrary, nevertheless, inasmuch as the Lateran Council held under Leo X (in the eighth session) condemns these tenets, and as Leo expressly ordains Christian philosophers to refute their arguments and to employ all their powers in making known the truth, I have ventured in this treatise to undertake the same task.

More than that, I am aware that the principal reason which causes many impious persons not to desire to believe that there is a God, and that the human soul is distinct from the body, is that they declare that hitherto no one has been able to demonstrate these two facts; and although I am not of their opinion but, on the contrary, hold that the greater part of the reasons which have been brought forward concerning these two questions by so many great men are, when they are rightly understood, equal to so many demonstrations, and that it is almost impossible to invent new ones, it is yet in my opinion the case that nothing more useful can be accomplished in philosophy than once for all to seek with care for the best of these reasons, and to set them forth in so clear and exact a manner, that it will henceforth be evident to everybody that they are veritable demonstrations. And, finally, inasmuch as it was desired that I should undertake this task by many who were aware that I had cultivated a certain Method for the resolution of difficulties of every kind in the Sciences – a method which it is true is not novel, since there is nothing more ancient than the truth, but of which they were aware that I had made use successfully enough in other matters of difficulty – I have thought that it was my duty also to make trial of it in the present matter.

Now all that I could accomplish in the matter is contained in this Treatise. Not that I have here drawn together all the different reasons which might be brought forward to serve as proofs of this subject: for that never seemed to be necessary excepting when there was no one single proof that was certain. But I have treated the first and principal ones in such a manner that I can venture to bring them forward as very evident and very certain demonstrations. And more than that, I will say that these proofs are such that I do not think that there is any way open to the human mind by which it can ever succeed in discovering better. For the importance of the subject, and the glory of God to which all this relates, constrain me to speak here somewhat more freely of myself than is my habit. Nevertheless, whatever certainty and evidence I find in my reasons, I cannot persuade myself that all the world is capable of understanding them. Still, just as in Geometry there are many demonstrations that have been left to us by Archimedes, by Apollonius, by Pappus, and others, which are accepted by everyone as perfectly certain and evident (because they clearly contain nothing which, considered by itself, is not very easy to understand, and as all through that which follows has an exact connection with, and dependence on that which precedes), nevertheless, because they are somewhat lengthy, and demand a mind wholly devoted to their consideration, they are only taken in and understood by a very limited number of persons. Similarly, although I judge that those of which I here make use are equal to, or even surpass in certainty and evidence, the demonstrations of Geometry, I yet apprehend that they cannot be adequately understood by many, both because they are also a little lengthy and dependent the one on the other, and principally because they demand a mind wholly free of prejudices, and one which can be easily detached from the affairs of the senses. And, truth to say, there are not so many in the world who are fitted for metaphysical speculations as there are for those of Geometry. And more than that; there is still this difference, that in Geometry, since each one is persuaded that nothing must be advanced of which there is not a certain demonstration, those who are not entirely adepts more frequently err in approving what is false, in order to give the impression that they understand it, than in refuting the true. But the case is different in philosophy where everyone believes that all is problematical, and few give themselves to the search after truth; and the greater number, in their desire to acquire a reputation for boldness of thought, arrogantly combat the most important of truths.

That is why, whatever force there may be in my reasonings, seeing they belong to philosophy, I cannot hope that they will have much effect on the minds of men, unless you extend to them your protection. But the estimation in which your Company is universally held is so great, and the name of SORBONNE carries with it so much authority, that, next to the Sacred Councils, never has such deference been paid to the judgment of any Body, not only in what concerns the faith, but also in what regards human philosophy as well: everyone indeed believes that it is not possible to discover elsewhere more perspicacity and solidity, or more integrity and wisdom in pronouncing judgment. For this reason I have no doubt that if you deign to take the trouble in the first place of correcting this work (for being conscious not only of my infirmity, but also of my ignorance, I should not dare to state that it was free from errors), and then, after adding to it these things that are lacking to it, completing those which are imperfect, and yourselves taking the trouble to give a more ample explanation of those things which have need of it, or at least making me aware of the defects so that I may apply myself to remedy them – when this is done and when finally the reasonings by which I prove that there is a God, and that the human soul differs from the body, shall be carried to that point of perspicuity to which I am sure they can be carried in order that they may be esteemed as perfectly exact demonstrations, if you deign to authorise your approbation and to render public testimony to their truth and certainty, I do not doubt, I say, that henceforward all the errors and false opinions which have ever existed regarding these two questions will soon be effaced from the minds of men. For the truth itself will easily cause all men of mind and learning to subscribe to your judgment; and your authority will cause the atheists, who are usually more arrogant than learned or judicious, to rid themselves of their spirit of contradiction or lead them possibly themselves to defend the reasonings which they find being received as demonstrations by all persons of consideration, lest they appear not to understand them. And, finally, all others will easily yield to such a mass of evidence, and there will be none who dares to doubt the existence of God and the real and true distinction between the human soul and the body. It is for you now in your singular wisdom to judge of the importance of the establishment of such beliefs [you who see the disorders produced by the doubt of them]. But it would not become me to say more in consideration of the cause of God and religion to those who have always been the most worthy supports of the Catholic Church.

Preface to the Reader

I have already slightly touched on these two questions of God and the human soul in the Discourse on the Method of rightly conducting the Reason and seeking truth in the Sciences, published in French in the year 1637. Not that I had the design of treating these with any thoroughness, but only so to speak in passing, and in order to ascertain by the judgment of the readers how I should treat them later on. For these questions have always appeared to me to be of such importance that I judged it suitable to speak of them more than once; and the road which I follow in the explanation of them is so little trodden, and so far removed from the ordinary path, that I did not judge it to be expedient to set it forth at length in French and in a Discourse which might be read by everyone, in case the feebler minds should believe that it was permitted to them to attempt to follow the same path.

But, having in this Discourse on Method begged all those who have found in my writings somewhat deserving of censure to do me the favour of acquainting me with the grounds of it, nothing worthy of remark has been objected to in them beyond two matters: to these two I wish here to reply in a few words before undertaking their more detailed discussion.

The first objection is that it does not follow from the fact that the human mind reflecting on itself does not perceive itself to be other than a thing that thinks, that its nature or its essence consists only in its being a thing that thinks, in the sense that this word *only* excludes all other things which might also be supposed to pertain to the nature of the soul. To this objection I reply that it was not my intention in that place to exclude these in accordance with the order that looks to the truth of the matter (as to which I was not then dealing), but only in accordance with the order of my thought [perception]; thus my meaning was that so far as I was aware, I knew nothing clearly as belonging to my essence, excepting that I was a thing that thinks, or a thing that has in itself the faculty of thinking. But I shall show hereafter how from the fact that I know no other thing which pertains to my essence, it follows that there is no other thing which really does belong to it.

The second objection is that it does not follow from the fact that I have in myself the idea of something more perfect than I am, that this idea is more perfect that I, and much less that what is represented by this idea exists. But I reply that in this term *idea* there is here something equivocal, for it may either be taken materially, as an act of my understanding, and in this sense it cannot be said that it is more perfect than I; or it may be taken objectively, as the thing which is represented by this act, which, although we do not suppose it to exist outside of my understanding, may, none the less, be more perfect than I, because of its essence. And in following out this Treatise I shall show more fully how, from the sole fact that I have in myself the idea of a thing more perfect than myself, it follows that this thing truly exists.

In addition to these two objections I have also seen two fairly lengthy works on this subject, which, however, did not so much impugn my reasonings as my conclusions, and this my arguments drawn from the ordinary atheistic sources. But, because such arguments cannot make any impression on the minds of those who really understand my reasonings, and as the judgments of many are so feeble and irrational that they very often allow themselves to be persuaded by the opinions which they have first formed, however false and far removed from reason they may be, rather than by a true and solid but subsequently received refutation of these opinions, I do not desire to reply here to their criticisms in case of being first of all obliged to state them. I shall only say in general that all that is said by the atheist against the existence of God, always depends either on the fact that we ascribe to God affections which are human, or that we attribute so much strength and wisdom to our minds that we even have the presumption to desire to determine and understand that which God can and ought to do. In this way all that they allege will cause us no difficulty, provided only we remember that we must consider our minds as things which are finite and limited, and God as a Being who is incomprehensible and infinite.

Now that I have once for all recognised and acknowledged the opinions of men, I at once begin to treat of God and the human soul, and at the same time to treat of the whole of the First Philosophy, without however expecting any praise from the vulgar and without the hope that my book will have many readers. On the contrary, I should never advise anyone to read it excepting those who desire to meditate seriously with me, and who can detach their minds from affairs of sense, and deliver themselves entirely from every sort of prejudice. I know too well that such men exist in a very small number. But for those who, without caring to comprehend the order and connections of my reasonings, form their criticisms on detached portions arbitrarily selected, as is the custom with many, these, I say, will not obtain much profit from reading this Treatise. And although they perhaps in several parts find occasion of cavilling, they can for all their pains make no objection which is urgent or deserving of reply.

And inasmuch as I make no promise to others to satisfy them at once, and as I do not presume so much on my own powers as to believe myself capable of foreseeing all that can cause difficulty to anyone, I shall first of all set forth in these Meditations the very considerations by which I persuade myself that I have reached a certain and evident knowledge of the truth, in order to see if, by the same reasons which persuaded me, I can also persuade others. And, after that, I shall reply to the objections which have been made to me by persons of genius and learning to whom I have sent my Meditations for examination, before submitting them to the press. For they have made so many objections and these so different, that I venture to promise that it will be difficult for anyone to bring to mind criticisms of any consequence which have not been already touched upon. This is why I beg those who read these Meditations to form no judgment upon them unless they have given themselves the trouble to read all the objections as well as the replies which I have made to them.

Synopsis of the Six Following Meditations

In the first Meditation I set forth the reasons for which we may, generally speaking, doubt about all things and especially about material things, at least so long as we have no other foundations for the science than those which we have hitherto possessed. But although the utility of a Doubt which is so general does not at first appear, it is at the same time very great, inasmuch as it delivers us from every kind of prejudice, and sets out for us a very simple way by which the mind may detach itself from the senses; and finally it makes it impossible for us ever to doubt those things which we have once discovered to be true.

In the second Meditation, mind, which making use of the liberty which pertains to it, takes for granted that all those things of whose existence it has the least doubt, are non-existent, recognises that it is however absolutely impossible that it does not itself exist. This point is likewise of the greatest moment, inasmuch as by this means a distinction is easily drawn between the things which pertain to mind – that is to say to the intellectual nature – and those which pertain to body.

But because it may be that some expect from me in this place a statement of the reasons establishing the immortality of the soul, I feel that I should here make known to them that having aimed at writing nothing in all this Treatise of which I do not possess very exact demonstrations, I am obliged to follow a similar order to that made use of by the geometers, which is to begin by putting forward as premises all those things upon which the proposition that we seek depends, before coming to any conclusion regarding it. Now the first and principal matter which is requisite for thoroughly understanding the immortality of the soul is to form the clearest possible conception of it, and one which will be entirely distinct from all the conceptions which we may have of body; and in this Meditation this has been done. In addition to this it is requisite that we may be assured that all the things which we conceive clearly and distinctly are true in the very way in which we think them; and this could not be proved previously to the Fourth Meditation. Further we must have a distinct conception of corporeal nature, which is given partly in this Second, and partly in the Fifth and Sixth Meditations. And finally we should conclude from all this, that those things which we conceive clearly and distinctly as being diverse substances, as we regard mind and body to be, are really substances essentially distinct one from the other; and this is the conclusion of the Sixth Meditation. This is further confirmed in this same Meditation by the fact that we cannot conceive of body excepting in so far as it is divisible, while the mind cannot be conceived of excepting as indivisible. For we are not able to conceive of the half of a mind as we can do of the smallest of all bodies; so that we see that not only are their natures different but even in some respects contrary to one another. I have not however dealt further with this matter in this treatise, both because what I have said is sufficient to show clearly enough that the extinction of the mind does not follow from the corruption of the body, and also to give men the hope of another life after death, as also because the premises from which the immortality of the soul may be deduced depend on an elucidation of a complete system of Physics. This would mean to establish in the first place that all substances generally – that is to say all things which cannot exist without being created by God – are in their nature incorruptible, and that they can never cease to exist unless God, in denying to them his concurrence, reduce them to nought; and secondly that body, regarded generally, is a substance, which is the reason why it also cannot perish, but that the human body, inasmuch as it differs from other bodies, is composed only of a certain configuration of members and of other similar accidents, while the human mind is not similarly composed of any accidents, but is a pure substance. For although all the accidents of mind be changed, although, for instance, it think certain things, will others, perceive others, etc., despite all this it does not emerge from these changes another mind: the human body on the other hand becomes a different thing from the sole fact that the figure or form of any of its portions is found to be changed. From this it follows that the human body may indeed easily enough perish, but the mind [or soul of man (I make no distinction between them)] is owing to its nature immortal.

In the third Meditation it seems to me that I have explained at sufficient length the principal argument of which I make use in order to prove the existence of God. But none the less, because I did not wish in that place to make use of any comparisons derived from corporeal things, so as to withdraw as much as I could the minds of readers from the senses, there may perhaps have remained many obscurities which, however, will, I hope, be entirely removed by the Replies which I have made to the Objections which have been set before me. Amongst others there is, for example, this one, 'How the idea in us of a being supremely perfect possesses so much objective reality [that is to say participates by representation in so many degrees of being and perfection] that it necessarily proceeds from a cause which is absolutely perfect. This is illustrated in these Replies by the comparison of a very perfect machine, the idea of which is found in the mind of some workman. For as the objective contrivance of this idea must have some cause, i.e. either the science of the workman or that of some other from whom he has received the idea, it is similarly impossible that the idea of God which is in us should not have God himself as its cause.

In the fourth Meditation it is shown that all these things which we very clearly and distinctly perceive are true, and at the same time it is explained in what the nature of error or falsity consists. This must of necessity be known both for the confirmation of the preceding truths and for the better comprehension of those that follow. (But it must meanwhile be remarked that I do not in any way there treat of sin – that is to say of the error which is committed in the pursuit of good and evil, but only of that which arises in the deciding between the true and the false. And I do not intend to speak of matters pertaining to the Faith or the conduct of life, but only of those which concern speculative truths, and which may be known by the sole aid of the light of nature.)

In the fifth Meditation corporeal nature generally is explained, and in addition to this the existence of God is demonstrated by a new proof in which there may possibly be certain difficulties also, but the solution of these will be seen in the Replies to the Objections. And further I show in what sense it is true to say that the certainty of geometrical demonstrations is itself dependent on the knowledge of God.

Finally in the Sixth I distinguish the action of the understanding from that of the imagination; the marks by which this distinction is made are described. I here show that the mind of man is really distinct from the body, and at the same time that the two are so closely joined together that they form, so to speak, a single thing. All the errors which proceed from the senses are then surveyed, while the means of avoiding them are demonstrated, and finally all the reasons from which we may deduce the existence of material things are set forth. Not that I judge them to be very useful in establishing that which they prove, to wit, that there is in truth a world, that men possess bodies, and other such things which never have been doubted by anyone of sense; but because in considering these closely we come to see that they are neither so strong nor so evident as those arguments which lead us to the knowledge of our mind and of God; so that these last must be the most certain and most evident facts which can fall within the cognizance of the human mind. And this is the whole matter that I have tried to prove in these Meditations, for which reason I here omit to speak of many other questions with which I dealt incidentally in this discussion.

Meditations on the First Philosophy in which the Existence of God and the Distinction Between Mind and Body are Demonstrated

Meditation I

Of the things which may be brought within the sphere of the doubtful

It is now some years since I detected how many were the false beliefs that I had from my earliest youth admitted as true, and how doubtful was everything I had since constructed on this basis; and from that time I was convinced that I must once for all seriously undertake to rid myself of all the opinions which I had formerly accepted, and commence to build anew from the foundation, if I wanted to establish any firm and permanent structure in the sciences. But as this enterprise appeared to be a very great one, I waited until I had attained an age so mature that I could not hope that at any later date I should be better fitted to execute my design. This reason caused me to delay so long that I should feel that I was doing wrong were I to occupy in deliberation the time that yet remains to me for action. To-day, then, since very opportunely for the plan I have in view I have delivered my mind from every care [and am happily agitated by no passions] and since I have procured for myself an assured leisure in a peaceable retirement, I shall at last seriously and freely address myself to the general upheaval of all my former opinions.

Now for this object it is not necessary that I should show that all of these are false – I shall perhaps never arrive at this end. But inasmuch as reason already persuades me that I ought no less carefully to withhold my assent from matters which are not entirely certain and indubitable than from those which appear to me manifestly to be false, if I am able to find in each one some reason to doubt, this will suffice to justify my rejecting the whole. And for that end it will not be requisite that I should examine each in particular, which would be an endless undertaking; for owing to the fact that the destruction of the foundations of necessity brings with it the downfall of the rest of the edifice, I shall only in the first place attack those principles upon which all my former opinions rested.

All that up to the present time I have accepted as most true and certain I have learned either from the senses or through the senses; but it is sometimes proved to me that these senses are deceptive, and it is wiser not to trust entirely to any thing by which we have once been deceived.

But it may be that although the senses sometimes deceive us concerning things which are hardly perceptible, or very far away, there are yet many others to be met with as to which we cannot reasonably have any doubt, although we recognise them by their means. For example, there is the fact that I am here, seated by the fire, attired in a dressing gown, having this paper in my hands and other similar matters. And how could I deny that these hands and this body are mine, were it not perhaps that I compare myself to certain persons, devoid of sense, whose cerebella are so troubled and clouded by the violent vapours of black bile, that they constantly assure us that they think they are kings when they are really quite poor, or that they are clothed in purple when they are really without covering, or who imagine that they have an earthenware head or are nothing but pumpkins or are made of glass. But they are mad, and I should not be any the less insane were I to follow examples so extravagant.

At the same time I must remember that I am a man, and that consequently I am in the habit of sleeping, and in my dreams representing to myself the same things or sometimes even less probable things, than do those who are insane in their waking moments. How often has it happened to me that in the night I dreamt that I found myself in this particular place, that I was dressed and seated near the fire, whilst in reality I was lying undressed in bed! At this moment it does indeed seem to me that it is with eyes awake that I am looking at this paper; that this head which I move is not asleep, that it is deliberately and of set purpose that I extend my hand and perceive it; what happens in sleep does not appear so clear nor so distinct as does all this. But in thinking over this I remind myself that on many occasions I have in sleep been deceived by similar illusions, and in dwelling carefully on this reflection I see so manifestly that there are no certain indications by which we may clearly distinguish wakefulness from sleep that I am lost in astonishment. And my astonishment is such that it is almost capable of persuading me that I now dream.

Now let us assume that we are asleep and that all these particulars, e.g. that we open our eyes, shake our head, extend our hands, and so on, are but false delusions; and let us reflect that possibly neither our hands nor our whole body are such as they appear to us to be. At the same time we must at least confess that the things which are represented to us in sleep are like painted representations which can only have been formed as the counterparts of something real and true, and that in this way those general things at least, i.e. eyes, a head, hands, and a whole body, are not imaginary things, but things really existent. For, as a matter of fact, painters, even when they study with the greatest skill to represent sirens and satyrs by forms the most strange and extraordinary, cannot give them natures which are entirely new, but merely make a certain medley of the members of different animals; or if their imagination is extravagant enough to invent something so novel that nothing similar has ever before been seen, and that then their work represents a thing purely fictitious and absolutely false, it is certain all the same that the colours of which this is composed are necessarily real. And for the same reason, although these general things, to wit, [a body], eyes, a head, hands, and such like, may be imaginary, we are bound at the same time to confess that there are at least some other objects yet more simple and more universal, which are real and true; and of these just in the same way as with certain real colours, all these images of things which dwell in our thoughts, whether true and real or false and fantastic, are formed.

To such a class of things pertains corporeal nature in general, and its extension, the figure of extended things, their quantity or magnitude and number, as also the place in which they are, the time which measures their duration, and so on.

That is possibly why our reasoning is not unjust when we conclude from this that Physics, Astronomy, Medicine and all other sciences which have as their end the consideration of composite things, are very dubious and uncertain; but that Arithmetic, Geometry and other sciences of that kind which only treat of things that are very simple and very general, without taking great trouble to ascertain whether they are actually existent or not, contain some measure of certainty and an element of the indubitable. For whether I am awake or asleep, two and three together always form five, and the square can never have more than four sides, and it does not seem possible that truths so clear and apparent can be suspected of any falsity [or uncertainty].

Nevertheless I have long had fixed in my mind the belief that an all-powerful God, existed by whom I have been created such as I am. But how do I know that He has not brought it to pass that there is no earth, no heaven, no extended body, no magnitude, no place, and that nevertheless [I possess the perceptions of all these things and that] they seem to me to exist just exactly as I now see them? And, besides, as I sometimes imagine that others deceive themselves in the things which they think they know best, how do I know that I am not deceived every time that I add two and three, or count the sides of a square, or judge of things yet simpler, if anything simpler can be imagined? But possibly God has not desired that I should be thus deceived, for He is said to be supremely good. If, however, it is contrary to His goodness to have made me such that I constantly deceive myself, it would also appear to be contrary to His goodness to permit me to be sometimes deceived, and nevertheless I cannot doubt that He does permit this.

There may indeed be those who would prefer to deny the existence of a God so powerful, rather than believe that all other things are uncertain. But let us not oppose them for the present, and grant that all that is here said of a God is a fable; nevertheless in whatever way they suppose that I have arrived at the state of being that I have reached – whether they attribute it to fate or to accident, or make out that it is by a continual succession of antecedents, or by some other method – since to err and deceive oneself is a defect, it is clear that the greater will be the probability of my being so imperfect as to deceive myself ever, as is the Author to whom they assign my origin the less powerful. To these reasons I have certainly nothing to reply, but at the end I feel constrained to confess that there is nothing in all that I formerly believed to be true, of which I cannot in some measure doubt, and that not merely through want of thought or through levity, but for reasons which are very powerful and maturely considered; so that henceforth I ought not the less carefully to refrain from giving credence to these opinions than to that which is manifestly false, if I desire to arrive at any certainty [in the sciences].

But it is not sufficient to have made these remarks, we must also be careful to keep them in mind. For these ancient and commonly held opinions still revert frequently to my mind, long and familiar custom having given them the right to occupy my mind against my inclination and rendered them almost masters of my belief; nor will I ever lose the habit of deferring to them or of placing my confidence in them, so long as I consider them as they really are, i.e. opinions in some measure doubtful, as I have just shown, and at the same time highly probable, so that there is much more reason to believe in than to deny them. That is why I consider that I shall not be acting amiss, if, taking of set purpose a contrary belief, I allow myself to be deceived, and for a certain time pretend that all these opinions are entirely false and imaginary, until at last, having thus balanced my former prejudices with my latter [so that they cannot divert my opinions more to one side than to the other], my judgment will no longer be dominated by bad usage or turned away from the right knowledge of the truth. For I am assured that there can be neither peril nor error in this course, and that I cannot at present yield too much to distrust, since I am not considering the question of action, but only of knowledge.

I shall then suppose, not that God who is supremely good and the fountain of truth, but some evil genius not less powerful than deceitful, has employed his whole energies in deceiving me; I shall consider that the heavens, the earth, colours, figures, sound, and all other external things are nought but the illusions and dreams of which this genius has availed himself in order to lay traps for my credulity; I shall consider myself as having no hands, no eyes, no flesh, no blood, nor any senses, yet falsely believing myself to possess all these things; I shall remain obstinately attached to this idea, and if by this means it is not in my power to arrive at the knowledge of any truth, I may at least do what is in my power [i.e. suspend my judgment], and with firm purpose avoid giving credence to any false thing, or being imposed upon by this arch deceiver, however powerful and deceptive he may be. But this task is a laborious one, and insensibly a certain lassitude leads me into the course of my ordinary life. And just as a captive who in sleep enjoys an imaginary liberty, when he begins to suspect that his liberty is but a dream, fears to awaken, and conspires with these agreeable illusions that the deception may be prolonged, so insensibly of my own accord I fall back into my former opinions, and I dread awakening from this slumber, lest the laborious wakefulness which would follow the tranquillity of this repose should have to be spent not in daylight, but in the excessive darkness of the difficulties which have just been discussed.

Meditation II

Of the Nature of the Human Mind; and that it is more easily known than the Body

The Meditation of yesterday filled my mind with so many doubts that it is no longer in my power to forget them. And yet I do not see in what manner I can resolve them; and, just as if I had all of a sudden fallen into very deep water, I am so disconcerted that I can neither make certain of setting my feet on the bottom, nor can I swim and so support myself on the surface. I shall nevertheless make an effort and follow anew the same path as that on which I yesterday entered, i.e. I shall proceed by setting aside all that in which the least doubt could be supposed to exist, just as if I had discovered that it was absolutely false; and I shall ever follow in this road until I have met with something which is certain, or at least, if I can do nothing else, until I have learned for certain that there is nothing in the world that is certain. Archimedes, in order that he might draw the terrestrial globe out of its place, and transport it elsewhere, demanded only that one point should be fixed and immoveable; in the same way I shall have the right to conceive high hopes if I am happy enough to discover one thing only which is certain and indubitable.

I suppose, then, that all the things that I see are false; I persuade myself that nothing has ever existed of all that my fallacious memory represents to me. I consider that I possess no senses; I imagine that body, figure, extension, movement and place are but the fictions of my mind. What, then, can be esteemed as true? Perhaps nothing at all, unless that there is nothing in the world that is certain.

But how can I know there is not something different from those things that I have just considered, of which one cannot have the slightest doubt? Is there not some God, or some other being by whatever name we call it, who puts these reflections into my mind? That is not necessary, for is it not possible that I am capable of producing them myself? I myself, am I not at least something? But I have already denied that I had senses and body. Yet I hesitate, for what follows from that? Am I so dependent on body and senses that I cannot exist without these? But I was persuaded that there was nothing in all the world, that there was no heaven, no earth, that there were no minds, nor any bodies: was I not then likewise persuaded that I did not exist? Not at all; of a surety I myself did exist since I persuaded myself of something [or merely because I thought of something]. But there is some deceiver or other, very powerful and very cunning, who ever employs his ingenuity in deceiving me. Then without doubt I exist also if he deceives me, and let him deceive me as much as he will, he can never cause me to be nothing so long as I think that I am something. So that after having reflected well and carefully examined all things, we must come to the definite conclusion that this proposition: I am, I exist, is necessarily true each time that I pronounce it, or that I mentally conceive it.

But I do not yet know clearly enough what I am, I who am certain that I am; and hence I must be careful to see that I do not imprudently take some other object in place of myself, and thus that I do not go astray in respect of this knowledge that I hold to be the most certain and most evident of all that I have formerly learned. That is why I shall now consider anew what I believed myself to be before I embarked upon these last reflections; and of my former opinions I shall withdraw all that might even in a small degree be invalidated by the reasons which I have just brought forward, in order that there may be nothing at all left beyond what is absolutely certain and indubitable.

What then did I formerly believe myself to be? Undoubtedly I believed myself to be a man. But what is a man? Shall I say a reasonable animal? Certainly not; for then I should have to inquire what an animal is, and what is reasonable; and thus from a single question I should insensibly fall into an infinitude of others more difficult; and I should not wish to waste the little time and leisure remaining to me in trying to unravel subtleties like these. But I shall rather stop here to consider the thoughts which of themselves spring up in my mind, and which were not inspired by anything beyond my own nature alone when I applied myself to the consideration of my being. In the first place, then, I considered myself as having a face, hands, arms, and all that system of members composed of bones and flesh as seen in a corpse which I designated by the name of body. In addition to this I considered that I was nourished, that I walked, that I felt, and that I thought, and I referred all these actions to the soul: but I did not stop to consider what the soul was, or if I did stop, I imagined that it was something extremely rare and subtle like a wind, a flame, or an ether, which was spread throughout my grosser parts. As to body I had no manner of doubt about its nature, but thought I had a very clear knowledge of it; and if I had desired to explain it according to the notions that I had then formed of it, I should have described it thus: By the body I understand all that which can be defined by a certain figure: something which can be confined in a certain place, and which can fill a given space in such a way that every other body will be excluded from it; which can be perceived either by touch, or by sight, or by hearing, or by taste, or by smell: which can be moved in many ways not, in truth, by itself, but by something which is foreign to it, by which it is touched [and from which it receives impressions]: for to have the power of self-movement, as also of feeling or of thinking, I did not consider to appertain to the nature of body: on the contrary, I was rather astonished to find that faculties similar to them existed in some bodies.

But what am I, now that I suppose that there is a certain genius which is extremely powerful, and, if I may say so, malicious, who employs all his powers in deceiving me? Can I affirm that I possess the least of all those things which I have just said pertain to the nature of body? I pause to consider, I revolve all these things in my mind, and I find none of which I can say that it pertains to me. It would be tedious to stop to enumerate them. Let us pass to the attributes of soul and see if there is any one which is in me? What of nutrition or walking [the first mentioned]? But if it is so that I have no body it is also true that I can neither walk nor take nourishment. Another attribute is sensation. But one cannot feel without body, and besides I have thought I perceived many things during sleep that I recognised in my waking moments as not having been experienced at all. What of thinking? I find here that thought is an attribute that belongs to me; it alone cannot be separated from me. I am, I exist, that is certain. But how often? Just when I think; for it might possibly be the case if I ceased entirely to think, that I should likewise cease altogether to exist I do not now admit anything which is not necessarily true: to speak accurately I am not more than a thing which thinks, that is to say a mind or a soul, or an understanding, or a reason, which are terms whose significance was formerly unknown to me. I am, however, a real thing and really exist; but what thing? I have answered: a thing which thinks.

And what more? I shall exercise my imagination [in order to see if I am not something more]. I am not a collection of members which we call the human body: I am not a subtle air distributed through these members, I am not a wind, a fire, a vapour, a breath, nor anything at all which I can imagine or conceive; because I have assumed that all these were nothing. Without changing that supposition I find that I only leave myself certain of the fact that I am somewhat. But perhaps it is true that these same things which I supposed were non-existent because they are unknown to me, are really not different from the self which I know. I am not sure about this, I shall not dispute about it now; I can only give judgment on things that are known to me. I know that I exist, and I inquire what I am, I whom I know to exist. But it is very certain that the knowledge of my existence taken in its precise significance does not depend on things whose existence is not yet known to me; consequently it does not depend on those which I can feign in imagination. And indeed the very term *feign* in imagination proves to me my error, for I really do this if I image myself a something, since to imagine is nothing else than to contemplate the figure or image of a corporeal thing. But I already know for certain that I am, and that it may be that all these images, and, speaking generally, all things that relate to the nature of body are nothing but dreams [and chimeras]. For this reason I see clearly that I have as little reason to say, 'I shall stimulate my imagination in order to know more distinctly what I am,' than if I were to say, 'I am now awake, and I perceive somewhat that is real and true: but because I do not yet perceive it distinctly enough, I shall go to sleep of express purpose, so that my dreams may represent the perception with greatest truth and evidence.' And, thus, I know for certain that nothing of all that I can understand by means of my imagination belongs to this knowledge which I have of myself, and that it is necessary to recall the mind from this mode of thought with the utmost diligence in order that it may be able to know its own nature with perfect distinctness.

But what then am I? A thing which thinks. What is a thing which thinks? It is a thing which doubts, understands, [conceives], affirms, denies, wills, refuses, which also imagines and feels.

Certainly it is no small matter if all these things pertain to my nature. But why should they not so pertain? Am I not that being who now doubts nearly everything, who nevertheless understands certain things, who affirms that one only is true, who denies all the others, who desires to know more, is averse from being deceived, who imagines many things, sometimes indeed despite his will, and who perceives many likewise, as by the intervention of the bodily organs? Is there nothing in all this which is as true as it is certain that I exist, even though I should always sleep and though he who has given me being employed all his ingenuity in deceiving me? Is there likewise any one of these attributes which can be distinguished from my thought, or which might be said to be separated from myself? For it is so evident of itself that it is I who doubts, who understands, and who desires, that there is no reason here to add anything to explain it. And I have certainly the power of imagining likewise; for although it may happen (as I formerly supposed) that none of the things which I imagine are true, nevertheless this power of imagining does not cease to be really in use, and it forms part of my thought. Finally, I am the same who feels, that is to say, who perceives certain things, as by the organs of sense, since in truth I see light, I hear noise, I feel heat. But it will be said that these phenomena are false and that I am dreaming. Let it be so; still it is at least quite certain that it seems to me that I see light, that I hear noise and that I feel heat. That cannot be false; properly speaking it is what is in me called feeling; and used in this precise sense that is no other thing than thinking.

From this time I begin to know what I am with a little more clearness and distinction than before; but nevertheless it still seems to me, and I cannot prevent myself from thinking, that corporeal things, whose images are framed by thought, which are tested by the senses, are much more distinctly known than that obscure part of me which does not come under the imagination. Although really it is very strange to say that I know and understand more distinctly these things whose existence seems to me dubious, which are unknown to me, and which do not belong to me, than others of the truth of which I am convinced, which are known to me and which pertain to my real nature, in a word, than myself. But I see clearly how the case stands: my mind loves to wander, and cannot yet suffer itself to be retained within the just limits of truth. Very good, let us once more give it the freest rein, so that, when afterwards we seize the proper occasion for pulling up, it may the more easily be regulated and controlled.

Let us begin by considering the commonest matters, those which we believe to be the most distinctly comprehended, to wit, the bodies which we touch and see; not indeed bodies in general, for these general ideas are usually a little more confused, but let us consider one body in particular. Let us take, for example, this piece of wax: it has been taken quite freshly from the hive, and it has not yet lost the sweetness of the honey which it contains; it still retains somewhat of the odour of the flowers from which it has been culled; its colour, its figure, its size are apparent; it is hard, cold, easily handled, and if you strike it with the finger, it will emit a sound. Finally all the things which are requisite to cause us distinctly to recognise a body, are met with in it. But notice that while I speak and approach the fire what remained of the taste is exhaled, the smell evaporates, the colour alters, the figure is destroyed, the size increases, it becomes liquid, it heats, scarcely can one handle it, and when one strikes it, no sound is emitted. Does the same wax remain after this change? We must confess that it remains; none would judge otherwise. What then did I know so distinctly in this piece of wax? It could certainly be nothing of all that the senses brought to my notice, since all these things which fall under taste, smell, sight, touch, and hearing, are found to be changed, and yet the same wax remains.

Perhaps it was what I now think, viz. that this wax was not that sweetness of honey, nor that agreeable scent of flowers, nor that particular whiteness, nor that figure, nor that sound, but simply a body which a little while before appeared to me as perceptible under these forms, and which is now perceptible under others. But what, precisely, is it that I imagine when I form such conceptions? Let us attentively consider this, and, abstracting from all that does not belong to the wax, let us see what remains. Certainly nothing remains excepting a certain extended thing which is flexible and movable. But what is the meaning of flexible and movable? Is it not that I imagine that this piece of wax being round is capable of becoming square and of passing from a square to a triangular figure? No, certainly it is not that, since I imagine it admits of an infinitude of similar changes, and I nevertheless do not know how to compass the infinitude by my imagination, and consequently this conception which I have of the wax is not brought about by the faculty of imagination. What now is this extension? Is it not also unknown? For it becomes greater when the wax is melted, greater when it is boiled, and greater still when the heat increases; and I should not conceive [clearly] according to truth what wax is, if I did not think that even this piece that we are considering is capable of receiving more variations in extension than I have ever imagined. We must then grant that I could not even understand through the imagination what this piece of wax is, and that it is my mind alone which perceives it. I say this piece of wax in particular, for as to wax in general it is yet clearer. But what is this piece of wax which cannot be understood excepting by the [understanding or] mind? It is certainly the same that I see, touch, imagine, and finally it is the same which I have always believed it to be from the beginning. But what must particularly be observed is that its perception is neither an act of vision, nor of touch, nor of imagination, and has never been such although it may have appeared formerly to be so, but only an intuition of the mind, which may be imperfect and confused as it was formerly, or clear and distinct as it is at present, according as my attention is more or less directed to the elements which are found in it, and of which it is composed.

Yet in the meantime I am greatly astonished when I consider [the great feebleness of mind] and its proneness to fall [insensibly] into error; for although without giving expression to my thoughts I consider all this in my own mind, words often impede me and I am almost deceived by the terms of ordinary language. For we say that we see the same wax, if it is present, and not that we simply judge that it is the same from its having the same colour and figure. From this I should conclude that I knew the wax by means of vision and not simply by the intuition of the mind; unless by chance I remember that, when looking from a window and saying I see men who pass in the street, I really do not see them, but infer that what I see is men, just as I say that I see wax. And yet what do I see from the window but hats and coats which may cover automatic machines? Yet I judge these to be men. And similarly solely by the faculty of judgment which rests in my mind, I comprehend that which I believed I saw with my eyes.

A man who makes it his aim to raise his knowledge above the common should be ashamed to derive the occasion for doubting from the forms of speech invented by the vulgar; I prefer to pass on and consider whether I had a more evident and perfect conception of what the wax was when I first perceived it, and when I believed I knew it by means of the external senses or at least by the common sense as it is called, that is to say by the imaginative faculty, or whether my present conception is clearer now that I have most carefully examined what it is, and in what way it can be known. It would certainly be absurd to doubt as to this. For what was there in this first perception which was distinct? What was there which might not as well have been perceived by any of the animals? But when I distinguish the wax from its external forms, and when, just as if I had taken from it its vestments, I consider it quite naked, it is certain that although some error may still be found in my judgment, I can nevertheless not perceive it thus without a human mind.

But finally what shall I say of this mind, that is, of myself, for up to this point I do not admit in myself anything but mind? What then, I who seem to perceive this piece of wax so distinctly, do I not know myself, not only with much more truth and certainty, but also with much more distinctness and clearness? For if I judge that the wax is or exists from the fact that I see it, it certainly follows much more clearly that I am or that I exist myself from the fact that I see it. For it may be that what I see is not really wax, it may also be that I do not possess eyes with which to see anything; but it cannot be that when I see, or (for I no longer take account of the distinction) when I think I see, that I myself who think am nought. So if I judge that the wax exists from the fact that I touch it, the same thing will follow, to wit, that I am; and if I judge that my imagination, or some other cause, whatever it is, persuades me that the wax exists, I shall still conclude the same. And what I have here remarked of wax may be applied to all other things which are external to me [and which are met with outside of me]. And further, if the [notion or] perception of wax has seemed to me clearer and more distinct, not only after the sight or the touch, but also after many other causes have rendered it quite manifest to me, with how much more [evidence] and distinctness must it be said that I now know myself, since all the reasons which contribute to the knowledge of wax, or any other body whatever, are yet better proofs of the nature of my mind! And there are so many other things in the mind itself which may contribute to the elucidation of its nature, that those which depend on body such as these just mentioned, hardly merit being taken into account.

But finally here I am, having insensibly reverted to the point I desired, for, since it is now manifest to me that even bodies are not properly speaking known by the senses or by the faculty of imagination, but by the understanding only, and since they are not known from the fact that they are seen or touched, but only because they are understood, I see clearly that there is nothing which is easier for me to know than my mind. But because it is difficult to rid oneself so promptly of an opinion to which one was accustomed for so long, it will be well that I should halt a little at this point, so that by the length of my meditation I may more deeply imprint on my memory this new knowledge.

Meditation III

Of God: that He exists

I shall now close my eyes, I shall stop my ears, I shall call away all my senses, I shall efface even from my thoughts all the images of corporeal things, or at least (for that is hardly possible) I shall esteem them as vain and false; and thus holding converse only with myself and considering my own nature, I shall try little by little to reach a better knowledge of and a more familiar acquaintanceship with myself. I am a thing that thinks, that is to say, that doubts, affirms, denies, that knows a few things, that is ignorant of many [that loves, that hates], that wills, that desires, that also imagines and perceives; for as I remarked before, although the things which I perceive and imagine are perhaps nothing at all apart from me and in themselves, I am nevertheless assured that these modes of thought that I call perceptions and imaginations, inasmuch only as they are modes of thought, certainly reside [and are met with] in me.

And in the little that I have just said, I think I have summed up all that I really know, or at least all that hitherto I was aware that I knew. In order to try to extend my knowledge further, I shall now look around more carefully and see whether I cannot still discover in myself some other things which I have not hitherto perceived. I am certain that I am a thing which thinks; but do I not then likewise know what is requisite to render me certain of a truth? Certainly in this first knowledge there is nothing that assures me of its truth, excepting the clear and distinct perception of that which I state, which would not indeed suffice of assure me that what I say is true, if it could ever happen that a thing which I conceived so clearly and distinctly could be false; and accordingly it seems to me that already I can establish as a general rule that all things which I perceive very clearly and very distinctly are true.

At the same time I have before received and admitted many things to be very certain and manifest, which yet I afterwards recognised as being dubious. What then were these things? They were the earth, sky, stars and all other objects which I apprehended by means of the senses. But what did I clearly [and distinctly] perceive in them? Nothing more than that the ideas or thoughts of these things were presented to my mind. And not even now do I deny that these ideas are met with in me. But there was yet another thing which I affirmed, and which, owing to the habit which I had formed of believing it, I thought I perceived very clearly, although in truth I did not perceive it at all, to wit, that there were objects outside of me from which these ideas proceeded, and to which they were entirely similar. And it was in this that I erred, or, if perchance my judgment was correct, this was not due to any knowledge arising from my perception.

But when I took anything very simple and easy in the sphere of arithmetic or geometry into consideration, e.g. that two and three together made five, and other things of the sort, were not these present to my mind so clearly as to enable me to affirm that they were true? Certainly if I judged that since such matters could be doubted, this would not have been so for any other reason than that it came into my mind that perhaps a God might have endowed me with such a nature that I may have been deceived even concerning things which seemed to me most manifest. But every time that this preconceived opinion of the sovereign power of a God presents itself to my thought, I am constrained to confess that it is easy to Him, if He wishes it, to cause me to err, even in matters in which I believe myself to have the best evidence. And, on the other hand, always when I direct my attention to things which I believe myself to perceive very clearly, I am so persuaded of their truth that I let myself break out into words such as these: Let who will deceive me, He can never cause me to be nothing while I think that I am, or some day cause it to be true to say that I have never been, it being true now to say that I am, or that two and three make more or less than five, or any such thing in which I see a manifest contradiction. And, certainly, since I have no reason to believe that there is a God who is a deceiver, and as I have not yet satisfied myself that there is a God at all, the reason for doubt which depends on this opinion alone is very slight, and so to speak metaphysical. But in order to be able altogether to remove it, I must inquire whether there is a God as soon as the occasion presents itself; and if I find that there is a God, I must also inquire whether He may be a deceiver; for without a knowledge of these two truths I do not see that I can ever be certain of anything.

And in order that I may have an opportunity of inquiring into this in an orderly way [without interrupting the order of meditation which I have proposed to myself, and which is little by little to pass from the notions which I find first of all in my mind to those which I shall later on discover in it] it is requisite that I should here divide my thoughts into certain kinds, and that I should consider in which of these kinds there is, properly speaking, truth or error to be found. Of my thoughts some are, so to speak, images of the things, and to these alone is the title 'idea' properly applied; examples are my thought of a man or of a chimera, of heaven, of an angel, or [even] of God. But other thoughts possess other forms as well. For example in willing, fearing, approving, denying, though I always perceive something as the subject of the action of my mind, yet by this action I always add something else to the idea which I have of that thing; and of the thoughts of this kind some are called volitions or affections, and others judgments.

Now as to what concerns ideas, if we consider them only in themselves and do not relate them to anything else beyond themselves, they cannot properly speaking be false; for whether I imagine a goat or a chimera, it is not less true that I imagine the one than the other. We must not fear likewise that falsity can enter into will and into affections, for although I may desire evil things, or even things that never existed, it is not the less true that I desire them. Thus there remains no more than the judgments which we make, in which I must take the greatest care not to deceive myself. But the principal error and the commonest which we may meet with in them, consists in my judging that the ideas which are in me are similar or conformable to the things which are outside me; for without doubt if I considered the ideas only as certain modes of my thoughts, without trying to relate them to anything beyond, they could scarcely give me material for error.

But among these ideas, some appear to me to be innate, some adventitious, and others to be formed [or invented] by myself; for, as I have the power of understanding what is called a thing, or a truth, or a thought, it appears to me that I hold this power from no other source than my own nature. But if I now hear some sound, if I see the sun, or feel heat, I have hitherto judged that these sensations proceeded from certain things that exist outside of me; and finally it appears to me that sirens, hippogryphs, and the like, are formed out of my own mind. But again I may possibly persuade myself that all these ideas are of the nature of those which I term adventitious, or else that they are all innate, or all fictitious: for I have not yet clearly discovered their true origin.

And my principal task in this place is to consider, in respect to those ideas which appear to me to proceed from certain objects that are outside me, what are the reasons which cause me to think them similar to these objects. It seems indeed in the first place that I am taught this lesson by nature; and, secondly, I experience in myself that these ideas do not depend on my will nor therefore on myself – for they often present themselves to my mind in spite of my will. Just now, for instance, whether I will or whether I do not will, I feel heat, and thus I persuade myself that this feeling, or at least this idea of heat, is produced in me by something which is different from me, i.e. by the heat of the fire near which I sit. And nothing seems to me more obvious than to judge that this object imprints its likeness rather than anything else upon me.

Now I must discover whether these proofs are sufficiently strong and convincing. When I say that I am so instructed by nature, I merely mean a certain spontaneous inclination which impels me to believe in this connection, and not a natural light which makes me recognise that it is true. But these two things are very different; for I cannot doubt that which the natural light causes me to believe to be true, as, for example, it has shown me that I am from the fact that I doubt, or other facts of the same kind. And I possess no other faculty whereby to distinguish truth from falsehood, which can teach me that what this light shows me to be true is not really true, and no other faculty that is equally trustworthy. But as far as [apparently] natural impulses are concerned, I have frequently remarked, when I had to make active choice between virtue and vice, that they often enough led me to the part that was worse; and this is why I do not see any reason for following them in what regards truth and error.

And as to the other reason, which is that these ideas must proceed from objects outside me, since they do not depend on my will, I do not find it any the more convincing. For just as these impulses of which I have spoken are found in me, notwithstanding that they do not always concur with my will, so perhaps there is in me some faculty fitted to produce these ideas without the assistance of any external things, even though it is not yet known by me; just as, apparently, they have hitherto always been found in me during sleep without the aid of any external objects.

And finally, though they did proceed from objects different from myself, it is not a necessary consequence that they should resemble these. On the contrary, I have noticed that in many cases there was a great difference between the object and its idea. I find, for example, two completely diverse ideas of the sun in my mind; the one derives its origin from the senses, and should be placed in the category of adventitious ideas; according to this idea the sun seems to be extremely small; but the other is derived from astronomical reasonings, i.e. is elicited from certain notions that are innate in me, or else it is formed by me in some other manner; in accordance with it the sun appears to be several times greater than the earth. These two ideas cannot, indeed, both resemble the same sun, and reason makes me believe that the one which seems to have originated directly from the sun itself, is the one which is most dissimilar to it.

All this causes me to believe that until the present time it has not been by a judgment that was certain [or premeditated], but only by a sort of blind impulse that I believed that things existed outside of, and different from me, which, by the organs of my senses, or by some other method whatever it might be, conveyed these ideas or images to me [and imprinted on me their similitudes].

But there is yet another method of inquiring whether any of the objects of which I have ideas within me exist outside of me. If ideas are only taken as certain modes of thought, I recognise amongst them no difference or inequality, and all appear to proceed from me in the same manner; but when we consider them as images, one representing one thing and the other another, it is clear that they are very different one from the other. There is no doubt that those which represent to me substances are something more, and contain so to speak more objective reality within them [that is to say, by representation participate in a higher degree of being or perfection] than those that simply represent modes or accidents; and that idea again by which I understand a supreme God, eternal, infinite, [immutable], omniscient, omnipotent, and Creator of all things which are outside of Himself, has certainly more objective reality in itself than those ideas by which finite substances are represented.

Now it is manifest by the natural light that there must at least be as much reality in the efficient and total cause as in its effect. For, pray, whence can the effect derive its reality, if not from its cause? And in what way can this cause communicate this reality to it, unless it possessed it in itself? And from this it follows, not only that something cannot proceed from nothing, but likewise that what is more perfect – that is to say, which has more reality within itself – cannot proceed from the less perfect. And this is not only evidently true of those effects which possess actual or formal reality, but also of the ideas in which we consider merely what is termed objective reality. To take an example, the stone which has not yet existed not only cannot now commence to be unless it has been produced by something which possesses within itself, either formally or eminently, all that enters into the composition of the stone [i.e. it must possess the same things or other more excellent things than those which exist in the stone] and heat can only be produced in a subject in which it did not previously exist by a cause that is of an order [degree or kind] at least as perfect as heat, and so in all other cases. But further, the idea of heat, or of a stone, cannot exist in me unless it has been placed within me by some cause which possesses within it at least as much reality as that which I conceive to exist in the heat or the stone. For although this cause does not transmit anything of its actual or formal reality to my idea, we must not for that reason imagine that it is necessarily a less real cause; we must remember that [since every idea is a work of the mind] its nature is such that it demands of itself no other formal reality than that which it borrows from my thought, of which it is only a mode [i.e. a manner or way of thinking]. But in order that an idea should contain some one certain objective reality rather than another, it must without doubt derive it from some cause in which there is at least as much formal reality as this idea contains of objective reality. For if we imagine that something is found in an idea which is not found in the cause, it must then have been derived from nought; but however imperfect may be this mode of being by which a thing is objectively [or by representation] in the understanding by its idea, we cannot certainly say that this mode of being is nothing, nor, consequently, that the idea derives its origin from nothing.

Nor must I imagine that, since the reality that I consider in these ideas is only objective, it is not essential that this reality should be formally in the causes of my ideas, but that it is sufficient that it should be found objectively. For just as this mode of objective existence pertains to ideas by their proper nature, so does the mode of formal existence pertain to the causes of those ideas (this is at least true of the first and principal) by the nature peculiar to them. And although it may be the case that one idea gives birth to another idea, that cannot continue to be so indefinitely; for in the end we must reach an idea whose cause shall be so to speak an archetype, in which the whole reality [or perfection] which is so to speak objectively [or by representation] in these ideas is contained formally [and really]. Thus the light of nature causes me to know clearly that the "ideas in me are like [pictures or] images which can, in truth, easily fall short of the perfection of the objects from which they have been derived, but which can never contain anything greater or more perfect."

And the longer and the more carefully that I investigate these matters, the more clearly and distinctly do I recognise their truth. But what am I to conclude from it all in the end? It is this, that if the objective reality of any one of my ideas is of such a nature as clearly to make me recognise that it is not in me either formally or eminently, and that consequently I cannot myself be the cause of it, it follows of necessity that I am not alone in the world, but that there is another being which exists, or which is the cause of this idea. On the other hand, had no such an idea existed in me, I should have had no sufficient argument to convince me of the existence of any being beyond myself; for I have made very careful investigation everywhere and up to the present time have been able to find no other ground.

But of my ideas, beyond that which represents me to myself, as to which there can here be no difficulty, there is another which represents a God, and there are others representing corporeal and inanimate things, others angels, others animals, and others again which represent to me men similar to myself.

As regards the ideas which represent to me other men or animals, or angels, I can however easily conceive that they might be formed by an admixture of the other ideas which I have of myself, of corporeal things, and of God, even although there were apart from me neither men nor animals, nor angels, in all the world.

And in regard to the ideas of corporeal objects, I do not recognise in them anything so great or so excellent that they might not have possibly proceeded from myself; for if I consider them more closely, and examine them individually, as I yesterday examined the idea of wax, I find that there is very little in them which I perceive clearly and distinctly. Magnitude or extension in length, breadth, or depth, I do so perceive; also figure which results from a termination of this extension, the situation which bodies of different figure preserve in relation to one another, and movement or change of situation; to which we may also add substance, duration and number. As to other things such as light, colours, sounds, scents, tastes, heat, cold and the other tactile qualities, they are thought by me with so much obscurity and confusion that I do not even know if they are true or false, i.e. whether the ideas which I form of these qualities are actually the ideas of real objects or not [or whether they only represent chimeras which cannot exist in fact]. For although I have before remarked that it is only in judgments that falsity, properly speaking, or formal falsity, can be met with, a certain material falsity may nevertheless be found in ideas, i.e. when these ideas represent what is nothing as though it were something. For example, the ideas which I have of cold and heat are so far from clear and distinct that by their means I cannot tell whether cold is merely a privation of heat, or heat a privation of cold, or whether both are real qualities, or are not such. And inasmuch as [since ideas resemble images] there cannot be any ideas which do not appear to represent some things, if it is correct to say that cold is merely a privation of heat, the idea which represents it to me as something real and positive will not be improperly termed false, and the same holds good of other similar ideas.

To these it is certainly not necessary that I should attribute any author other than myself. For if they are false, i.e. if they represent things which do not exist, the light of nature shows me that they issue from nought, that is to say, that they are only in me in so far as something is lacking to the perfection of my nature. But if they are true, nevertheless because they exhibit so little reality to me that I cannot even clearly distinguish the thing represented from non-being, I do not see any reason why they should not be produced by myself.

As to the clear and distinct idea which I have of corporeal things, some of them seem as though I might have derived them from the idea which I possess of myself, as those which I have of substance, duration, number, and such like. For [even] when I think that a stone is a substance, or at least a thing capable of existing of itself, and that I am a substance also, although I conceive that I am a thing that thinks and not one that is extended, and that the stone on the other hand is an extended thing which does not think, and that thus there is a notable difference between the two conceptions – they seem, nevertheless, to agree in this, that both represent substances. In the same way, when I perceive that I now exist and further recollect that I have in former times existed, and when I remember that I have various thoughts of which I can recognise the number, I acquire ideas of duration and number which I can afterwards transfer to any object that I please. But as to all the other qualities of which the ideas of corporeal things are composed, to wit, extension, figure, situation and motion, it is true that they are not formally in me, since I am only a thing that thinks; but because they are merely certain modes of substance [and so to speak the vestments under which corporeal substance appears to us] and because I myself am also a substance, it would seem that they might be contained in me eminently.

Hence there remains only the idea of God, concerning which we must consider whether it is something which cannot have proceeded from me myself. By the name God I understand a substance that is infinite [eternal, immutable], independent, all-knowing, all-powerful, and by which I myself and everything else, if anything else does exist, have been created. Now all these characteristics are such that the more diligently I attend to them, the less do they appear capable of proceeding from me alone; hence, from what has been already said, we must conclude that God necessarily exists.

For although the idea of substance is within me owing to the fact that I am substance, nevertheless I should not have the idea of an infinite substance – since I am finite – if it had not proceeded from some substance which was veritably infinite.

Nor should I imagine that I do not perceive the infinite by a true idea, but only by the negation of the finite, just as I perceive repose and darkness by the negation of movement and of light; for, on the contrary, I see that there is manifestly more reality in infinite substance than in finite, and therefore that in some way I have in me the notion of the infinite earlier than the finite – to wit, the notion of God before that of myself. For how would it be possible that I should know that I doubt and desire, that is to say, that something is lacking to me, and that I am not quite perfect, unless I had within me some idea of a Being more perfect than myself, in comparison with which I should recognise the deficiencies of my nature?

And we cannot say that this idea of God is perhaps materially false and that consequently I can derive it from nought [i.e. that possibly it exists in me because I am imperfect], as I have just said is the case with ideas of heat, cold and other such things; for, on the contrary, as this idea is very clear and distinct and contains within it more objective reality than any other, there can be none which is of itself more true, nor any in which there can be less suspicion of falsehood. The idea, I say, of this Being who is absolutely perfect and infinite, is entirely true; for although, perhaps, we can imagine that such a Being does not exist, we cannot nevertheless imagine that His idea represents nothing real to me, as I have said of the idea of cold. This idea is also very clear and distinct; since all that I conceive clearly and distinctly of the real and the true, and of what conveys some perfection, is in its entirety contained in this idea. And this does not cease to be true although I do not comprehend the infinite, or though in God there is an infinitude of things which I cannot comprehend, nor possibly even reach in any way by thought; for it is of the nature of the infinite that my nature, which is finite and limited, should not comprehend it; and it is sufficient that I should understand this, and that I should judge that all things which I clearly perceive and in which I know that there is some perfection, and possibly likewise an infinitude of properties of which I am ignorant, are in God formally or eminently, so that the idea which I have of Him may become the most true, most clear, and most distinct of all the ideas that are in my mind.

But possibly I am something more than I suppose myself to be, and perhaps all those perfections which I attribute to God are in some way potentially in me, although they do not yet disclose themselves, or issue in action. As a matter of fact I am already sensible that my knowledge increases [and perfects itself] little by little, and I see nothing which can prevent it from increasing more and more into infinitude; nor do I see, after it has thus been increased [or perfected], anything to prevent my being able to acquire by its means all the other perfections of the Divine nature; nor finally why the power I have of acquiring these perfections, if it really exists in me, shall not suffice to produce the ideas of them.

At the same time I recognise that this cannot be. For, in the first place, although it were true that every day my knowledge acquired new degrees of perfection, and that there were in my nature many things potentially which are not yet there actually, nevertheless these excellences do not pertain to [or make the smallest approach to] the idea which I have of God in whom there is nothing merely potential [but in whom all is present really and actually]; for it is an infallible token of imperfection in my knowledge that it increases little by little. And further, although my knowledge grows more and more, nevertheless I do not for that reason believe that it can ever be actually infinite, since it can never reach a point so high that it will be unable to attain to any greater increase. But I understand God to be actually infinite, so that He can add nothing to His supreme perfection. And finally I perceive that the objective being of an idea cannot be produced by a being that exists potentially only, which properly speaking is nothing, but only by a being which is formal or actual.

To speak the truth, I see nothing in all that I have just said which by the light of nature is not manifest to anyone who desires to think attentively on the subject; but when I slightly relax my attention, my mind, finding its vision somewhat obscured and so to speak blinded by the images of sensible objects, I do not easily recollect the reason why the idea that I possess of a being more perfect than I, must necessarily have been placed in me by a being which is really more perfect; and this is why I wish here to go on to inquire whether I, who have this idea, can exist if no such being exists.

And I ask, from whom do I then derive my existence? Perhaps from myself or from my parents, or from some other source less perfect than God; for we can imagine nothing more perfect than God, or even as perfect as He is.

But [were I independent of every other and] were I myself the author of my being, I should doubt nothing and I should desire nothing, and finally no perfection would be lacking to me; for I should have bestowed on myself every perfection of which I possessed any idea and should thus be God. And it must not be imagined that those things that are lacking to me are perhaps more difficult of attainment than those which I already possess; for, on the contrary, it is quite evident that it was a matter of much greater difficulty to bring to pass that I, that is to say, a thing or a substance that thinks, should emerge out of nothing, than it would be to attain to the knowledge of many things of which I am ignorant, and which are only the accidents of this thinking substance. But it is clear that if I had of myself possessed this greater perfection of which I have just spoken [that is to say, if I had been the author of my own existence], I should not at least have denied myself the things which are the more easy to acquire [to wit, many branches of knowledge of which my nature is destitute]; nor should I have deprived myself of any of the things contained in the idea which I form of God, because there are none of them which seem to me specially difficult to acquire: and if there were any that were more difficult to acquire, they would certainly appear to me to be such (supposing I myself were the origin of the other things which I possess) since I should discover in them that my powers were limited.

But though I assume that perhaps I have always existed just as I am at present, neither can I escape the force of this reasoning, and imagine that the conclusion to be drawn from this is, that I need not seek for any author of my existence. For all the course of my life may be divided into an infinite number of parts, none of which is in any way dependent on the other; and thus from the fact that I was in existence a short time ago it does not follow that I must be in existence now, unless some cause at this instant, so to speak, produces me anew, that is to say, conserves me. It is as a matter of fact perfectly clear and evident to all those who consider with attention the nature of time, that, in order to be conserved in each moment in which it endures, a substance has need of the same power and action as would be necessary to produce and create it anew, supposing it did not yet exist, so that the light of nature shows us clearly that the distinction between creation and conservation is solely a distinction of the reason.

All that I thus require here is that I should interrogate myself, if I wish to know whether I possess a power which is capable of bringing it to pass that I who now am shall still be in the future; for since I am nothing but a thinking thing, or at least since thus far it is only this portion of myself which is precisely in question at present, if such a power did reside in me, I should certainly be conscious of it. But I am conscious of nothing of the kind, and by this I know clearly that I depend on some being different from myself.

Possibly, however, this being on which I depend is not that which I call God, and I am created either by my parents or by some other cause less perfect than God. This cannot be, because, as I have just said, it is perfectly evident that there must be at least as much reality in the cause as in the effect; and thus since I am a thinking thing, and possess an idea of God within me, whatever in the end be the cause assigned to my existence, it must be allowed that it is likewise a thinking thing and that it possesses in itself the idea of all the perfections which I attribute to God. We may again inquire whether this cause derives its origin from itself or from some other thing. For if from itself, it follows by the reasons before brought forward, that this cause must itself be God; for since it possesses the virtue of self-existence, it must also without doubt have the power of actually possessing all the perfections of which it has the idea, that is, all those which I conceive as existing in God. But if it derives its existence from some other cause than itself, we shall again ask, for the same reason, whether this second cause exists by itself or through another, until from one step to another, we finally arrive at an ultimate cause, which will be God.

And it is perfectly manifest that in this there can be no regression into infinity, since what is in question is not so much the cause which formerly created me, as that which conserves me at the present time.

Nor can we suppose that several causes may have concurred in my production, and that from one I have received the idea of one of the perfections which I attribute to God, and from another the idea of some other, so that all these perfections indeed exist somewhere in the universe, but not as complete in one unity which is God. On the contrary, the unity, the simplicity or the inseparability of all things which are in God is one of the principal perfections which I conceive to be in Him. And certainly the idea of this unity of all Divine perfections cannot have been placed in me by any cause from which I have not likewise received the ideas of all the other perfections; for this cause could not make me able to comprehend them as joined together in an inseparable unity without having at the same time caused me in some measure to know what they are [and in some way to recognise each one of them].

Finally, so far as my parents [from whom it appears I have sprung] are concerned, although all that I have ever been able to believe of them were true, that does not make it follow that it is they who conserve me, nor are they even the authors of my being in any sense, in so far as I am a thinking being; since what they did was merely to implant certain dispositions in that matter in which the self – i.e. the mind, which alone I at present identify with myself – is by me deemed to exist. And thus there can be no difficulty in their regard, but we must of necessity conclude from the fact alone that I exist, or that the idea of a Being supremely perfect – that is of God – is in me, that the proof of God's existence is grounded on the highest evidence.

It only remains to me to examine into the manner in which I have acquired this idea from God; for I have not received it through the senses, and it is never presented to me unexpectedly, as is usual with the ideas of sensible things when these things present themselves, or seem to present themselves, to the external organs of my senses; nor is it likewise a fiction of my mind, for it is not in my power to take from or to add anything to it; and consequently the only alternative is that it is innate in me, just as the idea of myself is innate in me.

And one certainly ought not to find it strange that God, in creating me, placed this idea within me to be like the mark of the workman imprinted on his work; and it is likewise not essential that the mark shall be something different from the work itself. For from the sole fact that God created me it is most probable that in some way he has placed his image and similitude upon me, and that I perceive this similitude (in which the idea of God is contained) by means of the same faculty by which I perceive myself – that is to say, when I reflect on myself I not only know that I am something [imperfect], incomplete and dependent on another, which incessantly aspires after something which is better and greater than myself, but I also know that He on whom I depend possesses in Himself all the great things towards which I aspire [and the ideas of which I find within myself], and that not indefinitely or potentially alone, but really, actually and infinitely; and that thus He is God. And the whole strength of the argument which I have here made use of to prove the existence of God consists in this, that I recognise that it is not possible that my nature should be what it is, and indeed that I should have in myself the idea of a God, if God did not veritably exist – a God, I say, whose idea is in me, i.e. who possesses all those supreme perfections of which our mind may indeed have some idea but without understanding them all, who is liable to no errors or defect [and who has none of all those marks which denote imperfection]. From this it is manifest that He cannot be a deceiver, since the light of nature teaches us that fraud and deception necessarily proceed from some defect.

But before I examine this matter with more care, and pass on to the consideration of other truths which may be derived from it, it seems to me right to pause for a while in order to contemplate God Himself, to ponder at leisure His marvellous attributes, to consider, and admire, and adore, the beauty of this light so resplendent, at least as far as the strength of my mind, which is in some measure dazzled by the sight, will allow me to do so. For just as faith teaches us that the supreme felicity of the other life consists only in this contemplation of the Divine Majesty, so we continue to learn by experience that a similar meditation, though incomparably less perfect, causes us to enjoy the greatest satisfaction of which we are capable in this life.

Meditation IV

Of the True and the False

I have been well accustomed these past days to detach my mind from my senses, and I have accurately observed that there are very few things that one knows with certainty respecting corporeal objects, that there are many more which are known to us respecting the human mind, and yet more still regarding God Himself; so that I shall now without any difficulty abstract my thoughts from the consideration of [sensible or] imaginable objects, and carry them to those which, being withdrawn from all contact with matter, are purely intelligible. And certainly the idea which I possess of the human mind inasmuch as it is a thinking thing, and not extended in length, width and depth, nor participating in anything pertaining to body, is incomparably more distinct than is the idea of any corporeal thing. And when I consider that I doubt, that is to say, that I am an incomplete and dependent being, the idea of a being that is complete and independent, that is of God, presents itself to my mind with so much distinctness and clearness – and from the fact alone that this idea is found in me, or that I who possess this idea exist, I conclude so certainly that God exists, and that my existence depends entirely on Him in every moment of my life – that I do not think that the human mind is capable of knowing anything with more evidence and certitude. And it seems to me that I now have before me a road which will lead us from the contemplation of the true God (in whom all the treasures of science and wisdom are contained) to the knowledge of the other objects of the universe.

For, first of all, I recognise it to be impossible that He should ever deceive me; for in all fraud and deception some imperfection is to be found, and although it may appear that the power of deception is a mark of subtilty or power, yet the desire to deceive without doubt testifies to malice or feebleness, and accordingly cannot be found in God.

In the next place I experienced in myself a certain capacity for judging which I have doubtless received from God, like all the other things that I possess; and as He could not desire to deceive me, it is clear that He has not given me a faculty that will lead me to err if I use it aright.

And no doubt respecting this matter could remain, if it were not that the consequence would seem to follow that I can thus never be deceived; for if I hold all that I possess from God, and if He has not placed in me the capacity for error, it seems as though I could never fall into error. And it is true that when I think only of God [and direct my mind wholly to Him], I discover [in myself] no cause of error, or falsity; yet directly afterwards, when recurring to myself, experience shows me that I am nevertheless subject to an infinitude of errors, as to which, when we come to investigate them more closely, I notice that not only is there a real and positive idea of God or of a Being of supreme perfection present to my mind, but also, so to speak, a certain negative idea of nothing, that is, of that which is infinitely removed from any kind of perfection; and that I am in a sense something intermediate between God and nought, i.e. placed in such a manner between the supreme Being and non-being, that there is in truth nothing in me that can lead to error in so far as a sovereign Being has formed me; but that, as I in some degree participate likewise in nought or in non-being, i.e. in so far as I am not myself the supreme Being, and as I find myself subject to an infinitude of imperfections, I ought not to be astonished if I should fall into error. Thus do I recognise that error, in so far as it is such, is not a real thing depending on God, but simply a defect; and therefore, in order to fall into it, that I have no need to possess a special faculty given me by God for this very purpose, but that I fall into error from the fact that the power given me by God for the purpose of distinguishing truth from error is not infinite.

Nevertheless this does not quite satisfy me; for error is not a pure negation [i.e. is not the simple defect or want of some perfection which ought not to be mine], but it is a lack of some knowledge which it seems that I ought to possess. And on considering the nature of God it does not appear to me possible that He should have given me faculty which is not perfect of its kind, that is, which is wanting in some perfection due to it. For if it is true that the more skilful the artisan, the more perfect is the work of his hands, what can have been produced by this supreme Creator of all things that is not in all its parts perfect? And certainly there is no doubt that God could have created me so that I could never have been subject to error; it is also certain that He ever wills what is best; is it then better that I should be subject to err than that I should not?

In considering this more attentively, it occurs to me in the first place that I should not be astonished if my intelligence is not capable of comprehending why God acts as He does; and that there is thus no reason to doubt of His existence from the fact that I may perhaps find many other things besides this as to which I am able to understand neither for what reason nor how God has produced them. For, in the first place, knowing that my nature is extremely feeble and limited, and that the nature of God is on the contrary immense, incomprehensible, and infinite, I have no further difficulty in recognising that there is an infinitude of matters in His power, the causes of which transcend my knowledge; and this reason suffices to convince me that the species of cause termed final, finds no useful employment in physical [or natural] things; for it does not appear to me that I can without temerity seek to investigate the [inscrutable] ends of God.

It further occurs to me that we should not consider one single creature separately, when we inquire as to whether the works of God are perfect, but should regard all his creations together. For the same thing which might possibly seem very imperfect with some semblance of reason if regarded by itself, is found to be very perfect if regarded as part of the whole universe; and although, since I resolved to doubt all things, I as yet have only known certainly my own existence and that of God, nevertheless since I have recognised the infinite power of God, I cannot deny that He may have produced many other things, or at least that He has the power of producing them, so that I may obtain a place as a part of a great universe.

Whereupon, regarding myself more closely, and considering what are my errors (for they alone testify to there being any imperfection in me), I answer that they depend on a combination of two causes, to wit, on the faculty of knowledge that rests in me, and on the power of choice or of free will – that is to say, of the understanding and at the same time of the will. For by the understanding alone I [neither assert nor deny anything, but] apprehend the ideas of things as to which I can form a judgment. But no error is properly speaking found in it, provided the word error is taken in its proper signification; and though there is possibly an infinitude of things in the world of which I have no idea in my understanding, we cannot for all that say that it is deprived of these ideas [as we might say of something which is required by its nature], but simply it does not possess these; because in truth there is no reason to prove that God should have given me a greater faculty of knowledge than He has given me; and however skilful a workman I represent Him to be, I should not for all that consider that He was bound to have placed in each of His works all the perfections which He may have been able to place in some. I likewise cannot complain that God has not given me a free choice or a will which is sufficient, ample and perfect, since as a matter of fact I am conscious of a will so extended as to be subject to no limits. And what seems to me very remarkable in this regard is that of all the qualities which I possess there is no one so perfect and so comprehensive that I do not very clearly recognise that it might be yet greater and more perfect. For, to take an example, if I consider the faculty of comprehension which I possess, I find that it is of very small extent and extremely limited, and at the same time I find the idea of another faculty much more ample and even infinite, and seeing that I can form the idea of it, I recognise from this very fact that it pertains to the nature of God. If in the same way I examine the memory, the imagination, or some other faculty, I do not find any which is not small and circumscribed, while in God it is immense [or infinite]. It is free-will alone or liberty of choice which I find to be so great in me that I can conceive no other idea to be more great; it is indeed the case that it is for the most part this will that causes me to know that in some manner I bear the image and similitude of God. For although the power of will is incomparably greater in God than in me, both by reason of the knowledge and the power which, conjoined with it, render it stronger and more efficacious, and by reason of its object, inasmuch as in God it extends to a great many things; it nevertheless does not seem to me greater if I consider it formally and precisely in itself: for the faculty of will consists alone in our having the power of choosing to do a thing or choosing not to do it (that is, to affirm or deny, to pursue or to shun it), or rather it consists alone in the fact that in order to affirm or deny, pursue or shun those things placed before us by the understanding, we act so that we are unconscious that any outside force constrains us in doing so. For in order that I should be free it is not necessary that I should be indifferent as to the choice of one or the other of two contraries; but contrariwise the more I lean to the one – whether I recognise clearly that the reasons of the good and true are to be found in it, or whether God so disposes my inward thought – the more freely do I choose and embrace it. And undoubtedly both divine grace and natural knowledge, far from diminishing my liberty, rather increase it and strengthen it. Hence this indifference which I feel, when I am not swayed to one side rather than to the other by lack of reason, is the lowest grade of liberty, and rather evinces a lack or negation in knowledge than a perfection of will: for if I always recognised clearly what was true and good, I should never have trouble in deliberating as to what judgment or choice I should make, and then I should be entirely free without ever being indifferent.

From all this I recognise that the power of will which I have received from God is not of itself the source of my errors – for it is very ample and very perfect of its kind – any more than is the power of understanding; for since I understand nothing but by the power which God has given me for understanding, there is no doubt that all that I understand, I understand as I ought, and it is not possible that I err in this. Whence then come my errors? They come from the sole fact that since the will is much wider in its range and compass than the understanding, I do not restrain it within the same bounds, but extend it also to things which I do not understand: and as the will is of itself indifferent to these, it easily falls into error and sin, and chooses the evil for the good, or the false for the true.

For example, when I lately examined whether anything existed in the world, and found that from the very fact that I considered this question it followed very clearly that I myself existed, I could not prevent myself from believing that a thing I so clearly conceived was true: not that I found myself compelled to do so by some external cause, but simply because from great clearness in my mind there followed a great inclination of my will; and I believed this with so much the greater freedom or spontaneity as I possessed the less indifference towards it. Now, on the contrary, I not only know that I exist, inasmuch as I am a thinking thing, but a certain representation of corporeal nature is also presented to my mind; and it comes to pass that I doubt whether this thinking nature which is in me, or rather by which I am what I am, differs from this corporeal nature, or whether both are not simply the same thing; and I here suppose that I do not yet know any reason to persuade me to adopt the one belief rather than the other. From this it follows that I am entirely indifferent as to which of the two I affirm or deny, or even whether I abstain from forming any judgment in the matter.

And this indifference does not only extend to matters as to which the understanding has no knowledge, but also in general to all those which are not apprehended with perfect clearness at the moment when the will is deliberating upon them: for, however probable are the conjectures which render me disposed to form a judgment respecting anything, the simple knowledge that I have that those are conjectures alone and not certain and indubitable reasons, suffices to occasion me to judge the contrary. Of this I have had great experience of late when I set aside as false all that I had formerly held to be absolutely true, for the sole reason that I remarked that it might in some measure he doubted.

But if I abstain from giving my judgment on any thing when I do not perceive it with sufficient clearness and distinctness, it is plain that I act rightly and am not deceived. But if I determine to deny or affirm, I no longer make use as I should of my free will, and if I affirm what is not true, it is evident that I deceive myself; even though I judge according to truth, this comes about only by chance, and I do not escape the blame of misusing my freedom; for the light of nature teaches us that the knowledge of the understanding should always precede the determination of the will. And it is in the misuse of the free will that the privation which constitutes the characteristic nature of error is met with. Privation, I say, is found in the act, in so far as it proceeds from me, but it is not found in the faculty which I have received from God, nor even in the act in so far as it depends on Him.

For I have certainly no cause to complain that God has not given me an intelligence which is more powerful, or a natural light which is stronger than that which I have received from Him, since it is proper to the finite understanding not to comprehend a multitude of things, and it is proper to a created understanding to be finite; on the contrary, I have every reason to render thanks to God who owes me nothing and who has given me all the perfections I possess, and I should be far from charging Him with injustice, and with having deprived me of, or wrongfully withheld from me, these perfections which He has not bestowed upon me.

I have further no reason to complain that He has given me a will more ample than my understanding, for since the will consists only of one single element, and is so to speak indivisible, it appears that its nature is such that nothing can be abstracted from it [without destroying it]; and certainly the more comprehensive it is found to be, the more reason I have to render gratitude to the giver.

And, finally, I must also not complain that God concurs with me in forming the acts of the will, that is the judgment in which I go astray, because these acts are entirely true and good, inasmuch as they depend on God; and in a certain sense more perfection accrues to my nature from the fact that I can form them, than if I could not do so. As to the privation in which alone the formal reason of error or sin consists, it has no need of any concurrence from God, since it is not a thing [or an existence], and since it is not related to God as to a cause, but should be termed merely a negation [according to the significance given to these words in the Schools]. For in fact it is not an imperfection in God that He has given me the liberty to give or withhold my assent from certain things as to which He has not placed a clear and distinct knowledge in my understanding; but it is without doubt an imperfection in me not to make a good use of my freedom, and to give my judgment readily on matters which I only understand obscurely. I nevertheless perceive that God could easily have created me so that I never should err, although I still remained free, and endowed with a limited knowledge, viz. by giving to my understanding a clear and distinct intelligence of all things as to which I should ever have to deliberate; or simply by His engraving deeply in my memory the resolution never to form a judgment on anything without having a clear and distinct understanding of it, so that I could never forget it. And it is easy for me to understand that, in so far as I consider myself alone, and as if there were only myself in the world, I should have been much more perfect than I am, if God had created me so that I could never err. Nevertheless I cannot deny that in some sense it is a greater perfection in the whole universe that certain parts should not be exempt from error as others are than that all parts should be exactly similar. And I have no right to complain if God, having placed me in the world, has not called upon me to play a part that excels all others in distinction and perfection.

And further I have reason to be glad on the ground that if He has not given me the power of never going astray by the first means pointed out above, which depends on a clear and evident knowledge of all the things regarding which I can deliberate, He has at least left within my power the other means, which is firmly to adhere to the resolution never to give judgment on matters whose truth is not clearly known to me; for although I notice a certain weakness in my nature in that I cannot continually concentrate my mind on one single thought, I can yet, by attentive and frequently repeated meditation, impress it so forcibly on my memory that I shall never fail to recollect it whenever I have need of it, and thus acquire the habit of never going astray.

And inasmuch as it is in this that the greatest and principal perfection of man consists, it seems to me that I have not gained little by this day's Meditation, since I have discovered the source of falsity and error. And certainly there can be no other source than that which I have explained; for as often as I so restrain my will within the limits of my knowledge that it forms no judgment except on matters which are clearly and distinctly represented to it by the understanding, I can never be deceived; for every clear and distinct conception is without doubt something, and hence cannot derive its origin from what is nought, but must of necessity have God as its author – God, I say, who being supremely perfect, cannot be the cause of any error; and consequently we must conclude that such a conception [or such a judgment] is true. Nor have I only learned to-day what I should avoid in order that I may not err, but also how I should act in order to arrive at a knowledge of the truth; for without doubt I shall arrive at this end if I devote my attention sufficiently to those things which I perfectly understand; and if I separate from these that which I only understand confusedly and with obscurity. To these I shall henceforth diligently give heed.

Meditation V

Of the essence of material things, and, again, of God, that He exists

Many other matters respecting the attributes of God and my own nature or mind remain for consideration; but I shall possibly on another occasion resume the investigation of these. Now (after first noting what must be done or avoided, in order to arrive at a knowledge of the truth) my principal task is to endeavour to emerge from the state of doubt into which I have these last days fallen, and to see whether nothing certain can be known regarding material things.

But before examining whether any such objects as I conceive exist outside of me, I must consider the ideas of them in so far as they are in my thought, and see which of them are distinct and which confused.

In the first place, I am able distinctly to imagine that quantity which philosophers commonly call continuous, or the extension in length, breadth, or depth, that is in this quantity, or rather in the object to which it is attributed. Further, I can number in it many different parts, and attribute to each of its parts many sorts of size, figure, situation and local movement, and, finally, I can assign to each of these movements all degrees of duration.

And not only do I know these things with distinctness when I consider them in general, but, likewise [however little I apply my attention to the matter], I discover an infinitude of particulars respecting numbers, figures, movements, and other such things, whose truth is so manifest, and so well accords with my nature, that when I begin to discover them, it seems to me that I learn nothing new, or recollect what I formerly knew – that is to say, that I for the first time perceive things which were already present to my mind, although I had not as yet applied my mind to them.

And what I here find to be most important is that I discover in myself an infinitude of ideas of certain things which cannot be esteemed as pure negations, although they may possibly have no existence outside of my thought, and which are not framed by me, although it is within my power either to think or not to think them, but which possess natures which are true and immutable. For example, when I imagine a triangle, although there may nowhere in the world be such a figure outside my thought, or ever have been, there is nevertheless in this figure a certain determinate nature, form, or essence, which is immutable and eternal, which I have not invented, and which in no wise depends on my mind, as appears from the fact that diverse properties of that triangle can be demonstrated, viz. that its three angles are equal to two right angles, that the greatest side is subtended by the greatest angle, and the like, which now, whether I wish it or do not wish it, I recognise very clearly as pertaining to it, although I never thought of the matter at all when I imagined a triangle for the first time, and which therefore cannot be said to have been invented by me.

Nor does the objection hold good that possibly this idea of a triangle has reached my mind through the medium of my senses, since I have sometimes seen bodies triangular in shape; because I can form in my mind an infinitude of other figures regarding which we cannot have the least conception of their ever having been objects of sense, and I can nevertheless demonstrate various properties pertaining to their nature as well as to that of the triangle, and these must certainly all be true since I conceive them clearly. Hence they are something, and not pure negation; for it is perfectly clear that all that is true is something, and I have already fully demonstrated that all that I know clearly is true. And even although I had not demonstrated this, the nature of my mind is such that I could not prevent myself from holding them to be true so long as I conceive them clearly; and I recollect that even when I was still strongly attached to the objects of sense, I counted as the most certain those truths which I conceived clearly as regards figures, numbers, and the other matters which pertain to arithmetic and geometry, and, in general, to pure and abstract mathematics.

But now, if just because I can draw the idea of something from my thought, it follows that all which I know clearly and distinctly as pertaining to this object does really belong to it, may I not derive from this an argument demonstrating the existence of God? It is certain that I no less find the idea of God, that is to say, the idea of a supremely perfect Being, in me, than that of any figure or number whatever it is; and I do not know any less clearly and distinctly that an [actual and] eternal existence pertains to this nature than I know that all that which I am able to demonstrate of some figure or number truly pertains to the nature of this figure or number, and therefore, although all that I concluded in the preceding Meditations were found to be false, the existence of God would pass with me as at least as certain as I have ever held the truths of mathematics (which concern only numbers and figures) to be.

This indeed is not at first manifest, since it would seem to present some appearance of being a sophism. For being accustomed in all other things to make a distinction between existence and essence, I easily persuade myself that the existence can be separated from the essence of God, and that we can thus conceive God as not actually existing. But, nevertheless, when I think of it with more attention, I clearly see that existence can no more be separated from the essence of God than can its having its three angles equal to two right angles be separated from the essence of a [rectilinear] triangle, or the idea of a mountain from the idea of a valley; and so there is not any less repugnance to our conceiving a God (that is, a Being supremely perfect) to whom existence is lacking (that is to say, to whom a certain perfection is lacking), than to conceive of a mountain which has no valley.

But although I cannot really conceive of a God without existence any more than a mountain without a valley, still from the fact that I conceive of a mountain with a valley, it does not follow that there is such a mountain in the world; similarly although I conceive of God as possessing existence, it would seem that it does not follow that there is a God which exists; for my thought does not impose any necessity upon things, and just as I may imagine a winged horse, although no horse with wings exists, so I could perhaps attribute existence to God, although no God existed.

But a sophism is concealed in this objection; for from the fact that I cannot conceive a mountain without a valley, it does not follow that there is any mountain or any valley in existence, but only that the mountain and the valley, whether they exist or do not exist, cannot in any way be separated one from the other. While from the fact that I cannot conceive God without existence, it follows that existence is inseparable from Him, and hence that He really exists; not that my thought can bring this to pass, or impose any necessity on things, but, on the contrary, because the necessity which lies in the thing itself, i.e. the necessity of the existence of God determines me to think in this way. For it is not within my power to think of God without existence (that is of a supremely perfect Being devoid of a supreme perfection) though it is in my power to imagine a horse either with wings or without wings.

And we must not here object that it is in truth necessary for me to assert that God exists after having presupposed that He possesses every sort of perfection, since existence is one of these, but that as a matter of fact my original supposition was not necessary, just as it is not necessary to consider that all quadrilateral figures can be inscribed in the circle; for supposing I thought this, I should be constrained to admit that the rhombus might be inscribed in the circle since it is a quadrilateral figure, which, however, is manifestly false. [We must not, I say, make any such allegations because] although it is not necessary that I should at any time entertain the notion of God, nevertheless whenever it happens that I think of a first and a sovereign Being, and, so to speak, derive the idea of Him from the storehouse of my mind, it is necessary that I should attribute to Him every sort of perfection, although I do not get so far as to enumerate them all, or to apply my mind to each one in particular. And this necessity suffices to make me conclude (after having recognised that existence is a perfection) that this first and sovereign Being really exists; just as though it is not necessary for me ever to imagine any triangle, yet, whenever I wish to consider a rectilinear figure composed only of three angles, it is absolutely essential that I should attribute to it all those properties which serve to bring about the conclusion that its three angles are not greater than two right angles, even although I may not then be considering this point in particular. But when I consider which figures are capable of being inscribed in the circle, it is in no wise necessary that I should think that all quadrilateral figures are of this number; on the contrary, I cannot even pretend that this is the case, so long as I do not desire to accept anything which I cannot conceive clearly and distinctly. And in consequence there is a great difference between the false suppositions such as this, and the true ideas born within me, the first and principal of which is that of God. For really I discern in many ways that this idea is not something factitious, and depending solely on my thought, but that it is the image of a true and immutable nature; first of all, because I cannot conceive anything but God himself to whose essence existence [necessarily] pertains; in the second place because it is not possible for me to conceive two or more Gods in this same position; and, granted that there is one such God who now exists, I see clearly that it is necessary that He should have existed from all eternity, and that He must exist eternally; and finally, because I know an infinitude of other properties in God, none of which I can either diminish or change.

For the rest, whatever proof or argument I avail myself of, we must always return to the point that it is only those things which we conceive clearly and distinctly that have the power of persuading me entirely. And although amongst the matters which I conceive of in this way, some indeed are manifestly obvious to all, while others only manifest themselves to those who consider them closely and examine them attentively; still, after they have once been discovered, the latter are not esteemed as any less certain than the former. For example, in the case of every right-angled triangle, although it does not so manifestly appear that the square of the base is equal to the squares of the two other sides as that this base is opposite to the greatest angle; still, when this has once been apprehended, we are just as certain of its truth as of the truth of the other. And as regards God, if my mind were not pre-occupied with prejudices, and if my thought did not find itself on all hands diverted by the continual pressure of sensible things, there would be nothing which I could know more immediately and more easily than Him. For is there anything more manifest than that there is a God, that is to say, a Supreme Being, to whose essence alone existence pertains?

And although for a firm grasp of this truth I have need of a strenuous application of mind, at present I not only feel myself to be as assured of it as of all that I hold as most certain, but I also remark that the certainty of all other things depends on it so absolutely, that without this knowledge it is impossible ever to know anything perfectly.

For although I am of such a nature that as long as I understand anything very clearly and distinctly, I am naturally impelled to believe it to be true, yet because I am also of such a nature that I cannot have my mind constantly fixed on the same object in order to perceive it clearly, and as I often recollect having formed a past judgment without at the same time properly recollecting the reasons that led me to make it, it may happen meanwhile that other reasons present themselves to me, which would easily cause me to change my opinion, if I were ignorant of the facts of the existence of God, and thus I should have no true and certain knowledge, but only vague and vacillating opinions. Thus, for example, when I consider the nature of a [rectilinear] triangle, I who have some little knowledge of the principles of geometry recognise quite clearly that the three angles are equal to two right angles, and it is not possible for me not to believe this so long as I apply my mind to its demonstration; but so soon as I abstain from attending to the proof, although I still recollect having clearly comprehended it, it may easily occur that I come to doubt its truth, if I am ignorant of there being a God. For I can persuade myself of having been so constituted by nature that I can easily deceive myself even in those matters which I believe myself to apprehend with the greatest evidence and certainty, especially when I recollect that I have frequently judged matters to be true and certain which other reasons have afterwards impelled me to judge to be altogether false.

But after I have recognised that there is a God – because at the same time I have also recognised that all things depend upon Him, and that He is not a deceiver, and from that have inferred that what I perceive clearly and distinctly cannot fail to be true – although I no longer pay attention to the reasons for which I have judged this to be true, provided that I recollect having clearly and distinctly perceived it no contrary reason can be brought forward which could ever cause me to doubt of its truth; and thus I have a true and certain knowledge of it. And this same knowledge extends likewise to all other things which I recollect having formerly demonstrated, such as the truths of geometry and the like; for what can be alleged against them to cause me to place them in doubt? Will it be said that my nature is such as to cause me to be frequently deceived? But I already know that I cannot be deceived in the judgment whose grounds I know clearly. Will it be said that I formerly held many things to be true and certain which I have afterwards recognised to be false? But I had not had any clear and distinct knowledge of these things, and not as yet knowing the rule whereby I assure myself of the truth, I had been impelled to give my assent from reasons which I have since recognised to be less strong than I had at the time imagined them to be. What further objection can then be raised? That possibly I am dreaming (an objection I myself made a little while ago), or that all the thoughts which I now have are no more true than the phantasies of my dreams? But even though I slept the case would be the same, for all that is clearly present to my mind is absolutely true.

And so I very clearly recognise that the certainty and truth of all knowledge depends alone on the knowledge of the true God, in so much that, before I knew Him, I could not have a perfect knowledge of any other thing. And now that I know Him I have the means of acquiring a perfect knowledge of an infinitude of things, not only of those which relate to God Himself and other intellectual matters, but also of those which pertain to corporeal nature in so far as it is the object of pure mathematics [which have no concern with whether it exists or not].

Meditation VI

Of the Existence of Material Things, and of the real distinction between the Soul and Body of Man

Nothing further now remains but to inquire whether material things exist. And certainly I at least know that these may exist in so far as they are considered as the objects of pure mathematics, since in this aspect I perceive them clearly and distinctly. For there is no doubt that God possesses the power to produce everything that I am capable of perceiving with distinctness, and I have never deemed that anything was impossible for Him, unless I found a contradiction in attempting to conceive it clearly. Further, the faculty of imagination which I possess, and of which, experience tells me, I make use when I apply myself to the consideration of material things, is capable of persuading me of their existence; for when I attentively consider what imagination is, I find that it is nothing but a certain application of the faculty of knowledge to the body which is immediately present to it, and which therefore exists.

And to render this quite clear, I remark in the first place the difference that exists between the imagination and pure intellection [or conception]. For example, when I imagine a triangle, I do not conceive it only as a figure comprehended by three lines, but I also apprehend these three lines as present by the power and inward vision of my mind, and this is what I call imagining. But if I desire to think of a chiliagon, I certainly conceive truly that it is a figure composed of a thousand sides, just as easily as I conceive of a triangle that it is a figure of three sides only; but I cannot in any way imagine the thousand sides of a chiliagon [as I do the three sides of a triangle], nor do I, so to speak, regard them as present [with the eyes of my mind]. And although in accordance with the habit I have formed of always employing the aid of my imagination when I think of corporeal things, it may happen that in imagining a chiliagon I confusedly represent to myself some figure, yet it is very evident that this figure is not a chiliagon, since it in no way differs from that which I represent to myself when I think of a myriagon or any other many-sided figure; nor does it serve my purpose in discovering the properties which go to form the distinction between a chiliagon and other polygons. But if the question turns upon a pentagon, it is quite true that I can conceive its figure as well as that of a chiliagon without the help of my imagination; but I can also imagine it by applying the attention of my mind to each of its five sides, and at the same time to the space which they enclose. And thus I clearly recognise that I have need of a particular effort of mind in order to effect the act of imagination, such as I do not require in order to understand, and this particular effort of mind clearly manifests the difference which exists between imagination and pure intellection.

I remark besides that this power of imagination which is in one, inasmuch as it differs from the power of understanding, is in no wise a necessary element in my nature, or in [my essence, that is to say, in] the essence of my mind; for although I did not possess it I should doubtless ever remain the same as I now am, from which it appears that we might conclude that it depends on something which differs from me. And I easily conceive that if some body exists with which my mind is conjoined and united in such a way that it can apply itself to consider it when it pleases, it may be that by this means it can imagine corporeal objects; so that this mode of thinking differs from pure intellection only inasmuch as mind in its intellectual activity in some manner turns on itself, and considers some of the ideas which it possesses in itself; while in imagining it turns towards the body, and there beholds in it something conformable to the idea which it has either conceived of itself or perceived by the senses. I easily understand, I say, that the imagination could be thus constituted if it is true that body exists; and because I can discover no other convenient mode of explaining it, I conjecture with probability that body does exist; but this is only with probability, and although I examine all things with care, I nevertheless do not find that from this distinct idea of corporeal nature, which I have in my imagination, I can derive any argument from which there will necessarily be deduced the existence of body.

But I am in the habit of imagining many other things besides this corporeal nature which is the object of pure mathematics, to wit, the colours, sounds, scents, pain, and other such things, although less distinctly. And inasmuch as I perceive these things much better through the senses, by the medium of which, and by the memory, they seem to have reached my imagination, I believe that, in order to examine them more conveniently, it is right that I should at the same time investigate the nature of sense perception, and that I should see if from the ideas which I apprehend by this mode of thought, which I call feeling, I cannot derive some certain proof of the existence of corporeal objects.

And first of all I shall recall to my memory those matters which I hitherto held to be true, as having perceived them through the senses, and the foundations on which my belief has rested; in the next place I shall examine the reasons which have since obliged me to place them in doubt; in the last place I shall consider which of them I must now believe.

First of all, then, I perceived that I had a head, hands, feet, and all other members of which this body – which I considered as a part, or possibly even as the whole, of myself – is composed. Further I was sensible that this body was placed amidst many others, from which it was capable of being affected in many different ways, beneficial and hurtful, and I remarked that a certain feeling of pleasure accompanied those that were beneficial, and pain those which were harmful. And in addition to this pleasure and pain, I also experienced hunger, thirst, and other similar appetites, as also certain corporeal inclinations towards joy, sadness, anger, and other similar passions. And outside myself, in addition to extension, figure, and motions of bodies, I remarked in them hardness, heat, and all other tactile qualities, and, further, light and colour, and scents and sounds, the variety of which gave me the means of distinguishing the sky, the earth, the sea, and generally all the other bodies, one from the other. And certainly, considering the ideas of all these qualities which presented themselves to my mind, and which alone I perceived properly or immediately, it was not without reason that I believed myself to perceive objects quite different from my thought, to wit, bodies from which those ideas proceeded; for I found by experience that these ideas presented themselves to me without my consent being requisite, so that I could not perceive any object, however desirous I might be, unless it were present to the organs of sense; and it was not in my power not to perceive it, when it was present. And because the ideas which I received through the senses were much more lively, more clear, and even, in their own way, more distinct than any of those which I could of myself frame in meditation, or than those I found impressed on my memory, it appeared as though they could not have proceeded from my mind, so that they must necessarily have been produced in me by some other things. And having no knowledge of those objects excepting the knowledge which the ideas themselves gave me, nothing was more likely to occur to my mind than that the objects were similar to the ideas which were caused. And because I likewise remembered that I had formerly made use of my senses rather than my reason, and recognised that the ideas which I formed of myself were not so distinct as those which I perceived through the senses, and that they were most frequently even composed of portions of these last, I persuaded myself easily that I had no idea in my mind which had not formerly come to me through the senses. Nor was it without some reason that I believed that this body (which by a certain special right I call my own) belonged to me more properly and more strictly than any other; for in fact I could never be separated from it as from other bodies; I experienced in it and on account of it all my appetites and affections, and finally I was touched by the feeling of pain and the titillation of pleasure in its parts, and not in the parts of other bodies which were separated from it. But when I inquired, why, from some, I know not what, painful sensation, there follows sadness of mind, and from the pleasurable sensation there arises joy, or why this mysterious pinching of the stomach which I call hunger causes me to desire to eat, and dryness of throat causes a desire to drink, and so on, I could give no reason excepting that nature taught me so; for there is certainly no affinity (that I at least can understand) between the craving of the stomach and the desire to eat, any more than between the perception of whatever causes pain and the thought of sadness which arises from this perception. And in the same way it appeared to me that I had learned from nature all the other judgments which I formed regarding the objects of my senses, since I remarked that those judgments were formed in me before I had the leisure to weigh and consider any reasons which might oblige me to make them.

But afterwards many experiences little by little destroyed all the faith which I had rested in my senses; for I from time to time observed that those towers which from afar appeared to me to be round, more closely observed seemed square, and that colossal statues raised on the summit of these towers, appeared as quite tiny statues when viewed from the bottom; and so in an infinitude of other cases I found error in judgments founded on the external senses. And not only in those founded on the external senses, but even in those founded on the internal as well; for is there anything more intimate or more internal than pain? And yet I have learned from some persons whose arms or legs have been cut off, that they sometimes seemed to feel pain in the part which had been amputated, which made me think that I could not be quite certain that it was a certain member which pained me, even although I felt pain in it. And to those grounds of doubt I have lately added two others, which are very general; the first is that I never have believed myself to feel anything in waking moments which I cannot also sometimes believe myself to feel when I sleep, and as I do not think that these things which I seem to feel in sleep, proceed from objects outside of me, I do not see any reason why I should have this belief regarding objects which I seem to perceive while awake. The other was that being still ignorant, or rather supposing myself to be ignorant, of the author of my being, I saw nothing to prevent me from having been so constituted by nature that I might be deceived even in matters which seemed to me to be most certain. And as to the grounds on which I was formerly persuaded of the truth of sensible objects, I had not much trouble in replying to them. For since nature seemed to cause me to lean towards many things from which reason repelled me, I did not believe that I should trust much to the teachings of nature. And although the ideas which I receive by the senses do not depend on my will, I did not think that one should for that reason conclude that they proceeded from things different from myself, since possibly some faculty might be discovered in me – though hitherto unknown to me – which produced them.

But now that I begin to know myself better, and to discover more clearly the author of my being, I do not in truth think that I should rashly admit all the matters which the senses seem to teach us, but, on the other hand, I do not think that I should doubt them all universally.

And first of all, because I know that all things which I apprehend clearly and distinctly can be created by God as I apprehend them, it suffices that I am able to apprehend one thing apart from another clearly and distinctly in order to be certain that the one is different from the other, since they may be made to exist in separation at least by the omnipotence of God; and it does not signify by what power this separation is made in order to compel me to judge them to be different: and, therefore, just because I know certainly that I exist, and that meanwhile I do not remark that any other thing necessarily pertains to my nature or essence, excepting that I am a thinking thing, I rightly conclude that my essence consists solely in the fact that I am a thinking thing [or a substance whose whole essence or nature is to think]. And although possibly (or rather certainly, as I shall say in a moment) I possess a body with which I am very intimately conjoined, yet because, on the one side, I have a clear and distinct idea of myself inasmuch as I am only a thinking and unextended thing, and as, on the other, I possess a distinct idea of body, inasmuch as it is only an extended and unthinking thing, it is certain that this I [that is to say, my soul by which I am what I am], is entirely and absolutely distinct from my body, and can exist without it.

I further find in myself faculties employing modes of thinking peculiar to themselves, to wit, the faculties of imagination and feeling, without which I can easily conceive myself clearly and distinctly as a complete being; while, on the other hand, they cannot be so conceived apart from me, that is without an intelligent substance in which they reside, for [in the notion we have of these faculties, or, to use the language of the Schools] in their formal concept, some kind of intellection is comprised, from which I infer that they are distinct from me as its modes are from a thing. I observe also in me some other faculties such as that of change of position, the assumption of different figures and such like, which cannot be conceived, any more than can the preceding, apart from some substance to which they are attached, and consequently cannot exist without it; but it is very clear that these faculties, if it be true that they exist, must be attached to some corporeal or extended substance, and not to an intelligent substance, since in the clear and distinct conception of these there is some sort of extension found to be present, but no intellection at all. There is certainly further in me a certain passive faculty of perception, that is, of receiving and recognising the ideas of sensible things, but this would be useless to me [and I could in no way avail myself of it], if there were not either in me or in some other thing another active faculty capable of forming and producing these ideas. But this active faculty cannot exist in me [inasmuch as I am a thing that thinks] seeing that it does not presuppose thought, and also that those ideas are often produced in me without my contributing in any way to the same, and often even against my will; it is thus necessarily the case that the faculty resides in some substance different from me in which all the reality which is objectively in the ideas that are produced by this faculty is formally or eminently contained, as I remarked before. And this substance is either a body, that is, a corporeal nature in which there is contained formally [and really] all that which is objectively [and by representation] in those ideas, or it is God Himself, or some other creature more noble than body in which that same is contained eminently. But, since God is no deceiver, it is very manifest that He does not communicate to me these ideas immediately and by Himself, nor yet by the intervention of some creature in which their reality is not formally, but only eminently, contained. For since He has given me no faculty to recognise that this is the case, but, on the other hand, a very great inclination to believe [that they are sent to me or] that they are conveyed to me by corporeal objects, I do not see how He could be defended from the accusation of deceit if these ideas were produced by causes other than corporeal objects. Hence we must allow that corporeal things exist. However, they are perhaps not exactly what we perceive by the senses, since this comprehension by the senses is in many instances very obscure and confused; but we must at least admit that all things which I conceive in them clearly and distinctly, that is to say, all things which, speaking generally, are comprehended in the object of pure mathematics, are truly to be recognised as external objects.

As to other things, however, which are either particular only, as, for example, that the sun is of such and such a figure, etc., or which are less clearly and distinctly conceived, such as light, sound, pain and the like, it is certain that although they are very dubious and uncertain, yet on the sole ground that God is not a deceiver, and that consequently He has not permitted any falsity to exist in my opinion which He has not likewise given me the faculty of correcting, I may assuredly hope to conclude that I have within me the means of arriving at the truth even here. And first of all there is no doubt that in all things which nature teaches me there is some truth contained; for by nature, considered in general, I now understand no other thing than either God Himself or else the order and disposition which God has established in created things; and by my nature in particular I understand no other thing than the complexus of all the things which God has given me.

But there is nothing which this nature teaches me more expressly [nor more sensibly] than that I have a body which is adversely affected when I feel pain, which has need of food or drink when I experience the feelings of hunger and thirst, and so on; nor can I doubt there being some truth in all this.

Nature also teaches me by these sensations of pain, hunger, thirst, etc., that I am not only lodged in my body as a pilot in a vessel, but that I am very closely united to it, and so to speak so intermingled with it that I seem to compose with it one whole. For if that were not the case, when my body is hurt, I, who am merely a thinking thing, should not feel pain, for I should perceive this wound by the understanding only, just as the sailor perceives by sight when something is damaged in his vessel; and when my body has need of drink or food, I should clearly understand the fact without being warned of it by confused feelings of hunger and thirst. For all these sensations of hunger, thirst, pain, etc. are in truth none other than certain confused modes of thought which are produced by the union and apparent intermingling of mind and body.

Moreover, nature teaches me that many other bodies exist around mine, of which some are to be avoided, and others sought after. And certainly from the fact that I am sensible of different sorts of colours, sounds, scents, tastes, heat, hardness, etc., I very easily conclude that there are in the bodies from which all these diverse sense-perceptions proceed certain variations which answer to them, although possibly these are not really at all similar to them. And also from the fact that amongst these different sense-perceptions some are very agreeable to me and others disagreeable, it is quite certain that my body (or rather myself in my entirety, inasmuch as I am formed of body and soul) may receive different impressions agreeable and disagreeable from the other bodies which surround it.

But there are many other things which nature seems to have taught me, but which at the same time I have never really received from her, but which have been brought about in my mind by a certain habit which I have of forming inconsiderate judgments on things; and thus it may easily happen that these judgments contain some error. Take, for example, the opinion which I hold that all space in which there is nothing that affects [or makes an impression on] my senses is void; that in a body which is warm there is something entirely similar to the idea of heat which is in me; that in a white or green body there is the same whiteness or greenness that I perceive; that in a bitter or sweet body there is the same taste, and so on in other instances; that the stars, the towers, and all other distant bodies are of the same figure and size as they appear from far off to our eyes, etc. But in order that in this there should be nothing which I do not conceive distinctly, I should define exactly what I really understand when I say that I am taught somewhat by nature. For here I take nature in a more limited signification than when I term it the sum of all the things given me by God, since in this sum many things are comprehended which only pertain to mind (and to these I do not refer in speaking of nature) such as the notion which I have of the fact that what has once been done cannot ever be undone and an infinitude of such things which I know by the light of nature [without the help of the body]; and seeing that it comprehends many other matters besides which only pertain to body, and are no longer here contained under the name of nature, such as the quality of weight which it possesses and the like, with which I also do not deal; for in talking of nature I only treat of those things given by God to me as a being composed of mind and body. But the nature here described truly teaches me to flee from things which cause the sensation of pain, and seek after the things which communicate to me the sentiment of pleasure and so forth; but I do not see that beyond this it teaches me that from those diverse sense-perceptions we should ever form any conclusion regarding things outside of us, without having [carefully and maturely] mentally examined them beforehand. For it seems to me that it is mind alone, and not mind and body in conjunction, that is requisite to a knowledge of the truth in regard to such things. Thus, although a star makes no larger an impression on my eye than the flame of a little candle there is yet in me no real or positive propensity impelling me to believe that it is not greater than that flame; but I have judged it to be so from my earliest years, without any rational foundation. And although in approaching fire I feel heat, and in approaching it a little too near I even feel pain, there is at the same time no reason in this which could persuade me that there is in the fire something resembling this heat any more than there is in it something resembling the pain; all that I have any reason to believe from this is, that there is something in it, whatever it may be, which excites in me these sensations of heat or of pain. So also, although there are spaces in which I find nothing which excites my senses, I must not from that conclude that these spaces contain no body; for I see in this, as in other similar things, that I have been in the habit of perverting the order of nature, because these perceptions of sense having been placed within me by nature merely for the purpose of signifying to my mind what things are beneficial or hurtful to the composite whole of which it forms a part, and being up to that point sufficiently clear and distinct, I yet avail myself of them as though they were absolute rules by which I might immediately determine the essence of the bodies which are outside me, as to which, in fact, they can teach me nothing but what is most obscure and confused.

But I have already sufficiently considered how, notwithstanding the supreme goodness of God, falsity enters into the judgments I make. Only here a new difficulty is presented – one respecting those things the pursuit or avoidance of which is taught me by nature, and also respecting the internal sensations which I possess, and in which I seem to have sometimes detected error [and thus to be directly deceived by my own nature]. To take an example, the agreeable taste of some food in which poison has been intermingled may induce me to partake of the poison, and thus deceive me. It is true, at the same time, that in this case nature may be excused, for it only induces me to desire food in which I find a pleasant taste, and not to desire the poison which is unknown to it; and thus I can infer nothing from this fact, except that my nature is not omniscient, at which there is certainly no reason to be astonished, since man, being finite in nature, can only have knowledge the perfectness of which is limited.

But we not unfrequently deceive ourselves even in those things to which we are directly impelled by nature, as happens with those who when they are sick desire to drink or eat things hurtful to them. It will perhaps be said here that the cause of their deceptiveness is that their nature is corrupt, but that does not remove the difficulty, because a sick man is none the less truly God's creature than he who is in health; and it is therefore as repugnant to God's goodness for the one to have a deceitful nature as it is for the other. And as a clock composed of wheels and counter-weights no less exactly observes the laws of nature when it is badly made, and does not show the time properly, than when it entirely satisfies the wishes of its maker, and as, if I consider the body of a man as being a sort of machine so built up and composed of nerves, muscles, veins, blood and skin, that though there were no mind in it at all, it would not cease to have the same motions as at present, exception being made of those movements which are due to the direction of the will, and in consequence depend upon the mind [as opposed to those which operate by the disposition of its organs], I easily recognise that it would be as natural to this body, supposing it to be, for example, dropsical, to suffer the parchedness of the throat which usually signifies to the mind the feeling of thirst, and to be disposed by this parched feeling to move the nerves and other parts in the way requisite for drinking, and thus to augment its malady and do harm to itself, as it is natural to it, when it has no indisposition, to be impelled to drink for its good by a similar cause. And although, considering the use to which the clock has been destined by its maker, I may say that it deflects from the order of its nature when it does not indicate the hours correctly; and as, in the same way, considering the machine of the human body as having been formed by God in order to have in itself all the movements usually manifested there, I have reason for thinking that it does not follow the order of nature when, if the throat is dry, drinking does harm to the conservation of health, nevertheless I recognise at the same time that this last mode of explaining nature is very different from the other. For this is but a purely verbal characterisation depending entirely on my thought, which compares a sick man and a badly constructed clock with the idea which I have of a healthy man and a well made clock, and it is hence extrinsic to the things to which it is applied; but according to the other interpretation of the term nature I understand something which is truly found in things and which is therefore not without some truth.

But certainly although in regard to the dropsical body it is only so to speak to apply an extrinsic term when we say that its nature is corrupted, inasmuch as apart from the need to drink, the throat is parched; yet in regard to the composite whole, that is to say, to the mind or soul united to this body, it is not a purely verbal predicate, but a real error of nature, for it to have thirst when drinking would be hurtful to it. And thus it still remains to inquire how the goodness of God does not prevent the nature of man so regarded from being fallacious.

In order to begin this examination, then, I here say, in the first place, that there is a great difference between mind and body, inasmuch as body is by nature always divisible, and the mind is entirely indivisible. For, as a matter of fact, when I consider the mind, that is to say, myself inasmuch as I am only a thinking thing, I cannot distinguish in myself any parts, but apprehend myself to be clearly one and entire; and although the whole mind seems to be united to the whole body, yet if a foot, or an arm, or some other part, is separated from my body, I am aware that nothing has been taken way from my mind. And the faculties of willing, feeling, conceiving, etc. cannot be properly speaking said to be its parts, for it is one and the same mind which employs itself in willing and in feeling and understanding. But it is quite otherwise with corporeal or extended objects, for there is not one of these imaginable by me which my mind cannot easily divide into parts, and which consequently I do not recognise as being divisible; this would be sufficient to teach me that the mind or soul of man is entirely different from the body, if I had not already learned it from other sources.

I further notice that the mind does not receive the impressions from all parts of the body immediately, but only from the brain, or perhaps even from one of its smallest parts, to wit, from that in which the common sense is said to reside, which, whenever it is disposed in the same particular way, conveys the same thing to the mind, although meanwhile the other portions of the body may be differently disposed, as is testified by innumerable experiments which it is unnecessary here to recount.

I notice, also, that the nature of body is such that none of its parts can be moved by another part a little way off which cannot also be moved in the same way by each one of the parts which are between the two, although this more remote part does not act at all. As, for example, in the cord *ABCD* [which is in tension] if we pull the last part *D*, the first part *A* will not be moved in any way differently from what would be the case if one of the intervening parts *B* or *C* were pulled, and the last part *D* were to remain unmoved. And in the same way, when I feel pain in my foot, my knowledge of physics teaches me that this sensation is communicated by means of nerves dispersed through the foot, which, being extended like cords from there to the brain, when they are contracted in the foot, at the same time contract the inmost portions of the brain which is their extremity and place of origin, and then excite a certain movement which nature has established in order to cause the mind to be affected by a sensation of pain represented as existing in the foot. But because these nerves must pass through the tibia, the thigh, the loins, the back and the neck, in order to reach from the leg to the brain, it may happen that although their extremities which are in the foot are not affected, but only certain ones of their intervening parts [which pass by the loins or the neck], this action will excite the same movement in the brain that might have been excited there by a hurt received in the foot, in consequence of which the mind will necessarily feel in the foot the same pain as if it had received a hurt. And the same holds good of all the other perceptions of our senses.

I notice finally that since each of the movements which are in the portion of the brain by which the mind is immediately affected brings about one particular sensation only, we cannot under the circumstances imagine anything more likely than that this movement, amongst all the sensations which it is capable of impressing on it, causes mind to be affected by that one which is best fitted and most generally useful for the conservation of the human body when it is in health. But experience makes us aware that all the feelings with which nature inspires us are such as I have just spoken of; and there is therefore nothing in them which does not give testimony to the power and goodness of the God [who has produced them]. Thus, for example, when the nerves which are in the feet are violently or more than usually moved, their movement, passing through the medulla of the spine to the inmost parts of the brain, gives a sign to the mind which makes it feel somewhat, to wit, pain, as though in the foot, by which the mind is excited to do its utmost to remove the cause of the evil as dangerous and hurtful to the foot. It is true that God could have constituted the nature of man in such a way that this same movement in the brain would have conveyed something quite different to the mind; for example, it might have produced consciousness of itself either in so far as it is in the brain, or as it is in the foot, or as it is in some other place between the foot and the brain, or it might finally have produced consciousness of anything else whatsoever; but none of all this would have contributed so well to the conservation of the body. Similarly, when we desire to drink, a certain dryness of the throat is produced which moves its nerves, and by their means the internal portions of the brain; and this movement causes in the mind the sensation of thirst, because in this case there is nothing more useful to us than to become aware that we have need to drink for the conservation of our health; and the same holds good in other instances.

From this it is quite clear that, notwithstanding the supreme goodness of God, the nature of man, inasmuch as it is composed of mind and body, cannot be otherwise than sometimes a source of deception. For if there is any cause which excites, not in the foot but in some part of the nerves which are extended between the foot and the brain, or even in the brain itself, the same movement which usually is produced when the foot is detrimentally affected, pain will be experienced as though it were in the foot, and the sense will thus naturally be deceived; for since the same movement in the brain is capable of causing but one sensation in the mind, and this sensation is much more frequently excited by a cause which hurts the foot than by another existing in some other quarter, it is reasonable that it should convey to the mind pain in the foot rather than in any other part of the body. And although the parchedness of the throat does not always proceed, as it usually does, from the fact that drinking is necessary for the health of the body, but sometimes comes from quite a different cause, as is the case with dropsical patients, it is yet much better that it should mislead on this occasion than if, on the other hand, it were always to deceive us when the body is in good health; and so on in similar cases.

And certainly this consideration is of great service to me, not only in enabling me to recognise all the errors to which my nature is subject, but also in enabling me to avoid them or to correct them more easily. For knowing that all my senses more frequently indicate to me truth than falsehood respecting the things which concern that which is beneficial to the body, and being able almost always to avail myself of many of them in order to examine one particular thing, and, besides that, being able to make use of my memory in order to connect the present with the past, and of my understanding which already has discovered all the causes of my errors, I ought no longer to fear that falsity may be found in matters every day presented to me by my senses. And I ought to set aside all the doubts of these past days as hyperbolical and ridiculous, particularly that very common uncertainty respecting sleep, which I could not distinguish from the waking state; for at present I find a very notable difference between the two, inasmuch as our memory can never connect our dreams one with the other, or with the whole course of our lives, as it unites events which happen to us while we are awake. And, as a matter of fact, if someone, while I was awake, quite suddenly appeared to me and disappeared as fast as do the images which I see in sleep, so that I could not know from whence the form came nor whither it went, it would not be without reason that I should deem it a spectre or a phantom formed by my brain [and similar to those which I form in sleep], rather than a real man. But when I perceive things as to which I know distinctly both the place from which they proceed, and that in which they are, and the time at which they appeared to me; and when, without any interruption, I can connect the perceptions which I have of them with the whole course of my life, I am perfectly assured that these perceptions occur while I am waking and not during sleep. And I ought in no wise to doubt the truth of such matters, if, after having called up all my senses, my memory, and my understanding, to examine them, nothing is brought to evidence by any one of them which is repugnant to what is set forth by the others. For because God is in no wise a deceiver, it follows that I am not deceived in this. But because the exigencies of action often oblige us to make up our minds before having leisure to examine matters carefully, we must confess that the life of man is very frequently subject to error in respect to individual objects, and we must in the end acknowledge the infirmity of our nature.

8

The Second Set of Objections with Replies by Descartes

Collected by Marin Mersenne

Marin Mersenne (1588–1648) was one of the first graduates of the Jesuit college at La Flèche, the same school Descartes would later attend. Mersenne became a member of the Minim Friars and acquired a reputation for piety. In Paris, he organized a circle of intellectuals that included Descartes, Hobbes, and Pierre Gassendi. He was responsible for the publication of a large number of works attacking enemies of science and religion. Among others, he defended Galileo and, later, Hobbes.

Mersenne may be considered the founder of mitigated skepticism, which accepts the skeptical attacks against the proposition that people have absolute or necessary knowledge about reality, but defends the claim that people possess probable truths about appearances. Scientific and mathematical knowledge could not be absolutely doubted as a set of hypotheses and predictions about appearances. Human knowledge has pragmatic value. It is sufficient to act as a guide to action. Mersenne presented his position in *La Vérité des sciences, contre les Sceptiques ou Pyrrhoniens* (1624). This led the way for Pierre Gassendi's own mitigated skepticism.

It was Mersenne who was responsible for the publication of Descartes's *Meditations* with the objections and replies. The original title of the second set of objections was "The Second Objections Collected by the Rev. Father Mersenne from the utterances of Divers Theologians and Philosophers." Reproduced here are two objections: one is that the proof for the existence of God depends on the reliability of the criteria of clearness and distinctness even though the existence of God is also supposed to justify those criteria. The other objection is that, contrary to what Descartes claims, atheist mathematicians have mathematical knowledge, so such knowledge cannot depend on belief in the existence of God.

Since you are not yet certain of the aforesaid existence of God, and yet according to your statement, cannot be certain of anything or know anything clearly and distinctly unless previously you know certainly and clearly that God exists, it follows that you cannot clearly and distinctly know that you are a thinking thing, since, according to you, that knowledge depends on the clear knowledge of the existence of God, the proof of which you have not yet reached at that point where you draw the conclusion that you have a clear knowledge of what you are.

Take this also, that while an Atheist knows clearly and distinctly that the three angles of a triangle are equal to two right, yet he is far from believing in the existence of God; in fact he denies it, because if God existed there would be a supreme existence, a highest good, i.e. an infinite Being. But the infinite in every type of perfection precludes the existence of anything else whatsoever it be, e.g. of every variety of entity and good, nay even every sort of non-entity and evil; whereas there are in existence many entities, many good things, as well as many non-entities and many evil things. We consider that you should give a solution of this objection, lest the impious should still have some case left them.

[Reply]

When I said that *we could know nothing with certainty unless we were first aware that God existed*, I announced in express terms that I referred only to the science apprehending such conclusions *as can recur in memory without attending further to the proofs which led me to make them*. Further, knowledge of first principles is not usually called science by dialecticians. But when we become aware that we are thinking beings, this is a primitive act of knowledge derived from no syllogistic reasoning. He who says, '*I think, hence I am, or exist*,' does not deduce existence from thought by a syllogism, but, by a simple act of mental vision, recognises it as if it were a thing that is known *per se*. This is evident from the fact that if it were syllogistically deduced, the major premise, *that everything that thinks is, or exists*, would have to be known previously; but yet that has rather been learned from the experience of the individual – that unless he exists he cannot think. For our mind is so constituted by nature that general propositions are formed out of the knowledge of particulars.

That *an atheist can know clearly that the three angles of a triangle are equal to two right angles*, I do not deny, I merely affirm that, on the other hand, such knowledge on his part cannot constitute true science, because no knowledge that can be rendered doubtful should be called science. Since he is, as supposed, an Atheist, he cannot be sure that he is not deceived in the things that seem most evident to him, as has been sufficiently shown; and though perchance the doubt does not occur to him, nevertheless it may come up, if he examine the matter, or if another suggests it; he can never be safe from it unless he first recognises the existence of a God.

And it does not matter though he think he has demonstrations proving that there is no God. Since they are by no means true, the errors in them can always be pointed out to him, and when this takes place he will be driven from his opinion. [. . .]

To begin with, directly we think that we rightly perceive something, we spontaneously persuade ourselves that it is true. Further, if this conviction is so strong that we have no reason to doubt concerning that of the truth of which we have persuaded ourselves, there is nothing more to enquire about; we have here all the certainty that can reasonably be desired. What is it to us, though perchance some one feigns that that, of the truth of which we are so firmly persuaded, appears false to God or to an Angel, and hence is, absolutely speaking, false? What heed do we pay to that absolute falsity, when we by no means believe that it exists or even suspect its existence? We have assumed a conviction so strong that nothing can remove it, and this persuasion is clearly the same as perfect certitude.

But it may be doubted whether there is any such certitude whether such firm and immutable conviction exists.

[. . .]

It is indeed clear that no one possesses such certainty in those cases where there is the very least confusion and obscurity in our perception; for this obscurity, of whatsoever sort it be, is sufficient to make us doubt here. In matters perceived by sense alone, however clearly, certainty does not exist, because we have often noted that error can occur in sensation, as in the instance of the thirst of the dropsical man, or when one who is jaundiced sees snow as yellow; for he sees it thus with no less clearness and distinctness than we see it as white. If, then, any certitude does exist, it remains that it must be found only in the clear perceptions of the intellect.

But of these there are some so evident and at the same time so simple, that in their case we never doubt about believing them true: e.g. that I, while I think, exist; that what is once done cannot be undone, and other similar truths, about which clearly we can possess this certainty. For we cannot doubt them unless we think of them; but we cannot think of them without at the same time believing them to be true, the position taken up. Hence we can never doubt them without at the same time believing them to be true; i.e. we can never doubt them.

No difficulty is caused by the objection that *we have often found that others have been deceived in matters in which they believed they had knowledge as plain as daylight*. For we have never noticed that this has occurred, nor could anyone find it to occur with these persons who have sought to draw the clearness of their vision from the intellect alone, but only with those who have made either the senses or some erroneous preconception the source from which they derived that evidence.

[. . .]

Arguments Demonstrating the Existence of God and the Distinction Between Soul and Body, Drawn Up in Geometrical Fashion

Definitions

I. *Thought* is a word that covers everything that exists in us in such a way that we are immediately conscious of it. Thus all the operations of will, intellect, imagination, and of the senses are thoughts. But I have added *immediately*, for the purpose of excluding that which is a consequence of our thought; for example, voluntary movement, which, though indeed depending on thought as on a causal principle, is yet itself not thought.

II. *Idea* is a word by which I understand the form of any thought, that form by the immediate awareness of which I am conscious of that said thought; in such a way that, when understanding what I say, I can express nothing in words, without that very fact making it certain that I possess the idea of that which these words signify. And thus it is not only images depicted in the imagination that I call ideas; nay, to such images I here decidedly refuse the title of ideas, in so far as they are pictures in the corporeal imagination, i.e. in some part of the brain. They are ideas only in so far as they constitute the form of the mind itself that is directed towards that part of the brain.

III. By the *objective reality of an idea* I mean that in respect of which the thing represented in the idea is an entity, in so far as that exists in the idea; and in the same way we can talk of objective perfection, objective device, etc. For whatever we perceive as being as it were in the objects of our ideas, exists in the ideas themselves objectively.

IV. To exist *formally* is the term applied where the same thing exists in the object of an idea in such a manner that the way in which it exists in the object is exactly like what we know of it when aware of it; it exists *eminently* when, though not indeed of identical quality, it is yet of such amount as to be able to fulfil the function of an exact counterpart.

V. Everything in which there resides immediately, as in a subject, or by means of which there exists anything that we perceive, i.e. any property, quality, or attribute, of which we have a real idea, is called a *Substance*; neither do we have any other idea of substance itself, precisely taken, than that it is a thing in which this something that we perceive or which is present objectively in some of our ideas, exists formally or eminently. For by means of our natural light we know that a real attribute cannot be an attribute of nothing.

VI. That substance in which thought immediately resides, I call *Mind*. I use the term 'mind' here rather than 'spirit,' as 'spirit' is equivocal and is frequently applied to what is corporeal.

VII. That substance, which is the immediate subject of extension in space and of the accidents that presuppose extension, e.g. figure, situation, movement in space etc., is called *Body*. But we must postpone till later on the inquiry as to whether it is one and the same substance or whether there are two diverse substances to which the names Mind and Body apply.

VIII. That substance which we understand to be supremely perfect and in which we conceive absolutely nothing involving defect or limitation of its perfection, is called *God*.

IX. When we say that any attribute is contained in the nature or concept of anything, that is precisely the same as saying that it is true of that thing or can be affirmed of it.

X. Two substances are said to be really distinct, when each of them can exist apart from the other.

Postulates

The *First* request I press upon my readers is a recognition of the weakness of the reasons on account of which they have hitherto trusted their senses, and the insecurity of all the judgments they have based upon them. I beg them to revolve this in their minds so long and so frequently that at length they will acquire the habit of no longer reposing too much trust in them. For I deem that this is necessary in order to attain to a perception of the certainty of metaphysical truths [not dependent on the senses].

Secondly, I ask them to make an object of study of their own mind and all the attributes attaching to it, of which they find they cannot doubt, notwithstanding it be supposed that whatever they have at any time derived from their senses is false; and I beg them not to desist from attending to it, until they have acquired the habit of perceiving it distinctly and of believing that it can be more readily known than any corporeal thing.

Thirdly, I bid them carefully rehearse those propositions, intelligible *per se*, which they find they possess, e.g. *that the same thing cannot at the same time both be and not be; that nothing cannot be the efficient cause of anything*, and so forth; and thus employ in its purity, and in freedom from the interference of the senses, that clarity of understanding that nature has implanted in them, but which sensuous objects are wont to disturb and obscure. For by this means the truth of the following Axioms will easily become evident to them.

Fourthly, I postulate an examination of the ideas of those natures in which there is a complex of many coexistent attributes, such as e.g. the nature of the triangle or of the square, or of any other figure; and so too the nature of Mind, the nature of Body, and above all the nature of God, or of a supremely perfect entity. My readers must also notice that everything which we perceive to be contained in these natures can be truly predicated of the things themselves. For example, because the equality of its three angles to two right angles is contained in the idea of the Triangle, and divisibility is contained in the nature of Body or of extended thing (for we can conceive nothing that is extended as being so small as not to be capable of being divided in thought at least), we constantly assert that in every Triangle the angles are equal to two right angles, and that every Body is divisible.

Fifthly, I require my readers to dwell long and much in contemplation of the nature of the supremely perfect Being. Among other things they must reflect that while possible existence indeed attaches to the ideas of all other natures, in the case of the idea of God that existence is not possible but wholly necessary. For from this alone and without any train of reasoning they will learn that God exists, and it will be not less self evident to them than the fact that number two is even and number three odd, and similar truths. For there are certain truths evident to some people, without proof, that can be made intelligible to others only by a train of reasoning.

Sixthly, I ask people to go carefully over all the examples of clear and distinct perception, and likewise those that illustrate that which is obscure and confused, mentioned in my Meditations, and so accustom themselves to distinguish what is clearly known from what is obscure. For examples teach us better than rules how to do this; and I think that I have there either explained or at least to some extent touched upon all the instances of this subject.

Seventhly and finally, I require them, in virtue of their consciousness that falsity has never been found in matters of clear perception, while, on the contrary, amidst what is only obscurely comprehended they have never come upon the truth, except accidentally, to consider it wholly irrational to regard as doubtful matters that are perceived clearly and distinctly by the understanding in its purity, on account of mere prejudices of the senses and hypotheses in which there is an element of the unknown. By doing so they will readily admit the truth and certainty of the following axioms. Yet I admit that several of them might have been much better explained and should have been brought forward as theorems if I had wished to be more exact.

Axioms or Common Principles

I. Nothing exists concerning which the question may not be raised – 'what is the cause of its existence?' For this question may be asked even concerning God. Not that He requires any cause in order to exist, but because in the very immensity of His being lies the cause or reason why He needs no cause in order to exist.

II. The present time has no causal dependence on the time immediately preceding it. Hence, in order to secure the continued existence of a thing, no less a cause is required than that needed to produce it at the first.

III. A thing, and likewise an actually existing perfection belonging to anything, can never have *nothing*, or a non-existent thing, as the cause of its existence.

IV. Whatever reality or perfection exists in a thing, exists formally or else eminently in its first and adequate cause.

V. Whence it follows also that the objective reality of our ideas requires a cause in which the same reality is contained not indeed objectively, but formally or else eminently. We have to note that the admission of this axiom is highly necessary for the reason that we must account for our knowledge of all things, both of sensuous and of non-sensuous objects, and do so by means of it alone. For whence, e.g., comes our knowledge that there is a heaven? Because we behold it? But that vision does not reach the mind, except in so far as it is an idea, an idea, I say, inhering in the mind itself, and not an image depicted in the phantasy. But neither can we, in virtue of this idea, assert that there is a heaven, except because every idea needs to have some really existing cause of its objective reality; and this cause we judge to be the heaven itself, and so in other cases.

VI. There are diverse degrees of reality or (the quality of being an) entity. For substance has more reality than accident or mode; and infinite substance has more than finite substance. Hence there is more objective reality in the idea of substance than in that of accident; more in the idea of an infinite than in that of a finite substance.

VII. The will of a thinking being is borne, willingly indeed and freely (for that is of the essence of will), but none the less infallibly, towards the good that it clearly knows. Hence, if it knows certain perfections that it lacks, it will immediately give them to itself if they are in its power [for it will know that it is a greater good for it to possess them, than not to possess them].

VIII. That which can effect what is greater or more difficult, can also accomplish what is less.

IX. It is a greater thing to create or conserve substance than the attributes or properties of substance; it is not, moreover, a greater thing to create that than to conserve its existence, as I have already said.

X. Existence is contained in the idea or concept of everything, because we can conceive nothing except as existent, with this difference, that possible or contingent existence is contained in the concept of a limited thing, but necessary and perfect existence in the concept of a supremely perfect being.

Proposition I
The Knowledge of the Existence of God Proceeds from the Mere Consideration of His Nature

Demonstration

To say that something is contained in the nature or concept of anything is the same as to say that it is true of that thing (Def. IX). But necessary existence is contained in the concept of God (Ax. X). Hence it is true to affirm of God that necessary existence exists in Him, or that God Himself exists.

And this is the syllogism of which I made use above, in replying to the sixth objection. Its conclusion is self-evident to those who are free from prejudices, as was said in the fifth postulate. But, because it is not easy to arrive at such clearness of mind, we seek to establish it by other methods.

Proposition II
A Posteriori Demonstration of God's Existence from the Mere Fact that the Idea of God Exists in Us

Demonstration

The objective reality of any of our ideas must have a cause, in which the very same reality is contained, not merely objectively but formally, or else eminently (Ax. V). But we do possess the idea of God (Deff. II and VIII), and the objective reality of this idea is contained in us neither formally nor eminently (Ax. VI), nor can it be contained in anything other than God Himself (Def. VIII). Hence this idea of God, which exists in us, must have God as its cause, and hence God exists (Ax. III).

Proposition III
The Existence of God Is Proved by the Fact that We, who Possess This Idea, Ourselves Exist

Demonstration

If I had the power of conserving my own existence, I should have had a proportionately greater power of giving myself the perfections that I lack (Axx. VIII and IX); for they are only attributes of substance, whereas I am a substance. But I do not have the power of giving myself these perfections; otherwise I should already possess them (Ax. VII). Therefore I do not have the power of conserving myself.

Further, I cannot exist without being conserved, whilst I exist, either by myself, if I have that power, or by some other one who has that power (Axx. I and II); yet, though I do exist, I have not the power of conserving myself, as has just been proved. Consequently it is another being that conserves my existence.

Besides, He to whom my conservation is due contains within Himself formally or eminently everything that is in me (Ax. IV). But there exists in me the perception of many perfections that I do not possess, as well as of the idea of God (Deff. II and VIII). Therefore the perception of the same perfections exists in Him by whom I am conserved.

Finally this same Being cannot possess the perception of any perfections of which He is lacking, or which He does not possess within Himself either formally or eminently (Ax. VII). For, since He has the power of conserving me, as has been already said, He would have the power of bestowing these upon Himself, if He lacked them (Axx. VIII and IX). But He possesses the perception of all those that I lack, and which I conceive can exist in God alone, as has been lately proved. Therefore He possesses those formally or eminently within Himself, and hence is God.

Corollary
God Has Created the Heaven and the Earth and All that in Them Is. Moreover He Can Bring to Pass Whatever We Clearly Conceive, Exactly as We Conceive It

Demonstration

This all follows clearly from the previous proposition. For in it we prove that God exists, from the fact that some one must exist in whom are formally or eminently all the perfections of which we have any idea. But we possess the idea of a power so great that by Him and Him alone, in whom this power is found, must heaven and earth be created, and a power such that likewise whatever else is apprehended by me as possible must be created by Him too. Hence concurrently with God's existence we have proved all this likewise about him.

Proposition IV
There Is a Real Distinction Between Mind and Body

Demonstration

God can effect whatever we clearly perceive just as we perceive it (preceding Corollary). But we clearly perceive the mind, i.e. a thinking substance, apart from the body, i.e. apart from any extended substance (Post. II); and *vice versa* we can (as all admit) perceive body apart from mind. Hence, at least through the instrumentality of the Divine power, mind can exist apart from body, and body apart from mind.

But now, substances that can exist apart from each other, are really distinct (Def. X). But mind and body are substances (Deff. V, VI and VII), that can exist apart from each other (just proved). Hence there is a real distinction between mind and body.

Here it must be noted that I employed the Divine power as a means, not because any extraordinary power was needed to effect the separation of mind and body, but because, treating as I did of God alone in what precedes, there was nothing else for me to use. But our knowledge of the real distinctness of two things is unaffected by any question as to the power that disunites them.

9

Thomas Hobbes, *The Third Set of Objections with Replies by Descartes*

The following selection contains part of the objections that Thomas Hobbes (1588–1679) raised against Descartes's philosophy. Hobbes did not think that the *cogito* deserved a special place in knowledge. He also doubted the cogency of Descartes's proof of the existence of God because he believed that humans do not have a genuine idea of the nature of God.

Because Hobbes was a materialist and dogmatic, and because Descartes was a dualist and dogmatic, there was not much chance for an illuminating debate.

For Hobbes's life, see the introduction to part IV, selection 20.

[. . .]

Objection II

(In opposition to the Second Meditation, *Concerning the nature of the Human Mind.*)

I am a thing that thinks; *quite correct. From the fact that I think, or have an image, whether sleeping or waking, it is inferred that I am exercising thought; for* I think and I am exercising thought *mean the same thing. From the fact that I am exercising thought it follows that* I am, *since that which thinks is not nothing. But, where it is added,* this is the mind, the spirit, the understanding, the reason, *a doubt arises. For it does not seem to be good reasoning to say:* I am exercising thought, *hence* I am thought; *or* I am using my intellect, *hence* I am intellect. *For in the same way I might say,* I am walking; *hence* I am the walking. *It is hence an assumption on the part of M. Descartes that that which understands is the same as the exercise of understanding which is an act of that which understands, or, at least, that that which understands is the same as the understanding, which is a power possessed by that which thinks. Yet all Philosophers distinguish a subject from its faculties and activities, i.e. from its properties and essences; for the* entity *itself is one thing, its* essence *another. Hence it is possible for a thing that thinks to be the subject of the mind, reason, or understanding, and hence to be something corporeal; and the opposite of this has been assumed, not proved. Yet this inference is the basis of the conclusion that M. Descartes seems to wish to establish.*

In the same place he says, I know that I exist; the question is, who am I – the being that I know? It is certain that the knowledge of this being thus accurately determined does not depend on those things which I do not yet know to exist.

[. . .]

Objection V

[. . .]

When I think of a man, I recognize an idea, or image, with figure and colour as its constituents; and concerning this I can raise the question whether or not it is the likeness of a man. So it is also when I think of the heavens. When I think of the chimera, I recognize an idea or image, being able at the same time to doubt whether or not it is the likeness of an animal, which, though it does not exist, may yet exist or has at some other time existed.

But, when one thinks of an Angel, what is noticed in the mind is now the image of a flame, now that of a fair winged child, and this, I may be sure, has no likeness to an Angel, and hence is not the idea of an Angel. But believing that created beings exist that are the ministers of God, invisible and immaterial, we give the name of Angel to this object of belief, this supposed being, though the idea used in imagining an Angel is, nevertheless, constructed out of the ideas of visible things.

It is the same way with the most holy name of God; we have no image, no idea corresponding to it. Hence we are forbidden to worship God in the form of an image, lest we should think we could conceive Him who is inconceivable.

Hence it appears that we have no idea of God. But just as one born blind who has frequently been brought close to a fire and has felt himself growing warm, recognizes that there is something which made him warm, and, if he hears it called fire, concludes that fire exists, though he has no acquaintance with its shape or colour, and has no idea of fire nor image that he can discover in his mind; so a man, recognizing that there must be some cause of his images and ideas, and another previous cause of this cause and so on continuously, is finally carried on to a conclusion, or to the supposition of some eternal cause, which, never having begun to be, can have no cause prior to it: and hence he necessarily concludes that something eternal exists. But nevertheless he has no idea that he can assert to be that of this eternal being, and he merely gives a name to the object of his faith or reasoning and calls it God.

Since now it is from this position, viz. that there is an idea of God in our soul, that M. Descartes proceeds to prove the theorem that God (an all-powerful, all-wise Being, the creator of the world) exists, he should have explained this idea of God better, and he should have deduced from it not only God's existence, but also the creation of the world.

Reply

Here the meaning assigned to the term idea is merely that of images depicted in the corporeal imagination; and, that being agreed on, it is easy for my critic to prove that there is no proper idea of Angel or of God. But I have, everywhere, from time to time, and principally in this place, shown that I take the term idea to stand for whatever the mind directly perceives; and so when I will or when I fear, since at the same time I perceive that I will and fear, that very volition and apprehension are ranked among my ideas. I employed this term because it was the term currently used by Philosophers for the forms of perception of the Divine mind, though we can discover no imagery in God; besides I had no other more suitable term. But I think I have sufficiently well explained what the idea of God is for those who care to follow my meaning; those who prefer to wrest my words from the sense I give them, I can never satisfy. The objection that here follows, relative to the creation of the world, is plainly irrelevant [for I proved that God exists, before asking whether there is a world created by him, and from the mere fact that God, i.e. a supremely perfect being exists, it follows that if there be a world it must have been created by him].

10

Antoine Arnauld, *The Fourth Set of Objections with Replies by Descartes*

Antoine Arnauld (1612–94) was a theologian and philosopher, associated with the Jansenist community at Port-Royal, France. Jansenism was a reformist movement within the Roman Catholic Church. It emphasized predestination, irresistible grace, and limited atonement. It originated with Cornelius Jansen (1585–1638), a Flemish bishop, who drew upon the anti-Pelagian writings of Augustine of Hippo. Port-Royal, a convent of nuns, with male associates such as Arnauld and Saint Cyran, adopted Jansenism. Jansenists were chiefly opposed by the Jesuits. When Arnauld's writings were attacked by the Jesuits, Blaise Pascal wrote the *Provincial Letters* (1656–7) in defense of him. Pope Innocent X condemned Jansenism in 1653, but it survived.

Arnauld was the author of the fourth set of objections against Descartes's *Meditations*. Arnauld's most serious objection is the one called "the Cartesian circle." It appears that Descartes needs the existence of God to justify acceptance of the criteria of clarity and distinctness, but Descartes also relies on those criteria in his proof for the existence of God.

Nonetheless Arnauld accepted much of Descartes's philosophy, notably the latter's defense of the immortality of the soul. In later years, he wrote against Malebranche's view that people perceive ideas in God. (For Malebranche, see selection 15.) In contrast, Arnauld holds that ideas are mental acts that put people into direct contact with things in the world.

Objection IV

The only remaining scruple I have is an uncertainty as to how a circular reasoning is to be avoided in saying: the only secure reason we have for believing that what we clearly and distinctly perceive is true, is the fact that God exists.

But we can be sure that God exists, only because we clearly and evidently perceive that; therefore prior to being certain that God exists, we should be certain that whatever we clearly and evidently perceive is true.

[. . .]

[Reply]

Finally, to prove that I have not argued in a circle in saying, *that the only secure reason we have for believing that what we clearly and distinctly perceive is true, is the fact that God exists; but that clearly we can be sure that God exists only because we perceive that,* I may cite the explanations that I have already given at sufficient length in my reply to the second set of Objections, numbers 3 and 4. There I distinguished those matters that in actual truth we clearly perceive from those we remember to have formerly perceived. For first, we are sure that God exists because we have attended to the proofs that established this fact; but afterwards it is enough for us to remember that we have perceived something clearly, in order to be sure that it is true; but this would not suffice, unless we knew that God existed and that he did not deceive us.

The fact *that nothing can exist in the mind, in so far as it is a thinking thing, of which it is not conscious*, seems to me self-evident, because we conceive nothing to exist in it, viewed in this light, that is not thought, and something dependent on thought; for otherwise it would not belong to the mind, in so far as it is a thinking thing. But there can exist in us no thought of which, at the very moment that it is present in us, we are not conscious. Wherefore I have no doubt that the mind begins to think at the same time as it is infused into the body of an infant, and is at the same time conscious of its own thought, though afterwards it does not remember that, because the specific forms of these thoughts do not live in the memory.

But it has to be noted that, while indeed we are always in actuality conscious of acts or operations of the mind, that is not the case with the faculties or powers of mind, except potentially. So that when we dispose ourselves to the exercise of any faculty, if the faculty reside in us, we are immediately actually conscious of it; and hence we can deny that it exists in the mind, if we can form no consciousness of it.

11

Pierre Gassendi, *The Fifth Set of Objections with Replies by Descartes*

Pierre Gassendi (1592–1655) was a philosopher and scientist, a good friend of Thomas Hobbes, and a member of Marin Mersenne's intellectual circle in Paris. He defended a mitigated skepticism, which, *pace* Descartes, denied that any knowledge was certain, but, *pace* the dogmatic and the Pyrrhonian skeptics such as Michel de Montaigne and Pierre Charon, affirmed that some knowledge was probable. He did not think that the senses deceived humans, but he argued that they did not reveal the essences of things either.

In his first book, *Exercitationes Paradoxicae Adversis Aristoteleos* (1624), Gassendi attacked Aristotle's philosophy. Like Hobbes, Malebranche, and several other early modern philosophers, his ultimate goal was to reconcile modern science with orthodox Christian doctrine. Since Aristotelianism was the dominant philosophy used to explain Christian doctrine but incompatible with modern science, it was necessary to refute it.

But it was not enough to displace Aristotelianism; something had to replace it. Gassendi did not think that Descartes's *Meditations* could do the job, and explained why in the fifth set of objections, of which part is printed here. He rejects Descartes's claim to have discovered absolutely certain knowledge. He argues that an idea may be clear and distinct and not represent something outside the mind.

For his positive doctrine, Gassendi defended a version of Epicurus's atomism to explain how bodies act. His principal work in this regard is *Syntagma Philosophiae Epicuri* (1649).

[Objection V]

You next attempt the proof of God's existence and the vital part of your argument lies in these words: When I think attentively I clearly see that the existence can no more be separated from the essence of God than can there be separated from the essence of a triangle the equality in magnitude of its three angles to two right angles, or the idea of a mountain from the idea of a valley; so that there is no less incongruity in our conceiving a God (i.e. a Being who is supremely perfect) to Whom existence is lacking (i.e. in Whom a certain perfection is missing), than to think of a mountain which is not accompanied by a valley. *But we must note that a comparison of this kind is not sufficiently accurate.*

For though you properly enough compare essence with essence, in your next step it is neither existence with essence, nor property with property that you compare, but existence with property. Hence it seems that you either ought to have said that God's omnipotence can no more be separated from His essence than can that equality in magnitude of the angles of a triangle from its essence; or at least, that God's existence can no more be separated from His essence than the existence from the essence of a triangle. Thus taken, each comparison would have proceeded on correct lines, and the truth would have been conceded, not only of the former but of the latter, although this would not be evidence that you had established your conclusion that God necessarily exists, because neither does the triangle necessarily exist, although its essence and its existence cannot in reality be severed, howsoever much the mind separates them or thinks of them apart, in the same way as the Divine essence and existence may be thought of separately.

Next we must note that you place existence among the Divine perfections, without, however, putting it among the perfections of a triangle or of a mountain, though in exactly similar fashion, and in its own way, it may be said to be a perfection of each. But, sooth to say, existence is a perfection neither in God nor in anything else; it is rather that in the absence of which there is no perfection.

This must be so if, indeed, that which does not exist has neither perfection nor imperfection, and that which exists and has various perfections, does not have its existence as a particular perfection and as one of the number of its perfections, but as that by means of which the thing itself equally with its perfections is in existence, and without which neither can it be said to possess perfections, nor can perfections be said to be possessed by it. Hence neither is existence held to exist in a thing in the way that perfections do, nor if the thing lacks existence is it said to be imperfect (or deprived of a perfection), so much as to be nothing.

Wherefore, as in enumerating the perfections of a triangle you do not mention existence, nor hence conclude that the triangle exists, so, in enumerating the perfections of God, you ought not to have put existence among them, in order to draw the conclusion that God exists, unless you wanted to beg the question.

[Reply]

Here I do not see to what class of reality you wish to assign existence, nor do I see why it may not be said to be a property as well as omnipotence, taking the word property as equivalent to any attribute or anything which can be predicated of a thing, as in the present case it should be by all means regarded. Nay, necessary existence in the case of God is also a true property in the strictest sense of the word, because it belongs to Him and forms part of His essence alone. Hence the existence of a triangle cannot be compared with the existence of God, because existence manifestly has a different relation to essence in the case of God and in the case of a triangle.

Nor is it more a begging of the question, *to enumerate existence among the things belonging to the essence of God*, than to reckon the equality of the three angles of a triangle to two right angles among the properties of the triangle.

Nor is it true *that essence and existence can be thought, the one apart from the other in God*, as in a triangle, because God *is* His existence, while a triangle is not its own existence. I do not, nevertheless, deny that existence is a possible perfection in the idea of a triangle, as it is a necessary one in the idea of God; for this fact makes the idea of the triangle one of higher rank than the ideas of those chimerical things whose existence can never be supposed. Hence you have not diminished the force of this argument of mine in the slightest, and you still remain deluded *by that fallacy, which you say I could have exposed so easily.*

I have elsewhere given a sufficient answer to your next objections. You are plainly in error when you say *that existence is not demonstrated of God, as it is demonstrated of the triangle that its three angles are equal to two right angles*; for the way in which both are proved is alike, except that the demonstration proving existence in God is much simpler and clearer. I pass over the rest, because, though saying *that I explain nothing*, you yourself explain nothing and prove nothing, save only that you are able to prove nothing.

12

Letters to and from Princess Elizabeth of Bohemia

Elizabeth of Bohemia (1618–80) was the daughter of Frederick, the Elector Palatine, and Elizabeth Stuart, the daughter of King James I and VI of England and Scotland. Born at Heidelberg, she spent a large part of her childhood in Silesia, because her father was then living in exile. She corresponded with Descartes, and after his death retired to a convent in Westphalia, where she eventually became its abbess and later died.

Elizabeth, probably better than any other philosopher, revealed the underlying problem of mind–body interaction. Since a body moves only by contact with another body, and since mind is altogether a different kind of thing from body, it appears that Descartes has no cogent explanation for how the body affects the mind and the mind the body. In some places, Descartes says that the interaction must occur in the tiny pineal gland, which has the general shape of a human being. Perhaps Descartes thought that, because the gland was so small, the problem of interaction was made so small as to cease to be a problem. That does not work in philosophy. If a body can be moved only by a body, then no matter how small the body is, it must be moved by a body; nothing else.

Princess Elizabeth to Descartes

The Hague, 6–16 May 1643

. . . I beg of you to tell me how the human soul can determine the movement of the animal spirits in the body so as to perform voluntary acts – being as it is merely a conscious (*pensante*) substance. For the determination of movement seems always to come about from the moving body's being propelled – to depend on the kind of impulse it gets from what sets it in motion, or again, on the nature and shape of this latter thing's surface. Now the first two conditions involve contact, and the third involves that the impelling thing has extension; but you utterly exclude extension from your notion of soul, and contact seems to me incompatible with a thing's being immaterial.

I therefore ask you for a more specific definition of the soul than you give in your metaphysics: a definition of its substance, as distinct from its activity, consciousness (*pensée*). Even if we supposed these to be in fact inseparable – a matter hard to prove in regard to children in their mother's womb and severe fainting-fits – to be inseparable as the divine attributes are: nevertheless we may get a more perfect idea of them by considering them apart.

Descartes to Princess Elizabeth

Egmond, 21 May 1643

. . . I may truly say that what your Highness is propounding seems to me to be the question people have most right to ask me in view of my published works. For there are two facts about the human soul on which there depends any knowledge we may have as to its nature: first, that it is conscious; secondly, that, being united to a body, it is able to act and suffer along with it. Of the second fact I said almost nothing; my aim was simply to make the first properly understood; for my main object was to prove the distinction of soul and body; and to this end only the first was serviceable, the second might have been prejudicial. But since your Highness sees too clearly for dissimulation to be possible, I will here try to explain how I conceive the union of soul and body and how the soul has the power of moving the body.

My first observation is that there are in us certain primitive notions – the originals, so to say, on the pattern of which we form all other knowledge. These notions are very few in number. First, there are the most general ones, existence, number, duration, etc., which apply to everything we can conceive. As regards body in particular, we have merely the notion of extension and the consequent notions of shape and movement. As regards the soul taken by itself, we have merely the notion of consciousness, which comprises the conceptions [*perceptions*] of the intellect and the inclinations of the will. Finally, as regards the soul and body together, we have merely the notion of their union; and on this there depend our notions of the soul's power to move the body, and of the body's power to act on the soul and cause sensations and emotions.

I would also observe that all human knowledge consists just in properly distinguishing these notions and attaching each of them only to the objects that it applies to. If we try to explain some problem by means of a notion that does not apply, we cannot help making mistakes; we are just as wrong if we try to explain one of these notions in terms of another, since, being primitive, each such notion has to be understood in itself. The use of our senses has made us much more familiar with notions of extension, shape, and movement than with others; thus the chief cause of our errors is that ordinarily we try to use these notions to explain matters to which they do not apply; e.g. we try to use our imagination in conceiving the nature of the soul, or to conceive the way the soul moves the body in terms of the way that one body is moved by another body.

In the Meditations that your Highness condescended to read, I tried to bring before the mind the notions that apply to the soul taken by itself, and to distinguish them from those that apply to the body taken by itself. Accordingly, the next thing I have to explain is how we are to form the notions that apply to the union of the soul with the body, as opposed to those that apply to the body taken by itself or the mind taken by itself. . . . These simple notions are to be sought only within the soul, which is naturally endowed with all of them, but does not always adequately distinguish between them, or again does not always attach them to the right objects.

So I think people have hitherto confused the notions of the soul's power to act within the body and the power one body has act within another; and they have ascribed both powers not to soul, whose nature was so far unknown, but to various qualities of bodies – gravity, heat, etc. These qualities were imagined to be real, i.e. to have an existence distinct from the existence of bodies; consequently, they were imagined to be substances, although they were called qualities. In order to conceive of them, people have used sometimes notions that we have for the purpose of knowing body, and sometimes those that we have for the purpose of knowing the soul, according as they were ascribing to them a material or an immaterial nature. For example, on the supposition that gravity is a real quality, about which we know no more than its power of moving the body in which it occurs towards the centre of the Earth, we find no difficulty in conceiving how it moves the body or how it is united to it; and we do not think of this as taking place by means of real mutual contact between two surfaces; our inner experience shows [*nous expérimentons*] that that notion is a specific one. Now I hold that we misuse this notion by applying it to gravity (which, as I hope to show in my *Physics*, is nothing really distinct from body), but that it has been given to us in order that we may conceive of the way that the soul moves the body.

Princess Elizabeth to Descartes

The Hague, 10–20 June 1643

. . . . <I cannot>* understand the idea by means of which we are to judge of the way that the soul, unextended and immaterial, moves the body, in terms of the idea you used to have about gravity. You used falsely to ascribe to gravity, under the style of a 'quality', the power of carrying bodies towards the centre of the Earth. But I cannot see why this should convince us that a body may be impelled by something immaterial; why we should not rather be confirmed in the view that this is impossible, by the demonstration of a true <view of gravity>, opposed <to this>, which you promise us in your *Physics*; especially as the idea <that a body may be so impelled> cannot claim the same degree of perfection and representative reality [*réalité objective*] as the idea of God, and may be a figment resulting from ignorance of what really moves bodies towards the centre. Since no material cause was apparent to the senses, people may well have ascribed this to the opposite cause, the immaterial; but I have never been able to conceive *that*, except as a negation of matter, which can have no communication with matter.

And I must confess that I could more readily allow that the soul has matter and extension than that an immaterial being has the capacity of moving a body and being affected by it. If the first, <the soul's moving the body>, took place by <the soul's giving> information <to the body>, then the <animal> spirits, which carry out the movement, would have to be intelligent; but you do not allow intelligence to anything corporeal. You do indeed show the possibility of the second thing <the body's affecting the soul>, in your Metaphysical Meditations; but it is very hard to see how a soul such as you describe, after possessing the power and the habit of correct reasoning, may lose all that because of some vapours <in the brain>; or why the soul is so much governed by the body, when it can subsist separately, and has nothing in common with it. . . .

* Words in angle brackets are editorial conjecture. A.P.M.

Descartes to Princess Elizabeth

Egmond, 28 June 1643

I am most deeply obliged to your Highness for condescending, after experience of my previous ill success in explaining the problem you were pleased to propound to me, to be patient enough to listen to me once more on the same subject, and to give me an opportunity of making remarks on matters I had passed over. My chief omissions seem to be the following. I began by distinguishing three kinds of primitive ideas or notions, each of which is known in a specific way and not by comparison to another kind; viz. the notion of soul, the notion of body, and the notion of the union between soul and body. I still had to explain the difference between these three kinds of notions, and again between the operations of the soul by means of which we get them, and to show the means of becoming readily familiar with each kind. Further, I had to explain why I used the comparison of gravity. Next, I had to show that even if we try to conceive of the soul as material (which means, properly speaking, to conceive of its union with the body), we cannot help going on to recognise that it is separable from the body. This, I think, is the sum of the task your Highness has set me.

In the first place, then, I discern this great difference between the three kinds of notions: the soul is conceived only by pure intellect; body (i.e. extension, shape, and movement) can likewise be known by pure intellect, but is known much better when intellect is aided by imagination; finally, what belongs to the union of soul and body can be understood only in an obscure way either by pure intellect or even when the intellect is aided by imagination, but is understood very clearly by means of the senses. Consequently, those who never do philosophise and make use only of their senses have no doubt that the soul moves the body and the body acts on the soul; indeed, they consider the two as a single thing, i.e. they conceive of their union; for to conceive of the union between two things is to conceive of them as a single thing. Metaphysical reflections, which exercise the pure intellect, are what make us familiar with the notion of soul; the study of mathematics, which chiefly exercises the imagination in considering figures and movements, accustoms us to form very distinct notions of body; finally, it is just by means of ordinary life and conversation, by abstaining from meditating and from studying things that exercise the imagination, that one learns to conceive the union of soul and body.

I am half afraid that your Highness may think I am not speaking seriously here; but that would be contrary to the respect that I owe to your Highness and will never fail to pay. I can truly say that the chief rule I have always observed in my studies, and the one I think has been most serviceable to me in acquiring some measure of knowledge, has been never to spend more than a few hours a day in thoughts that demand imagination, or more than a few hours a year in thoughts that demand pure intellect; I have given all the rest of my time to the relaxation of my senses and the repose of my mind. I here count among exercises of imagination all serious conversations, and everything that demands attention. This is what made me retire to the country; it is true that in the busiest city in the world I might have as many hours to myself as I now spend in study, but I could not employ them so usefully when my mind was wearied by the attention that the troubles of life demand.

I take the liberty of writing thus to your Highness, to express my sincere admiration of your Highness's ability, among all the business and cares that are never lacking to persons who combine high intelligence and high birth, to find leisure for the meditations that are necessary for proper understanding of the distinction between soul and body. I formed the opinion that it was these meditations, rather than thoughts demanding less attention, that made your Highness find some obscurity in our notion of their union. It seems to me that the human mind is incapable of distinctly conceiving both the distinction between body and soul and their union, at one and the same time; for that requires our conceiving them as a single thing and simultaneously conceiving them as two things, which is self-contradictory. I supposed that your Highness still had very much in mind the arguments proving the distinction of soul and body; and I did not wish to ask you to lay them aside, in order to represent to yourself that notion of their union which everybody always has in himself without doing philosophy – viz. that there is one single person who has at once body and consciousness, so that this consciousness can move the body and be aware of the events that happen to it. Accordingly, I used in my previous letter the simile of gravity and other qualities, which we imagine to be united to bodies as consciousness is united to ours. I did not worry over the fact that this simile is lame, because these qualities are not, as one imagines, realities; for I thought your Highness was already fully convinced that the soul is a substance distinct from the body.

Your Highness, however, makes the remark that it is easier to ascribe matter and extension to the soul than to ascribe to it the power of moving a body and being moved by it without having any matter. Now I would ask your Highness to hold yourself free to ascribe 'matter and extension' to the soul; for this is nothing else than to conceive the soul as united to the body. After forming a proper conception of this, and experiencing it in your own case, your Highness will find it easy to reflect that the matter you thus ascribe to your consciousness [*pensée*] is not the consciousness itself; again, the extension of the matter is essentially different from the extension of the consciousness, for the first extension is determined to a certain place, and excludes any other corporeal extension from that place, whereas the second does not. In this way your Highness will assuredly find it easy to come back to a realisation of the distinction between soul and body, in spite of having conceived of them as united.

Finally, I think it is very necessary to have got a good understanding, for once in one's life, of the principles of metaphysics, because it is from these that we have knowledge of God and of our soul. But I also think it would be very harmful to occupy one's intellect often with meditating on them, for it would be the less able to find leisure for the functioning of the imagination and the senses; the best thing is to be content with retaining in memory and in belief the conclusions one has drawn once for all, and to spend the rest of one's time for study in reflections in which the intellect co-operates with the imagination and the senses. . . .

13

Blaise Pascal, *Pensées*

Blaise Pascal (1623–62), born in the Auvergne, was educated by his father, who moved to Paris in 1631. He was a distinguished mathematician and scientist. He founded the modern theory of probability, contributed to the mathematics that led to the discovery of the infinitesimal calculus, and conducted experiments with fluids that led to the invention of the hydraulic press. Some of his experiments confirmed Torricelli's discovery of the vacuum. Given these achievements one might expect him to criticize Descartes for not being rationalist enough. But the opposite is true.

Two years after his sister became a member of Port-Royal in 1652, Pascal underwent a spiritual experience and became acquainted with members of Port-Royal, although he denied that he was a member. After Jansenism was condemned by the pope in 1653, Pascal agreed that the doctrines deserved to be condemned, but denied that they were doctrines that he held. The pope thought this maneuver was dishonest. When Antoine Arnauld was attacked for his Jansenist views, Pascal defended him in the *Provincial Letters* (1655–7).

Pascal's spirituality led him to criticize Descartes's philosophy, which ignored the deepest, inescapable needs of human beings: "The heart has its reasons, which reason does not know. . . . It is the heart which experiences God, and not the reason." He said he could not forgive Descartes because Descartes's God was used for nothing other than to set the world in motion.

Although Pascal had deep doubts, they were not Cartesian ones. He had doubts about the existence of God that were related to doubts about the meaning of life. He thought that humans could not have an adequate idea of God and thus could not know what he is. To rely on reason is to know that, if God exists, he is "infinitely incomprehensible" since he is completely unlike creatures.

Sometimes he denied that people could know by reason that God existed. Instead, it is "by faith" that he is known. This denial of a rational proof of the existence of God should not be confused with his proof that it is rational to *believe* that God exists. It is the difference between proving that *p* and proving that one should believe that *p*. Pascal begins his proof with the observation that a person must make a decision as to whether he will believe that God exists or believe that God does not exist. If one believes that God exists, then if God does exist, God will eternally reward the person for his belief. This is a winning outcome of infinite worth. If one believes that God does not exist and if God does, then God will eternally punish this person. This is a losing outcome, with an infinitely high penalty. Whether one believes that God exists or not, if he does not exist, the person loses very little since his existence will end at death. On a risk–reward basis, the rational thing to do is believe in God's existence. Because winning and losing are the outcomes this argument is called Pascal's wager.

There are all sorts of problems with the argument as presented. Here are some. Pascal talks about belief as if it were voluntary, but it is not. A person can't choose to believe or not to believe something. Belief is caused by evidence. This leads to another problem. The evidence may not cause a person to believe or to disbelieve in the existence of God. If the evidence is not compelling, a person may be agnostic, that is, have no belief about the existence or nonexistence of God.

Another problem is that there is some reason to doubt that God would reward a person for choosing to believe in God out of self-interest. Wouldn't God require love or a desire for the truth? Perhaps the self-interested belief in God would cause God to damn the person eternally. This leads to a related problem. The proposition that God exists is logically independent of the proposition that a person who believes in God gets rewarded after death. Perhaps there is no afterlife. Alternatively, perhaps there is an afterlife but no God. Think of Cartesian minds without God.

Pascal's actual argument is too subtle to be discussed here at length. He has replies to at least some of the objections just made. For example, to the first, that belief is involuntary, he makes the insightful remark that one can do things or put oneself into a position that would likely cause one to acquire a belief. By acting as if one believed, by going to mass and using holy water, one may come to believe.

77

I cannot forgive Descartes. In all his philosophy he would have been quite willing to dispense with God. But he had to make Him give a fillip to set the world in motion; beyond this, he has no further need of God.

78

Descartes useless and uncertain.

[. . .]

229

This is what I see and what troubles me. I look on all sides, and I see only darkness everywhere. Nature presents to me nothing which is not matter of doubt and concern. If I saw nothing there which revealed a Divinity, I would come to a negative conclusion; if I saw everywhere the signs of a Creator, I would remain peacefully in faith. But, seeing too much to deny and too little to be sure, I am in a state to be pitied; wherefore I have a hundred time wished that if a God maintains nature, she should testify to Him unequivocally, and that, if the signs she gives are deceptive, she should suppress them altogether; that she should say everything or nothing, that I might see which cause I ought to follow. Whereas in my present state, ignorant of what I am or of what I ought to do, I know neither my condition nor my duty. My heart inclines wholly to know where is the true good, in order to follow it; nothing would be too dear to me for eternity.

I envy those whom I see living in the faith with such carelessness, and who make such a bad use of a gift of which it seems to me I would make such a different use.

[. . .]

233

Infinite – nothing.

[. . .]

We know that there is an infinite, and are ignorant of its nature. As we know it to be false that numbers are finite, it is therefore true that there is an infinity in number. But we do not know what it is. It is false that it is even, it is false that it is odd; for the addition of a unit can make no change in its nature. Yet it is a number, and every number is odd or even (this is certainly true of every finite number). So we may well know that there is a God without knowing what He is. Is there not one substantial truth, seeing there are so many things which are not the truth itself?

We know then the existence and nature of the finite, because we also are finite and have extension. We know the existence of the infinite, and are ignorant of its nature, because it has extension like us, but not limits like us. But we know neither the existence nor the nature of God, because He has neither extension nor limits.

But by faith we know His existence; in glory we shall know His nature. Now, I have already shown that we may well know the existence of a thing, without knowing its nature.

Let us now speak according to natural lights.

If there is a God, He is infinitely incomprehensible, since, having neither parts nor limits, He has no affinity to us. We are then incapable of knowing either what He is or if He is. This being so, who will dare to undertake the decision of the question? Not we, who have no affinity to Him.

Who then will blame Christians for not being able to give a reason for their belief, since they profess a religion for which they cannot give a reason? They declare, in expounding it to the world, that it is a foolishness, *stultitiam*; and then you complain that they do not prove it! If they proved it, they would not keep their word; it is in lacking proofs, that they are not lacking in sense. "Yes, but although this excuses those who offer it as such, and takes away from them the blame of putting it forward without reason, it does not excuse those who receive it." Let us then examine this point, and say, "God is, or He is not." But to which side shall we incline? Reason can decide nothing here. There is an infinite chaos which separated us. A game is being played at the extremity of this infinite distance where heads or tails will turn up. What will you wager? According to reason, you can do neither the one thing nor the other; according to reason, you can defend neither of the propositions.

Do not then reprove for error those who have made a choice; for you know nothing about it. "No, but I blame them for having made, not this choice, but a choice; for again both he who chooses heads and he who chooses tails are equally at fault, they are both in the wrong. The true course is not to wager at all."

Yes; but you must wager. It is not optional. You are embarked. Which will you choose then? Let us see. Since you must choose, let us see which interests you least. You have two things to lose, the true and the good; and two things to stake, your reason and your will, your knowledge and your happiness; and your nature has two things to shun, error and misery. Your reason is no more shocked in choosing one rather than the other, since you must of necessity choose. This is one point settled. But your happiness? Let us weigh the gain and the loss in wagering that God is. Let us estimate these two chances. If you gain, you gain all; if you lose, you lose nothing. Wager, then, without hesitation that He is. – "That is very fine. Yes, I must wager; but I may perhaps wager too much." – Let us see. Since there is an equal risk of gain and of loss, if you had only to gain two lives, instead of one, you might still wager. But if there were three lives to gain, you would have to play (since you are under the necessity of playing), and you would be imprudent, when you are forced to play, not to chance your life to gain three at a game where there is an equal risk of loss and gain. But there is an eternity of life and happiness. And this being so, if there were an infinity of chances, of which one only would be for you, you would still be right in wagering one to win two, and you would act stupidly, being obliged to play, by refusing to stake one life against three at a game in which out of an infinity of chances there is one for you, if there were an infinity of an infinitely happy life to gain. But there is here an infinity of an infinitely happy life to gain, a chance of gain against a finite number of chances of loss, and what you stake is finite. It is all divided; wherever the infinite is and there is not an infinity of chances of loss against that of gain, there is no time to hesitate, you must give all. And thus, when one is forced to play, he must renounce reason to preserve his life, rather than risk it for infinite gain, as likely to happen as the loss of nothingness.

For it is no use to say it is uncertain if we will gain, and it is certain that we risk, and that the infinite distance between the *certainty* of what is staked and the *uncertainty* of what will be gained, equals the finite good which is certainly staked against the uncertain infinite. It is not so, as every player stakes a certainty to gain an uncertainty, and yet he stakes a finite certainty to gain a finite uncertainty, without transgressing against reason. There is not an infinite distance between the certainty staked and the uncertainty of the gain; that is untrue. In truth, there is an infinity between the certainty of gain and the certainty of loss. But the uncertainty of the gain is proportioned to the certainty of the stake according to the proportion of the chances of gain and loss. Hence it comes that, if there are as many risks on one side as on the other, the course is to play even; and then the certainty of the stake is equal to the uncertainty of the gain, so far is it from fact that there is an infinite distance between them. And so our proposition is of infinite force, when there is the finite to stake in a game where there are equal risks of gain and of loss, and the infinite to gain. This is demonstrable; and if men are capable of any truths, this is one.

"I confess it, I admit it. But, still, is there no means of seeing the faces of the cards?" – Yes, Scripture and the rest, etc. "Yes, but I have my hands tied and my mouth closed; I am forced to wager, and am not free. I am not released, and am so made that I cannot believe. What, then, would you have me do?"

True. But at least learn your inability to believe, since reason brings you to this, and yet you cannot believe. Endeavour then to convince yourself, not by increase of proofs of God, but by the abatement of your passions. You would like to attain faith, and do not know the way; you would like to cure yourself of unbelief, and ask the remedy for it. Learn of those who have been bound like you, and who now stake all their possessions. These are people who know the way which you would follow, and who are cured of an ill of which you would be cured. Follow the way by which they began; by acting as if they believed, taking the holy water, having masses said, etc. Even this will naturally make you believe, and deaden your acuteness. – "But this is what I am afraid of." – And why? What have you to lose?

But to show you that this leads you there, it is this which will lessen the passions, which are your stumbling-blocks.

The end of this discourse. – Now, what harm will befall you in taking this side? You will be faithful, honest, humble, grateful, generous, a sincere friend, truthful. Certainly you will not have those poisonous pleasures, glory and luxury; but will you not have others? I will tell you that you will thereby gain in this life, and that, at each step you take on this road, you will see so great certainty of gain, so much nothingness in what you risk, that you will at last recognise that you have wagered for something certain and infinite, for which you have given nothing.

"Ah! This discourse transports me, charms me," etc.

If this discourse pleases you and seems impressive, know that it is made by a man who has knelt, both before and after it, in prayer to that Being, infinite and without parts, before whom he lays all he has, for you also to lay before Him all you have for your own good and for His glory, that so strength may be given to lowliness.

234

If we must not act save on a certainty, we ought not to act on religion, for it is not certain. But how many things we do on an uncertainty, sea voyages, battles! I say then we must do nothing at all, for nothing is certain, and that there is more certainty in religion than there is as to whether we may see to-morrow; for it is not certain that we may see to-morrow, and it is certainly possible that we may not see it. We cannot say as much about religion. It is not certain that it is; but who will venture to say that it is certainly possible that it is not? Now when we work for to-morrow, and so on an uncertainty, we act reasonably; for we ought to work for an uncertainty according to the doctrine of chance which was demonstrated above.

Saint Augustine has seen that we work for an uncertainty, on sea, in battle, etc. But he has not seen the doctrine of chance which proves that we should do so. Montaigne has seen that we are shocked at a fool, and that habit is all-powerful; but he has not seen the reason of this effect.

All these persons have seen the effects, but they have not seen the causes. They are, in comparison with those who have discovered the causes, as those who have only eyes are in comparison with those who have intellect. For the effects are perceptible by sense, and the causes are visible only to the intellect. And although these effects are seen by the mind, this mind is, in comparison with the mind which sees the causes, as the bodily senses are in comparison with the intellect.

[...]

282

We know truth, not only by the reason, but also by the heart, and it is in this last way that we know first principles; and reason, which has no part in it, tries in vain to impugn them. The sceptics, who have only this for their object, labour to no purpose. We know that we do not dream, and however impossible it is for us to prove it by reason, this inability demonstrates only the weakness of our reason, but not, as they affirm, the uncertainty of all our knowledge. For the knowledge of first principles, as space, time, motion, number, is as sure as any of those which we get from reasoning. And reason must trust these intuitions of the heart, and must base them on every argument. (We have intuitive knowledge of the tridimensional nature of space, and of the infinity of number, and reason then shows that there are no two square numbers one of which is double of the other. Principles are intuited, propositions are inferred, all with certainty, though in different ways.)

[. . .]

339

I can well conceive a man without hands, feet, head (for it is only experience which teaches us that the head is more necessary than feet). But I cannot conceive man without thought; he would be a stone or a brute.

[. . .]

346

Thought constitutes the greatness of man.

347

Man is but a reed, the most feeble thing in nature; but he is a thinking reed. The entire universe need not arm itself to crush him. A vapour, a drop of water suffices to kill him. But, if the universe were to crush him, man would still be more noble than that which killed him, because he knows that he dies and the advantage which the universe has over him; the universe knows nothing of this.

All our dignity consists, then, in thought. By it we must elevate ourselves, and not by space and time which we cannot fill. Let us endeavour, then, to think well; this is the principle of morality.

348

A thinking reed. – It is not from space that I must seek my dignity, but from the government of my thought. I shall have no more if I possess worlds. By space the universe encompasses and swallows me up like an atom; by thought I comprehend the world.

Part III

Rationalism

Introduction

Descartes converted almost no Aristotelian scholastic philosophers to Cartesianism. Once people have a well-integrated system of beliefs, especially theoretical beliefs, it is psychologically difficult to conceive of the benefits of another, substantially different system, or, conceiving them, to slough off the old beliefs and put on the new ones. New adherents to a new philosophy come from the ranks of the young, not the old.

Similarly, it is difficult for the person who has devised a substantially different system to see its defects even when they are pointed out to him several times by different people. Few parents think their own child is ugly. So Descartes could not see the force of the objections directed against his philosophy. The biggest problem was Descartes's dualism. If matter and mind are completely different, the first being either space or what fills up space, and the second having no spatial properties, and if matter moves only by being touched, how can there be any mind–matter interaction? How can the mind move the body? How can changes in the body cause changes in the mind?

There seemed to be three basic solutions to the problem. One was to assert that there is only one substance. A second was to assert that there are many substances but that they are all of the same kind, that is, all material or all mental. A third was to assert that there are two substances, but to deny that they interact.

Benedict Spinoza adopted the first solution. He is a monist because for him there is only one substance, which human beings represent sometimes as material and sometimes as mental. The problem of interaction is forestalled by not allowing the existence of two kinds of substance. Gottfried Leibniz adopted the second solution. There is only one kind of substance, but there are innumerably many of them and they are infinitesimally small. When these substances cluster together, they give rise to the appearance of material objects. But the substances themselves, things Leibniz calls "monads," are not material. It might seem to be a contradiction to hold that all the parts of reality are nonmaterial but that groups of nonmaterial objects are material, but it is not. Consider that a skyscraper has the property of being enormous, even though none of its parts has the property of being enormous. All the stone, steel, glass, and what have you that make up the skyscraper are less than enormous.

In theory, a skyscraper could be made up of small bricks. Or consider a black stone, that is, a stone with the property of being black. If it is broken into small enough parts, one can discover that none of the parts has the property of being black. In short, wholes can have properties that none of their parts have. Because the basic parts of bodies, monads, are not material, no monad can touch any other; and if no monad can touch any other, no monad can affect any other. Each monad is in effect a closed room with no windows; each, however, reflects every other. The apparent causal relations that people observe in the world are the result of a harmony, pre-established by God.

A problem with both Spinoza's philosophy and Leibniz's is that they go against a deep intuition that people had in the seventeenth century, namely, that there are two kinds of substance: matter and mind. Descartes accepted this intuition and built his metaphysics around it. Malebranche respected that intuition, but gave up the idea that mind could actually affect matter. He posited a variation of Leibniz's idea of pre-established harmony; according to him, the activity of the mental was the occasion for the activity of the material. Orchestrating this "occasionalism" was God, who orders the universe.

The selections in this part show how Spinoza, Malebranche, and Leibniz worked out alternatives to Descartes's interactive dualism.

14

Benedict Spinoza, *The Ethics*

Spinoza (1632–77), born in Amsterdam, Holland, was the son of a family of Jews who had fled Portugal to escape persecution. The name he was given at birth, Baruch, was rejected by him after he was expelled from the synagogue for his heretical views. He took for himself the name Benedict; in order to honor his self-definition, that name is used here to refer to him.

Spinoza received a good education in Jewish religion and philosophy. He studied the Hebrew Bible, the Talmud, and the writings of Moses Maimonides. After being overheard expressing heretical views about Judaism, he was ordered to renounce them. As a matter of personal integrity he refused, and was consequently excommunicated in July 1656. Several years later, Spinoza left Amsterdam and eventually settled in The Hague, where he worked as a lens grinder, so that he would not have to worry about being dismissed from a teaching position for his views. He also received some financial support from his Christian friends and corresponded with some of the most important intellectuals of the time, such as Henry Oldenburg, Secretary of the Royal Society in London, who may have hoped that Spinoza would convert to Christianity. Spinoza admired Jesus but did not accept any revealed religion.

Like Descartes and Hobbes, whom he read and admired, he wanted to bring mathematical certainty to philosophy. His *magnum opus*, *Ethics* (published posthumously in 1678), begins with definitions, axioms, and postulates, just as Euclid's *Elements* does. The only works he published during his lifetime were *Principles of Descartes's Philosophy*, a critical exposition, and the *Theologico-Political Treatise*, published anonymously. Influenced by Hobbes's philosophy, Spinoza presents a social contract theory of government, but he advocates limited government, in contrast with Hobbes's advocacy of absolute sovereignty. True to his philosophy, Spinoza aligned himself with the De Witt brothers, who were republicans (supporters of citizen-controlled government), and against the monarchical House of Orange. The *Theologico-Political Treatise* also contains a long discussion of the composition and reliability of the Bible, a discussion that greatly extends the work of Hobbes and others on biblical criticism. Though not a believer, Spinoza explicitly argues that religious toleration is justified by both Judaism and Christianity.

Spinoza was internationally known as a philosopher of genius and renowned for his integrity, the Socrates of modern philosophy, even though many thought he was a despicable atheist. He died in 1677.

The *Ethics* contains five parts: (1) "Of God" (presented in full here); (2) "Of the Nature and Origin of the Mind" (presented in part); (3) "Of the Origin and Nature of the Affects [Emotions]" (not included); (4) "Of Human Bondage, *or* the Powers of the Affects" (not included); and (5) "Of the Power of the Intellect, *or* on Human Freedom" (presented in part).

Like Descartes and Hobbes, Spinoza thought that philosophy consisted of propositions proved by reason alone. Like Hobbes and unlike Descartes, Spinoza was a monist, not a dualist. Unlike both Hobbes and Descartes, Spinoza was not a materialist. He believed that reality or substance is infinite and consists of an infinite number of attributes. Humans, however, know of only two of them: extension and thought. The intuition that drove Spinoza to his monism was the idea that everything is connected. In being completely connected, reality is one (see below part I, proposition 14).

One way to understand his monism is to begin with a concept that is central to a philosophy that initially seems to be completely alien to his, namely, the concept of substance in Aristotelian scholastic philosophy. Spinoza accepts the scholastic definition that a substance exists in itself or on its own or does not depend on anything else for its existence (*Ethics*, D3). The contrasting term in scholastic philosophy is an "accident," which can exist only in a substance and hence depends on a substance for its existence. (What scholastic philosophers called "accidents" philosophers today typically call "properties.") Scholastic philosophers would count trees, dogs, and humans as examples of substances. Trees have the accident (property) of being strong. The tree's strength depends on the tree and cannot exist apart from the tree. A brown dog has the accident of being brown, and the dog's brownness cannot exist apart from the dog. A wise human has the accident of being wise, and that wisdom cannot exist apart from the human.

As apparently sensible as this view is, it does not stand up to reflection, according to Spinoza. What he does is to draw out the consequences of the Aristotelian conception of substance more rigorously than any scholastic had.[1] Trees, dogs, and humans do not exist independently; they depend on other things. Trees, dogs, and humans require air, water, warmth, and nutriments to survive.

We have just observed that a tree depends on several things. Now consider an individual tree with all of its properties. A particular tree is not just a complex of roots, trunk, branches, and leaves, unrelated to anything else. It is anchored in some particular soil, absorbing certain water, and surrounded by some particular air. That is, an individual tree has the properties of being in a certain soil, surrounded by certain water and certain air. And, if we are rigorous, we will not stop with these properties. The tree we are focusing on has such properties as, say, being 51 feet from the house at 6823 Willamette Drive in Cleveland, Ohio, USA, being 11′3″ from an elm that is 8′ from a barbeque pit, and so on. Further, the tree's spatial properties are not exhausted by the ones it has in virtue of relationships to other things on earth. It is related by innumerable relations to all the things in the solar system, and to the Milky Way galaxy, and to the universe as a whole. And we have been talking now only about the spatial properties. Think of all the other properties it has in virtue of being connected with everything else in the universe. Reality is one.

1 In *Principles of First Philosophy*, Descartes mentions that "properly speaking" only God is a substance (*Principles*, I.51).

One might protest that although all created reality is one, it does not follow that all reality is absolutely one. There could be at least two realities, God and creation. Let's see whether this protest bears scrutiny. Creation does not exist in itself. It depends on God. The standard Judaeo-Christian scholastic view of creation in the seventeenth century maintained that creation depended for its existence upon God's creative act at every moment. God continuously conserves creation; and conserving, as Descartes pointed out, is essentially the same as creating. So, "creation" does not exist in itself. (I will explain the scare quotes in a moment.) It exists from God.

Now, what is God? As Spinoza defines him, and this definition also agrees with the scholastic tradition, God is "a being absolutely infinite." Since God is absolutely infinite, nothing limits him. If "creation" were something different from God, then it would limit him; but this is impossible, as we have just seen. So what we call "creation" is nothing other than God. That is why I put "creation" in scare quotes above. In other words, "creation" is a misnomer, a name that wrongly connotes that it ("creation") is something other than God. There is literally no creation, because for something literally to be creation, it must not only depend on God but be different from God. But nothing can be different from God, because if something were, then God would be limited.

When ordinary people use the word "creation," they are unwittingly designating Nature. Nature, according to Spinoza, is God conceived of as extension. God, however, cannot be simply Nature and nothing more, because then God would be limited. He would be only Nature and not other things. So God has an infinite number of "attributes" although humans can conceive of only one more of these, thought. ("Attribute" is a technical term in Spinoza's philosophy and means something like "essential accident or essential property.") In short, God is everything.

This is a shocking result, and many of his contemporaries were shocked, not to mention outraged. For many people, to say that everything is God is to say that nothing is God (Compare: if everyone is guilty, no one is guilty.) So, if Spinoza holds that everything is God, he is an atheist. The other interpretation of Spinoza, proposed by Novalis (1772–1801), a German Romantic poet and philosopher, is that Spinoza's identification of everything with God shows that he was a God-intoxicated man. Part of the intoxication is his belief that "the human mind is part of the infinite intellect of God," because God is the only substance and his essence is mind (part II, proposition 11).

So far, I have been discussing Spinoza's philosophy from a metaphysical perspective. I have been talking about the properties of trees, dogs, and human beings, and about the nature of substance and God. Spinoza often indicated that the very same metaphysical results can be generated epistemically, that is, by considering how things are known or conceived. A complete understanding of anything requires an understanding of everything. (This was shown in effect when we discussed what trees depend on.) For example, in his definition of a substance, Spinoza says that it is what is "conceived through itself." The epistemic aspect of things also comes out in his definition of an attribute as "what the *intellect perceives* of a substance, as constituting its essence" (my italics), and in his definition of a mode as "that which is in another through which *it is also conceived*" (my italics), more simply, what is in something that makes us conceive it the way we do. Something in a brown dog makes us conceive it as being brown. This thing is a mode. ("Mode" is a technical term that is roughly equivalent to "accident" in scholastic philosophy.)

Let's move on to other aspects of Spinoza's philosophy. He defines a cause of itself as "that whose essence involves existence." This is the same as saying that it is something "whose nature cannot be conceived except as existing" (*Ethics*, D1). Two things are worth noting. First, in philosophy today, causality is understood to be an irreflexive relation.[2] That is, it is not the case that *x* is the cause of *x*. You could not have caused yourself to exist. To be caused is to be dependent on something else. Do not think that the world caused itself to exist. According to the Big Bang Theory, the world began with a big explosion of matter, but neither the world nor the matter (nor anything else) caused the explosion. The world did not bang itself into existence. Nonetheless, Spinoza did not make a mistake in thinking of something as its own cause. He uses the word "cause" for something different than we do. For him, like many of his predecessors, a cause is either a cause in our sense or a reason or explanation for the existence of something. So when Spinoza says that a substance is the cause of itself, he means that the explanation of its existence is itself.[3]

In other words, the conception of a substance is something that contains within itself the idea of its own existence. This conception of a substance has a notable consequence. In scholastic philosophy, the thing that "cannot be conceived except as existing" is God. Descartes used this fact in his ontological argument. God's essence includes his existence. Spinoza then had his own version of the ontological argument (see proposition 9). It differs from traditional ontological arguments in that for Spinoza Nature is the thing whose essence includes its own existence.

Since the idea that there is only one substance, God, which is the same as Nature is a shocking position, it is worth giving another of Spinoza's proofs that there can be only one substance. Let's begin by proving that there cannot be two or more substances of the same nature or attribute (proposition 5). The proof is a *reductio ad absurdum* argument. Suppose that there are two substances of the same kind, A and B. If A and B are different, then they must be different either with respect to their attributes or with respect to their affections (modes). They cannot have different attributes, because it is in virtue of having the same attribute that they are substances "of the same kind." The attribute makes them to be a substance of the kind that they are. So, since they are identical with respect to the attribute they have, the attribute cannot make them two things. Now consider the possibility that they are made different by their affections. Since a substance is prior to its affections, the substances must be different before the affections come into play at all. Since they are not different before the affections come into play, the supposed two substances are actually only one substance.[4]

In part II of the *Ethics*, Spinoza gives his explanation of the nature and origin of the mind by talking extensively about God. Body is the essence of God "considered as a thing extended," and thought is "an attribute of God," and so on. Since only God is a substance, human beings are not substances, they are modes of God. It is important, however, not to isolate particular human bodies from the entire course of reality. Human beings are in every respect a part of nature.

2 Causation is also usually thought to be transitive: if *x* causes *y* and y causes *z*, then *x* is the cause of *z*; and asymmetric: if *x* causes *y*, then *y* does not cause *x*.

3 Can anything be the explanation for itself?

4 This argument seems to beg the question or confuse temporal priority with ontological priority. Even if the two substances are the same in nature, their different affections would distinguish them. Although substances are ontologically prior to affections, they are not temporally prior. To say that the substances must be different "before" the affections are considered is to confuse the logical sense with the temporal sense.

This raises the difficult and vexed issue concerning the freedom of human beings. Are people free or not? If they are free, is it because they have free will or for some other reason? These were particularly pressing questions because the modern science of Galileo, Hobbes, Descartes, and others was deterministic. Every event was held to have a cause, which itself is an event. So it seems that human actions, which are events, have causes and hence are not free. All events are determined by their causes, and whatever is determined is necessary.

There are three basic philosophical options: libertarianism (not to be confused with political libertarianism), according to which human actions are not caused by any preceding event other than an act of free will; soft determinism, according to which human actions are both caused by a preceding event and free; and hard determinism, according to which every event is caused and human actions are not free. Spinoza may be thought to support a soft determinist position, but of a unique sort, divine soft determinism. His view turns on his definition of "free." An action is free just in case it comes from the nature of a substance and nothing else. For Spinoza God is free in the sense that all of his actions result from his nature and not from anything external to his nature. At the same time, all of God's actions are necessary because they are determined by God's nature. In short, freedom is compatible with necessity. As regards human freedom, people are free to the extent that they understand the causes of their actions. People think that many events are contingent (not the result of necessary causes) because they do not know the causes of those events. Complete knowledge of the world or Nature would eliminate the appearance of contingency and unpleasant emotions. It would also reveal the way in which every part of Nature is perfect insofar as it contributes to Nature as a whole, which is perfect.[5] Spinoza has to hold this view because Nature is God, and hence perfect.

As in the grand scheme of things, so in Spinoza's philosophy, individuals are unimportant. Within extension and thought are chains of modes, individual bodies and thoughts, respectively, and the objects in each chain correlate with each other. For each body there is an idea of that body, and for each causal connection between one body or event and another there is an idea of that causal connection. The human mind, then, is the idea of a human body, and both of these things, like everything else, exist in God.

Spinoza's philosophy seems to have a problem. If each part of Nature is perfect insofar as it contributes to the whole of Nature, how can any idea be false? Spinoza thinks that all ideas, insofar as they are related to God, are true. But that fact is irrelevant to, and in fact apparently inconsistent with, the claim that some ideas are inadequate and not properly related to other ideas. Another apparent problem is that, for Spinoza, emotions are modifications of the body's power to act, and emotions inhibit a person's causal power to act. To this latter problem he might respond that emotions seem to be imperfections only when they are considered in themselves, and not as parts of the whole. But this answer does not seem adequate, because Spinoza also thinks that emotions are responses to the level of one's being, and some levels are higher than others. The distinction between higher and lower levels should have no place in a theory that makes the whole perfect.

A large part of part V, "The Intellectual Love of God," is a secular and semi-mystical celebration of God.

5 The phrase "insofar as" is necessary in order to avoid committing the fallacy of composition. In itself, a theft or murder is not perfect. But one cannot go from "a murder is not perfect" to "Nature is not perfect."

> He who understands himself and his affects clearly and distinctly loves God and does so the more, the more he understands himself and his affects....
>
> This Love toward God must engage the Mind most.... No one can hate God.... The greatest virtue of the Mind is to know God. The intellectual love of God is eternal.

Spinoza attributes to God many of the same properties that scholastic philosophers did: "God is without passions, and is not affected with any affect of... sadness.... God can pass neither to a greater nor a lesser perfection." However, he departs from the scholastics in other ways. For him, God loves no one and does not experience joy.

Demonstrated in Geometric Order
and Divided into Five Parts,
Which Treat

I. Of God
II. Of the Nature and Origin of the Mind
III. Of the Origin and Nature of the Affects
IV. Of Human Bondage, *or* the Powers of the Affects
V. Of the Power of the Intellect, *or* on Human Freedom*

First Part of the Ethics
Of God

Definitions

D1: By cause of itself I understand that whose essence involves existence, *or* that whose nature cannot be conceived except as existing.

D2: That thing is said to be finite in its own kind that can be limited by another of the same nature.

For example, a body is called finite because we always conceive another that is greater. Thus a thought is limited by another thought. But a body is not limited by a thought nor a thought by a body.

D3: By substance I understand what is in itself and is conceived through itself, that is, that whose concept does not require the concept of another thing, from which it must be formed.

D4: By attribute I understand what the intellect perceives of a substance, as constituting its essence.

D5: By mode I understand the affections of a substance, *or* that which is in another through which it is also conceived.

D6: By God I understand a being absolutely infinite, that is, a substance consisting of an infinity of attributes, of which each one expresses an eternal and infinite essence.

* Spinoza's *Ethics* includes numerous cross-references. In this selection all such cross-references have been retained, including those which relate to sections which do not appear here, to enable readers to refer to a complete edition if they wish.

Exp.: I say absolutely infinite, not infinite in its own kind; for if something is only infinite in its own kind, we can deny infinite attributes of it [NS: (i.e., we can conceive infinite attributes which do not pertain to its nature)]; but if something is absolutely infinite, whatever expresses essence and involves no negation pertains to its essence.

D7: That thing is called free which exists from the necessity of its nature alone, and is determined to act by itself alone. But a thing is called necessary, or rather compelled, which is determined by another to exist and to produce an effect in a certain and determinate manner.

D8: By eternity I understand existence itself, insofar as it is conceived to follow necessarily from the definition alone of the eternal thing.

Exp.: For such existence, like the essence of a thing, is conceived as an eternal truth, and on that account cannot be explained by duration or time, even if the duration is conceived to be without beginning or end.

Axioms

A1: Whatever is, is either in itself or in another.

A2: What cannot be conceived through another, must be conceived through itself.

A3: From a given determinate cause the effect follows necessarily; and conversely, if there is no determinate cause, it is impossible for an effect to follow.

A4: The knowledge of an effect depends on, and involves, the knowledge of its cause.

A5: Things that have nothing in common with one another also cannot be understood through one another, *or* the concept of the one does not involve the concept of the other.

A6: A true idea must agree with its object.

A7: If a thing can be conceived as not existing, its essence does not involve existence.

P1: *A substance is prior in nature to its affections.*

Dem.: This is evident from D3 and D5.

P2: *Two substances having different attributes have nothing in common with one another.*

Dem.: This is also evident from D3. For each must be in itself and be conceived through itself, *or* the concept of the one does not involve the concept of the other.

P3: *If things have nothing in common with one another, one of them cannot be the cause of the other.*

Dem.: If they have nothing in common with one another, then (by A5) they cannot be understood through one another, and so (by A4) one cannot be the cause of the other, q.e.d.

P4: *Two or more distinct things are distinguished from one another, either by a difference in the attributes of the substances or by a difference in their affections.*

Dem.: Whatever is, is either in itself or in another (by A1), that is (by D3 and D5), outside the intellect there is nothing except substances and their affections. Therefore, there is nothing outside the intellect through which a number of things can be distinguished from one another except substances, *or* what is the same (by D4), their attributes, and their affections, q.e.d.

P5: *In Nature there cannot be two or more substances of the same nature* or *attribute.*

Dem.: If there were two or more distinct substances, they would have to be distinguished from one another either by a difference in their attributes, or by a difference in their affections (by P4). If only by a difference in their attributes, then it will be conceded that there is only one of the same attribute. But if by a difference in their affections, then since a substance is prior in nature to its affections (by P1), if the affections are put to one side and [the substance] is considered in itself, that is (by D3 and A6), considered truly, one cannot be conceived to be distinguished from another, that is (by P4), there cannot be many, but only one [of the same nature *or* attribute], q.e.d.

P6: *One substance cannot be produced by another substance.*

Dem.: In Nature there cannot be two substances of the same attribute (by P5), that is (by P2), which have something in common with each other. Therefore (by P3) one cannot be the cause of the other, *or* cannot be produced by the other, q.e.d.

Cor.: From this it follows that a substance cannot be produced by anything else. For in Nature there is nothing except substances and their affections, as is evident from A1, D3, and D5. But it cannot be produced by a substance (by P6). Therefore, substance absolutely cannot be produced by anything else, q.e.d.

Alternatively: This is demonstrated even more easily from the absurdity of its contradictory. For if a substance could be produced by something else, the knowledge of it would have to depend on the knowledge of its cause (by A4). And so (by D3) it would not be a substance.

P7: *It pertains to the nature of a substance to exist.*

Dem.: A substance cannot be produced by anything else (by P6C); therefore it will be the cause of itself, that is (by D1), its essence necessarily involves existence, *or* it pertains to its nature to exist, q.e.d.

P8: *Every substance is necessarily infinite.*

Dem.: A substance of one attribute does not exist unless it is unique (P5), and it pertains to its nature to exist (P7). Of its nature, therefore, it will exist either as finite or as infinite. But not as finite. For then (by D2) it would have to be limited by something else of the same nature, which would also have to exist necessarily (by P7), and so there would be two substances of the same attribute, which is absurd (by P5). Therefore, it exists as infinite, q.e.d.

Schol. 1: Since being finite is really, in part, a negation, and being infinite is an absolute affirmation of the existence of some nature, it follows from P7 alone that every substance must be infinite. [NS: For if we assumed a finite substance, we would, in part, deny existence to its nature, which (by P7) is absurd.*].

Schol. 2: I do not doubt that the demonstration of P7 will be difficult to conceive for all who judge things confusedly, and have not been accustomed to know things through their first causes – because they do not distinguish between the modifications of substances and the substances themselves, nor do they know how things are produced. So it happens that they fictitiously ascribe to substances the beginning which they see that natural things have; for those who do not know the true causes of things confuse everything and without any conflict of mind feign that both trees and men speak, imagine that men are formed both from stones and from seed, and that any form whatever is changed into any other. So also, those who confuse the divine nature with the human easily ascribe human affects to God, particularly so long as they are also ignorant of how those affects are produced in the mind.

* NS: These are notes by the editor and translator, Edwin Curley, and introduce a variant reading from the Dutch translation of Spinoza's works which appeared at the same time as *Opera posthuma*. A.P.M.

But if men would attend to the nature of substance, they would have no doubt at all of the truth of P7. Indeed, this proposition would be an axiom for everyone, and would be numbered among the common notions. For by substance they would understand what is in itself and is conceived through itself, that is, that the knowledge of which does not require the knowledge of any other thing. But by modifications they would understand what is in another, those things whose concept is formed from the concept of the thing in which they are.

This is how we can have true ideas of modifications which do not exist; for though they do not actually exist outside the intellect, nevertheless their essences are comprehended in another in such a way that they can be conceived through it. But the truth of substances is not outside the intellect unless it is in them themselves, because they are conceived through themselves.

Hence, if someone were to say that he had a clear and distinct, that is, true, idea of a substance, and nevertheless doubted whether such a substance existed, that would indeed be the same as if he were to say that he had a true idea, and nevertheless doubted whether it was false (as is evident to anyone who is sufficiently attentive). Or if someone maintains that a substance is created, he maintains at the same time that a false idea has become true. Of course nothing more absurd can be conceived. So it must be confessed that the existence of a substance, like its essence, is an eternal truth.

And from this we can infer in another way that there is only one [substance] of the same nature, which I have considered it worth the trouble of showing here. But to do this in order, it must be noted,

> I. that the true definition of each thing neither involves nor expresses anything except the nature of the thing defined.

From which it follows,

> II. that no definition involves or expresses any certain number of individuals,

since it expresses nothing other than the nature of the thing defined. For example, the definition of the triangle expresses nothing but the simple nature of the triangle, but not any certain number of triangles. It is to be noted,

> III. that there must be, for each existing thing, a certain cause on account of which it exists.

Finally, it is to be noted,

> IV. that this cause, on account of which a thing exists, either must be contained in the very nature and definition of the existing thing (*viz. that it pertains to its nature to exist*) or must be outside it.

From these propositions it follows that if, in Nature, a certain number of individuals exists, there must be a cause why those individuals, and why neither more nor fewer, exist.

For example, if twenty men exist in Nature (*to make the matter clearer, I assume that they exist at the same time, and that no others previously existed in Nature*), it will not be enough (*i.e., to give a reason why twenty men exist*) to show the cause of human nature in general; but it will be necessary in addition to show the cause why not more and not fewer than twenty exist. For (by III) there must necessarily be a cause why each [NS: particular man] exists. But this cause (by II and III) cannot be contained in human nature itself, since the true definition of man does not involve the number 20. So (by IV) the cause why these twenty men exist, and consequently, why each of them exists, must necessarily be outside each of them.

For that reason it is to be inferred absolutely that whatever is of such a nature that there can be many individuals [of that nature] must, to exist, have an external cause to exist. Now since it pertains to the nature of a substance to exist (by what we have already shown in this scholium), its definition must involve necessary existence, and consequently its existence must be inferred from its definition alone. But from its definition (as we have shown from II and III) the existence of a number of substances cannot follow. Therefore it follows necessarily from this, that there exists only one of the same nature, as was proposed.

P9: *The more reality or being each thing has, the more attributes belong to it.*

Dem.: This is evident from D4.

P10: *Each attribute of a substance must be conceived through itself.*

Dem.: For an attribute is what the intellect perceives concerning a substance, as constituting its essence (by D4); so (by D3) it must be conceived through itself, q.e.d.

Schol.: From these propositions it is evident that although two attributes may be conceived to be really distinct (i.e., one may be conceived without the aid of the other), we still cannot infer from that that they constitute two beings, *or* two different substances. For it is of the nature of a substance that each of its attributes is conceived through itself, since all the attributes it has have always been in it together, and one could not be produced by another, but each expresses the reality, *or* being of substance.

So it is far from absurd to attribute many attributes to one substance. Indeed, nothing in Nature is clearer than that each being must be conceived under some attribute, and the more reality, or being it has, the more it has attributes which express necessity, *or* eternity, and infinity. And consequently there is also nothing clearer than that a being absolutely infinite must be defined (as we taught in D6) as a being that consists of infinite attributes, each of which expresses a certain eternal and infinite essence.

But if someone now asks by what sign we shall be able to distinguish the diversity of substances, let him read the following propositions, which show that in Nature there exists only one substance, and that it is absolutely infinite. So that sign would be sought in vain.

P11: *God,* or *a substance consisting of infinite attributes, each of which expresses eternal and infinite essence, necessarily exists.*

Dem.: If you deny this, conceive, if you can, that God does not exist. Therefore (by A7) his essence does not involve existence. But this (by P7) is absurd. Therefore God necessarily exists, q.e.d.

Alternatively: For each thing there must be assigned a cause, *or* reason, both for its existence and for its nonexistence. For example, if a triangle exists, there must be a reason *or* cause why it exists; but if it does not exist, there must also be a reason *or* cause which prevents it from existing, *or* which takes its existence away.

But this reason, *or* cause, must either be contained in the nature of the thing, or be outside it. For example, the very nature of a square circle indicates the reason why it does not exist, namely, because it involves a contradiction. On the other hand, the reason why a substance exists also follows from its nature alone, because it involves existence (see P7). But the reason why a circle or triangle exists, or why it does not exist, does not follow from the nature of these things, but from the order of the whole of corporeal Nature. For from this [order] it must follow either that the triangle necessarily exists now or that it is impossible for it to exist now. These things are evident through themselves; from them it follows that a thing necessarily exists if there is no reason or cause which prevents it from existing. Therefore, if there can be no reason or cause which prevents God from existing, or which takes his existence away, it must certainly be inferred that he necessarily exists.

But if there were such a reason, *or* cause, it would have to be either in God's very nature or outside it, that is, in another substance of another nature. For if it were of the same nature, that very supposition would concede that God exists. But a substance which was of another nature [NS: than the divine] would have nothing in common with God (by P2), and therefore could neither give him existence nor take it away. Since, then, there can be, outside the divine nature, no reason, *or*, cause which takes away the divine existence, the reason will necessarily have to be in his nature itself, if indeed he does not exist. That is, his nature would involve a contradiction [NS: as in our second example]. But it is absurd to affirm this of a Being absolutely infinite and supremely perfect. Therefore, there is no cause, *or* reason, either in God or outside God, which takes his existence away. And therefore, God necessarily exists, q.e.d.

Alternatively: To be able not to exist is to lack power, and conversely, to be able to exist is to have power (as is known through itself). So, if what now necessarily exists are only finite beings, then finite beings are more powerful than an absolutely infinite Being. But this, as is known through itself, is absurd. So, either nothing exists or an absolutely infinite Being also exists. But we exist, either in ourselves, or in something else, which necessarily exists (see A1 and P7). Therefore an absolutely infinite Being – that is (by D6), God – necessarily exists, q.e.d.

Schol.: In this last demonstration I wanted to show God's existence a posteriori, so that the demonstration would be perceived more easily – but not because God's existence does not follow a priori from the same foundation. For since being able to exist is power, it follows that the more reality belongs to the nature of a thing the more powers it has, of itself, to exist. Therefore, an absolutely infinite Being, *or* God, has, of himself, an absolutely infinite power of existing. For that reason, he exists absolutely.

Still, there may be many who will not easily be able to see how evident this demonstration is, because they have been accustomed to contemplate only those things that flow from external causes. And of these, they see that those which quickly come to be, that is, which easily exist, also easily perish. And conversely, they judge that those things to which they conceive more things to pertain are more difficult to do, that is, that they do not exist so easily. But to free them from these prejudices I have no need to show here in what manner this proposition – *what quickly comes to be, quickly perishes* – is true, nor whether or not all things are equally easy in respect to the whole of Nature. It is sufficient to note only this, that I am not here speaking of things that come to be from external causes, but only of substances that (by P6) can be produced by no external cause.

For things that come to be from external causes – whether they consist of many parts or of few – owe all the perfection or reality they have to the power of the external cause; and therefore their existence arises only from the perfection of their external cause, and not from their own perfection. On the other hand, whatever perfection substance has is not owed to any external cause. So its existence must follow from its nature alone; hence its existence is nothing but its essence.

Perfection, therefore, does not take away the existence of a thing, but on the contrary asserts it. But imperfection takes it away. So there is nothing of whose existence we can be more certain than we are of the existence of an absolutely infinite, *or* perfect, Being – that is, God. For since his essence excludes all imperfection, and involves absolute perfection, by that very fact it takes away every cause of doubting his existence, and gives the greatest certainty concerning it. I believe this will be clear even to those who are only moderately attentive.

P12: *No attribute of a substance can be truly conceived from which it follows that the substance can be divided.*

Dem.: For the parts into which a substance so conceived would be divided either will retain the nature of the substance or will not. If the first [NS: viz. they retain the nature of the substance], then (by P8) each part will have to be infinite, and (by P7) its own cause, and (by P5) each part will have to consist of a different attribute. And so many substances will be able to be formed from one, which is absurd (by P6). Furthermore, the parts (by P2) would have nothing in common with their whole, and the whole (by D4 and P10) could both be and be conceived without its parts, which is absurd, as no one will be able to doubt.

But if the second is asserted, namely, that the parts will not retain the nature of substance, then since the whole substance would be divided into equal parts, it would lose the nature of substance, and would cease to be, which (by P7) is absurd.

P13: *A substance which is absolutely infinite is indivisible.*

Dem.: For if it were divisible, the parts into which it would be divided will either retain the nature of an absolutely infinite substance or they will not. If the first, then there will be a number of substances of the same nature, which (by P5) is absurd. But if the second is asserted, then (as above [NS: P12]), an absolutely infinite substance will be able to cease to be, which (by P11) is also absurd.

Cor.: From these [propositions] it follows that no substance, and consequently no corporeal substance, insofar as it is a substance, is divisible.

Schol.: That substance is indivisible, is understood more simply merely from this, that the nature of substance cannot be conceived unless as infinite, and that by a part of substance nothing can be understood except a finite substance, which (by P8) implies a plain contradiction.

P14: *Except God, no substance can be or be conceived.*

Dem.: Since God is an absolutely infinite being, of whom no attribute which expresses an essence of substance can be denied (by D6), and he necessarily exists (by P11), if there were any substance except God, it would have to be explained through some attribute of God, and so two substances of the same attribute would exist, which (by P5) is absurd. And so except God, no substance can be or, consequently, be conceived. For if it could be conceived, it would have to be conceived as existing. But this (by the first part of this demonstration) is absurd. Therefore, except for God no substance can be or be conceived, q.e.d.

Cor. 1: From this it follows most clearly, first, that God is unique, that is (by D6), that in Nature there is only one substance, and that it is absolutely infinite (as we indicated in P10S).

Cor. 2: It follows, second, that an extended thing and a thinking thing are either attributes of God, or (by A1) affections of God's attributes.

P15: *Whatever is, is in God, and nothing can be or be conceived without God.*

Dem.: Except for God, there neither is, nor can be conceived, any substance (by P14), that is (by D3), thing that is in itself and is conceived through itself. But modes (by D5) can neither be nor be conceived without substance. So they can be in the divine nature alone, and can be conceived through it alone. But except for substances and modes there is nothing (by A1). Therefore, [NS: everything is in God and] nothing can be or be conceived without God, q.e.d.

Schol.: [I.] There are those who feign a God, like man, consisting of a body and a mind, and subject to passions. But how far they wander from the true knowledge of God, is sufficiently established by what has already been demonstrated. Them I dismiss. For everyone who has to any extent contemplated the divine nature denies that God is corporeal. They prove this best from the fact that by body we understand any quantity, with length, breadth, and depth, limited by some certain figure. Nothing more absurd than this can be said of God, namely, of a being absolutely infinite. But meanwhile, by the other arguments by which they strive to demonstrate this same conclusion they clearly show that they entirely remove corporeal, *or* extended, substance itself from the divine nature. And they maintain that it has been created by God. But by what divine power could it be created? They are completely ignorant of that. And this shows clearly that they do not understand what they themselves say. At any rate, I have demonstrated clearly enough – in my judgment, at least – that no substance can be produced or created by another thing (see P6C and P8S2). Next, we have shown (P14) that except for God, no substance can either be or be conceived, and hence [in P14C2] we have concluded that extended substance is one of God's infinite attributes. But to provide a fuller explanation, I shall refute my opponents' arguments, which all reduce to these.

[II.] *First*, they think that corporeal substance, insofar as it is substance, consists of parts. And therefore they deny that it can be infinite, and consequently, that it can pertain to God. They explain this by many examples, of which I shall mention one or two.

[i] If corporeal substance is infinite, they say, let us conceive it to be divided in two parts. Each part will be either finite or infinite. If the former, then an infinite is composed of two finite parts, which is absurd. If the latter [NS: i.e., if each part is infinite], then there is one infinite twice as large as another, which is also absurd. [ii] Again, if an infinite quantity is measured by parts [each] equal to a foot, it will consist of infinitely many such parts, as it will also, if it is measured by parts [each] equal to an inch. And therefore, one infinite number will be twelve times greater than another [NS: which is no less absurd]. [iii] Finally, if we conceive that from one point of a certain infinite quantity two lines, say AB and AC, are extended to infinity, it is certain that, although in the beginning they are a certain, determinate distance apart, the distance between B and C is continuously increased, and at last, from being determinate, it will become indeterminable. Since these absurdities follow – so they think – from the fact that an infinite quantity is supposed, they infer that corporeal substance must be finite, and consequently cannot pertain to God's essence.

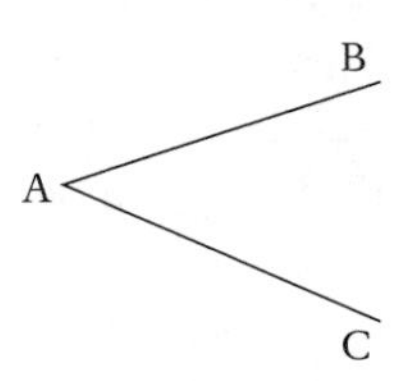

[III.] Their *second* argument is also drawn from God's supreme perfection. For God, they say, since he is a supremely perfect being, cannot be acted on. But corporeal substance, since it is divisible, can be acted on. It follows, therefore, that it does not pertain to God's essence.

[IV.] These are the arguments which I find Authors using, to try to show that corporeal substance is unworthy of the divine nature, and cannot pertain to it. But anyone who is properly attentive will find that I have already replied to them, since these arguments are founded only on their supposition that corporeal substance is composed of parts, which I have already (P12 and P13C) shown to be absurd. And then anyone who wishes to consider the matter rightly will see that all those absurdities (*if indeed they are all absurd, which I am not now disputing*), from which they wish to infer that extended substance is finite, do not follow at all from the fact that an infinite quantity is supposed, but from the fact that they suppose an infinite quantity to be measurable and composed of finite parts. So from the absurdities which follow from that they can infer only that infinite quantity is not measurable, and that it is not composed of finite parts. This is the same thing we have already demonstrated above (P12, etc.). So the weapon they aim at us, they really turn against themselves. If, therefore, they still wish to infer from this absurdity of theirs that extended substance must be finite, they are indeed doing nothing more than if someone feigned that a circle has the properties of a square, and inferred from that the circle has no center, from which all lines drawn to the circumference are equal. For corporeal substance, which cannot be conceived except as infinite, unique, and indivisible (see P8, 5, and 12), they conceive to be composed of finite parts, to be many, and to be divisible, in order to infer that it is finite.

So also others, after they feign that a line is composed of points, know how to invent many arguments, by which they show that a line cannot be divided to infinity. And indeed it is no less absurd to assert that corporeal substance is composed of bodies, *or* parts, than that a body is composed of surfaces, the surfaces of lines, and the lines, finally, of points. All those who know that clear reason is infallible must confess this – particularly those who deny that there is a vacuum. For if corporeal substance could be so divided that its parts were really distinct, why, then, could one part not be annihilated, the rest remaining connected with one another as before? And why must they all be so fitted together that there is no vacuum? Truly, of things which are really distinct from one another, one can be, and remain in its condition, without the other. Since, therefore, there is no vacuum in Nature (a subject I discuss elsewhere), but all its parts must so concur that there is no vacuum, it follows also that they cannot be really distinguished, that is, that corporeal substance, insofar as it is a substance, cannot be divided.

[V.] If someone should now ask why we are, by nature, so inclined to divide quantity, I shall answer that we conceive quantity in two ways: abstractly, *or* superficially, as we [NS: commonly] imagine it, or as substance, which is done by the intellect alone [NS: without the help of the imagination]. So if we attend to quantity as it is in the imagination, which we do often and more easily, it will be found to be finite, divisible, and composed of parts; but if we attend to it as it is in the intellect, and conceive it insofar as it is a substance, which happens [NS: seldom and] with great difficulty, then (as we have already sufficiently demonstrated) it will be found to be infinite, unique, and indivisible.

This will be sufficiently plain to everyone who knows how to distinguish between the intellect and the imagination – particularly if it is also noted that matter is everywhere the same, and that parts are distinguished in it only insofar as we conceive matter to be affected in different ways, so that its parts are distinguished only modally, but not really.

For example, we conceive that water is divided and its parts separated from one another – insofar as it is water, but not insofar as it is corporeal substance. For insofar as it is substance, it is neither separated nor divided. Again, water, insofar as it is water, is generated and corrupted, but insofar as it is substance, it is neither generated nor corrupted.

[VI.] And with this I think I have replied to the second argument also, since it is based on the supposition that matter, insofar as it is substance, is divisible, and composed of parts. Even if this [reply] were not [sufficient], I do not know why [matter] would be unworthy of the divine nature. For (by P14) apart from God there can be no substance by which [the divine nature] would be acted on. All things, I say, are in God, and all things that happen, happen only through the laws of God's infinite nature and follow (as I shall show) from the necessity of his essence. So it cannot be said in any way that God is acted on by another, or that extended substance is unworthy of the divine nature, even if it is supposed to be divisible, so long as it is granted to be eternal and infinite. But enough of this for the present.

P16: *From the necessity of the divine nature there must follow infinitely many things in infinitely many modes, (i.e., everything which can fall under an infinite intellect).*

Dem.: This proposition must be plain to anyone, provided he attends to the fact that the intellect infers from the given definition of any thing a number of properties that really do follow necessarily from it (that is, from the very essence of the thing); and that it infers more properties the more the definition of the thing expresses reality, that is, the more reality the essence of the defined thing involves. But since the divine nature has absolutely infinite attributes (by D6), each of which also expresses an essence infinite in its own kind, from its necessity there must follow infinitely many things in infinite modes (i.e., everything which can fall under an infinite intellect), q.e.d.

Cor. 1: From this it follows that God is the efficient cause of all things which can fall under an infinite intellect.

Cor. 2: It follows, second, that God is a cause through himself and not an accidental cause.

Cor. 3: It follows, third, that God is absolutely the first cause.

P17: *God acts from the laws of his nature alone, and is compelled by no one.*

Dem.: We have just shown (P16) that from the necessity of the divine nature alone, or (what is the same thing) from the laws of his nature alone, absolutely infite things follow, and in P15 we have demonstrated that nothing can be or be conceived without God, but that all things are in God. So there can be nothing outside him by which he is determined or compelled to act. Therefore, God acts from the laws of his nature alone, and is compelled by no one, q.e.d.

Cor. 1: From this it follows, first, that there is no cause, either extrinsically or intrinsically, which prompts God to action, except the perfection of his nature.

Cor. 2: It follows, second, that God alone is a free cause. For God alone exists only from the necessity of his nature (by P11 and P14C1), and acts from the necessity of his nature (by P17). Therefore (by D7) God alone is a free cause, q.e.d.

Schol.: [I.] Others think that God is a free cause because he can (so they think) bring it about that the things which we have said follow from his nature (i.e., which are in his power) do not happen or are not produced by him. But this is the same as if they were to say that God can bring it about that it would not follow from the nature of a triangle that its three angles are equal to two right angles; *or* that from a given cause the effect would not follow – which is absurd.

Further, I shall show later, without the aid of this proposition, that neither intellect nor will pertain to God's nature. Of course I know there are many who think they can demonstrate that a supreme intellect and a free will pertain to God's nature. For they say they know nothing they can ascribe to God more perfect than what is the highest perfection in us.

Moreover, though they conceive God to actually understand in the highest degree, they still do not believe that he can bring it about that all the things he actually understands exist. For they think that in that way they would destroy God's power. If he had created all the things in his intellect (they say), then he would have been able to create nothing more, which they believe to be incompatible with God's omnipotence. So they prefer to maintain that God is indifferent to all things, not creating anything except what he has decreed to create by some absolute will.

But I think I have shown clearly enough (see P16) that from God's supreme power, *or* infinite nature, infinitely many things in infinitely many modes, that is, all things, have necessarily flowed, or always follow, by the same necessity and in the same way as from the nature of a triangle it follows, from eternity and to eternity, that its three angles are equal to two right angles. So God's omnipotence has been actual from eternity and will remain in the same actuality to eternity. And in this way, at least in my opinion, God's omnipotence is maintained far more perfectly.

Indeed – to speak openly – my opponents seem to deny God's omnipotence. For they are forced to confess that God understands infinitely many creatable things, which nevertheless he will never be able to create. For otherwise, if he created everything he understood [NS: to be creatable] he would (according to them) exhaust his omnipotence and render himself imperfect. Therefore to maintain that God is perfect, they are driven to maintain at the same time that he cannot bring about everything to which his power extends. I do not see what could be feigned which would be more absurd than this or more contrary to God's omnipotence.

[II.] Further – to say something here also about the intellect and will which we commonly attribute to God – if will and intellect do pertain to the eternal essence of God, we must of course understand by each of these attributes something different from what men commonly understand. For the intellect and will which would constitute God's essence would have to differ entirely from our intellect and will, and could not agree with them in anything except the name. They would not agree with one another any more than do the dog that is a heavenly constellation and the dog that is a barking animal. I shall demonstrate this.

If intellect pertains to the divine nature, it will not be able to be (like our intellect) by nature either posterior to (as most would have it), or simultaneous with, the things understood, since God is prior in causality to all things (by P16C1). On the contrary, the truth and formal essence of things is what it is because it exists objectively in that way in God's intellect. So God's intellect, insofar as it is conceived to constitute God's essence, is really the cause both of the essence and of the existence of things. This seems also to have been noticed by those who asserted that God's intellect, will, and power are one and the same.

Therefore, since God's intellect is the only cause of things (viz. as we have shown, both of their essence and of their existence), he must necessarily differ from them both as to his essence and as to his existence. For what is caused differs from its cause precisely in what it has from the cause [NS: for that reason it is called the effect of such a cause]. For example, a man is the cause of the existence of another man, but not of his essence, for the latter is an eternal truth. Hence, they can agree entirely according to their essence. But in existing they must differ. And for that reason, if the existence of one perishes, the other's existence will not thereby perish. But if the essence of one could be destroyed, and become false, the other's essence would also be destroyed [NS: and become false].

So the thing that is the cause both of the essence and of the existence of some effect, must differ from such an effect, both as to its essence and as to its existence. But God's intellect is the cause both of the essence and of the existence of our intellect. Therefore, God's intellect, insofar as it is conceived to constitute the divine essence, differs from our intellect both as to its essence and as to its existence, and cannot agree with it in anything except in name, as we supposed. The proof proceeds in the same way concerning the will, as anyone can easily see.

P18: *God is the immanent, not the transitive, cause of all things.*

Dem.: Everything that is, is in God, and must be conceived through God (by P15), and so (by P16C1) God is the cause of [NS: all] things, which are in him. That is the first [thing to be proven]. And then outside God there can be no substance (by P14), that is (by D3), thing which is in itself outside God. That was the second. God, therefore, is the immanent, not the transitive cause of all things, q.e.d.

P19: *God is eternal, or all God's attributes are eternal.*

Dem.: For God (by D6) is substance, which (by P11) necessarily exists, that is (by P7), to whose nature it pertains to exist, or (what is the same) from whose definition it follows that he exists; and therefore (by D8), he is eternal.

Next, by God's attributes are to be understood what (by D4) expresses an essence of the divine substance, that is, what pertains to substance. The attributes themselves, I say, must involve it itself. But eternity pertains to the nature of substance (as I have already demonstrated from P7). Therefore each of the attributes must involve eternity, and so, they are all eternal, q.e.d.

Schol.: This proposition is also as clear as possible from the way I have demonstrated God's existence (P11). For from that demonstration, I say, it is established that God's existence, like his essence, is an eternal truth. And then I have also demonstrated God's eternity in another way (*Descartes' Principles* IP19), and there is no need to repeat it here.

P20: *God's existence and his essence are one and the same.*

Dem.: God (by P19) and all of his attributes are eternal, that is (by D8), each of his attributes expresses existence. Therefore, the same attributes of God which (by D4) explain God's eternal essence at the same time explain his eternal existence, that is, that itself which constitutes God's essence at the same time constitutes his existence. So his existence and his essence are one and the same, q.e.d.

Cor. 1: From this it follows, first, that God's existence, like his essence, is an eternal truth.

Cor. 2: It follows, second, that God, *or* all of God's attributes, are immutable. For if they changed as to their existence, they would also (by P20) change as to their essence, that is (as is known through itself), from being true become false, which is absurd.

P21: *All the things which follow from the absolute nature of any of God's attributes have always had to exist and be infinite,* or *are, through the same attribute, eternal and infinite.*

Dem.: If you deny this, then conceive (if you can) that in some attribute of God there follows from its absolute nature something that is finite and has a determinate existence, *or* duration, for example, God's idea in thought. Now since thought is supposed to be an attribute of God, it is necessarily (by P11) infinite by its nature. But insofar as it has God's idea, [thought] is supposed to be finite. But (by D2) [thought] cannot be conceived to be finite unless it is determined through thought itself. But [thought can] not [be determined] through thought itself, insofar as it constitutes God's idea, for to that extent [thought] is supposed to be finite. Therefore, [thought must be determined] through thought insofar as it does not constitute God's idea, which [thought] nevertheless (by P11) must necessarily exist. Therefore, there is thought which does not constitute God's idea, and on that account God's idea does not follow necessarily from the nature [of this thought] insofar as it is absolute thought (for [thought] is conceived both as constituting God's idea and as not constituting it). [That God's idea does not follow from thought, insofar as it is absolute thought] is contrary to the hypothesis. So if God's idea in thought, or anything else in any attribute of God (for it does not matter what example is taken, since the demonstration is universal), follows from the necessity of the absolute nature of the attribute itself, it must necessarily be infinite. This was the first thing to be proven.

Next, what follows in this way from the necessity of the nature of any attribute cannot have a determinate [NS: existence, or] duration. For if you deny this, then suppose there is, in some attribute of God, a thing which follows from the necessity of the nature of that attribute – for example, God's idea in thought – and suppose that at some time [this idea] did not exist or will not exist. But since thought is supposed to be an attribute of God, it must exist necessarily and be immutable (by P11 and P20C2). So beyond the limits of the duration of God's idea (for it is supposed that at some time [this idea] did not exist or will not exist) thought will have to exist without God's idea. But this is contrary to the hypothesis, for it is supposed that God's idea follows necessarily from the given thought. Therefore, God's idea in thought, or anything else which follows necessarily from the absolute nature of some attribute of God, cannot have a determinate duration, but through the same attribute is eternal. This was the second thing [NS: to be proven]. Note that the same is to be affirmed of any thing which, in some attribute of God, follows necessarily from God's absolute nature.

P22: *Whatever follows from some attribute of God insofar as it is modified by a modification which, through the same attribute, exists necessarily and is infinite, must also exist necessarily and be infinite.*

Dem.: The demonstration of this proposition proceeds in the same way as the demonstration of the preceding one.

P23: *Every mode which exists necessarily and is infinite has necessarily had to follow either from the absolute nature of some attribute of God, or from some attribute, modified by a modification which exists necessarily and is infinite.*

Dem.: For a mode is in another, through which it must be conceived (by D5), that is (by P15), it is in God alone, and can be conceived through God alone. So if a mode is conceived to exist necessarily and be infinite, [its necessary existence and infinity] must necessarily be inferred, *or* perceived through some attribute of God, insofar as that attribute is conceived to express infinity and necessity of existence, *or* (what is the same, by D8) eternity, that is (by D6 and P19), insofar as it is considered absolutely. Therefore, the mode, which exists necessarily and is infinite, has had to follow from the absolute nature of some attribute of God – either immediately (see P21) or by some mediating modification, which follows from its absolute nature, that is (by P22), which exists necessarily and is infinite, q.e.d.

P24: *The essence of things produced by God does not involve existence.*

Dem.: This is evident from D1. For that whose nature involves existence (considered in itself), is its own cause, and exists only from the necessity of its nature.

Cor.: From this it follows that God is not only the cause of things' beginning to exist, but also of their persevering in existing, *or* (to use a Scholastic term) God is the cause of the being of things. For – whether the things [NS: produced] exist or not – so long as we attend to their essence, we shall find that it involves neither existence nor duration. So their essence can be the cause neither of their existence nor of their duration, but only God, to whose nature alone it pertains to exist [, can be the cause] (by P14C1).

P25: *God is the efficient cause, not only of the existence of things, but also of their essence.*

Dem.: If you deny this, then God is not the cause of the essence of things; and so (by A4) the essence of things can be conceived without God. But (by P15) this is absurd. Therefore God is also the cause of the essence of things, q.e.d.

Schol.: This proposition follows more clearly from P16. For from that it follows that from the given divine nature both the essence of things and their existence must necessarily be inferred; and in a word, God must be called the cause of all things in the same sense in which he is called the cause of himself. This will be established still more clearly from the following corollary.

Cor.: Particular things are nothing but affections of God's attributes, *or* modes by which God's attributes are expressed in a certain and determinate way. The demonstration is evident from P15 and D5.

P26: *A thing which has been determined to produce an effect has necessarily been determined in this way by God; and one which has not been determined by God cannot determine itself to produce an effect.*

Dem.: That through which things are said to be determined to produce an effect must be something positive (as is known through itself). And so, God, from the necessity of his nature, is the efficient cause both of its essence and of its existence (by P25 and 16); this was the first thing. And from it the second thing asserted also follows very clearly. For if a thing which has not been determined by God could determine itself, the first part of this [NS: proposition] would be false, which is absurd, as we have shown.

P27: *A thing which has been determined by God to produce an effect, cannot render itself undetermined.*

Dem.: This proposition is evident from A3.

P28: *Every singular thing,* or *any thing which is finite and has a determinate existence, can neither exist nor be determined to produce an effect unless it is determined to exist and produce an effect by another cause, which is also finite and has a determinate existence; and again, this cause also can neither exist nor be determined to produce an effect unless it is determined to exist and produce an effect by another, which is also finite and has a determinate existence, and so on, to infinity.*

Dem.: Whatever has been determined to exist and produce an effect has been so determined by God (by P26 and P24C). But what is finite and has a determinate existence could not have been produced by the absolute nature of an attribute of God; for whatever follows from the absolute nature of an attribute of God is eternal and infinite (by P21). It had, therefore, to follow either from God or from an attribute of God insofar as it is considered to be affected by some mode. For there is nothing except substance and its modes (by A1, D3, and D5) and modes (by P25C) are nothing but affections of God's attributes. But it also could not follow from God, or from an attribute of God, insofar as it is affected by a modification which is eternal and infinite (by P22). It had, therefore, to follow from, or be determined to exist and produce an effect by God or an attribute of God insofar as it is modified by a modification which is finite and has a determinate existence. This was the first thing to be proven.

And in turn, this cause, *or* this mode (by the same reasoning by which we have already demonstrated the first part of this proposition) had also to be determined by another, which is also finite and has a determinate existence; and again, this last (by the same reasoning) by another, and so always (by the same reasoning) to infinity, q.e.d.

Schol.: Since certain things had to be produced by God immediately, namely, those which follow necessarily from his absolute nature, and others (which nevertheless can neither be nor be conceived without God) had to be produced by the mediation of these first things, it follows:

I. That God is absolutely the proximate cause of the things produced immediately by him, and not [a proximate cause] in his own kind, as they say. For God's effects can neither be nor be conceived without their cause (by P15 and P24C).

II. That God cannot properly be called the remote cause of singular things, except perhaps so that we may distinguish them from those things that he has produced immediately, or rather, that follow from his absolute nature. For by a remote cause we understand one which is not conjoined in any way with its effect. But all things that are, are in God, and so depend on God that they can neither be nor be conceived without him.

P29: *In nature there is nothing contingent, but all things have been determined from the necessity of the divine nature to exist and produce an effect in a certain way.*

Dem.: Whatever is, is in God (by P15); but God cannot be called a contingent thing. For (by P11) he exists necessarily, not contingently. Next, the modes of the divine nature have also followed from it necessarily and not contingently (by P16) – either insofar as the divine nature is considered absolutely (by P21) or insofar as it is considered to be determined to act in a certain way (by P28). Further, God is the cause of these modes not only insofar as they simply exist (by P24C), but also (by P26) insofar as they are considered to be determined to produce an effect. For if they have not been determined by God, then (by P26) it is impossible, not contingent, that they should determine themselves. Conversely (by P27) if they have been determined by God, it is not contingent, but impossible, that they should render themselves undetermined. So all things have been determined from the necessity of the divine nature, not only to exist, but to exist in a certain way, and to produce effects in a certain way. There is nothing contingent, q.e.d.

Schol.: Before I proceed further, I wish to explain here – or rather to advise [the reader] – what we must understand by *Natura naturans* and *Natura naturata*. For from the preceding I think it is already established that by *Natura naturans* we must understand what is in itself and is conceived through itself, *or* such attributes of substance as express an eternal and infinite essence, that is (by P14C1 and P17C2), God, insofar as he is considered as a free cause.

But by *Natura naturata* I understand whatever follows from the necessity of God's nature, *or* from any of God's attributes, that is, all the modes of God's attributes insofar as they are considered as things which are in God, and can neither be nor be conceived without God.

P30: *An actual intellect, whether finite or infinite, must comprehend God's attributes and God's affections, and nothing else.*

Dem.: A true idea must agree with its object (by A6), that is (as is known through itself), what is contained objectively in the intellect must necessarily be in Nature. But in Nature (by P14C1) there is only one substance, namely, God, and there are no affections other than those which are in God (by P15) and which can neither be nor be conceived without God (by P15). Therefore, an actual intellect, whether finite or infinite, must comprehend God's attributes and God's affections, and nothing else, q.e.d.

P31: *The actual intellect, whether finite or infinite, like will, desire, love, and the like, must be referred to* Natura naturata, *not to* Natura naturans.

Dem.: By intellect (as is known through itself) we understand not absolute thought, but only a certain mode of thinking, which mode differs from the others, such as desire, love, and the like, and so (by D5) must be conceived through absolute thought, that is (by P15 and D6), it must be so conceived through an attribute of God, which expresses the eternal and infinite essence of thought, that it can neither be nor be conceived without [that attribute]; and so (by P29S), like the other modes of thinking, it must be referred to *Natura naturata*, not to *Natura naturans*, q.e.d.

Schol.: The reason why I speak here of actual intellect is not because I concede that there is any potential intellect, but because, wishing to avoid all confusion, I wanted to speak only of what we perceive as clearly as possible, that is, of the intellection itself. We perceive nothing more clearly than that. For we can understand nothing that does not lead to more perfect knowledge of the intellection.

P32: *The will cannot be called a free cause, but only a necessary one.*

Dem.: The will, like the intellect, is only a certain mode of thinking. And so (by P28) each volition can neither exist nor be determined to produce an effect unless it is determined by another cause, and this Cause again by another, and so on, to infinity. Even if the will be supposed to be infinite, it must still be determined to exist and produce an effect by God, not insofar as he is an absolutely infinite substance, but insofar as he has an attribute that expresses the infinite and eternal essence of thought (by P23). So in whatever way it is conceived, whether as finite or as infinite, it requires a cause by which it is determined to exist and produce an effect. And so (by D7) it cannot be called a free cause, but only a necessary or compelled one, q.e.d.

Cor. 1: From this it follows, first, that God does not produce any effect by freedom of the will.

Cor. 2: It follows, second, that will and intellect are related to God's nature as motion and rest are, and as are absolutely all natural things, which (by P29) must be determined by God to exist and produce an effect in a certain way. For the will, like all other things, requires a cause by which it is determined to exist and produce an effect in a certain way. And although from a given will, *or* intellect infinitely many things may follow, God still cannot be said, on that account, to act from freedom of the will, any more than he can be said to act from freedom of motion and rest on account of those things that follow from motion and rest (for infinitely many things also follow from motion and rest). So will does not pertain to God's nature any more than do the other natural things, but is related to him in the same way as motion and rest, and all the other things which, as we have shown, follow from the necessity of the divine nature and are determined by it to exist and produce an effect in a certain way.

P33: *Things could have been produced by God in no other way, and in no other order than they have been produced.*

Dem.: For all things have necessarily followed from God's given nature (by P16), and have been determined from the necessity of God's nature to exist and produce an effect in a certain way (by P29). Therefore, if things could have been of another nature, or could have been determined to produce an effect in another way, so that the order of Nature was different, then God's nature could also have been other than it is now, and therefore (by P11) that [other nature] would also have had to exist, and consequently, there could have been two or more Gods, which is absurd (by P14C1). So things could have been produced in no other way and no other order, and so on, q.e.d.

Schol. 1: Since by these propositions I have shown more clearly than the noon light that there is absolutely nothing in things on account of which they can be called contingent, I wish now to explain briefly what we must understand by contingent – but first, what [we must understand] by necessary and impossible.

A thing is called necessary either by reason of its essence or by reason of its cause. For a thing's existence follows necessarily either from its essence and definition or from a given efficient cause. And a thing is also called impossible from these same causes – namely, either because its essence, *or* definition, involves a contradiction, or because there is no external cause which has been determined to produce such a thing.

But a thing is called contingent only because of a defect of our knowledge. For if we do not know that the thing's essence involves a contradiction, or if we do know very well that its essence does not involve a contradiction, and nevertheless can affirm nothing certainly about its existence, because the order of causes is hidden from us, it can never seem to us either necessary or impossible. So we call it contingent or possible.

Schol. 2: From the preceding it clearly follows that things have been produced by God with the highest perfection, since they have followed necessarily from a given most perfect nature. Nor does this convict God of any imperfection, for his perfection compels us to affirm this. Indeed, from the opposite, it would clearly follow (as I have just shown), that God is not supremely perfect; because if things had been produced by God in another way, we would have to attribute to God another nature, different from that which we have been compelled to attribute to him from the consideration of the most perfect being.

However, I have no doubt that many will reject this opinion as absurd, without even being willing to examine it – for no other reason than because they have been accustomed to attribute another freedom to God, far different from that we have taught (D7), namely, an absolute will. But I also have no doubt that, if they are willing to reflect on the matter, and consider properly the chain of our demonstrations, in the end they will utterly reject the freedom they now attribute to God, not only as futile, but as a great obstacle to science. Nor is it necessary for me to repeat here what I said in P17S.

Nevertheless, to please them, I shall show that even if it is conceded that will pertains to God's essence, it still follows from his perfection that things could have been created by God in no other way or order. It will be easy to show this if we consider, first, what they themselves concede, namely, that it depends on God's decree and will alone that each thing is what it is. For otherwise God would not be the cause of all things. Next, that all God's decrees have been established by God himself from eternity. For otherwise he would be convicted of imperfection and inconstancy. But since, in eternity, there is neither *when*, nor *before*, nor *after*, it follows, from God's perfection alone, that he can never decree anything different, and never could have, *or* that God was not before his decrees, and cannot be without them.

But they will say that even if it were supposed that God had made another nature of things, or that from eternity he decreed something else concerning Nature and its order, no imperfection in God would follow from that.

Still, if they say this, they will concede at the same time that God can change his decrees. For if God had decreed, concerning Nature and its order, something other than what he did decree, that is, had willed and conceived something else concerning Nature, he would necessarily have had an intellect other than he now has, and a will other than he now has. And if it is permitted to attribute to God another intellect and another will, without any change of his essence and of his perfection, why can he not now change his decrees concerning created things, and nevertheless remain equally perfect? For his intellect and will concerning created things and their order are the same in respect to his essence and his perfection, however his will and intellect may be conceived.

Further, all the philosophers I have seen concede that in God there is no potential intellect, but only an actual one. But since his intellect and his will are not distinguished from his essence, as they all also concede, it follows that if God had another actual intellect, and another will, his essence would also necessarily be other. And therefore (as I inferred at the beginning) if things had been produced by God otherwise than they now are, God's intellect and his will, that is (as is conceded), his essence, would have to be different [NS: from what it now is]. And this is absurd.

Therefore, since things could have been produced by God in no other way, and no other order, and since it follows from God's supreme perfection that this is true, no truly sound reason can persuade us to believe that God did not will to create all the things which are in his intellect, with that same perfection with which he understands them.

But they will say that there is no perfection or imperfection in things; what is in them, on account of which they are perfect or imperfect, and are called good or bad, depends only on God's will. And so, if God had willed, he could have brought it about that what is now perfection would have been the greatest imperfection, and conversely [NS: that what is now an imperfection in things would have been the most perfect]. How would this be different from saying openly that God, who necessarily understands what he wills, can bring it about by his will that he understands things in another way than he does understand them? As I have just shown, this is a great absurdity.

So I can turn the argument against them in the following way. All things depend on God's power. So in order for things to be able to be different, God's will would necessarily also have to be different. But God's will cannot be different (as we have just shown most evidently from God's perfection). So things also cannot be different.

I confess that this opinion, which subjects all things to a certain indifferent will of God, and makes all things depend on his good pleasure, is nearer the truth than that of those who maintain that God does all things for the sake of the good. For they seem to place something outside God, which does not depend on God, to which God attends, as a model, in what he does, and at which he aims, as at a certain goal. This is simply to subject God to fate. Nothing more absurd can be maintained about God, whom we have shown to be the first and only free cause, both of the essence of all things, and of their existence. So I shall waste no time in refuting this absurdity.

P34: *God's power is his essence itself.*

Dem.: For from the necessity alone of God's essence it follows that God is the cause of himself (by P11) and (by P16 and P16C) of all things. Therefore, God's power, by which he and all things are and act, is his essence itself, q.e.d.

P35: *Whatever we conceive to be in God's power, necessarily exists.*

Dem.: For whatever is in God's power must (by P34) be so comprehended by his essence that it necessarily follows from it, and therefore necessarily exists, q.e.d.

P36: *Nothing exists from whose nature some effect does not follow.*

Dem.: Whatever exists expresses the nature, *or* essence of God in a certain and determinate way (by P25C), that is (by P34), whatever exists expresses in a certain and determinate way the power of God, which is cause of all things. So (by P16), from [NS: everything which exists] some effect must follow, q.e.d.

Appendix

With these [demonstrations] I have explained God's nature and properties: that he exists necessarily; that he is unique; that he is and acts from the necessity alone of his nature; that (and how) he is the free cause of all things; that all things are in God and so depend on him that without him they can neither be nor be conceived; and finally, that all things have been predetermined by God, not from freedom of the will *or* absolute good pleasure, but from God's absolute nature, *or* infinite power. Further, I have taken care, whenever the occasion arose, to remove prejudices that could prevent my demonstrations from being perceived. But because many prejudices remain that could, and can, be a great obstacle to men's understanding the connection of things in the way I have explained it, I considered it worthwhile to submit them here to the scrutiny of reason. All the prejudices I here undertake to expose depend on this one: that men commonly suppose that all natural things act, as men do, on account of an end; indeed, they maintain as certain that God himself directs all things to some certain end, for they say that God has made all things for man, and man that he might worship God.

So I shall begin by considering this one prejudice, asking *first* [I] why most people are satisfied that it is true, and why all are so inclined by nature to embrace it. *Then* [II] I shall show its falsity, and *finally* [III] how, from this, prejudices have arisen concerning *good* and *evil*, *merit* and *sin*, *praise* and *blame*, *order* and *confusion*, *beauty* and *ugliness*, and other things of this kind.

[I.] Of course this is not the place to deduce these things from the nature of the human mind. It will be sufficient here if I take as a foundation what everyone must acknowledge: that all men are born ignorant of the causes of things, and that they all want to seek their own advantage, and are conscious of this appetite. From these [assumptions] it follows, *first*, that men think themselves free, because they are conscious of their volitions and their appetite, and do not think, even in their dreams, of the causes by which they are disposed to wanting and willing, because they are ignorant of [those causes]. It follows, *second*, that men act always on account of an end, namely, on account of their advantage, which they want. Hence they seek to know only the final causes of what has been done, and when they have heard them, they are satisfied, because they have no reason to doubt further. But if they cannot hear them from another, nothing remains for them but to turn toward themselves, and reflect on the ends by which they are usually determined to do such things; so they necessarily judge the temperament of the other from their own temperament.

Furthermore, they find – both in themselves and outside themselves – many means that are very helpful in seeking their own advantage, for example, eyes for seeing, teeth for chewing, plants and animals for food, the sun for light, the sea for supporting fish [NS: and so with almost all other things whose natural causes they have no reason to doubt]. Hence, they consider all natural things as means to their own advantage. And knowing that they had found these means, not provided them for themselves, they had reason to believe that there was someone else who had prepared those means for their use. For after they considered things as means, they could not believe that the things had made themselves; but from the means they were accustomed to prepare for themselves, they had to infer that there was a ruler, or a number of rulers, of Nature, endowed with human freedom, who had taken care of all things for them, and made all things for their use.

And since they had never heard anything about the temperament of these rulers, they had to judge it from their own. Hence, they maintained that the gods direct all things for the use of men in order to bind men to them and be held by men in the highest honor. So it has happened that each of them has thought up from his own temperament different ways of worshiping God, so that God might love him above all the rest, and direct the whole of Nature according to the needs of their blind desire and insatiable greed. Thus this prejudice was changed into superstition, and struck deep roots in their minds. This was why each of them strove with great diligence to understand and explain the final causes of all things.

But while they sought to show that Nature does nothing in vain (i.e., nothing not of use to men), they seem to have shown only that Nature and the gods are as mad as men. See, I ask you, how the matter has turned out! Among so many conveniences in Nature they had to find many inconveniences: storms, earthquakes, diseases, and the like. These, they maintain, happen because the gods [NS: (whom they judge to be of the same nature as themselves)] are angry on account of wrongs done to them by men, *or* on account of sins committed in their worship. And though their daily experience contradicted this, and though infinitely many examples showed that conveniences and inconveniences happen indiscriminately to the pious and the impious alike, they did not on that account give up their long-standing prejudice. It was easier for them to put this among the other unknown things, whose use they were ignorant of, and so remain in the state of ignorance in which they had been born, than to destroy that whole construction, and think up a new one.

So they maintained it as certain that the judgments of the gods far surpass man's grasp. This alone, of course, would have caused the truth to be hidden from the human race to eternity, if mathematics, which is concerned not with ends, but only with the essences and properties of figures, had not shown men another standard of truth. And besides mathematics, we can assign other causes also (which it is unnecessary to enumerate here), which were able to bring it about that men [NS: – but very few, in relation to the whole human race –] would notice these common prejudices and be led to the true knowledge of things.

[II.] With this I have sufficiently explained what I promised in the first place [viz. why men are so inclined to believe that all things act for an end]. Not many words will be required now to show that Nature has no end set before it, and that all final causes are nothing but human fictions. For I believe I have already sufficiently established it, both by the foundations and causes from which I have shown this prejudice to have had its origin, and also by P16, P32C1, and C2, and all those [propositions] by which I have shown that all things proceed by a certain eternal necessity of Nature, and with the greatest perfection.

I shall, however, add this: this doctrine concerning the end turns Nature completely upside down. For what is really a cause, it considers as an effect, and conversely [NS: what is an effect it considers as a cause]. What is by nature prior, it makes posterior. And finally, what is supreme and most perfect, it makes imperfect. For – to pass over the first two, since they are manifest through themselves – as has been established in PP21–23, that effect is most perfect which is produced immediately by God, and the more something requires several intermediate causes to produce it, the more imperfect it is. But if the things which have been produced immediately by God had been made so that God would achieve his end, then the last things, for the sake of which the first would have been made, would be the most excellent of all.

Again, this doctrine takes away God's perfection. For if God acts for the sake of an end, he necessarily wants something which he lacks. And though the theologians and metaphysicians distinguish between an end of need and an end of assimilation, they nevertheless confess that God did all things for his own sake, not for the sake of the things to be created. For before creation they can assign nothing except God for whose sake God would act. And so they are necessarily compelled to confess that God lacked those things for the sake of which he willed to prepare means, and that he desired them. This is clear through itself.

Nor ought we here to pass over the fact that the Followers of this doctrine, who have wanted to show off their cleverness in assigning the ends of things, have introduced – to prove this doctrine of theirs – a new way of arguing: by reducing things, not to the impossible, but to ignorance. This shows that no other way of defending their doctrine was open to them. For example, if a stone has fallen from a roof onto someone's head and killed him, they will show, in the following way, that the stone fell in order to kill the man. For if it did not fall to that end, God willing it, how could so many circumstances have concurred by chance (for often many circumstances do concur at once)? Perhaps you will answer that it happened because the wind was blowing hard and the man was walking that way. But they will persist: why was the wind blowing hard at that time? why was the man walking that way at that same time? If you answer again that the wind arose then because on the preceding day, while the weather was still calm, the sea began to toss, and that the man had been invited by a friend, they will press on – for there is no end to the questions which can be asked: but why was the sea tossing? why was the man invited at just that time? And so they will not stop asking for the causes of causes until you take refuge in the will of God, that is, the sanctuary of ignorance.

Similarly, when they see the structure of the human body, they are struck by a foolish wonder, and because they do not know the causes of so great an art, they infer that it is constructed, not by mechanical, but by divine, or supernatural art, and constituted in such a way that one part does not injure another.

Hence it happens that one who seeks the true causes of miracles, and is eager, like an educated man, to understand natural things, not to wonder at them, like a fool, is generally considered an impious heretic and denounced as such by those whom the people honor as interpreters of Nature and the gods. For they know that if ignorance is taken away, then foolish wonder, the only means they have of arguing and defending their authority, is also taken away. But I leave these things, and pass on to what I have decided to treat here in the *third* place.

[III.] After men persuaded themselves that everything which happens, happens on their account, they had to judge that what is most important in each thing is what is most useful to them, and to rate as most excellent all those things by which they were most pleased. Hence, they had to form these notions, by which they explained natural things: *good*, *evil*, *order*, *confusion*, *warm*, *cold*, *beauty*, *ugliness*. And because they think themselves free, those notions have arisen: *praise* and *blame*, *sin* and *merit*. The latter I shall explain after I have treated human nature; but the former I shall briefly explain here.

Whatever conduces to health and the worship of God, they have called *good*; but what is contrary to these, *evil*.

And because those who do not understand the nature of things, but only imagine them, affirm nothing concerning things, and take the imagination for the intellect, they firmly believe, in their ignorance of things and of their own nature, that there is an order in things. For when things are so disposed that, when they are presented to us through the senses, we can easily imagine them, and so can easily remember them, we say that they are well-ordered; but if the opposite is true, we say that they are badly ordered, or confused.

And since those things we can easily imagine are especially pleasing to us, men prefer order to confusion, as if order were anything in Nature more than a relation to our imagination. They also say that God has created all things in order, and so, unknowingly attribute imagination to God – unless, perhaps, they mean that God, to provide for human imagination, has disposed all things so that men can very easily imagine them. Nor will it, perhaps, give them pause that infinitely many things are found which far surpass our imagination, and a great many which confuse it on account of its weakness. But enough of this.

The other notions are also nothing but modes of imagining, by which the imagination is variously affected; and yet the ignorant consider them the chief attributes of things, because, as we have already said, they believe all things have been made for their sake, and call the nature of a thing good or evil, sound or rotten and corrupt, as they are affected by it. For example, if the motion the nerves receive from objects presented through the eyes is conducive to health, the objects by which it is caused are called beautiful; those which cause a contrary motion are called ugly. Those which move the sense through the nose, they call pleasant-smelling or stinking; through the tongue, sweet or bitter, tasty or tasteless; through touch, hard or soft, rough or smooth, and the like; and finally, those which move the ears are said to produce noise, sound, or harmony. Men have been so mad as to believe that God is pleased by harmony. Indeed there are philosophers who have persuaded themselves that the motions of the heavens produce a harmony.

All of these things show sufficiently that each one has judged things according to the disposition of his brain; or rather, has accepted affections of the imagination as things. So it is no wonder (to note this, too, in passing) that we find so many controversies to have arisen among men, and that they have finally given rise to skepticism. For although human bodies agree in many things, they still differ in very many. And for that reason what seems good to one, seems bad to another; what seems ordered to one, seems confused to another; what seems pleasing to one, seems displeasing to another, and so on.

I pass over the [other notions] here, both because this is not the place to treat them at length, and because everyone has experienced this [variability] sufficiently for himself. That is why we have such sayings as "So many heads, so many attitudes," "everyone finds his own judgment more than enough," and "there are as many differences of brains as of palates." These proverbs show sufficiently that men judge things according to the disposition of their brain, and imagine, rather than understand them. For if men had understood them, the things would at least convince them all, even if they did not attract them all, as the example of mathematics shows.

We see, therefore, that all the notions by which ordinary people are accustomed to explain Nature are only modes of imagining, and do not indicate the nature of anything, only the constitution of the imagination. And because they have names, as if they were [notions] of beings existing outside the imagination, I call them beings, not of reason, but of imagination. So all the arguments in which people try to use such notions against us can easily be warded off.

For many are accustomed to arguing in this way: if all things have followed from the necessity of God's most perfect nature, why are there so many imperfections in Nature? why are things corrupt to the point where they stink? so ugly that they produce nausea? why is there confusion, evil, and sin?

As I have just said, those who argue in this way are easily answered. For the perfection of things is to be judged solely from their nature and power; things are not more or less perfect because they please or offend men's senses, or because they are of use to, or are incompatible with, human nature.

But to those who ask "why God did not create all men so that they would be governed by the command of reason?" I answer only "because he did not lack material to create all things, from the highest degree of perfection to the lowest"; or, to speak more properly, "because the laws of his nature have been so ample that they sufficed for producing all things which can be conceived by an infinite intellect" (as I have demonstrated in P16).

These are the prejudices I undertook to note here. If any of this kind still remain, they can be corrected by anyone with only a little meditation. [NS: And so I find no reason to devote more time to these matters, and so on.]

Second Part of the Ethics
Of the Nature and Origin of the Mind

I pass now to explaining those things which must necessarily follow from the essence of God, or the infinite and eternal being – not, indeed, all of them, for we have demonstrated (IP16) that infinitely many things must follow from it in infinitely many modes, but only those that can lead us, by the hand, as it were, to the knowledge of the human mind and its highest blessedness.

Definitions

D1: By body I understand a mode that in a certain and determinate way expresses God's essence insofar as he is considered as an extended thing (see IP25C).

D2: I say that to the essence of any thing belongs that which, being given, the thing is [NS: also] necessarily posited and which, being taken away, the thing is necessarily [NS: also] taken away; or that without which the thing can neither be nor be conceived, and which can neither be nor be conceived without the thing.

D3: By idea I understand a concept of the mind which the mind forms because it is a thinking thing.

Exp.: *I say concept rather than perception, because the word perception seems to indicate that the mind is acted on by the object. But concept seems to express an action of the mind.*

D4: By adequate idea I understand an idea which, insofar as it is considered in itself, without relation to an object, has all the properties, *or* intrinsic denominations of a true idea.

Exp.: *I say intrinsic to exclude what is extrinsic, namely, the agreement of the idea with its object.*

D5: Duration is an indefinite continuation of existing.

Exp.: *I say indefinite because it cannot be determined at all through the very nature of the existing thing, nor even by the efficient cause, which necessarily posits the existence of the thing, and does not take it away.*

D6: By reality and perfection I understand the same thing.

D7: By singular things I understand things that are finite and have a determinate existence. And if a number of individuals so concur in one action that together they are all the cause of one effect, I consider them all, to that extent, as one singular thing.

Axioms

A1: The essence of man does not involve necessary existence, that is, from the order of Nature it can happen equally that this or that man does exist, or that he does not exist.

A2: Man thinks [NS: or, to put it differently, we know that we think].

A3: There are no modes of thinking, such as love, desire, or whatever is designated by the word affects of the mind, unless there is in the same individual the idea of the thing loved, desired, and the like. But there can be an idea, even though there is no other mode of thinking.

A4: We feel that a certain body [NS: our body] is affected in many ways.

A5: We neither feel nor perceive any singular things [NS: or anything of *Natura naturata*], except bodies and modes of thinking.

See the postulates after P13.

P1: *Thought is an attribute of God,* or *God is a thinking thing.*

Dem.: Singular thoughts, *or* this or that thought, are modes which express God's nature in a certain and determinate way (by IP25C). Therefore (by ID5) there belongs to God an attribute whose concept all singular thoughts involve, and through which they are also conceived. Therefore, thought is one of God's infinite attributes, which expresses an eternal and infinite essence of God (see ID6), *or* God is a thinking thing, q.e.d.

Schol.: This proposition is also evident from the fact that we can conceive an infinite thinking being. For the more things a thinking being can think, the more reality, *or* perfection, we conceive it to contain. Therefore, a being which can think infinitely many things in infinitely many ways is necessarily infinite in its power of thinking. So since we can conceive an infinite being by attending to thought alone, thought (by ID4 and D6) is necessarily one of God's infinite attributes, as we maintained.

P2: *Extension is an attribute of God,* or *God is an extended thing.*

Dem.: The demonstration of this proceeds in the same way as that of the preceding proposition.

P3: *In God there is necessarily an idea, both of his essence and of everything which necessarily follows from his essence.*

Dem.: For God (by P1) can think infinitely many things in infinitely many modes, *or* (what is the same, by IP16) can form the idea of his essence and of all the things which necessarily follow from it. But whatever is in God's power necessarily exists (by IP35); therefore, there is necessarily such an idea, and (by IP15) it is only in God, q.e.d.

Schol.: By God's power ordinary people understand God's free will and his right over all things which are, things which on that account are commonly considered to be contingent. For they say that God has the power of destroying all things and reducing them to nothing. Further, they very often compare God's power with the power of kings.

But we have refuted this in IP32C1 and C2, and we have shown in IP16 that God acts with the same necessity by which he understands himself, that is, just as it follows from the necessity of the divine nature (as everyone maintains unanimously) that God understands himself, with the same necessity it also follows that God does infinitely many things in infinitely many modes. And then we have shown in IP34 that God's power is nothing except God's active essence. And so it is as impossible for us to conceive that God does not act as it is to conceive that he does not exist.

Again, if it were agreeable to pursue these matters further, I could also show here that power which ordinary people fictitiously ascribe to God is not only human (which shows that ordinary people conceive God as a man, or as like a man), but also involves lack of power. But I do not wish to speak so often about the same topic. I only ask the reader to reflect repeatedly on what is said concerning this matter in Part I, from P16 to the end. For no one will be able to perceive rightly the things I maintain unless he takes great care not to confuse God's power with the human power or right of kings.

P4: *God's idea, from which infinitely many things follow in infinitely many modes, must be unique.*

Dem.: An infinite intellect comprehends nothing except God's attributes and his affections (by IP30). But God is unique (by IP14C1). Therefore God's idea, from which infinitely many things follow in infinitely many modes, must be unique, q.e.d.

P5: *The formal being of ideas admits God as a cause only insofar as he is considered as a thinking thing, and not insofar as he is explained by any other attribute. That is, ideas, both of God's attributes and of singular things, admit not the objects themselves, or the things perceived, as their efficient cause, but God himself, insofar as he is a thinking thing.*

Dem.: This is evident from P3. For there we inferred that God can form the idea of his essence, and of all the things that follow necessarily from it, solely from the fact that God is a thinking thing, and not from the fact that he is the object of his own idea. So the formal being of ideas admits God as its cause insofar as he is a thinking thing.

But another way of demonstrating this is the following. The formal being of ideas is a mode of thinking (as is known through itself), that is (by IP25C), a mode which expresses, in a certain way, God's nature insofar as he is a thinking thing. And so (by IP10) it involves the concept of no other attribute of God, and consequently (by IA4) is the effect of no other attribute than thought. And so the formal being of ideas admits God as its cause insofar as he is considered only as a thinking thing, and so on, q.e.d.

P6: *The modes of each attribute have God for their cause only insofar as he is considered under the attribute of which they are modes, and not insofar as he is considered under any other attribute.*

Dem.: For each attribute is conceived through itself without any other (by IP10). So the modes of each attribute involve the concept of their own attribute, but not of another one; and so (by IA4) they have God for their cause only insofar as he is considered under the attribute of which they are modes, and not insofar as he is considered under any other, q.e.d.

Cor.: From this it follows that the formal being of things which are not modes of thinking does not follow from the divine nature because [God] has first known the things; rather the objects of ideas follow and are inferred from their attributes in the same way and by the same necessity as that with which we have shown ideas to follow from the attribute of thought.

P7: *The order and connection of ideas is the same as the order and connection of things.*

Dem.: This is clear from IA4. For the idea of each thing caused depends on the knowledge of the cause of which it is the effect.

Cor.: From this it follows that God's [NS: actual] power of thinking is equal to his actual power of acting. That is, whatever follows formally from God's infinite nature follows objectively in God from his idea in the same order and with the same connection.

Schol.: Before we proceed further, we must recall here what we showed [NS: in the First Part], namely, that whatever can be perceived by an infinite intellect as constituting an essence of substance pertains to one substance only, and consequently that the thinking substance and the extended substance are one and the same substance, which is now comprehended under this attribute, now under that. So also a mode of extension and the idea of that mode are one and the same thing, but expressed in two ways. Some of the Hebrews seem to have seen this, as if through a cloud, when they maintained that God, God's intellect, and the things understood by him are one and the same.

For example, a circle existing in Nature and the idea of the existing circle, which is also in God, are one and the same thing, which is explained through different attributes. Therefore, whether we conceive Nature under the attribute of extension, or under the attribute of thought, or under any other attribute, we shall find one and the same order, or one and the same connection of causes, that is, that the same things follow one another.

When I said [NS: before] that God is the cause of the idea, say of a circle, only insofar as he is a thinking thing, and [the cause] of the circle, only insofar as he is an extended thing, this was for no other reason than because the formal being of the idea of the circle can be perceived only through another mode of thinking, as its proximate cause, and that mode again through another, and so on, to infinity. Hence, so long as things are considered as modes of thinking, we must explain the order of the whole of Nature, or the connection of causes, through the attribute of though alone. And insofar as they are considered as modes of extension, the order of the whole of Nature must be explained through the attribute of extension alone. I understand the same concerning the other attributes.

So of things as they are in themselves, God is really the cause insofar as he consists of infinite attributes. For the present, I cannot explain these matters more clearly.

P8: *The ideas of singular things, or of modes, that do not exist must be comprehended in God's infinite idea in the same way as the formal essences of the singular things, or modes, are contained in God's attributes.*

Dem.: This proposition is evident from the preceding one, but is understood more clearly from the preceding scholium.

Cor.: From this it follows that so long as singular things do not exist, except insofar as they are comprehended in God's attributes, their objective being, or ideas, do not exist except insofar as God's infinite idea exists. And when singular things are said to exist, not only insofar as they are comprehended in God's attributes, but insofar also as they are said to have duration, their ideas also involve the existence through which they are said to have duration.

[. . .]

P9: *The idea of a singular thing which actually exists has God for a cause not insofar as he is infinite, but insofar as he is considered to be affected by another idea of a singular thing which actually exists; and of this [idea] God is also the cause, insofar as he is affected by another third [NS: idea], and so on, to infinity.*

Dem.: The idea of a singular thing which actually exists is a singular mode of thinking, and distinct from the others (by P8C and S), and so (by P6) has God for a cause only insofar as he is a thinking thing. But not (by IP28) insofar as he is a thing thinking absolutely; rather insofar as he is considered to be affected by another [NS: determinate] mode of thinking. And God is also the cause of this mode, insofar as he is affected by another [NS: determinate mode of thinking], and so on, to infinity. But the order and connection of ideas (by P7) is the same as the order and connection of causes. Therefore, the cause of one singular idea is another idea, *or* God, insofar as he is considered to be affected by another idea; and of this also [God is the cause], insofar as he is affected by another, and so on, to infinity, q.e.d.

Cor.: Whatever happens in the singular object of any idea, there is knowledge of it in God, only insofar as he has the idea of the same object.

Dem.: Whatever happens in the object of any idea, there is an idea of it in God (by P3), not insofar as he is infinite, but insofar as he is considered to be affected by another idea of [NS: an existing] singular thing (by P9); but the order and connection of ideas (by P7) is the same as the order and connection of things; therefore, knowledge of what happens in a singular object will be in God only insofar as he has the idea of the same object, q.e.d.

P10: *The being of substance does not pertain to the essence of man, or substance does not constitute the form of man.*

Dem.: For the being of substance involves necessary existence (by IP7). Therefore, if the being of substance pertained to the essence of man, then substance being given, man would necessarily be given (by D2), and consequently man would exist necessarily, which (by A1) is absurd, q.e.d.

Schol.: This proposition is also demonstrated from IP5, namely, that there are not two substances of the same nature. Since a number of men can exist, what constitutes the form of man is not the being of substance. Further, this proposition is evident from the other properties of substance, namely, that substance is, by its nature, infinite, immutable, indivisible, and so forth, as anyone can easily see.

Cor.: From this it follows that the essence of man is constituted by certain modifications of God's attributes.

Dem.: For the being of substance does not pertain to the essence of man (by P10). Therefore, it is something (by IP15) which is in God, and which can neither be nor be conceived without God, *or* (by IP25C) an affection, *or* mode, which expresses God's nature in a certain and determinate way.

Schol.: Everyone, of course, must concede that nothing can either be or be conceived without God. For all confess that God is the only cause of all things, both of their essence and of their existence. That is, God is not only the cause of the coming to be of things, as they say, but also of their being.

But in the meantime many say that anything without which a thing can neither be nor be conceived pertains to the nature of the thing. And so they believe either that the nature of God pertains to the essence of created things, or that created things can be or be conceived without God – or what is more certain, they are not sufficiently consistent.

The cause of this, I believe, was that they did not observe the [proper] order of philosophizing. For they believed that the divine nature, which they should have contemplated before all else (because it is prior both in knowledge and in nature) is last in the order of knowledge, and that the things which are called objects of the senses are prior to all. That is why, when they contemplated natural things, they thought of nothing less than they did of the divine nature; and when afterwards they directed their minds to contemplating the divine nature, they could think of nothing less than of their first fictions, on which they had built the knowledge of natural things, because these could not assist knowledge of the divine nature. So it is no wonder that they have generally contradicted themselves.

But I pass over this. For my intent here was only to give a reason why I did not say that anything without which a thing can neither be nor be conceived pertains to its essence – namely, because singular things can neither be nor be conceived without God, and nevertheless, God does not pertain to their essence. But I have said that what necessarily constitutes the essence of a thing is that which, if it is given, the thing is posited, and if it is taken away, the thing is taken away, that is, the essence is what the thing can neither be nor be conceived without, and vice versa, what can neither be nor be conceived without the thing.

P11: *The first thing which constitutes the actual being of a human Mind is nothing but the idea of a singular thing which actually exists.*

Dem.: The essence of man (by P10C) is constituted by certain modes of God's attributes, namely (by A2), by modes of thinking, of all of which (by A3) the idea is prior in nature, and when it is given, the other modes (to which the idea is prior in nature) must be in the same individual (by A3). And therefore an idea is the first thing which constitutes the being of a human mind. But not the idea of a thing which does not exist. For then (by P8C) the idea itself could not be said to exist. Therefore, it will be the idea of a thing which actually exists. But not of an infinite thing. For an infinite thing (by IP21 and 22) must always exist necessarily. But (by A1) it is absurd [that this idea should be of a necessarily existing object]. Therefore, the first thing which constitutes the actual being of a human mind is the idea of a singular thing which actually exists, q.e.d.

Cor.: From this it follows that the human mind is a part of the infinite intellect of God. Therefore, when we say that the human mind perceives this or that, we are saying nothing but that God, not insofar as he is infinite, but insofar as he is explained through the nature of the human mind, *or* insofar as he constitutes the essence of the human mind, has this or that idea; and when we say that God has this or that idea, not only insofar as he constitutes the nature of the human mind, but insofar as he also has the idea of another thing together with the human mind, then we say that the human mind perceives the thing only partially, *or* inadequately.

Schol.: Here, no doubt, my readers will come to a halt, and think of many things which will give them pause. For this reason I ask them to continue on with me slowly, step by step, and to make no judgment on these matters until they have read through them all.

P12: *Whatever happens in the object of the idea constituting the human mind must be perceived by the human mind,* or *there will necessarily be an idea of that thing in the mind; that is, if the object of the idea constituting a human mind is a body, nothing can happen in that body which is not perceived by the mind.*

Dem.: For whatever happens in the object of any idea, the knowledge of that thing is necessarily in God (by P9C), insofar as he is considered to be affected by the idea of the same object, that is (by P11), insofar as he constitutes the mind of some thing. Therefore, whatever happens in the object of the idea constituting the human mind, the knowledge of it is necessarily in God insofar as he constitutes the nature of the human mind, that is (by P11C), knowledge of this thing will necessarily be in the mind, *or* the mind will perceive it, q.e.d.

Schol.: This proposition is also evident, and more clearly understood from P7S, which you should consult.

P13: *The object of the idea constituting the human mind is the body,* or *a certain mode of extension which actually exists, and nothing else.*

Dem.: For if the object of the human mind were not the body, the ideas of the affections of the body would not be in God (by P9C) insofar as he constituted our mind, but insofar as he constituted the mind of another thing, that is (by P11C), the ideas of the affections of the body would not be in our mind; but (by A4) we have ideas of the affections of the body. Therefore, the object of the idea which constitutes the human mind is the body, and it (by P11) actually exists.

Next, if the object of the mind were something else also, in addition to the body, then since (by IP36) nothing exists from which there does not follow some effect, there would necessarily (by P12) be an idea in our mind of some effect of it. But (by A5) there is no idea of it. Therefore, the object of our mind is the existing body and nothing else, q.e.d.

Cor.: From this it follows that man consists of a mind and a body, and that the human body exists, as we are aware of it.

Schol.: From these [propositions] we understand not only that the human mind is united to the body, but also what should be understood by the union of mind and body. But no one will be able to understand it adequately, *or* distinctly, unless he first knows adequately the nature of our body. For the things we have shown so far are completely general and do not pertain more to man than to other individuals, all of which, though in different degrees, are nevertheless animate. For of each thing there is necessarily an idea in God, of which God is the cause in the same way as he is of the idea of the human body. And so, whatever we have said of the idea of the human body must also be said of the idea of any thing.

However, we also cannot deny that ideas differ among themselves, as the objects themselves do, and that one is more excellent than the other, and contains more reality, just as the object of the one is more excellent than the object of the other and contains more reality. And so to determine what is the difference between the human mind and the others, and how it surpasses them, it is necessary for us, as we have said, to know the nature of its object, that is, of the human body. I cannot explain this here, nor is that necessary for the things I wish to demonstrate. Nevertheless, I say this in general, that in proportion as a body is more capable than others of doing many things at once, or being acted on in many ways at once, so its mind is more capable than others of perceiving many things at once. And in proportion as the actions of a body depend more on itself alone, and as other bodies concur with it less in acting, so its mind is more capable of understanding distinctly. And from these [truths] we can know the excellence of one mind over the others, and also see the cause why we have only a completely confused knowledge of our body, and many other things which I shall deduce from them in the following [propositions]. For this reason I have thought it worthwhile to explain and demonstrate these things more accurately. To do this it is necessary to premise a few things concerning the nature of bodies.

A1′: All bodies either move or are at rest.

A2′: Each body moves now more slowly, now more quickly.

L1: *Bodies are distinguished from one another by reason of motion and rest, speed and slowness, and not by reason of substance.*

Dem.: I suppose that the first part of this is known through itself. But that bodies are not distinguished by reason of substance is evident both from IP5 and from IP8. But it is more clearly evident from those things which are said in IP15S.

L2: *All bodies agree in certain things.*

Dem.: For all bodies agree in that they involve the concept of one and the same attribute (by D1), and in that they can move now more slowly, now more quickly, and absolutely, that now they move, now they are at rest.

L3: *A body which moves* or *is at rest must be determined to motion or rest by another body, which has also been determined to motion or rest by another, and that again by another, and so on, to infinity.*

Dem.: Bodies (by D1) are singular things which (by L1) are distinguished from one another by reason of motion and rest; and so (by IP28), each must be determined necessarily to motion or rest by another singular thing, namely (by P6), by another body, which (by A1′) either moves or is at rest. But this body also (by the same reasoning) could not move or be at rest if it had not been determined by another to motion or rest, and this again (by the same reasoning) by another, and so on, to infinity, q.e.d.

Cor.: From this it follows that a body in motion moves until it is determined by another body to rest; and that a body at rest also remains at rest until it is determined to motion by another.

This is also known through itself. For when I suppose that body A, say, is at rest, and do not attend to any other body in motion, I can say nothing about body A except that it is at rest. If afterwards it happens that body A moves, that of course could not have come about from the fact that it was at rest. For from that nothing else could follow but that body A would be at rest.

If, on the other hand, A is supposed to move, then as often as we attend only to A, we shall be able to affirm nothing concerning it except that it moves. If afterwards it happens that A is at rest, that of course also could not have come about from the motion it had. For from the motion nothing else could follow but that A would move. Therefore, it happens by a thing which was not in A, namely, by an external cause, by which [NS: the body in motion, A] has been determined to rest.

A1″: All modes by which a body is affected by another body follow both from the nature of the body affected and at the same time from the nature of the affecting body, so that one and the same body may be moved differently according to differences in the nature of the bodies moving it. And conversely, different bodies may be moved differently by one and the same body.

A2″: When a body in motion strikes against another which is at rest and cannot give way, then it is reflected, so that it continues to move, and the angle of the line of the reflected motion with the surface of the body at rest which it struck against will be equal to the angle which the line of the incident motion makes with the same surface.

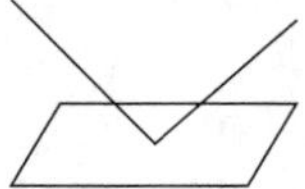

This will be sufficient concerning the simplest bodies, which are distinguished from one another only by motion and rest, speed and slowness. Now let us move up to composite bodies.

Definition: *When a number of bodies, whether of the same or of different size, are so constrained by other bodies that they lie upon one another, or if they so move, whether with the same degree or different degrees of speed, that they communicate their motions to each other in a certain fixed manner, we shall say that those bodies are united with one another and that they all together compose one* body or *individual, which is distinguished from the others by this union of bodies.*

A3″: As the parts of an individual, or composite body, lie upon one another over a larger or smaller surface, so they can be forced to change their position with more or less difficulty; and consequently the more or less will be the difficulty of bringing it about that the individual changes its shape. And therefore the bodies whose parts lie upon one another over a large surface, I shall call *hard*; those whose parts lie upon one another over a small surface, I shall call *soft*; and finally those whose parts are in motion, I shall call *fluid*.

L4: *If, of a body,* or *of an individual, which is composed of a number of bodies, some are removed, and at the same time as many others of the same nature take their place, the [NS: body, or the] individual will retain its nature, as before, without any change of its form.*

Dem.: For (by L1) bodies are not distinguished in respect to substance; what constitutes the form of the individual consists [NS: only] in the union of the bodies (by the preceding definition). But this [NS: union] (by hypothesis) is retained even if a continual change of bodies occurs. Therefore, the individual will retain its nature, as before, both in respect to substance, and in respect to mode, q.e.d.

L5: *If the parts composing an individual become greater or less, but in such a proportion that they all keep the same ratio of motion and rest to each other as before, then the individual will likewise retain its nature, as before, without any change of form.*

Dem.: The demonstration of this is the same as that of the preceding lemma.

L6: *If certain bodies composing an individual are compelled to alter the motion they have from one direction to another, but so that they can continue their motions and communicate them to each other in the same ratio as before, the individual will likewise retain its nature, without any change of form.*

Dem.: This is evident through itself. For it is supposed that it retains everything which, in its definition, we said constitutes its form. [NS: See the definition before L4.]

L7: *Furthermore, the individual so composed retains its nature, whether it, as a whole, moves or is at rest, or whether it moves in this or that direction, so long as each part retains its motion, and communicates it, as before, to the others.*

Dem.: This [NS: also] is evident from the definition preceding L4.

Schol.: By this, then, we see how a composite individual can be affected in many ways, and still preserve its nature. So far we have conceived an individual which is composed only of bodies which are distinguished from one another only by motion and rest, speed and slowness, that is, which is composed of the simplest bodies. But if we should now conceive of another, composed of a number of individuals of a different nature, we shall find that it can be affected in a great many other ways, and still preserve its nature. For since each part of it is composed of a number of bodies, each part will therefore (by L7) be able, without any change of its nature, to move now more slowly, now more quickly, and consequently communicate its motion more quickly or more slowly to the others.

But if we should further conceive a third kind of individual, composed [NS: of many individuals] of this second kind, we shall find that it can be affected in many other ways, without any change of its form. And if we proceed in this way to infinity, we shall easily conceive that the whole of nature is one individual, whose parts, that is, all bodies, vary in infinite ways, without any change of the whole individual.

If it had been my intention to deal expressly with body, I ought to have explained and demonstrated these things more fully. But I have already said that I intended something else, and brought these things forward only because I can easily deduce from them the things I have decided to demonstrate.

Postulates

I. The human body is composed of a great many individuals of different natures, each of which is highly composite.

II. Some of the individuals of which the human body is composed are fluid, some soft, and others, finally, are hard.

III. The individuals composing the human body, and consequently, the human body itself, are affected by external bodies in very many ways.

IV. The human body, to be preserved, requires a great many other bodies, by which it is, as it were, continually regenerated.

V. When a fluid part of the human body is determined by an external body so that it frequently thrusts against a soft part [of the body], it changes its surface and, as it were, impresses on [the soft part] certain traces of the external body striking against [the fluid part].

VI. The human body can move and dispose external bodies in a great many ways.

P14: *The human mind is capable of perceiving a great many things, and is the more capable, the more its body can be disposed in a great many ways.*

Dem.: For the human body (by Post. 3 and 6) is affected in a great many ways by external bodies, and is disposed to affect external bodies in a great many ways. But the human mind must perceive everything which happens in the human body (by P12). Therefore, the human mind is capable of perceiving a great many things, and is the more capable [NS: as the human body is more capable], q.e.d.

P15: *The idea that constitutes the formal being* [esse] *of the human mind is not simple, but composed of a great many ideas.*

Dem.: The idea that constitutes the formal being of the human mind is the idea of a body (by P13), which (by Post. 1) is composed of a great many highly composite individuals. But of each individual composing the body, there is necessarily (by P8C) an idea in God. Therefore (by P7), the idea of the human body is composed of these many ideas of the parts composing the body, q.e.d.

P16: *The idea of any mode in which the human body is affected by external bodies must involve the nature of the human body and at the same time the nature of the external body.*

Dem.: For all the modes in which a body is affected follow from the nature of the affected body, and at the same time from the nature of the affecting body (by A1″ [II/99]). So the idea of them (by IA4) will necessarily involve the nature of each body. And so the idea of each mode in which the human body is affected by an external body involves the nature of the human body and of the external body, q.e.d.

Cor. 1: From this it follows, first, that the human mind perceives the nature of a great many bodies together with the nature of its own body.

Cor. 2: It follows, second, that the ideas which we have of external bodies indicate the condition of our own body more than the nature of the external bodies. I have explained this by many examples in the Appendix of Part I.

P17: *If the human body is affected with a mode that involves the nature of an external body, the human mind will regard the same external body as actually existing, or as present to it, until the body is affected by an affect that excludes the existence or presence of that body.*

Dem.: This is evident. For so long as the human body is so affected, the human mind (by P12) will regard this affection of the body, that is (by P16), it will have the idea of a mode that actually exists, an idea which involves the nature of the external body, that is, an idea which does not exclude, but posits, the existence or presence of the nature of the external body. And so the mind (by P16C1) will regard the external body as actually existing, or as present, until it is affected, and so on, q.e.d.

Cor.: Although the external bodies by which the human body has once been affected neither exist nor are present, the mind will still be able to regard them as if they were present.

Dem.: While external bodies so determine the fluid parts of the human body that they often thrust against the softer parts, they change (by Post. 5) their surfaces with the result (see A2″ after L3) that they are reflected from it in another way than they used to be before, and still later, when the fluid parts, by their spontaneous motion, encounter those new surfaces, they are reflected in the same way as when they were driven against those surfaces by the external bodies. Consequently, while, thus reflected, they continue to move, they will affect the human body with the same mode, concerning which the mind (by P12) will think again, that is (by P17), the mind will again regard the external body as present; this will happen as often as the fluid parts of the human body encounter the same surfaces by their spontaneous motion. So although the external bodies by which the human body has once been affected do not exist, the mind will still regard them as present, as often as this action of the body is repeated, q.e.d.

Schol.: We see, therefore, how it can happen (as it often does) that we regard as present things which do not exist. This can happen from other causes also, but it is sufficient for me here to have shown one through which I can explain it as if I had shown it through its true cause; still, I do not believe that I wander far from the true [cause] since all those postulates which I have assumed contain hardly anything which is not established by experience which we cannot doubt, after we have shown that the human body exists as we are aware of it (see P13C).

Furthermore (from P17C and P16C2), we clearly understand what is the difference between the idea of, say, Peter, which constitutes the essence of Peter's mind, and the idea of Peter which is in another man, say in Paul. For the former directly explains the essence of Peter's body, and does not involve existence, except so long as Peter exists; but the latter indicates the condition of Paul's body more than Peter's nature [NS: see P16C2], and therefore, while that condition of Paul's body lasts, Paul's mind will still regard Peter as present to itself, even though Peter does not exist.

Next, to retain the customary words, the affections of the human body whose ideas present external bodies as present to us, we shall call images of things, though they do not reproduce the [NS: external] figures of things. And when the mind regards bodies in this way, we shall say that it imagines.

And here, in order to begin to indicate what error is, I should like you to note that the imaginations of the mind, considered in themselves contain no error, *or* that the mind does not err from the fact that it imagines, but only insofar as it is considered to lack an idea which excludes the existence of those things which it imagines to be present to it. For if the mind, while it imagined nonexistent things as present to it, at the same time knew that those things did not exist, it would, of course, attribute this power of imagining to a virtue of its nature, not to a vice – especially if this faculty of imagining depended only on its own nature, that is (by ID7), if the mind's faculty of imagining were free.

P18: *If the human body has once been affected by two or more bodies at the same time, then when the mind subsequently imagines one of them, it will immediately recollect the others also.*

Dem.: The mind (by P17C) imagines a body because the human body is affected and disposed as it was affected when certain of its parts were struck by the external body itself. But (by hypothesis) the body was then so disposed that the mind imagined two [or more] bodies at once; therefore it will now also imagine two [or more] at once, and when the mind imagines one, it will immediately recollect the other also, q.e.d.

Schol.: From this we clearly understand what memory is. For it is nothing other than a certain connection of ideas involving the nature of things which are outside the human body – a connection which is in the mind according to the order and connection of the affections of the human body.

I say, *first*, that the connection is only of those ideas which involve the nature of things outside the human body, but not of the ideas which explain the nature of the same things. For they are really (by P16) ideas of affections of the human body which involve both its nature and that of external bodies.

I say, *second*, that this connection happens according to the order and connection of the affections of the human body in order to distinguish it from the connection of ideas which happens according to the order of the intellect, by which the mind perceives things through their first causes, and which is the same in all men.

And from this we clearly understand why the mind, from the thought of one thing, immediately passes to the thought of another, which has no likeness to the first: as, for example, from the thought of the word *pomum* a Roman will immediately pass to the thought of the fruit [viz. an apple], which has no similarity to that articulate sound and nothing in common with it except that the body of the same man has often been affected by these two

[NS: at the same time], that is, that the man often heard the word *pomum* while he saw the fruit.

And in this way each of us will pass from one thought to another, as each one's association has ordered the images of things in the body. For example, a soldier, having seen traces of a horse in the sand, will immediately pass from the thought of a horse to the thought of a horseman, and from that to the thought of war, and so on. But a farmer will pass from the thought of a horse to the thought of a plow, and then to that of a field, and so on. And so each one, according as he has been accustomed to join and connect the images of things in this or that way, will pass from one thought to another.

P19: *The human mind does not know the human body itself, nor does it know that it exists, except through ideas of affections by which the body is affected.*

Dem.: For the human mind is the idea itself, *or* knowledge of the human body (by P13), which (by P9) is indeed in God insofar as he is considered to be affected by another idea of a singular thing, or because (by Post. 4) the human body requires a great many bodies by which it is, as it were, continually regenerated; and [NS: because] the order and connection of ideas is (by P7) the same as the order and connection of causes, this idea will be in God insofar as he is considered to be affected by the ideas of a great many singular things. Therefore, God has the idea of the human body, *or* knows the human body, insofar as he is affected by a great many other ideas, and not insofar as he constitutes the nature of the human mind, that is (by P11C), the human mind does not know the human body.

But the ideas of affections of the body are in God insofar as he constitutes the nature of the human mind, *or* the human mind perceives the same affections (by P12), and consequently (by P16) the human body itself, as actually existing (by P17).

Therefore to that extent only, the human mind perceives the human body itself, q.e.d.

P20: *There is also in God an idea,* or *knowledge, of the human mind, which follows in God in the same way and is related to God in the same way as the idea,* or *knowledge, of the human body.*

Dem.: Thought is an attribute of God (by P1), and so (by P3) there must necessarily be in God an idea both of [NS: thought] and of all of its affections, and consequently (by P11), of the human mind also. Next, this idea, *or* knowledge, of the mind does not follow in God insofar as he is infinite, but insofar as he is affected by another idea of a singular thing (by P9). But the order and connection of ideas is the same as the order and connection of causes (by P7). Therefore, this idea, *or* knowledge, of the mind follows in God and is related to God in the same way as the idea, *or* knowledge, of the body, q.e.d.

P21: *This idea of the mind is united to the mind in the same way as the mind is united to the body.*

Dem.: We have shown that the mind is united to the body from the fact that the body is the object of the mind (see P12 and 13); and so by the same reasoning the idea of the mind must be united with its own object, that is, with the mind itself, in the same way as the mind is united with the body, q.e.d.

Schol.: This proposition is understood far more clearly from what is said in P7S; for there we have shown that the idea of the body and the body, that is (by P13), the mind and the body, are one and the same individual, which is conceived now under the attribute of thought, now under the attribute of extension. So the idea of the mind and the mind itself are one and the same thing, which is conceived under one and the same attribute, namely, thought. The idea of the mind, I say, and the mind itself follow in God from the same power of thinking and by the same necessity. For the idea of the mind, that is, the idea of the idea, is nothing but the form of the idea insofar as this is considered as a mode of thinking without relation to the object. For as soon as someone knows something, he thereby knows that he knows it, and at the same time knows that he knows that he knows, and so on, to infinity. But more on these matters later.

P22: *The human mind perceives not only the affections of the body, but also the ideas of these affections.*

Dem.: The ideas of the ideas of the affections follow in God in the same way and are related to God in the same way as the ideas themselves of the affections (this is demonstrated in the same way as P20). But the ideas of the affections of the body are in the human mind (by P12), that is (by P11C), in God, insofar as he constitutes the essence of the human mind. Therefore, the ideas of these ideas will be in God insofar as he has the knowledge, *or* idea, of the human mind, that is (by P21), they will be in the human mind itself, which for that reason perceives not only the affections of the body, but also their ideas, q.e.d.

P23: *The mind does not know itself, except insofar as it perceives the ideas of the affections of the body.*

[. . .]

P24: *The human mind does not involve adequate knowledge of the parts composing the human body.*

[. . .]

P25: *The idea of any affection of the human body does not involve adequate knowledge of an external body.*

Dem.: We have shown (P16) that the idea of an affection of the human body involves the nature of an external body insofar as the external body determines the human body in a certain fixed way. But insofar as the external body is an Individual which is not related to the human body, the idea, *or* knowledge, of it is in God (by P9) insofar as God is considered to be affected with the idea of another thing which (by P7) is prior in nature to the external body itself. So adequate knowledge of the external body is not in God insofar as he has the idea of an affection of the human body, *or* the idea of an affection of the human body does not involve adequate knowledge of the external body, q.e.d.

P26: *The human mind does not perceive any external body as actually existing, except through the ideas of the affections of its own body.*

Dem.: If the human body is not affected by an external body in any way, then (by P7) the idea of the human body, that is (by P13) the human mind, is also not affected in any way by the idea of the existence of that body, *or* it does not perceive the existence of that external body in any way. But insofar as the human body is affected by an external body in some way, to that extent [the human mind] (by P16 and P16C1) perceives the external body, q.e.d.

Cor.: Insofar as the human mind imagines an external body, it does not have adequate knowledge of it.

Dem.: When the human mind regards external bodies through ideas of the affections of its own body, then we say that it imagines (see P17S); and the mind cannot in any other way (by P26) imagine external bodies as actually existing. And so (by P25), insofar as the mind imagines external bodies, it does not have adequate knowledge of them, q.e.d.

P27: *The idea of any affection of the human body does not involve adequate knowledge of the human body itself.*

Dem.: Any idea of any affection of the human body involves the nature of the human body insofar as the human body itself is considered to be affected with a certain definite mode (see P16). But insofar as the human body is an individual, which can be affected with many other modes, the idea of this [affection] and so on. (See P25D.)

P28: *The ideas of the affections of the human body, insofar as they are related only to the human mind, are not clear and distinct, but confused.*

[. . .]

P29: *The idea of the idea of any affection of the human body does not involve adequate knowledge of the human mind.*

Dem.: For the idea of an affection of the human body (by P27) does not involve adequate knowledge of the body itself, *or* does not express its nature adequately, that is (by P13), does not agree adequately with the nature of the mind; and so (by IA6) the idea of this idea does not express the nature of the human mind adequately, *or* does not involve adequate knowledge of it, q.e.d.

Cor.: From this it follows that so long as the human mind perceives things from the common order of Nature, it does not have an adequate, but only a confused and mutilated knowledge of itself, of its own body, and of external bodies. For the mind does not know itself except insofar as it perceives ideas of the affections of the body (by P23). But it does not perceive its own body (by P19) except through the very ideas themselves of the affections [of the body], and it is also through them alone that it perceives external bodies (by P26). And so, insofar as it has these [ideas], then neither of itself (by P29), nor of its own body (by P27), nor of external bodies (by P25) does it have an adequate knowledge, but only (by P28 and P28S) a mutilated and confused knowledge, q.e.d.

Schol.: I say expressly that the mind has, not an adequate, but only a confused [NS: and mutilated] knowledge, of itself, of its own body, and of external bodies, so long as it perceives things from the common order of Nature, that is, so long as it is determined externally, from fortuitous encounters with things, to regard this or that, and not so long as it is determined internally, from the fact that it regards a number of things at once, to understand their agreements, differences, and oppositions. For so often as it is disposed internally, in this or another way, then it regards things clearly and distinctly, as I shall show below.

P30: *We can have only an entirely inadequate knowledge of the duration of our body.*

Dem.: Our body's duration depends neither on its essence (by A1), nor even on God's absolute nature (by IP21). But (by IP28) it is determined to exist and produce an effect from such [NS: other] causes as are also determined by others to exist and produce an effect in a certain and determinate manner, and these again by others, and so to infinity. Therefore, the duration of our body depends on the common order of Nature and the constitution of things. But adequate knowledge of how things are constituted is in God, insofar as he has the ideas of all of them, and not insofar as he has only the idea of the human body (by P9C). So the knowledge of the duration of our body is quite inadequate in God, insofar as he is considered to constitute only the nature of the human mind, that is (by P11C), this knowledge is quite inadequate in our mind, q.e.d.

P31: *We can have only an entirely inadequate knowledge of the duration of the singular things which are outside us.*

Dem.: For each singular thing, like the human body, must be determined by another singular thing to exist and produce effects in a certain and determinate way, and this again by another, and so to infinity (by IP28). But since (in P30) we have demonstrated from this common property of singular things that we have only a very inadequate knowledge of the duration of our body, we shall have to draw the same conclusion concerning the duration of singular things [outside us], namely, that we can have only a very inadequate knowledge of their duration, q.e.d.

Cor.: From this it follows that all particular things are contingent and corruptible. For we can have no adequate knowledge of their duration (by P31), and that is what we must understand by the contingency of things and the possibility of their corruption (see IP33S1). For (by IP29) beyond that there is no contingency.

P32: *All ideas, insofar as they are related to God, are true.*

Dem.: For all ideas which are in God agree entirely with their objects (by P7C), and so (by IA6) they are all true, q.e.d.

P33: *There is nothing positive in ideas on account of which they are called false.*

Dem.: If you deny this, conceive (if possible) a positive mode of thinking which constitutes the form of error, *or* falsity. This mode of thinking cannot be in God (by P32). But it also can neither be nor be conceived outside God (by IP15). And so there can be nothing positive in ideas on account of which they are called false, q.e.d.

P34: *Every idea which in us is absolute,* or *adequate and perfect, is true.*

Dem.: When we say that there is in us an adequate and perfect idea, we are saying nothing but that (by P11C) there is an adequate and perfect idea in God insofar as he constitutes the essence of our mind, and consequently (by P32) we are saying nothing but that such an idea is true, q.e.d.

P35: *Falsity consists in the privation of knowledge which inadequate,* or *mutilated and confused, ideas involve.*

Dem.: There is nothing positive in ideas which constitutes the form of falsity (by P33); but falsity cannot consist in an absolute privation (for it is minds, not bodies, which are said to err, or be deceived), nor also in absolute ignorance. For to be ignorant and to err are different. So it consists in the privation of knowledge which inadequate knowledge of things, *or* inadequate and confused ideas, involve, q.e.d.

Schol.: In P17S I explained how error consists in the privation of knowledge. But to explain the matter more fully, I shall give [NS: one or two examples]: men are deceived in that they think themselves free [NS. i.e., they think that, of their own free will, they can either do a thing or forbear doing it], an opinion which consists only in this, that they are conscious of their actions and ignorant of the causes by which they are determined. This, then, is their idea of freedom – that they do not know any cause of their actions. They say, of course, that human actions depend on the will, but these are only words for which they have no idea. For all are ignorant of what the will is, and how it moves the body; those who boast of something else, who feign seats and dwelling places of the soul, usually provoke either ridicule or disgust.

Similarly, when we look at the sun, we imagine it as about two hundred feet away from us, an error which does not consist simply in this imagining, but in the fact that while we imagine it in this way, we are ignorant of its true distance and of the cause of this imagining. For even if we later come to know that it is more than six hundred diameters of the earth away from us, we nevertheless imagine it as near. For we imagine the sun so near not because we do not know its true distance, but because an affection of our body involves the essence of the sun insofar as our body is affected by the sun.

P36: *Inadequate and confused ideas follow with the same necessity as adequate, or clear and distinct ideas.*

[. . .]

P37: *What is common to all things* (on this see L2, above) *and is equally in the part and in the whole, does not constitute the essence of any singular thing.*

Dem.: If you deny this, conceive (if possible) that it does constitute the essence of some singular thing, say the essence of B. Then (by D2) it can neither be nor be conceived without B. But this is contrary to the hypothesis. Therefore, it does not pertain to the essence of B, nor does it constitute the essence of any other singular thing, q.e.d.

P38: *Those things which are common to all, and which are equally in the part and in the whole, can only be conceived adequately.*

[. . .]

P39: *If something is common to, and peculiar to, the human body and certain external bodies by which the human body is usually affected, and is equally in the part and in the whole of each of them, its idea will also be adequate in the mind.*

[. . .]

P40: *Whatever ideas follow in the mind from ideas which are adequate in the mind are also adequate.*

Dem.: This is evident. For when we say that an idea in the human mind follows from ideas which are adequate in it, we are saying nothing but that (by P11C) in the divine intellect there is an idea of which God is the cause, not insofar as he is infinite, nor insofar as he is affected with the ideas of a great many singular things, but insofar as he constitutes only the essence of the human mind [NS: and therefore, it must be adequate].

Schol. 1: With this I have explained the cause of those notions which are called *common*, and which are the foundations of our reasoning.

But some axioms, *or* notions, result from other causes which it would be helpful to explain by this method of ours. For from these [explanations] it would be established which notions are more useful than the others, and which are of hardly any use; and then, which are common, which are clear and distinct only to those who have no prejudices, and finally, which are ill-founded. Moreover, we would establish what is the origin of those notions they call *Second*, and consequently of the axioms founded on them, and other things I have thought about, from time to time, concerning these matters. But since I have set these aside for another treatise, and do not wish to give rise to disgust by too long a discussion, I have decided to pass over them here.

But not to omit anything it is necessary to know, I shall briefly add something about the causes from which the terms called *Transcendental* have had their origin – I mean term like

Being, Thing, and Something. These terms arise from the fact that the human body, being limited, is capable of forming distinctly only a certain number of images at the same time (I have explained what an image is in P17S). If that number is exceeded, the images will begin to be confused, and if the number of images the body is capable of forming distinctly in itself at once is greatly exceeded, they will all be completely confused with one another.

Since this is so, it is evident from P17C and P18, that the human mind will be able to imagine distinctly, at the same time, as many bodies as there can be images formed at the same time in its body. But when the images in the body are completely confused, the mind also will imagine all the bodies confusedly, without any distinction, and comprehend them as if under one attribute, namely, under the attribute of Being, Thing, and so forth. This can also be deduced from the fact that images are not always equally vigorous and from other causes like these, which it is not necessary to explain here. For our purpose it is sufficient to consider only one. For they all reduce to this: these terms signify ideas that are confused in the highest degree.

Those notions they call *Universal*, like Man, Horse, Dog, and the like, have arisen from similar causes, namely, because so many images (e.g., of men) are formed at one time in the human body that they surpass the power of imagining – not entirely, of course, but still to the point where the mind can imagine neither slight differences of the singular [men] (such as the color and size of each one, etc.) nor their determinate number, and imagines distinctly only what they all agree in, insofar as they affect the body. For the body has been affected most [NS: forcefully] by [what is common], since each singular has affected it [by this property]. And [NS: the mind] expresses this by the word *man*, and predicates it of infinitely many singulars. For as we have said, it cannot imagine a determinate number of singulars.

But it should be noted that these notions are not formed by all [NS: men] in the same way, but vary from one to another, in accordance with what the body has more often been affected by, and what the mind imagines or recollects more easily. For example, those who have more often regarded men's stature with wonder will understand by the word *man* an animal of erect stature. But those who have been accustomed to consider something else, will form another common image of men – for example, that man is an animal capable of laughter, or a featherless biped, or a rational animal.

And similarly concerning the others – each will form universal images of things according to the disposition of his body. Hence it is not surprising that so many controversies have arisen among the philosophers, who have wished to explain natural things by mere images of things.

Schol. 2: From what has been said above, it is clear that we perceive many things and form universal notions:

I. from singular things which have been represented to us through the senses in a way which is mutilated, confused, and without order for the intellect (see P29C); for that reason I have been accustomed to call such perceptions knowledge from random experience;

II. from signs, for example, from the fact that, having heard or read certain words, we recollect things, and form certain ideas of them, like those through which we imagine the things (P18S); these two ways of regarding things I shall henceforth call knowledge of the first kind, opinion or imagination;

III. finally, from the fact that we have common notions and adequate ideas of the properties of things (see P38C, P39, P39C, and P40). This I shall call reason and the second kind of knowledge.

[IV.] In addition to these two kinds of knowledge, there is (as I shall show in what follows) another, third kind, which we shall call intuitive knowledge. And this kind of knowing proceeds from an adequate idea of the formal essence of certain attributes of God to the adequate knowledge of the [NS: formal] essence of things.

I shall explain all these with one example. Suppose there are three numbers, and the problem is to find a fourth which is to the third as the second is to the first. Merchants do not hesitate to multiply the second by the third, and divide the product by the first, because they have not yet forgotten what they heard from their teacher without any demonstration, or because they have often found this in the simplest numbers, or from the force of the demonstration of P19 in Book VII of Euclid, namely, from the common property of proportionals. But in the simplest numbers none of this is necessary. Given the numbers 1, 2, and 3, no one fails to see that the fourth proportional number is 6 – and we see this much more clearly because we infer the fourth number from the ratio which, in one glance, we see the first number to have to the second.

P41: *Knowledge of the first kind is the only cause of falsity, whereas knowledge of the second and of the third kind is necessarily true.*

Dem.: We have said in the preceding scholium that to knowledge of the first kind pertain all those ideas which are inadequate and confused; and so (by P35) this knowledge is the only cause of falsity. Next, we have said that to knowledge of the second and third kinds pertain those which are adequate; and so (by P34) this knowledge is necessarily true.

P42: *Knowledge of the second and third kinds, and not of the first kind, teaches us to distinguish the true from the false.*

Dem.: This proposition is evident through itself. For he who knows how to distinguish between the true and the false must have an adequate idea of the true and of the false that is (P40S2), must know the true and the false by the second or third kind of knowledge.

P43: *He who has a true idea at the same time knows that he has a true idea, and cannot doubt the truth of the thing.*

Dem.: An idea true in us is that which is adequate in God insofar as he is explained through the nature of the human mind (by P11C). Let us posit, therefore, that there is in God, insofar as he is explained through the nature of the human mind, an adequate idea, A. Of this idea there must necessarily also be in God an idea which is related to God in the same way as idea A (by P20, whose demonstration is universal [NS: and can be applied to all ideas]). But idea A is supposed to be related to God insofar as he is explained through the nature of the human mind; therefore the idea of idea A must also be related to God in the same way, that is (by the same P11C), this adequate idea of idea A will be in the mind itself which has the adequate idea A. And so he who has an adequate idea, *or* (by P34) who knows a thing truly, must at the same time have an adequate idea, *or* true knowledge, of his own knowledge. That is (as is manifest through itself), he must at the same time be certain, q.e.d.

Schol.: In P21S I have explained what an idea of an idea is. But it should be noted that the preceding proposition is sufficiently manifest through itself. For no one who has a true idea is unaware that a true idea involves the highest certainty. For to have a true idea means nothing other than knowing a thing perfectly, *or* in the best way. And of course no one can doubt this unless he thinks that an idea is something mute, like a picture on a tablet, and not a mode of thinking, namely, the very [act of] understanding. And I ask, who can know that he understands some thing unless he first understands it? That is, who can know that he is certain about some thing unless he is first certain about it? What can there be which is clearer and more certain than a true idea, to serve as a standard of truth? As the light makes both itself and the darkness plain, so truth is the standard both of itself and of the false.

By this I think we have replied to these questions: if a true idea is distinguished from a false one, [NS: not insofar as it is said to be a mode of thinking, but] only insofar as it is said to agree with its object, then a true idea has no more reality or perfection than a false one (since they are distinguished only through the extrinsic denomination [NS: and not through the intrinsic denomination]) – and so, does the man who has true ideas [NS: have any more reality or perfection] than he who has only false ideas? Again, why do men have false ideas? And finally, how can someone know certainly that he has ideas which agree with their objects?

To these questions, I say, I think I have already replied. For as far as the difference between a true and a false idea is concerned, it is established from P35 that the true is related to the false as being is to nonbeing. And the causes of falsity I have shown most clearly from P19 to P35S. From this it is also clear what is the difference between the man who has true ideas and the man who has only false ideas. Finally, as to the last, namely, how a man can know that he has an idea which agrees with its object? I have just shown, more than sufficiently, that this arises solely from his having an idea which does agree with its object – *or* that truth is its own standard. Add to this that our mind, insofar as it perceives things truly, is part of the infinite intellect of God (by P11C); hence, it is as necessary that the mind's clear and distinct ideas are true as that God's ideas are.

P44: *It is of the nature of reason to regard things as necessary, not as contingent.*

Dem.: It is of the nature of reason to perceive things truly (by P41), namely (by IA6), as they are in themselves, that is (by IP29), not as contingent but as necessary, q.e.d.

Cor. 1: From this it follows that it depends only on the imagination that we regard things as contingent, both in respect to the past and in respect to the future.

Schol.: I shall explain briefly how this happens. We have shown above (by P17 and P17C) that even though things do not exist, the mind still imagines them always as present to itself, unless causes occur which exclude their present existence. Next, we have shown (P18) that if the human body has once been affected by two external bodies at the same time, then afterwards, when the mind imagines one of them, it will immediately recollect the other also, that is, it will regard both as present to itself unless causes occur which exclude their present existence. Moreover, no one doubts but what we also imagine time, namely, from the fact that we imagine some bodies to move more slowly than others, or more quickly, or with the same speed.

Let us suppose, then, a child, who saw Peter for the first time yesterday, in the morning, but saw Paul at noon, and Simon in the evening, and today again saw Peter in the morning. It is clear from P18 that as soon as he sees the morning light, he will immediately imagine the sun taking the same course through the sky as he saw on the preceding day, *or* he will imagine the whole day, and Peter together with the morning, Paul with noon, and Simon with the evening. That is, he will imagine the existence of Paul and of Simon with a relation to future time. On the other hand, if he sees Simon in the evening, he will relate Paul and Peter to the time past, by imagining them together with past time. And he will do this more uniformly, the more often he has seen them in this same order.

But if it should happen at some time that on some other evening he sees James instead of Simon, then on the following morning he will imagine now Simon, now James, together with the evening time, but not both at once. For it is supposed that he has seen one or the other of them in the evening, but not both at once. His imagination, therefore, will vacillate and he will imagine now this one, now that one, with the future evening time, that is, he will regard neither of them as certainly future, but both of them as contingently future.

And this vacillation of the imagination will be the same if the imagination is of things we regard in the same way with relation to past time or to present time. Consequently we shall imagine things as contingent in relation to present time as well as to past and future time.

Cor. 2: It is of the nature of reason to perceive things under a certain species of eternity.

Dem.: It is of the nature of reason to regard things as necessary and not as contingent (by P44). And it perceives this necessity of things truly (by P41), that is (by IA6), as it is in itself. But (by IP16) this necessity of things is the very necessity of God's eternal nature. Therefore, it is of the nature of reason to regard things under this species of eternity.

Add to this that the foundations of reason are notions which explain those things which are common to all, and which (by P37) do not explain the essence of any singular thing. On that account, they must be conceived without any relation to time, but under a certain species of eternity, q.e.d.

P45: *Each idea of each body, or of each singular thing which actually exists, necessarily involves an eternal and infinite essence of God.*

Dem.: The idea of a singular thing which actually exists necessarily involves both the essence of the thing and its existence (by P8C). But singular things (by IP15) cannot be conceived without God – on the contrary; because (by P6) they have God for a cause insofar as he is considered under the attribute of which the things are modes, their ideas must involve the concept of their attribute (by IA4), that is (by ID6), must involve an eternal and infinite essence of God, q.e.d.

Schol.: By existence here I do not understand duration, that is, existence insofar as it is conceived abstractly, and as a certain species of quantity. For I am speaking of the very nature of existence, which is attributed to singular things because infinitely many things follow from the eternal necessity of God's nature in infinitely many modes (see IP16). I am speaking, I say, of the very existence of singular things insofar as they are in God. For even if each one is determined by another singular thing to exist in a certain way, still the force by which each one perseveres in existing follows from the eternal necessity of God's nature. Concerning this, see IP24C.

P46: *The knowledge of God's eternal and infinite essence which each idea involves is adequate and perfect.*

Dem.: The demonstration of the preceding proposition is universal, and whether the thing is considered as a part or as a whole, its idea, whether of the whole or of a part (by P45), will involve God's eternal and infinite essence. So what gives knowledge of an eternal and infinite essence of God is common to all, and is equally in the part and in the whole. And so this knowledge will be adequate, q.e.d.

P47: *The human mind has an adequate knowledge of God's eternal and infinite essence.*

Dem.: The human mind has ideas (by P22) from which it perceives (by P23) itself, (by P19) its own body, and (by P16C1 and P17) external bodies as actually existing. And so (by P45 and P46) it has an adequate knowledge of God's eternal and infinite essence, q.e.d.

Schol.: From this we see that God's infinite essence and his eternity are known to all. And since all things are in God and are conceived through God, it follows that we can deduce from this knowledge a great many things which we know adequately, and so can form that third kind of knowledge of which we spoke in P40S2 and of whose excellence and utility we shall speak in Part V.

But that men do not have so clear a knowledge of God as they do of the common notions comes from the fact that they cannot imagine God, as they can bodies, and that they have joined the name *God* to the images of things which they are used to seeing. Men can hardly avoid this, because they are continually affected by external bodies.

And indeed, most errors consist only in our not rightly applying names to things. For when someone says that the lines which are drawn from the center of a circle to its circumference are unequal, he surely understands (then at least) by a circle something different from what mathematicians understand. Similarly, when men err in calculating, they have certain numbers in their mind and different ones on the paper. So if you consider what they have in mind, they really do not err, though they seem to err because we think they have in their mind the numbers which are on the paper. If this were not so, we would not believe that they were erring, just as I did not believe that he was erring whom I recently heard cry out that his courtyard had flown into his neighbor's hen [NS: although his words were absurd], because what he had in mind seemed sufficiently clear to me [viz. that his hen had flown into his neighbor's courtyard].

And most controversies have arisen from this, that men do not rightly explain their own mind, or interpret the mind of the other man badly. For really, when they contradict one another most vehemently, they either have the same thoughts, or they are thinking of different things, so that what they think are errors and absurdities in the other are not.

P48: *In the mind there is no absolute, or free, will, but the mind is determined to will this or that by a cause which is also determined by another, and this again by another, and so to infinity.*

Dem.: The mind is a certain and determinate mode of thinking (by P11), and so (by IP17C2) cannot be a free cause of its own actions, *or* cannot have an absolute faculty of willing and not willing. Rather, it must be determined to willing this or that (by IP28) by a cause which is also determined by another, and this cause again by another, and so on, q.e.d.

Schol.: In this same way it is also demonstrated that there is in the mind no absolute faculty of understanding, desiring, loving, and the like. From this it follows that these and similar faculties are either complete fictions or nothing but metaphysical beings, *or* universals, which we are used to forming from particulars. So intellect and will are to this or that idea, or to this or that volition as 'stone-ness' is to this or that stone, or man to Peter or Paul.

We have explained the cause of men's thinking themselves free in the Appendix of Part I. But before I proceed further, it should be noted here that by will I understand a faculty of affirming and denying, and not desire. I say that I understand the faculty by which the mind affirms or denies something true or something false, and not the desire by which the mind wants a thing or avoids it.

But after we have demonstrated that these faculties are universal notions which are not distinguished from the singulars from which we form them, we must now investigate whether the volitions themselves are anything beyond the very ideas of things. We must investigate, I say, whether there is any other affirmation or negation in the mind except that which the idea involves, insofar as it is an idea – on this see the following proposition and also D3 – so that our thought does not fall into pictures. For by ideas I understand, not the images which are formed at the back of the eye (and, if you like, in the middle of the brain), but concepts of thought [NS: or the objective being of a thing insofar as it consists only in thought].

P49: *In the mind there is no volition,* or *affirmation and negation, except that which the idea involves insofar as it is an idea.*

Dem.: In the mind (by P48) there is no absolute faculty of willing and not willing, but only singular volitions, namely, this and that affirmation, and this and that negation. Let us conceive, therefore, some singular volition, say a mode of thinking by which the mind affirms that the three angles of a triangle are equal to two right angles.

This affirmation involves the concept, *or* idea, of the triangle, that is, it cannot be conceived without the idea of the triangle. For to say that A must involve the concept of B is the same as to say that A cannot be conceived without B. Further, this affirmation (by A3) also cannot be without the idea of the triangle. Therefore, this affirmation can neither be nor be conceived without the idea of the triangle.

Next, this idea of the triangle must involve this same affirmation, namely, that its three angles equal two right angles. So conversely, this idea of the triangle also can neither be nor be conceived without this affirmation.

So (by D2) this affirmation pertains to the essence of the idea of the triangle and is nothing beyond it. And what we have said concerning this volition (since we have selected it at random), must also be said concerning any volition, namely, that it is nothing apart from the idea, q.e.d.

Cor.: The will and the intellect are one and the same.

Dem.: The will and the intellect are nothing apart from the singular volitions and ideas themselves (by P48 and P48S). But the singular volitions and ideas are one and the same (by P49). Therefore the will and the intellect are one and the same, q.e.d.

Schol.: [I.] By this we have removed what is commonly maintained to be the cause of error. Moreover, we have shown above that falsity consists only in the privation which mutilated and confused ideas involve. So a false idea, insofar as it is false, does not involve certainty. When we say that a man rests in false ideas, and does not doubt them, we do not, on that account, say that he is certain, but only that he does not doubt, or that he rests in false ideas because there are no causes to bring it about that his imagination wavers [NS: or to cause him to doubt them]. On this, see P44S.

Therefore, however stubbornly a man may cling to something false [NS: so that we cannot in any way make him doubt it], we shall still never say that he is certain of it. For by certainty we understand something positive (see P43 and P43S), not the privation of doubt. But by the privation of certainty, we understand falsity.

However, to explain the preceding proposition more fully, there remain certain things I must warn you of. And then I must reply to the objections which can be made against this doctrine of ours. And finally, to remove every uneasiness, I thought it worthwhile to indicate some of the advantages of this doctrine. Some, I say – for the most important ones will be better understood from what we shall say in Part V.

[II.] I begin, therefore, by warning my readers, first, to distinguish accurately between an idea, *or* concept, of the mind, and the images of things which we imagine. And then it is necessary to distinguish between ideas and the words by which we signify things. For because many people either completely confuse these three – ideas, images, and words – or do not distinguish them accurately enough, or carefully enough, they have been completely ignorant of this doctrine concerning the will. But it is quite necessary to know it, both for the sake of speculation and in order to arrange one's life wisely.

Indeed, those who think that ideas consist in images which are formed in us from encounters with [NS: external] bodies, are convinced that those ideas of things [NS: which can make no trace in our brains, or] of which we can form no similar image [NS: in our brain] are not ideas, but only fictions which we feign from a free choice of the will. They look on ideas, therefore, as mute pictures on a panel, and preoccupied with this prejudice, do not see that an idea, insofar as it is an idea, involves an affirmation or negation.

And then, those who confuse words with the idea, or with the very affirmation which the idea involves, think that they can will something contrary to what they are aware of, when they only affirm or deny with words something contrary to what they are aware of. But these prejudices can easily be put aside by anyone who attends to the nature of thought, which does not at all involve the concept of extension. He will then understand clearly that an idea (since it is a mode of thinking) consists neither in the image of anything, nor in words. For the essence of words and of images is constituted only by corporeal motions, which do not at all involve the concept of thought.

It should suffice to have issued these few words of warning on this matter, so I pass to the objections mentioned above.

[III.A.(i)] The first of these is that they think it clear that the will extends more widely than the intellect, and so is different from the intellect. The reason why they think the will extends more widely than the intellect is that they say they know by experience that they do not require a greater faculty of assenting, *or* affirming, and denying, than we already have, in order to assent to infinitely many other things which we do not perceive – but they do require a greater faculty of understanding. The will, therefore, is distinguished from the intellect because the intellect is finite and the will is infinite.

[III.A.(ii)] Second, it can be objected to us that experience seems to teach nothing more clearly than that we can suspend our judgment so as not to assent to things we perceive. This also seems to be confirmed from the fact that no one is said to be deceived insofar as he perceives something, but only insofar as he assents or dissents. For example, someone who feigns a winged horse does not on that account grant that there is a winged horse, that is, he is not on that account deceived unless at the same time he grants that there is a winged horse. Therefore, experience seems to teach nothing more clearly than that the will, *or* faculty of assenting, is free, and different from the faculty of understanding.

[III.A.(iii)] Third, it can be objected that one affirmation does not seem to contain more reality than another, that is, we do not seem to require a greater power to affirm that what is true, is true, than to affirm that something false is true. But [NS: with ideas it is different, for] we perceive that one idea has more reality, *or* perfection, than another. As some objects are more excellent than others, so also some ideas of objects are more perfect than others. This also seems to establish a difference between the will and the intellect.

[III.A.(iv)] Fourth, it can be objected that if man does not act from freedom of the will, what will happen if he is in a state of equilibrium, like Buridan's ass? Will he perish of hunger and of thirst? If I concede that he will, I would seem to conceive an ass, or a statue of a man, not a man. But if I deny that he will, then he will determine himself, and consequently have the faculty of going where he wills and doing what he wills.

Perhaps other things in addition to these can be objected. But because I am not bound to force on you what anyone can dream, I shall only take the trouble to reply to these objections – and that as briefly as I can.

[III.B.(i)] To the first I say that I grant that the will extends more widely than the intellect, if by intellect they understand only clear and distinct ideas. But I deny that the will extends more widely than perceptions, *or* the faculty of conceiving. And indeed, I do not see why the faculty of willing should be called infinite, when the faculty of sensing is not. For just as we can affirm infinitely many things by the same faculty of willing (but one after another for we cannot affirm infinitely many things at once), so also we can sense, *or* perceive, infinitely many bodies by the same faculty of sensing (viz. one after another [NS: and not at once]).

If they say that there are infinitely many things which we cannot perceive, I reply that we cannot reach them by any thought, and consequently, not by any faculty of willing. But, they say, if God willed to bring it about that we should perceive them also, he would have to give us a greater faculty of perceiving, but not a greater faculty of willing than he has given us. This is the same as if they said that, if God should will to bring it about that we understood infinitely many other beings, it would indeed be necessary for him to give us a greater intellect, but not a more universal idea of being, in order for us to embrace the same infinity of beings. For we have shown that the will is a universal being, *or* idea, by which we explain all the singular volitions, that is, it is what is common to them all.

Therefore, since they believe that this common *or* universal idea of all volitions is a faculty, it is not at all surprising if they say that this faculty extends beyond the limits of the intellect to infinity. For the universal is said equally of one, a great many, or infinitely many individuals.

[III.B(ii)] To the second objection I reply by denying that we have a free power of suspending judgment. For when we say that someone suspends judgment, we are saying nothing but that he sees that he does not perceive the thing adequately. Suspension of judgment, therefore, is really a perception, not [an act of] free will.

To understand this clearly, let us conceive a child imagining a winged horse, and not perceiving anything else. Since this imagination involves the existence of the horse (by P17C), and the child does not perceive anything else which excludes the existence of the horse, he will necessarily regard the horse as present. Nor will he be able to doubt its existence, though he will not be certain of it.

We find this daily in our dreams, and I do not believe there is anyone who thinks that while he is dreaming he has a free power of suspending judgment concerning the things he dreams, and of bringing it about that he does not dream the things he dreams he sees. Nevertheless, it happens that even in dreams we suspend judgment, namely, when we dream that we dream.

Next, I grant that no one is deceived insofar as he perceives, that is, I grant that the imaginations of the mind, considered in themselves, involve no error. But I deny that a man affirms nothing insofar as he perceives. For what is perceiving a winged horse other than affirming wings of the horse? For if the mind perceived nothing else except the winged horse, it would regard it as present to itself, and would not have any cause of doubting its existence, or any faculty of dissenting, unless either the imagination of the winged horse were joined to an idea which excluded the existence of the same horse, or the mind perceived that its idea of a winged horse was inadequate. And then either it will necessarily deny the horse's existence, or it will necessarily doubt it.

[III.B.(iii)] As for the third objection, I think what has been said will be an answer to it too: namely, that the will is something universal, which is predicated of all ideas, and which signifies only what is common to all ideas, namely, the affirmation, whose adequate essence, therefore, insofar as it is thus conceived abstractly, must be in each idea and in this way only must be the same in all, but not insofar as it is considered to constitute the idea's essence; for in that regard the singular affirmations differ from one another as much as the ideas themselves do. For example, the affirmation which the idea of a circle involves differs from that which the idea of a triangle involves as much as the idea of the circle differs from the idea of the triangle.

Next, I deny absolutely that we require an equal power of thinking, to affirm that what is true is true, as to affirm that what is false is true. For if you consider the mind, they are related to one another as being to not-being. For there is nothing positive in ideas which constitutes the form of falsity (see P35, P35S, and P47S). So the thing to note here, above all, is how easily we are deceived when we confuse universals with singulars, and beings of reason and abstractions with real beings.

[III.B.(iv)] Finally, as far as the fourth objection is concerned, I say that I grant entirely that a man placed in such an equilibrium (viz. who perceives nothing but thirst and hunger, and such food and drink as are equally distant from him) will perish of hunger and thirst. If they ask me whether such a man should not be thought an ass, rather than a man, I say that I do not know – just as I also do not know how highly we should esteem one who hangs himself, or children, fools, and madmen, and so on.

[IV.] It remains now to indicate how much knowledge of this doctrine is to our advantage in life. We shall see this easily from the following considerations:

[A.] Insofar as it teaches that we act only from God's command, that we share in the divine nature, and that we do this the more, the more perfect our actions are, and the more and more we understand God. This doctrine, then, in addition to giving us complete peace of mind, also teaches us wherein our greatest happiness, *or* blessedness, consists: namely, in the knowledge of God alone, by which we are led to do only those things which love and morality advise. From this we clearly understand how far they stray from the true valuation of virtue, who expect to be honored by God with the greatest rewards for their virtue and best actions, as for the greatest bondage – as if virtue itself, and the service of God, were not happiness itself, and the greatest freedom.

[B.] Insofar as it teaches us how we must bear ourselves concerning matters of fortune, *or* things which are not in our power, that is, concerning things which do not follow from our nature – that we must expect and bear calmly both good fortune and bad. For all things follow from God's eternal decree with the same necessity as from the essence of a triangle it follows that its three angles are equal to two right angles.

[C.] This doctrine contributes to social life, insofar as it teaches us to hate no one, to disesteem no one, to mock no one, to be angry at no one, to envy no one; and also insofar as it teaches that each of us should be content with his own things, and should be helpful to his neighbor, not from unmanly compassion, partiality, or superstition, but from the guidance of reason, as the time and occasion demand. I shall show this in the Fourth Part.

[D.] Finally, this doctrine also contributes, to no small extent, to the common society insofar as it teaches how citizens are to be governed and led, not so that they may be slaves, but that they may do freely the things which are best.

And with this I have finished what I had decided to treat in this scholium, and put an end to this our Second Part. In it I think that I have explained the nature and properties of the human mind in sufficient detail, and as clearly as the difficulty of the subject allows, and that I have set out doctrines from which we can infer many excellent things, which are highly useful and necessary to know, as will be established partly in what follows.

Fifth Part of the Ethics
Of the Power of the Intellect

P14: *The Mind can bring it about that all the Body's affections*, or *images of things, are related to the idea of God.*

Dem.: There is no affection of the Body of which the Mind cannot form some clear and distinct concept (by P4). And so it can bring it about (by IP15) that they are related to the idea of God, q.e.d.

P15: *He who understands himself and his affects clearly and distinctly loves God, and does so the more, the more he understands himself and his affects.*

Dem.: He who understands himself and his affects clearly and distinctly rejoices (by IIIP53), and this Joy is accompanied by the idea of God (by P14). Hence (by Def. Aff. VI), he loves God, and (by the same reasoning) does so the more, the more he understands himself and his affects, q.e.d.

P16: *This Love toward God must engage the Mind most.*

Dem.: For this Love is joined to all the affections of the Body (by P14), which all encourage it (by P15). And so (by P11), it must engage the Mind most, q.e.d.

P17: *God is without passions, and is not affected with any affect of Joy or Sadness.*

Dem.: All ideas, insofar as they are related to God, are true (by IIP32), i.e. (by IID4), adequate. And so (by Gen. Def. Aff.), God is without passions.

Next, God can pass neither to a greater nor a lesser perfection, (by IP20C2); hence (by Defs. Aff. II, III) he is not affected with any affect of Joy or Sadness, q.e.d.

Cor.: Strictly speaking, God loves no one, and hates no one. For God (by P17) is not affected with any affect of Joy or Sadness. Consequently (by Defs. Aff. VI, VII), he also loves no one and hates no one.

P18: *No one can hate God.*

Dem.: The idea of God which is in us is adequate and perfect (by IIP46, P47). So insofar as we consider God, we act (by IIIP3). Consequently (by IIIP59), there can be no Sadness accompanied by the idea of God, i.e. (by Def. Aff. VII), no one can hate God, q.e.d.

Cor.: Love toward God cannot be turned into hate.

Schol.: But, it can be objected, while we understand God to be the cause of all things, we thereby consider God to be the cause of Sadness. To this I reply that insofar as we understand the causes of Sadness, it ceases (by P3) to be a passion, i.e. (by IIIP59), to that extent it ceases to be Sadness. And so, insofar as we understand God to be the cause of Sadness, we rejoice.

P19: *He who loves God cannot strive that God should love him in return.*

Dem.: If a man were to strive for this, he would desire (by P17C) that God, whom he loves, not be God. Consequently (by IIIP19), he would desire to be saddened, which is absurd (by IIIP28). Therefore, he who loves God, etc., q.e.d.

P20: *This Love toward God cannot be tainted by an affect of Envy or Jealousy: instead, the more men we imagine to be joined to God by the same bond of Love, the more it is encouraged.*

Dem.: This Love toward God is the highest good which we can want from the dictate of reason (by IVP28), and is common to all men (by IVP36); we desire that all should enjoy it (by IVP37). And so (by Def. Aff. XXIII), it cannot be stained by an affect of Envy, nor (by P18 and the Def. of Jealousy, see IIIP35S) by an affect of Jealousy. On the contrary (by IIIP31), the more men we imagine to enjoy it, the more it must be encouraged, q.e.d.

Schol.: Similarly we can show that there is no affect which is directly contrary to this Love and by which it can be destroyed. So we can conclude that this Love is the most constant of all the affects, and insofar as it is related to the Body, cannot be destroyed, unless it is destroyed with the Body itself. What the nature of this Love is insofar as it is related only to the Mind, we shall see later.

And with this, I have covered all the remedies for the affects, *or* all that the Mind, considered only in itself, can do against the affects. From this it is clear that the power of the Mind over the affects consists:

I. In the knowledge itself of the affects (see P4S);

II. In the fact that it separates the affects from the thought of an external cause, which we imagine confusedly (see P2 and P4S);

III. In the time by which the affections related to things we understand surpass those related to things we conceive confusedly, *or* in a mutilated way (see P7);

IV. In the multiplicity of causes by which affections related to common properties or to God are encouraged (see P9 and P11);

V. Finally, in the order by which the Mind can order its affects and connect them to one another (see P10, and in addition, P12, P13, and P14).

But to understand better this power of the Mind over the affects, the most important thing to note is that we call affects great when we compare the affect of one man with that of another, and see that the same affect troubles one more than the other, or when we compare the affects of one and the same man with each other, and find that he is affected, *or* moved, more by one affect than by another. For (by IVP5) the force of each affect is defined by the power of the external cause compared with our own. But the power of the Mind is defined by knowledge alone, whereas lack of power, *or* passion, is judged solely by the privation of knowledge, i.e., by that through which ideas are called inadequate.

From this it follows that that Mind is most acted on, of which inadequate ideas constitute the greatest part, so that it is distinguished more by what it undergoes than by what it does. On the other hand, that Mind acts most, of which adequate ideas constitute the greatest part, so that though it may have as many inadequate ideas as the other, it is still distinguished more by those which are attributed to human virtue than by those which betray man's lack of power.

Next, it should be noted that sickness of the mind and misfortunes take their origin especially from too much Love toward a thing which is liable to many variations and which we can never fully possess. For no one is disturbed or anxious concerning anything unless he loves it, nor do wrongs, suspicions, and enmities arise except from Love for a thing which no one can really fully possess.

From what we have said, we easily conceive what clear and distinct knowledge – and especially that third kind of knowledge (see IIP47S), whose foundation is the knowledge of God itself – can accomplish against the affects. Insofar as the affects are passions, if clear and distinct knowledge does not absolutely remove them (see P3 and P4S), at least it brings it about that they constitute the smallest part of the Mind (see P14). And then it begets a Love toward a thing immutable and eternal (see P15), which we really fully possess (see IIP45), and which therefore cannot be tainted by any of the vices which are in ordinary Love, but can always be greater and greater (by P15), and occupy the greatest part of the Mind (by P16), and affect it extensively.

With this I have completed everything which concerns this present life. Anyone who attends to what we have said in this Scholium, and at the same time, to the definitions of the Mind and its affects, and finally to IIIP1 and P3, will easily be able to see what I said at the beginning of this Scholium, viz. that in these few words I have covered all the remedies for the affects. So it is time now to pass to those things which pertain to the Mind's duration without relation to the body.

P21: *The Mind can neither imagine anything, nor recollect past things, except while the Body endures.*

Dem.: The Mind neither expresses the actual existence of its Body, nor conceives the Body's affections as actual, except while the Body endures (by IIP8C); consequently (by IIP26), it conceives no body as actually existing except while its body endures. Therefore, it can neither imagine anything (see the Def. of Imagination in IIP17S) nor recollect past things (see the Def. of Memory in IIP18S) except while the body endures, q.e.d.

P22: *Nevertheless, in God there is necessarily an idea that expresses the essence of this or that human Body, under a species of eternity.*

Dem.: God is the cause, not only of the existence of this or that human Body, but also of its essence (by IP25), which therefore must be conceived through the very essence of God (by IA4), by a certain eternal necessity (by IP16), and this concept must be in God (by IIP3), q.e.d.

P23: *The human Mind cannot be absolutely destroyed with the Body, but something of it remains which is eternal.*

Dem.: In God there is necessarily a concept, *or* idea, which expresses the essence of the human Body (by P22), an idea, therefore, which is necessarily something that pertains to the essence of the human Mind (by IIP13). But we do not attribute to the human Mind any duration that can be defined by time, except insofar as it expresses the actual existence of the Body, which is explained by duration, and can be defined by time, i.e. (by IIP8C), we do not attribute duration to it except while the Body endures. However, since what is conceived, with a certain eternal necessity, through God's essence itself (by P22) is nevertheless something, this something that pertains to the essence of the Mind will necessarily be eternal, q.e.d.

Schol.: There is, as we have said, this idea, which expresses the essence of the body under a species of eternity, a certain mode of thinking, which pertains to the essence of the Mind, and which is necessarily eternal. And though it is impossible that we should recollect that we existed before the Body – since there cannot be any traces of this in the body, and eternity can neither be defined by time nor have any relation to time – still, we feel and know by experience that we are eternal. For the Mind feels those things that it conceives in understanding no less than those it has in the memory. For the eyes of the mind, by which it sees and observes things, are the demonstrations themselves.

Therefore, though we do not recollect that we existed before the body, we nevertheless feel that our mind, insofar as it involves the essence of the body under a species of eternity, is eternal, and that this existence it has cannot be defined by time *or* explained through duration. Our mind, therefore, can be said to endure, and its existence can be defined by a certain time, only insofar as it involves the actual existence of the body, and to that extent only does it have the power of determining the existence of things by time, and of conceiving them under duration.

P24: *The more we understand singular things, the more we understand God.*

Dem.: This is evident from IP25C.

P25: *The greatest striving of the Mind, and its greatest virtue is understanding things by the third kind of knowledge.*

Dem.: The third kind of knowledge proceeds from an adequate idea of certain attributes of God to an adequate knowledge of the essence of things (see its Def. in IIP40S2), and the more we understand things in this way, the more we understand God (by P24). Therefore (by IVP28), the greatest virtue of the Mind, i.e. (by IVD8), the Mind's power, *or* nature, *or* (by IIIP7) its greatest striving, is to understand things by the third kind of knowledge, q.e.d.

P26: *The more the Mind is capable of understanding things by the third kind of knowledge, the more it desires to understand them by this kind of knowledge.*

Dem.: This is evident. For insofar as we conceive the Mind to be capable of understanding things by this kind of knowledge, we conceive it as determined to understand things by the same kind of knowledge. Consequently (by Def. Aff. I), the more the Mind is capable of this, the more it desires it, q.e.d.

P27: *The greatest satisfaction of Mind there can be arises from this third kind of knowledge.*

Dem.: The greatest virtue of the Mind is to know God (by IVP28), *or* to understand things by the third kind of knowledge (by P25). Indeed, this virtue is the greater, the more the Mind knows things by this kind of knowledge (by P24). So he who knows things by this kind of knowledge passes to the greatest human perfection, and consequently (by Def. Aff. II), is affected with the greatest Joy, accompanied (by IIP43) by the idea of himself and his virtue. Therefore (by Def. Aff. XXV), the greatest satisfaction there can be arises from this kind of knowledge, q.e.d.

P28: *The Striving, or Desire, to know things by the third kind of knowledge cannot arise from the first kind of knowledge, but can indeed arise from the second.*

Dem.: This Proposition is evident through itself. For whatever we understand clearly and distinctly, we understand either through itself, or through something else which is conceived through itself; i.e., the ideas which are clear and distinct in us, *or* which are related to the third kind of knowledge (see IIP40S2), cannot follow from mutilated and confused ideas, which (by IIP40S2) are related to the first kind of knowledge; but they can follow from adequate ideas, *or* (by IIP40S2) from the second and third kind of knowledge. Therefore (by Def. Aff. I), the Desire to know things by the third kind of knowledge cannot arise from the first kind of knowledge, but can from the second, q.e.d.

P29: *Whatever the Mind understands under a species of eternity, it understands not from the fact that it conceives the Body's present actual existence, but from the fact that it conceives the Body's essence under a species of eternity.*

Dem.: Insofar as the Mind conceives the present existence of its Body, it conceives duration, which can be determined by time, and to that extent it has only the power of conceiving things in relation to time (by P21 and IIP26). But eternity cannot be explained by duration (by ID8 and its explanation). Therefore, to that extent the Mind does not have the power of conceiving things under a species of eternity.

But because it is of the nature of reason to conceive things under a species of eternity (by IIP44C2), and it also pertains to the nature of the Mind to conceive the Body's essence under a species of eternity (by P23), and beyond these two, nothing else pertains to the Mind's essence (by IIP13), this power of conceiving things under a species of eternity pertains to the Mind only insofar as it conceives the Body's essence under a species of eternity, q.e.d.

Schol.: We conceive things as actual in two ways: either insofar as we conceive them to exist in relation to a certain time and place, or insofar as we conceive them to be contained in God and to follow from the necessity of the divine nature. But the things we conceive in this second way as true, *or* real, we conceive under a species of eternity, and to that extent they involve the eternal and infinite essence of God (as we have shown in IIP45 and P45S).

P30: *Insofar as our Mind knows itself and the Body under a species of eternity, it necessarily has knowledge of God, and knows that it is in God and is conceived through God.*

Dem.: Eternity is the very essence of God insofar as this involves necessary existence (by ID8). To conceive things under a species of eternity, therefore, is to conceive things insofar as they are conceived through God's essence, as real beings, *or* insofar as through God's essence they involve existence. Hence, insofar as our Mind conceives itself and the Body under a species of eternity, it necessarily has knowledge of God, and knows, etc., q.e.d.

P31: *The third kind of knowledge depends on the Mind, as on a formal cause, insofar as the Mind itself is eternal.*

[. . .]

Schol.: Therefore, the more each of us is able to achieve in this kind of knowledge, the more he is conscious of himself and of God, i.e., the more perfect and blessed he is. This will be even clearer from what follows.

But here it should be noted that although we are already certain that the Mind is eternal, insofar as it conceives things under a species of eternity, nevertheless, for an easier explanation and better understanding of the things we wish to show, we shall consider it as if it were now beginning to be, and were now beginning to understand things under a species of eternity, as we have done up to this point. We may do this without danger of error, provided we are careful to draw our conclusions only from evident premises.

P32: *Whatever we understand by the third kind of knowledge we take pleasure in, and our pleasure is accompanied by the idea of God as a cause.*

[. . .]

Cor.: From the third kind of knowledge, there necessarily arises an intellectual Love of God. For from this kind of knowledge there arises (by P32) Joy, accompanied by the idea of God as its cause, i.e. (by Def. Aff. VI), Love of God, not insofar as we imagine him as present (by P29), but insofar as we understand God to be eternal. And this is what I call intellectual love of God.

P33: *The intellectual Love of God, which arises from the third kind of knowledge, is eternal.*

Dem.: For the third kind of knowledge (by P31 and by IA3) is eternal. And so (by IA3), the Love that arises from it must also be eternal, q.e.d.

Schol.: Although this Love toward God has had no beginning (by P33), it still has all the perfections of Love, just as if it had come to be (as we have feigned in P32C). There is no difference here, except that the Mind has had eternally the same perfections which, in our fiction, now come to it, and that it is accompanied by the idea of God as an eternal cause. If Joy, then, consists in the passage to a greater perfection, blessedness must surely consist in the fact that the Mind is endowed with perfection itself.

P34: *Only while the Body endures is the Mind subject to affects which are related to the passions.*

Dem.: An imagination is an idea by which the Mind considers a thing as present (see its Def. in IIP17S), which nevertheless indicates the present constitution of the human Body more than the nature of the external thing (by IIP16C2). An imagination, then, is an affect (by the gen. Def. Aff.), insofar as it indicates the present constitution of the Body. So (by P21) only while the body endures is the Mind subject to affects which are related to passions, q.e.d.

Cor.: From this it follows that no Love except intellectual Love is eternal.

[. . .]

P35: *God loves himself with an infinite intellectual Love.*

Dem.: God is absolutely infinite (by ID6), i.e. (by IID6), the nature of God enjoys infinite perfection, accompanied (by IIP3) by the idea of himself, i.e. (by IP11 and D1), by the idea of his cause. And this is what we said (P32C) intellectual Love is.

P36: *The Mind's intellectual Love of God is the very Love of God by which God loves himself, not insofar as he is infinite, but insofar as he can be explained by the human Mind's essence, considered under a species of eternity; i.e., the Mind's intellectual Love of God is part of the infinite Love by which God loves himself.*

Dem.: This Love the Mind has must be related to its actions (by P32C and IIIP3); it is, then, an action by which the Mind contemplates itself, with the accompanying idea of God as its cause (by P32 and P32C), i.e. (by IP25C and IIP11C), an action by which God, insofar as he can be explained through the human Mind, contemplates himself, with the accompanying idea of himself [as the cause]; so (by P35), this Love the Mind has is part of the infinite love by which God loves himself, q.e.d.

Cor.: From this it follows that insofar as God loves himself, he loves men, and consequently that God's love of men and the Mind's intellectual Love of God are one and the same.

Schol.: From this we clearly understand wherein our salvation, *or* blessedness, *or* Freedom, consists, viz. in a constant and eternal Love of God, *or* in God's Love for men. And this Love, *or* blessedness, is called Glory in the Sacred Scriptures – not without reason. For whether this Love is related to God or to the Mind, it can rightly be called satisfaction of mind, which is really not distinguished from Glory (by Defs. Aff. XXV and XXX). For insofar as it is related to God (by P35), it is Joy (if I may still be permitted to use this term), accompanied by the idea of himself [as its cause]. And similarly insofar as it is related to the Mind (by P27).

Again, because the essence of our Mind consists only in knowledge, of which God is the beginning and foundation (by IP15 and IIP47S), it is clear to us how our Mind, with respect both to essence and existence, follows from the divine nature, and continually depends on God.

I thought this worth the trouble of noting here, in order to show by this example how much the knowledge of singular things I have called intuitive, *or* knowledge of the third kind (see IIP40S2), can accomplish, and how much more powerful it is than the universal knowledge I have called knowledge of the second kind. For although I have shown generally in Part I that all things (and consequently the human Mind also) depend on God both for their essence and their existence, nevertheless, that demonstration, though legitimate and put beyond all chance of doubt, still does not affect our Mind as much as when this is inferred from the very essence of any singular thing which we say depends on God.

P37: *There is nothing in nature which is contrary to this intellectual Love,* or *which can take it away.*

Dem.: This intellectual Love follows necessarily from the nature of the Mind insofar as it is considered as an eternal truth, through God's nature (by P33 and P29). So if there were something contrary to this Love, it would be contrary to the true; consequently, what could remove this Love would bring it about that what is true would be false. This (as is known through itself) is absurd. Therefore, there is nothing in nature, etc., q.e.d.

Schol.: IVA1 concerns singular things insofar as they are considered in relation to a certain time and place. I believe no one doubts this.

P38: *The more the Mind understands things by the second and third kind of knowledge, the less it is acted on by affects which are evil, and the less it fears death.*

Dem.: The Mind's essence consists in knowledge (by IIP11); therefore, the more the Mind knows things by the second and third kind of knowledge, the greater the part of it that remains (by P23 and P29), and consequently (by P37), the greater the part of it that is not touched by affects which are contrary to our nature, i.e., which (by IVP30) are evil. Therefore, the more the Mind understands things by the second and third kind of knowledge, the greater the part of it that remains unharmed, and hence, the less it is acted on by affects, etc., q.e.d.

Schol.: [. . .] [D]eath is less harmful to us, the greater the Mind's clear and distinct knowledge, and hence, the more the Mind loves God.

Next, because (by P27) the highest satisfaction there can be arises from the third kind of knowledge, it follows from this that the human Mind can be of such a nature that the part of the Mind which we have shown perishes with the body (see P21) is of no moment in relation to what remains. But I shall soon treat this more fully.

P39: *He who has a Body capable of a great many things has a Mind whose greatest part is eternal.*

Dem.: He who has a Body capable of doing a great many things is least troubled by evil affects (by IVP38), i.e. (by IVP30), by affects contrary to our nature. So (by P10) he has a power of ordering and connecting the affections of his Body according to the order of the intellect, and consequently (by P14), of bringing it about that all the affections of the Body are related to the idea of God. The result (by P15) is that it is affected with a Love of God, which (by P16) must occupy, *or* constitute the greatest part of the Mind. Therefore (by P33), he has a Mind whose greatest part is eternal, q.e.d.

Schol.: Because human Bodies are capable of a great many things, there is no doubt but what they can be of such a nature that they are related to Minds which have a great knowledge of themselves and of God, and of which the greatest, *or* chief, part is eternal. So they hardly fear death.

But for a clearer understanding of these things, we must note here that we live in continuous change, and that as we change for the better or worse, we are called happy or unhappy. For he who has passed from being an infant or child to being a corpse is called unhappy. On the other hand, if we pass the whole length of our life with a sound Mind in a sound Body, that is considered happiness. And really, he who, like an infant or child, has a Body capable of very few things, and very heavily dependent on external causes, has a Mind which considered solely in itself is conscious of almost nothing of itself, or of God, or of things. On the other hand, he who has a Body capable of a great many things, has a Mind which considered only in itself is very much conscious of itself, and of God, and of things.

In this life, then, we strive especially that the infant's Body may change (as much as its nature allows and assists) into another, capable of a great many things and related to a Mind very much conscious of itself, of God, and of things. We strive, that is, that whatever is related to its memory or imagination is of hardly any moment in relation to the intellect (as I have already said in P38S).

P40: *The more perfection each thing has, the more it acts and the less it is acted on; and conversely, the more it acts, the more perfect it is.*

Dem.: The more each thing is perfect, the more reality it has (by IID6), and consequently, the more it acts and the less it is acted on. This Demonstration indeed proceeds in the same way in reverse, from which it follows that the more a thing acts, the more perfect it is, q.e.d.

Cor.: From this it follows that the part of the Mind that remains, however great it is, is more perfect than the rest.

For the eternal part of the Mind (by P23 and P29) is the intellect, through which alone we are said to act (by IIIP3). But what we have shown to perish is the imagination (by P21), through which alone we are said to be acted on (by IIIP3 and the gen. Def. Aff.). So (by P40), the intellect, however extensive it is, is more perfect than the imagination, q.e.d.

Schol.: These are the things I have decided to show concerning the Mind, insofar as it is considered without relation to the Body's existence. From them – and at the same time from IP21 and other things – it is clear that our Mind, insofar as it understands, is an eternal mode of thinking, which is determined by another eternal mode of thinking, and this again by another, and so on, to infinity; so that together, they all constitute God's eternal and infinite intellect.

P41: *Even if we did not know that our Mind is eternal, we would still regard as of the first importance Morality, Religion, and absolutely all the things we have shown (in Part IV) to be related to Tenacity and Nobility.*

Dem.: The first and only foundation of virtue, *or* of the method of living rightly (by IVP22C and P24) is the seeking of our own advantage. But to determine what reason prescribes as useful, we took no account of the eternity of the Mind, which we only came to know in the Fifth Part. Therefore, though we did not know then that the Mind is eternal, we still regarded as of the first importance the things we showed to be related to Tenacity and Nobility. And so, even if we also did not know this now, we would still regard as of the first importance the same rules of reason, q.e.d.

Schol.: The usual conviction of the multitude seems to be different. For most people apparently believe that they are free to the extent that they are permitted to yield to their lust, and that they give up their right to the extent that they are bound to live according to the rule of the divine law. Morality, then, and Religion, and absolutely everything related to Strength of Character, they believe to be burdens, which they hope to put down after death, when they also hope to receive a reward for their bondage, that is, for their Morality and Religion. They are induced to live according to the rule of the divine law (as far as their weakness and lack of character allows) not only by this hope, but also, and especially, by the fear that they may he punished horribly after death. If men did not have this Hope and Fear, but believed instead that minds die with the body, and that the wretched, exhausted with the burden of Morality, cannot look forward to a life to come, they would return to their natural disposition, and would prefer to govern all their actions according to lust, and to obey fortune rather than themselves.

These opinions seem no less absurd to me than if someone, because he does not believe he can nourish his body with good food to eternity, should prefer to fill himself with poisons and other deadly things, or because he sees that the Mind is not eternal, *or* immortal, should prefer to be mindless, and to live without reason. These [common beliefs] are so absurd they are hardly worth mentioning.

P42: *Blessedness is not the reward of virtue, but virtue itself; nor do we enjoy it because we restrain our lusts; on the contrary, because we enjoy it, we are able to restrain them.*

Dem.: Blessedness consists in Love of God (by P36 and P36S), a Love which arises from the third kind of knowledge (by P32C). So this Love (by IIIP59 and P3) must be related to the Mind insofar as it acts. Therefore (by IVD8), it is virtue itself. This was the first point.

Next, the more the Mind enjoys this divine Love, *or* blessedness, the more it understands (by P32), i.e. (by P3C), the greater the power it has over the affects, and (by P38) the less it is acted on by evil affects. So because the Mind enjoys this divine Love *or* blessedness, it has the power of restraining lusts. And because human power to restrain the affects consists only in the intellect, no one enjoys blessedness because he has restrained the affects. Instead, the power to restrain lusts arises from blessedness itself, q.e.d.

Schol.: With this I have finished all the things I wished to show concerning the Mind's power over the affects and its Freedom. From what has been shown, it is clear how much the Wise man is capable of, and how much more powerful he is than one who is ignorant and is driven only by lust. For not only is the ignorant man troubled in many ways by external causes, and unable ever to possess true peace of mind, but he also lives as if he knew neither himself, nor God, nor things; and as soon as he ceases to be acted on, he ceases to be. On the other hand, the wise man, insofar as he is considered as such, is hardly troubled in spirit, but being, by a certain eternal necessity, conscious of himself, and of God, and of things, he never ceases to be, but always possesses true peace of mind.

If the way I have shown to lead to these things now seems very hard, still, it can be found. And of course, what is found so rarely must be hard. For if salvation were at hand, and could be found without great effort, how could nearly everyone neglect it? But all things excellent are as difficult as they are rare.

15

Nicolas Malebranche, *The Search After Truth*

Nicolas Malebranche (1638–1715) was the youngest child of a secretary to Louis XIII. He was deformed at birth and had fragile health. After studying theology at the Sorbonne, he joined the congregation of the Oratory. He then studied Descartes's philosophy before publishing *De la recherche de la vérité* (*The Search After Truth*), which was critical of Descartes on a number of points, but essentially Cartesian. One of the points of criticism involved causation. Malebranche denied Descartes's belief that the mind can have an effect on the body, because they are different kinds of things. Malebranche claimed that some disposition of matter was the occasion for God to produce some idea in a person's mind. This view is called "occasionalism." Thus, what looks like causal interaction is merely a correspondence between mental states and bodily states. In 1678 he published an edition of *The Search After Truth* that included sixteen *éclaircissements*, clarifications of some of his doctrines.

In 1680 Malebranche published *Traité de la nature et de la grâce* (*Treatise on Nature and Grace*), which led to a long and bitter debate with Antoine Arnauld, who wrote the fourth set of objections to Descartes's *Meditations*. (See selection 10.) The debate led to Malebranche's *Méditations chrétiennes et métaphysiques* (*Christian and Metaphysical Meditations*), in which the Word, the Second Person of the Trinity, summarizes Malebranche's system and emphasizes the sense in which God is the cause of all things. His *Entretiens sur la métaphysique et la religion* (*Dialogues on Metaphysics and Religion*) is a summary of his major doctrines, especially the vision in God, occasionalism, and the problem of evil.

The selection printed here comes from *The Search After Truth*. It begins with the claim that "everyone agrees" that people see ideas, not things in themselves. (Let the reader beware when a philosopher says that something is obvious or believed by everyone.) According to Malebranche, an idea is the immediate object perceived; it is the object closest to the mind. Of course sometimes, he goes on, "we perceive things that do not exist, and that have never existed."

Everything the soul perceives belongs to two kinds of things: its own operations, for example thoughts and sensations, and the ideas of things that are outside the soul or mind. The latter kind of thing is either spiritual or material. Spiritual things, like minds and God, cannot be joined to material things, because the latter are extended and the former not extended. "In this everyone must agree."

Malebranche criticizes the views of (a) the Aristotelians ("Peripatetics"), according to whom the ideas of bodies come to people from the bodies themselves, (b) those who hold that the soul produces its own ideas, (c) those who hold that people perceive innate ideas, and (d) those who hold that the soul has all the perfections it sees in bodies. Even if Malebranche's criticisms are not compelling, he makes a number of clever points. For example, it is easier to make an angel from nothing than from a stone since a stone is completely unlike an angel. (For Malebranche and other philosophers, angels were immaterial substances; they did not have bodies.)

Only one possible theory remains, namely that the soul is joined to a perfect being "that contains all intelligible perfections, or all the ideas of created beings." Malebranche has a positive argument in favor of this view. Since God created all things, he has to have within himself the ideas of all of these things. Since God is present to our minds, we see these ideas in him. What is seen is not the same as seeing God's essence, which is invisible to us. Malebranche thinks that an advantage of his view is that it "places created minds in a position of complete dependence on God." His view was criticized by other Cartesian philosophers, notably Arnauld.

Concerning the Cartesian issue of whether soul is better known than body, Malebranche says that it is in a certain sense. People know their own soul through consciousness, but know it imperfectly because what they know of it is limited to what it actually experiences.

Book Three
Part Two: The Pure Understanding
The Nature of Ideas

Chapter One

[I. What is meant by ideas]

I think everyone agrees that we do not perceive objects external to us by themselves. We see the sun, the stars, and an infinity of objects external to us; and it is not likely that the soul should leave the body to stroll about the heavens, as it were, in order to behold all these objects. Thus, it does not see them by themselves, and our mind's immediate object when it sees the sun, for example, is not the sun, but something that is intimately joined to our soul, and this is what I call an *idea*. Thus, by the word *idea*, I mean here nothing other than the immediate object, or the object closest to the mind, when it perceives something, i.e., that which affects and modifies the mind with the perception it has of an object.

It should be carefully noted that for the mind to perceive an object, it is absolutely necessary for the idea of that object to be actually present to it – and about this there can be no doubt; but there need not be any external thing like that idea. For it often happens that we perceive things that do not exist, and that even have never existed – thus our mind often has real ideas of things that have never existed. When, for example, a man imagines a golden mountain, it is absolutely necessary that the idea of this mountain really be present to his mind. When a madman or someone asleep or in a high fever sees some animal before his eyes, it is certain that what he sees is not nothing, and that therefore the idea of this animal really does exist, though the golden mountain and the animal have never existed.

Yet given that men are naturally led, as it were, to believe that only corporeal objects exist, they judge of the reality and existence of things other than as they should. For as soon as they perceive an object, they would have it as quite certain that it exists, although it often happens that there is nothing external. In addition, they would have the object be exactly as they see it, which never happens. But as for the idea that necessarily exists, and that cannot be other than as it is seen, they ordinarily judge unreflectingly that it is nothing – as if ideas did not have a great number of properties, as if the idea of a square, for example, were not different from that of a circle or a number, and did not represent completely different things, which can never be the case for nonbeing, since nonbeing has no properties. It is therefore indubitable that ideas have a very real existence. But now let us examine their nature and essence, and let us see what there can be in the soul that might represent all things to it.

Everything the soul perceives belongs to either one of two sorts: either it is in the soul, or outside the soul. The things that are in the soul are its own thoughts, i.e., all its various modifications – for by the words *thought*, *mode of thinking*, or *modification of the soul*, I generally understand all those things that cannot be in the soul without the soul being aware of them through the inner sensation it has of itself – such as its sensations, imaginings, pure intellections, or simply conceptions, as well as its passions and natural inclinations. Now, our soul has no need of ideas in order to perceive these things in the way it does, because these things are in the soul, or rather because they are but the soul itself existing in this or that way – just as the actual roundness and motion of a body are but that body shaped and moved in this or that way.

But as for things outside the soul, we can perceive them only by means of ideas, given that these things cannot be intimately joined to the soul. Of these, there are two sorts: spiritual and material. As for the spiritual, there is reason to believe they can be revealed to the soul by themselves and without ideas. For although experience teaches us that we cannot communicate our thoughts to one another immediately and by ourselves, but only through speech or some other sensible sign to which we have attached our ideas, still it might be said that God has established this state of affairs only for the duration of this life in order to prevent the disorder that would now prevail if men could communicate as they pleased. But when order and justice reign, and we are delivered from the captivity of our body, we shall perhaps be able to communicate through the intimate union among ourselves, as the angels seem to be able to do in heaven. Accordingly, it does not seem to be absolutely necessary to have ideas in order to represent spiritual things to the soul, because they might be seen through themselves, though in imperfect fashion.

I shall not inquire here how two minds can be united, or whether they can in this way reveal their thoughts to each other. I believe, however, that the only purely intelligible substance is God's, that nothing can be revealed with clarity except in the light of this substance, and that a union of minds cannot make them visible to each other. For although we may be closely joined together, we are and shall be unintelligible to each other until we see each other in God, and until He presents us with the perfectly intelligible idea He has of our being contained in His being. Thus, although I may seem to allow that angels can by themselves show to each other both what they are and what they are thinking (which I really do not believe), I warn that it is only because I have no desire to dispute the point*

* This paragraph is italicized because you may omit it as being too difficult to understand unless you know my views about the soul and the nature of ideas. [original footnote]

– provided that you grant me what cannot be disputed, to wit, that you cannot see material things by themselves and without ideas.

In the seventh chapter I shall explain my view on how we know minds, and I shall show that for the moment we cannot know them entirely by themselves, although they might be capable of union with us. But here I am speaking mainly about material things, which certainly cannot be joined to our soul in the way necessary for it to perceive them, because with them extended and the soul unextended, there is no relation between them. Besides which, our souls do not leave the body to measure the heavens, and as a result, they can see bodies outside only through the ideas representing them. In this everyone must agree.

II. A classification of all the ways external objects can be seen

We assert the absolute necessity, then, of the following: either (a) the ideas we have of bodies and of all other objects we do not perceive by themselves come from these bodies or objects; or (b) our soul has the power of producing these ideas; or (c) God has produced them in us while creating the soul or produces them every time we think about a given object; or (d) the soul has in itself all the perfections it sees in bodies; or else (e) the soul is joined to a completely perfect being that contains all intelligible perfections, or all the ideas of created beings.

We can know objects in only one of these ways. Let us examine, without prejudice, and without fear of the difficulty of the question, which is the likeliest way. Perhaps we can resolve the question with some clarity though we do not pretend to give demonstrations that will seem incontrovertible to everyone; rather, we merely give proofs that will seem very persuasive to those who consider them carefully, for one would appear presumptuous were one to speak otherwise.

Chapter Two

That material objects do not transmit species resembling them

The most commonly held opinion is that of the Peripatetics, who hold that external objects transmit species that resemble them, and that these species are carried to the common sense by the external senses. They call these species *impressed*, because objects impress them on the external senses. These impressed species, being material and sensible, are made intelligible by the *agent*, or *active intellect*, and can then be received in the *passive intellect*. These species, thus spiritualized, are called *expressed* species, because they are expressed from the impressed species, and through them the *passive intellect* knows material things.

We shall not pause here to further investigate these lovely things and the different ways different philosophers conceive of them. For although they disagree about the number of faculties they attribute to the interior sense and to the understanding, and although there are many of them who doubt whether an *agent intellect* is needed in order to know sensible objects, still they practically all agree that external objects transmit species or images that resemble them, and with only this as their basis, they multiply their faculties and defend their *agent intellect*. As this basis has no solidity, as will be shown, it is not necessary to pause further in order to overthrow everything that has been built upon it.

We assert, then, that it is unlikely that objects transmit images, or species, that resemble them, and here are some reasons why. The first is drawn from the impenetrability of bodies. All objects (such as the sun, the stars, as well as those closer to our eyes) are unable to transmit species of a nature other than their own. This is why philosophers commonly say that these species are gross and material as opposed to the expressed species, which are spiritualized. These impressed species are therefore little bodies. They therefore cannot penetrate each other or the whole of the space between the earth and the heavens, which must be full of them. From this it is easy to conclude that they must run against and batter each other from all directions, and that hence they cannot make objects visible.

Furthermore, a great number of objects located in the sky and on earth can be seen from the same place or the same point; the species of all these objects would then have to be capable of being reduced to a point. Now since they are extended they are impenetrable; therefore, . . . and so on.

But not only can a great number of very large objects be seen from the same point; there is no point in the universe's vast stretches from which an almost infinite number of objects cannot be discovered, and even objects as large as the sun, moon, and heavens. In the entire world there is no point where the species of all these things ought not meet – which is contrary to all indications of the truth.

The second reason is based on the change that occurs in the species. It is certain that the closer an object is, the larger its species must be, since we see the object as larger. Now, I do not see what can make this species diminish or what can become of the parts composing it when it was larger. But what is even harder to understand on their view is how, if we look at this object with magnifying glasses or a microscope, the species suddenly becomes five or six hundred times larger than it was before, for still less do we see with what parts it can so greatly increase its size in an instant.

The third reason is that when we look at a perfect cube, all the species of its sides are unequal, and yet we see all its sides as equally square. And likewise when we look at a picture of ovals and parallelograms, which can transmit only species of the same shape, we see in it only circles and squares. This clearly shows that the object we are looking at need not produce species that resemble it in order for us to see it.

Finally, it is inconceivable how a body that does not sensibly diminish could continually emit species in all directions, or how it could continually fill the vast spaces around it with them – and all this with inconceivable speed. For a hidden object can be seen at the very moment of its discovery from several million leagues away and from every direction. And, what seems stranger still, very active bodies, such as air and a few others, lack the force to emit images resembling them – as coarser and less active bodies, such as earth, stones, and almost all hard bodies do.

But I do not wish to linger to adduce all the reasons opposed to this view, since it would be an endless task and the least mental effort will yield an inexhaustible number of them. Those we have just given are enough, and even they are not necessary after what was said about this subject in the first book, where the errors of the senses were explained. But so many philosophers hold this view that I thought it necessary to say something about it in order to provoke them to reflect on their thoughts.

Chapter Three

That the soul does not have the power to produce ideas. The cause of our error in this matter

The second view belongs to those who believe that our souls have the power of producing the ideas of the things they wish to think about, and that our souls are moved to produce them by the impressions that objects make on the body, though these impressions are not images resembling the objects causing them. According to them, it is in this that man is made after the image of God and shares in His power. Further, just as God created all things from nothing, and can annihilate them and create new things in their place, so man can create and annihilate ideas of anything he pleases. But there is good reason to distrust all these views that elevate man. These are generally thoughts that come from his pride and vanity, and not from the Father of lights.

This share in God's power that men boast of for representing objects to themselves and for several other particular actions is a share that seems to involve a certain independence (as it is generally explained). But it is also an illusory share, which men's ignorance and vanity makes them imagine. Their dependence upon the power and goodness of God is much greater than they think, but this is not the place to explain the matter. Let us try only to show that men do not have the power to form ideas of the things they perceive.

Since ideas have real properties, no one can doubt that they are real beings, or that they differ from one another, and that they represent altogether different things. Nor can it be reasonably doubted that they are spiritual and are very different from the bodies they represent. This seems to raise a doubt whether the ideas by means of which bodies are seen are not more noble than the bodies themselves. Indeed, the intelligible world must be more perfect than the material, terrestrial world, as we shall see in what follows. Thus, when it is claimed that men have the power to form such ideas as please them, one runs the risk of claiming that men have the power of creating beings worthier and more perfect than the world God has created. Yet this is never thought about, because an idea is fancied to be nothing since it cannot be sensed – or if it is considered as a being, it is only as a meager and insignificant being, because it is thought to be annihilated as soon as it is no longer present to the mind.

But even if it were true that ideas were only lesser and insignificant beings, still they are beings, and spiritual beings at that, and given that men do not have the power of creation, it follows that they are unable to produce them. For the production of ideas in the way they explain it is a true creation, and although they may try to palliate the temerity and soften the harshness of this view by saying that the production of ideas presupposes something whereas creation presupposes nothing, still they have not resolved the fundamental difficulty.

For it ought to be carefully noted that it is no more difficult to produce something from nothing than to produce it by positing another thing from which it cannot be made and which can contribute nothing to its production. For example, it is no more difficult to create an angel than to produce it from a stone, because given that a stone is of a totally contrary kind of being, it can contribute nothing to the production of an angel. But it can contribute to the production of bread, of gold, and such, because stone, gold, and bread are but the same extension differently configured, and they are all material things.

It is even more difficult to produce an angel from a stone than to produce it from nothing, because to make an angel from a stone (insofar as it can be done), the stone must first be annihilated and then the angel must be created, whereas simply creating an angel does not require anything to be annihilated. If, then, the mind produces its own ideas from the material impressions the brain receives from objects, it continuously does the same thing, or something as difficult, or even more difficult, as if it created them. Since ideas are spiritual, they cannot be produced from material images in the brain, with which they are incommensurable.

But if it be said that an idea is not a substance, I would agree – but it is still a spiritual thing, and as it is impossible to make a square out of a mind, though a square is not a substance, so a spiritual idea cannot be formed from a material substance, even though an idea is not a substance.

But even if the mind of man were granted a sovereign power of annihilating and creating the ideas of things, still it would never use it to produce them. For just as a painter, no matter how good he is at his art, cannot represent an animal he has never seen and of which he has no idea – so that the painting he would be required to produce could not be like this unknown animal – so a man could not form the idea of an object unless he knew it beforehand, i.e., unless he already had the idea of it, which idea does not depend on his will. But if he already has an idea of it, he knows the object, and it is useless for him to form another idea of it. It is therefore useless to attribute to the mind of man the power of producing its ideas.

It might be said that the mind has general and confused ideas that it does not produce, and that those of its own making are clearer, more distinct, particular ideas. But this amounts to the same thing. For just as an artist cannot draw the portrait of an individual in such fashion that he could be certain of having done a proper job unless he had a distinct idea of the individual, and indeed unless the subject were to sit for it – so a mind that, for example, has only the idea of being or of animal in general cannot represent a horse to itself, or form a very distinct idea of it, or be sure that the idea exactly resembles a horse, unless it already has an initial idea against which it compares the second. Now if it already has one idea, it is useless to form a second, and therefore the question about the first idea, . . . , and so on.

It is true that when we conceive of a square through pure intellection, we can still imagine it, i.e., perceive it by tracing an image of it for ourselves in the brain. But it should be noted, first, that we are neither the true nor the principal cause of the image (but this is too long a matter to be explained here), and second, that far from being more distinct and more accurate than the first idea, the second idea accompanying the image is accurate only because it resembles the first, which serves as a model [*regle*] for the second. For ultimately, the imagination and the senses themselves should not be taken as representing objects to us more distinctly than does the pure understanding, but only as affecting and moving the mind more. For the ideas of the senses and of the imagination are distinct only to the extent that they conform to the ideas of pure intellection. The image of a square that the imagination traces in the brain, for example, is accurate and well formed only to the extent that it conforms to the idea of a square we conceive through pure intellection. It is this idea that governs the image. It is the mind that conducts the imagination and requires it, as it were, to consider occasionally whether the image it depicts is a figure composed of four straight and equal lines, and exactly right-angled – in a word, whether what one is imagining is like what one conceives.

After what has been said, I do not think anyone can doubt that those who claim the mind can form its own ideas of objects are mistaken, since they attribute to the mind the power of creating, and even of creating wisely and with order, although it has no knowledge of what it does – which is inconceivable. But the cause of their error is that men never fail to judge that a thing is the cause of a given effect when the two are conjoined, given that the true cause of the effect is unknown to them. This is why everyone concludes that a moving ball which strikes another is the true and principal cause of the motion it communicates to the other, and that the soul's will is the true and principal cause of movement in the arms, and other such prejudices – because it always happens that a ball moves when struck by another, that our arms move almost every time we want them to, and that we do not sensibly perceive what else could be the cause of these movements.

But when an effect does not so frequently follow something not its cause, there are still people who believe it to be caused by that thing, though not everyone falls into this error. For example, a comet appears and a prince dies, stones are exposed to the moon and are eaten by worms, the sun is in conjunction with Mars at the birth of a child and something extraordinary happens to the child. This is enough to convince many people that the comet, the moon, and the conjunction of the sun and Mars are the causes of the effects just noted and others like them; and the reason why not everyone is of the same belief is that these effects are not always observed to follow these things.

But given that all men generally have ideas of things present to the mind as soon as they want them, and that this occurs many times daily, practically everyone concludes that the will attending the production, or rather, the presence of ideas is their true cause, because at the time they see nothing they can assign as their cause, and because they believe that ideas cease to exist as soon as the mind ceases to perceive them and begin to exist again when they are represented to the mind. This is also why some people judge that external objects transmit images resembling them, as we have just pointed out in the preceeding chapter. Unable to see objects by themselves, but only through their ideas, they judge that the object produces the idea – because as soon as it is present, they see it; as soon as it is absent, they no longer see it; and because the presence of the object almost always attends the idea representing it to us.

Yet if men were not so rash in their judgments, they would conclude from the fact that the ideas of things are present to their mind as soon as they wish, only this, that in the order of nature their will is generally necessary for them to have these ideas, but not that the will is the true and principal cause that presents ideas to their mind, and still less that the will produces them from nothing or in the way they explain it. They should conclude not that objects transmit species resembling them because the soul ordinarily perceives them only when they are present, but only that the object is ordinarily necessary for the idea to be present to the mind. Finally, because a ball does not have the power to move itself, they should not judge that a ball in motion is the true and principal cause of the movement of the ball it finds in its path. They can judge only that the collision of the two balls is the occasion for the Author of all motion in matter to carry out the decree of His will, which is the universal cause of all things. He does so by communicating to the second ball part of the motion of the first, i.e., to speak more clearly, by willing that the latter ball should acquire as much motion in the same direction as the former loses, for the motor force of bodies can only be the will of Him who preserves them. [. . .]

Chapter Four

That we do not perceive objects by means of ideas created with us. That God does not produce ideas in us each time we need them

The third view is held by those who would have it that all ideas are innate or created with us.

To see the implausibility of this view, it should be considered that there are in the world many totally different things of which we have ideas. But to mention only simple figures, it is certain that their number is infinite, and even if we fix upon only one, such as the ellipse, the mind undoubtedly conceives of an infinite number of different kinds of them when it conceives that one of its diameters may be infinitely lengthened while the other remains constant.

Likewise, an infinite number of different kinds of triangles can be conceived, given that the altitude can be infinitely increased or decreased while the base remains the same; moreover, and this is what I ask be noted here, the mind to some extent perceives this infinite number of triangles, although we can imagine very few of them and cannot simultaneously have particular and distinct ideas of many triangles of different kinds. But it should be especially noted that the mind's general idea of this infinite number of different kinds of triangles suffices to prove that if we do not conceive of all these different triangles by means of particular ideas, in short, if we do not comprehend the infinite, it is not for want of ideas or because the infinite is not present to us, but only because of a lack of capacity and scope of mind. If a man were to apply himself to an investigation of the properties of all the different kinds of triangles, and even if he should continue his investigation forever, he would never want for further particular ideas. But his mind would exhaust itself for no purpose.

What I have just said about triangles is applicable to figures of five, six, a hundred, a thousand, of ten thousand sides, and so on to infinity. And if the sides of a triangle can have infinite relations with each other, making an infinity of different kinds of triangles, it is easy to see that figures of four, five, or a million sides can have even greater differences, since they can have a greater number of relations and combinations of their sides than can simple triangles.

The mind, then, perceives all these things; it has ideas of them; it is certain that it will never want for ideas should it spend countless centuries investigating even a single figure, and that if it does not perceive these figures in an instant, or if it does not comprehend the infinite, this is only because of its very limited scope. It has, then, an infinite number of ideas – what am I saying? – it has as many infinite numbers of ideas as there are different figures; consequently, since there is an infinite number of different figures, the mind must have an infinity of infinite numbers of ideas just to know the figures.

Now, I ask whether it is likely that God created so many things along with the mind of man. My own view is that such is not the case, especially since all this could be done in another, much simpler and easier way, as we shall see shortly. For as God always acts in the simplest ways, it does not seem reasonable to explain how we know objects by assuming the creation of an infinity of beings, since the difficulty can be resolved in an easier and more straightforward fashion.

But even if the mind had a store of all the ideas necessary for it to perceive objects, yet it would be impossible to explain how the soul could choose them to represent them to itself, how, for example, the soul could make itself instantly perceive all the different objects whose size, figure, distance and motion it discovers when it opens its eyes in the countryside. Through this means it could not even perceive a single object such as the sun when it is before the body's eyes. For, since the image the sun imprints in the brain does not resemble the idea we have of it (as we have proved elsewhere), and as the soul does not perceive the motion the sun produces in the brain and in the fundus of the eyes, it is inconceivable that it should be able to determine precisely which among the infinite number of its ideas it would have to represent to itself in order to imagine or see the sun and to see it as having a given size. It cannot be said, then, that ideas of things are created with us, or that this suffices for us to see the objects surrounding us.

Nor can it be said that God constantly produces as many new ideas as there are different things we perceive. This view is refuted well enough by what has just been said in this chapter. Furthermore, we must at all times actually have in us the ideas of all things, since we can at all times will to think about anything – which we could not do unless we already perceived them confusedly, i.e., unless an infinite number of ideas were present to the mind; for after all, one cannot will to think about objects of which one has no idea. Furthermore, it is clear that the idea, or immediate object of our mind, when we think about limitless space, or a circle in general, or indeterminate being, is nothing created. For no created reality can be either infinite or even general, as is what we perceive in these cases. But all this will be seen more clearly in what follows.

[...]

Chapter Six

That we see all things in God

In the preceding chapters we have examined four different ways in which the soul might see external objects, all of which seem to us very unlikely. There remains only the fifth, which alone seems to conform to reason and to be most appropriate for exhibiting the dependence that minds have on God in all their thoughts.

To understand this fifth way, we must remember what was just said in the preceding chapter – that God must have within Himself the ideas of all the beings He has created (since otherwise He could not have created them), and thus He sees all these beings by considering the perfections He contains to which they are related. We should know, furthermore, that through His presence God is in close union with our minds, such that He might be said to be the place of minds as space is, in a sense, the place of bodies. Given these two things, the mind surely can see what in God represents created beings, since what in God represents created beings is very spiritual, intelligible, and present to the mind. Thus, the mind can see God's works in Him, provided that God wills to reveal to it what in Him represents them. The following are the reasons that seem to prove that He wills this rather than the creation of an infinite number of ideas in each mind.

Not only does it strictly conform to reason, but it is also apparent from the economy found throughout nature that God never does in very complicated fashion what can be done in a very simple and straightforward way. For God never does anything uselessly and without reason. His power and wisdom are not shown by doing lesser things with greater means – this is contrary to reason and indicates a limited intelligence. Rather, they are shown by doing greater things with very simple and straightforward means. Thus, it was with extension alone that He produced everything admirable we see in nature and even what gives life and movement to animals. For those who absolutely insist on substantial forms, faculties, and souls in animals (different from their blood and bodily organs) to perform their functions, at the same time would have it that God lacks intelligence, or that He cannot make all these remarkable things with extension alone. They measure the power and sovereign wisdom of God by the pettiness of their own mind. Thus, since God can reveal everything to minds simply by willing that they see what is in their midst, i.e., what in Him is related to and represents these things, there is no likelihood that He does otherwise, or that He does so by producing as many infinities of infinite numbers of ideas as there are created minds.

But it should be carefully noted that we cannot conclude from their seeing all things in God in this way that our minds see the essence of God. God's essence is His own absolute being, and minds do not see the divine substance taken absolutely but only as relative to creatures and to the degree that they can participate in it. What they see in God is very imperfect, whereas God is most perfect. They see matter that is shaped, divisible, and so on, but there is nothing divisible or shaped in God, for God is all being, since He is infinite and comprehends everything; but He is no being in particular. Yet what we see is but one or more particular beings, and we do not understand this perfect simplicity of God, which includes all beings. In addition, it might be said that we do not so much see the ideas of things as the things themselves that are represented by ideas, for when we see a square, for example, we do not say that we see the idea of the square, which is joined to the mind, but only the square that is external to it.

The second reason for thinking that we see beings because God wills that what in Him representing them should be revealed to us (and not because there are as many ideas created with us as there are things we can perceive) is that this view places created minds in a position of complete dependence on God – the most complete there can be. For on this view, not only could we see nothing but what He wills that we see, but we could see nothing but what He makes us see. [. . .]

But the strongest argument of all is the mind's way of perceiving anything. It is certain, and everyone knows this from experience, that when we want to think about some particular thing, we first glance over all beings and then apply ourselves to the consideration of the object we wish to think about. Now, it is indubitable that we could not desire to see a particular object unless we already saw it, though in a general and confused fashion. As a result of this, given that we can desire to see all beings, now one, now another, it is certain that all beings are present to our mind; and it seems that all beings can be present to our mind only because God, i.e., He who includes all things in the simplicity of His being, is present to it.

It even seems that the mind would be incapable of representing universal ideas of genus, species, and so on, to itself if it did not see all beings contained in one. For, given that every creature is a particular being, we cannot say that we see a created thing when, for example, we see a triangle in general. Finally, I think that sense can be made of the way the mind knows certain abstract and general truths only through the presence of Him who can enlighten the mind in an infinity of different ways.

Finally, of the proofs of God's existence, the loftiest and most beautiful, the primary and most solid (or the one that assumes the least) is the idea we have of the infinite. For it is certain that (a) the mind perceives the infinite, though it does not comprehend it, and (b) it has a very distinct idea of God, which it can have only by means of its union with Him, since it is inconceivable that the idea of an infinitely perfect being (which is what we have of God) should be something created.

But not only does the mind have the idea of the infinite, it even has it before that of the finite. For we conceive of infinite being simply because we conceive of being, without thinking whether it is finite or infinite. In order for us to conceive of a finite being, something must necessarily be eliminated from this general notion of being, which consequently must come first. Thus, the mind perceives nothing except in the idea it has of the infinite, and far from this idea being formed from the confused collection of all our ideas of particular beings (as philosphers think), all these particular ideas are in fact but participations in the general idea of the infinite; just as God does not draw His being from creatures, while every creature is but an imperfect participation in the divine being.

Here is an argument that may prove demonstrative for those accustomed to abstract reasoning. It is certain that ideas are efficacious, since they act upon the mind and enlighten it, and since they make it happy or unhappy through the pleasant or unpleasant perceptions by which they affect it. Now nothing can act immediately upon the mind unless it is superior to it – nothing but God alone; for only the Author of our being can change its modifications. [. . .] Finally, God can have no other special end for His actions than Himself. [. . .]

God can make a mind in order for it to know His works, then, only if that mind to some extent sees God in seeing His works. As a result, it might be said that if we do not to some extent see God, we see nothing, just as if we do not love God, i.e., if God were not continuously impressing upon us the love of good in general, we would love nothing. For, given that this love is our will, we could neither love nor will anything without it, since we can love particular goods only by directing toward these goods the impulse of love that God gives us for Himself. Thus, as we love something only through our necessary love for God, we see something only through our natural knowledge of God; and all our particular ideas of creatures are but limitations of the idea of the Creator, as all the impulses of the will toward creatures are only determinations of its impulse toward the Creator.

[. . .]

We are of the opinion, then, that truths (and even those that are eternal, such as that twice two is four) are not absolute beings, much less that they are God Himself. For clearly, this truth consists only in the relation of equality between twice two and four. Thus, we do not claim, as does Saint Augustine, that we see God in seeing truths, but in seeing the *ideas* of these truths – for the ideas are real, whereas the equality between the ideas, which is the truth, is nothing real. When we say, for example, that the cloth we are measuring is three ells long, the cloth and the ells are real. But the equality between them is not a real being – it is only a relation found between the three ells and the cloth. When we say that twice two is four, the ideas of the numbers are real, but the equality between them is only a relation. Thus, our view is that we see God when we see eternal truths, and not that these truths are God, because the ideas on which these truths depend are in God – it might even be that this was Saint Augustine's meaning. We further believe that changeable and corruptible things are known in God, though Saint Augustine speaks only of immutable and incorruptible things, because for this to be so, no imperfection need be placed in God, since, as we have already said, it is enough that God should reveal to us what in Him is related to these things.

But although I may say that we see material and sensible things in God, it must be carefully noted that I am not saying we have sensations of them in God, but only that it is God who acts in us; for God surely knows sensible things, but He does not sense them. When we perceive something sensible, two things are found in our perception: *sensation* and pure *idea*. The sensation is a modification of our soul, and it is God who causes it in us. He can cause this modification even though He does not have it Himself, because He sees in the idea He has of our soul that it is capable of it. As for the idea found in conjunction with the sensation, it is in God, and we see it because it pleases God to reveal it to us. God joins the sensation to the idea when objects are present so that we may believe them to be present and that we may have all the feelings and passions that we should have in relation to them.

[. . .]

Chapter Seven

In order to clarify and simplify the view I have just laid out concerning the way in which the mind perceives all the various objects of its knowledge, I must distinguish its four ways of knowing.

I. The four ways of perceiving things

The first is to know things by themselves.

The second is to know them through their ideas, i.e., as I mean it here, through something different from themselves.

The third is to know them through *consciousness*, or inner sensation.

The fourth is to know them through conjecture.

We know things by themselves and without ideas when they are intelligible by themselves, i.e., when they can act on the mind and thereby reveal themselves to it. For the understanding is a purely passive faculty of the soul, whereas activity is found only in the will. Even its desires are not the true causes of ideas – they are but the occasional or natural causes of their presence as a result of the natural laws concerning the union of our soul with universal Reason, as I have explained elsewhere. We know things through their ideas when they are not intelligible by themselves, whether because they are corporeal or because they cannot affect the mind or reveal themselves to it. Through consciousness we know everything that is not distinct from ourselves. Finally, through conjecture we know those things that are different both from ourselves and from what we know either in itself or through ideas, such as when we believe that certain things are like certain others we know.

II. How we know God

Only God do we know through Himself, for though there are other spiritual beings besides Him, which seem intelligible by their nature, only He can act on our mind and reveal Himself to it. Only God do we perceive by a direct and immediate perception. Only He can enlighten our mind with His own substance. Finally, only through the union we have with Him are we capable in this life of knowing what we know, as we have explained in the preceding chapter; for He is the only master, according to Saint Augustine, ruling our mind without the mediation of any creature.

I cannot conceive how a created thing can represent the infinite, how being that is without restriction, immense and universal, can be perceived through an idea, i.e., through a particular being different from universal and infinite being. But as far as particular beings are concerned, there is no difficulty in conceiving how they can be represented by the infinite being that contains them in His most efficacious and, consequently, most intelligible substance. Thus, it must be said that (a) we know God through Himself, though our knowledge of Him in this life is very imperfect, and (b) we know corporeal things through their ideas, i.e., in God, since only God contains the intelligible world, where the ideas of all things are located.

But while we can see all things in God, it does not follow that we in fact do so – we see in God only the things of which we have ideas, and there are things we perceive without ideas, or know only through sensation.

III. How we know bodies

Everything in this world of which we have some knowledge is either a mind or a body, a property of a mind or a property of a body. Undoubtedly, we know bodies with their properties through their ideas, because given that they are not intelligible by themselves, we can perceive them only in that being which contains them in an intelligible way. Thus, it is in God and through their ideas that we perceive bodies and their properties, and for this reason, the knowledge we have of them is quite perfect – i.e., our idea of extension suffices to inform us of all the properties of which extension is capable, and we could not wish for an idea of extension, figure, or motion more distinct or more fruitful than the one God gives us.

As the ideas of things in God include all their properties, whoever sees their ideas can also see all their properties successively; for when we see things as they are in God, we always see them in perfect fashion, and the way we see them would be infinitely perfect if the mind seeing them were infinite. What is lacking to our knowledge of extension, figures, and motion is the shortcoming not of the idea representing it but of our mind considering it.

IV. How we know our own soul

Such is not the case with the soul, [which] we do not know through its idea – we do not see it in God; we know it only through *consciousness*, and because of this, our knowledge of it is imperfect. Our knowledge of our soul is limited to what we sense taking place in us. If we had never sensed pain, heat, light, and such, we would be unable to know whether the soul was capable of sensing these things, because we do not know it through its idea. But if we saw in God the idea corresponding to our soul, we would at the same time know, or at least could know all the properties of which it is capable – as we know, or at least can know, all the properties of which extension is capable, because we know extension, through its idea.

It is true that we know well enough through our consciousness, or the inner sensation we have of ourselves, that our soul is something of importance. But what we know of it might be almost nothing compared to what it is in itself. If all we knew about matter were some twenty or thirty figures it had been modified by, we certainly would know almost nothing about it in comparison with what we can know about it through the idea representing it. To know the soul perfectly, then, it is not enough to know only what we know through inner sensation – since the consciousness we have of ourselves perhaps shows us only the least part of our being.

From what we have just said it might be concluded that although we know the existence of our soul more distinctly than the existence of both our own body and those surrounding us, still our knowledge of the soul's nature is not as perfect as our knowledge of the nature of bodies, and this might serve to reconcile the differing views of those who say that nothing is known better than the soul, and those who claim to know nothing less.

This might also serve to prove that the ideas which represent to us things outside us are not modifications of our soul. For if the soul saw all things by considering its own modifications, it would have to know its own nature or essence more clearly than that of bodies, and all the sensations or modifications of which it is capable more clearly than the figures or modifications of which bodies are capable. However, it knows itself capable of a given sensation not through the perception it has of itself in consulting its idea but only through experience, whereas it knows that extension is capable of an infinite number of figures through the idea it has of extension. There are even certain sensations like colors and sounds which are such that most people cannot tell whether or not they are modification of the soul, but there is no figure that everyone, through the idea he has of extension, does not recognize as the modification of a body.

[. . .]

Although our knowledge of our soul is not complete, what we do know of it through consciousness or inner sensation is enough to demonstrate its immortality, spirituality, freedom, and several other attributes we need to know. And this seems to be why God does not cause us to know the soul, as He causes us to know bodies, through its idea. The knowledge that we have of our soul through consciousness is imperfect, granted; but it is not false. On the other hand, that knowledge we have of bodies through sensation or consciousness, if the confused sensation we have of what takes place in our body can be called consciousness, is not only imperfect, but also false. We therefore needed an idea of the body to correct our sensations of it – but we need no idea of our soul, since our consciousness of it does not involve us in error, and since to avoid being mistaken in our knowledge of it, it is enough not to confuse it with the body – and reason enables us to do this since our idea of the body reveals to us that the modalities of which it is capable are quite different from those we sense. Finally, if we had an idea of the soul as clear as that which we have of the body, that idea would have inclined us too much to view the soul as separated from the body. It would have thus diminished the union between our soul and body by preventing us from regarding it as dispersed through all our members, though I shall not further explain the matter here.

V. How we know other men's souls

Of all the objects of our knowledge, only the souls of other men and pure intelligences remain; and clearly we know them only through conjecture. At present we do not know them either in themselves or through their ideas, and as they are different from ourselves, we cannot know them through consciousness. We conjecture that the souls of other men are of the same sort as our own. We suppose them to feel what we feel in ourselves, and even when these sensations have no relation to the body, we are certain we are not mistaken because we see in God certain ideas and immutable laws from which we know with certainty that God acts uniformly in all minds.

[. . .]

16

G. W. F. Leibniz, *Discourse on Metaphysics*

Gottfried Wilhelm von Leibniz (1646–1716) was born in Leipzig and died in Hanover, Germany. He was a polymath. He discovered calculus independently of Isaac Newton, contributed to logic and mechanics, and was an expert in law and history, and chemistry. He founded the Academy of Berlin and corresponded with most of the distinguished philosophers and scientists of his time.

During his lifetime, he published many articles in learned journals but only one book, *Theodicy* (1710). He intended to publish a book-length criticism of John Locke's *Essay concerning Human Understanding*, with the title *New Essays on Human Understanding*, but changed his mind when he learned that Locke had died. Two of his masterpieces are *Discourse on Metaphysics*, written early in his philosophical career, and the *Monadology* (1714), written late. Both are included in this volume, in addition to his summary of the *Theodicy*.

The Discourse on Metaphysics begins with the standard definition of God in the early modern period, not to mention the Middle Ages. God is "an absolutely perfect being." Leibniz wants to explore the consequences of this definition. This includes an investigation into what perfection is and how many kinds of perfection there are. Two perfections are omnipotence and omniscience since there is no contradiction, according to Leibniz, in knowing everything and being all-powerful. It follows from omnipotence and omniscience that whatever God makes is perfect in the highest degree. In other words, God creates the best of all possible worlds, the view that Voltaire satirized in *Candide*. The goodness of God's creation is the basis of our love for God.

It is possible that what motivated Leibniz to write *The Discourse* was not so much the logical properties of perfection as the question of human freedom, given the theological commitment to the omniscience and omnipotence of God. If God knows that a person *P* will do some action *A* before *P* does *A*, then it is *certain* that *P* will do *A*. Does it follow that it is *necessary* that *P* will do *A*? Leibniz thinks it is not necessary, even though it is true that if *P* will do *A*, then *P*'s-doing-*A* is part of *P* as soon as he is created.

Related to the question of human freedom is the problem of predestination. If it is true that as soon as a person *P* is created, *P* do *A* – doing *P* is part of *P*'s essence – why does God choose to create that person? Leibniz's solution is essentially tied to God's perfection. Since he makes the best of all possible worlds, he must have a good reason, even if humans do not or cannot know what that reason is. The issue of human freedom and predestination is continued in *The Theodicy* (see selection 17).

I. Concerning the divine perfection and that God does everything in the most desirable way.

The conception of God which is the most common and the most full of meaning is expressed well enough in the words: God is an absolutely perfect being. The implications, however, of these words fail to receive sufficient consideration. For instance, there are many different kinds of perfection, all of which God possesses, and each one of them pertains to him in the highest degree.

We must also know what perfection is. One thing which can surely be affirmed about it is that those forms or natures which are not susceptible of it to the highest degree, say the nature of numbers or of figures, do not permit of perfection. This is because the number which is the greatest of all (that is, the sum of all the numbers), and likewise the greatest of all figures, imply contradictions. The greatest knowledge, however, and omnipotence contain no impossibility. Consequently power and knowledge do admit of perfection, and in so far as they pertain to God they have no limits.

Whence it follows that God who possesses supreme and infinite wisdom acts in the most perfect manner not only metaphysically, but also from the moral standpoint. And with respect to ourselves it can be said that the more we are enlightened and informed in regard to the works of God the more will we be disposed to find them excellent and conforming entirely to that which we might desire.

II. Against those who hold that there is in the works of God no goodness, or that the principles of goodness and beauty are arbitrary.

Therefore I am far removed from the opinion of those who maintain that there are no principles of goodness or perfection in the nature of things, or in the ideas which God has about them, and who say that the works of God are good only through the formal reason that God has made them. If this position were true, God, knowing that he is the author of things, would not have to regard them afterwards and find them good, as the Holy Scripture witnesses. Such anthropological expressions are used only to let us know that excellence is recognized in regarding the works themselves, even if we do not consider their evident dependence on their author. This is confirmed by the fact that it is in reflecting upon the works that we are able to discover the one who wrought. They must therefore bear in themselves his character. I confess that the contrary opinion seems to me extremely dangerous and closely approaches that of recent innovators who hold that the beauty of the universe and the goodness which we attribute to the works of God are chimeras of human beings who think of God in human terms. In saying, therefore, that things are not good according to any standard of goodness, but simply by the will of God it seems to me that one destroys, without realizing it, all the love of God and all his glory; for why praise him for what he has done, if he would be equally praiseworthy in doing the contrary? Where will be his justice and his wisdom if he has only a certain despotic power, if arbitrary will takes the place of reasonableness, and if in accord with the definition of tyrants, justice consists in that which is pleasing to the most powerful? Besides it seems that every act of willing supposes some reason for the willing and this reason, of course, must precede the act. This is why, accordingly, I find so strange those expressions of certain philosophers who say that the eternal truths of metaphysics and Geometry, and consequently the principles of goodness, of justice, and of perfection, are effects only of the will of God. To me it seems that all these follow from his understanding, which does not depend upon his will any more than does his essence.

III. Against those who think that God might have made things better than he has.

No more am I able to approve of the opinion of certain modern writers who boldly maintain that that which God has made is not perfect in the highest degree, and that he might have done better. It seems to me that the consequence of such an opinion are wholly inconsistent with the glory of God. *Uti minus malum habet rationem boni, ita minus bonum habet rationem mali.* I think that one acts imperfectly if he acts with less perfection than he is capable of. To show that an architect could have done better is to find fault with his work. Furthermore this opinion is contrary to the Holy Scriptures when they assure us of the goodness of God's work. For if comparative perfection were sufficient, then in whatever way God had accomplished his work, since there is an infinitude of possible imperfections, it would always have been good in comparison with the less perfect; but a thing is little praiseworthy when it can be praised only in this way.

I believe that a great many passages from the divine writings and from the holy fathers will be found favoring my position, while hardly any will be found in favor of that of these modern thinkers. Their opinion is, in my judgment, unknown to the writers of antiquity and is a deduction based upon the too slight acquaintaince which we have with the general harmony of the universe and with the hidden reasons for God's conduct. In our ignorance, therefore, we are tempted to decide audaciously that many things might have been done better.

These modern thinkers insist upon certain hardly tenable subtleties, for they imagine that nothing is so perfect that there might not have been something more perfect. This is an error. They think, indeed, that they are thus safeguarding the liberty of God. As if it were not the highest liberty to act in perfection according to the sovereign reason. For to think that God acts in anything without having any reason for his willing, even if we overlook the fact that such action seems impossible, is an opinion which conforms little to God's glory. For example, let us suppose that God chooses between A and B, and that he takes A without any reason for preferring it to B. I say that this action on the part of God is at least not praiseworthy, for all praise ought to be founded upon reason which *ex hypothesi* is not present here. My opinion is that God does nothing for which he does not deserve to be glorified.

IV. That love for God demands on our part complete satisfaction with and acquiescence in that which he has done.

The general knowledge of this great truth that God acts always in the most perfect and most desirable manner possible, is in my opinion the basis of the love which we owe to God in all things; for he who loves seeks his satisfaction in the felicity or perfection of the object loved and in the perfection of his actions. *Idem velle et idem nolle vera amicitia est.* I believe that it is difficult to love God truly when one, having the power to change his disposition, is not disposed to wish for that which God desires. In fact those who are not satisfied with what God does seem to me like dissatisfied subjects whose attitude is not very different from that of rebels. I hold therefore, that on these principles, to act conformably to the love of God it is not sufficient to force oneself to be patient, we must be really satisfied with all that comes to us according to his will. I mean this acquiescence in regard to the past; for as regards the future one should not be a quietist with the arms folded, open to ridicule, awaiting that which God will do; according to the sophism which the ancients called *λόγον ἄεργον*, the lazy reason. It is necessary to act conformably to the presumptive will of God as far as we are able to judge of it, trying with all our might to contribute to the general welfare and particularly to the ornamentation and the perfection of that which touches us, or of that which is nigh and so to speak at our hand. For if the future shall perhaps show that God has not wished our good intention to have its way, it does not follow that he has not wished us to act as we have; on the contrary, since he is the best of all masters, he ever demands only the right intentions, and it is for him to know the hour and the proper place to let good designs succeed.

V. In what the principles of the divine perfection consist, and that the simplicity of the means counter-balances the richness of the effects.

It is sufficient therefore to have this confidence in God, that he has done everything for the best and that nothing will be able to injure those who love him. To know in particular, however, the reasons which have moved him to choose this order of the universe, to permit sin, to dispense his salutary grace in a certain manner, – this passes the capacity of a finite mind, above all when such a mind has not come into the joy of the vision of God. Yet it is possible to make some general remarks touching the course of providence in the government of things. One is able to say, therefore, that he who acts perfectly is like an excellent Geometer who knows how to find the best construction for a problem; like a good architect who utilizes his location and the funds destined for the building in the most advantageous manner, leaving nothing which shocks or which does not display that beauty of which it is capable; like a good householder who employs his property in such a way that there shall be nothing uncultivated or sterile; like a clever machinist who makes his production in the least difficult way possible; and like an intelligent author who encloses the most of reality in the least possible compass.

Of all beings those which are the most perfect and occupy the least possible space, that is to say those which interfere with one another the least, are the spirits whose perfections are the virtues. That is why we may not doubt that the felicity of the spirits is the principal aim of God and that he puts this purpose into execution, as far as the general harmony will permit. We will recur to this subject again.

When the simplicity of God's way is spoken of, reference is specially made to the means which he employs, and on the other hand when the variety, richness and abundance are referred to, the ends or effects are had in mind. Thus one ought to be proportioned to the other, just as the cost of a building should balance the beauty and grandeur which is expected. It is true that nothing costs God anything, just as there is no cost for a philosopher who makes hypotheses in constructing his imaginary world, because God has only to make decrees in order that a real world come into being; but in matters of wisdom the decrees or hypotheses meet the expenditure in proportion as they are more independent of one another. The reason wishes to avoid multiplicity in hypotheses or principles very much as the simplest system is preferred in Astronomy.

VI. That God does nothing which is not orderly, and that it is not even possible to conceive of events which are not regular.

The activities or the acts of will of God are commonly divided into ordinary and extraordinary. But it is well to bear in mind that God does nothing out of order. Therefore, that which passes for extraordinary is so only with regard to a particular order established among the created things, for as regards the universal order, everything conforms to it. This is so true that not only does nothing occur in this world which is absolutely irregular, but it is even impossible to conceive of such an occurrence. Because, let us suppose for example that some one jots down a quantity of paints upon a sheet of paper helter skelter, as do those who exercise the ridiculous art of Geomancy; now I say that it is possible to find a geometrical line whose concept shall be uniform and constant, that is, in accordance with a certain formula, and which line at the same time shall pass through all of those points, and in the same order in which the hand jotted them down; also if a continuous line be traced, which is now straight, now circular, and now of any other description, it is possible to find a mental equivalent, a formula or an equation common to all the points of this line by virtue of which formula the changes in the direction of the line must occur. There is no instance of a face whose contour does not form part of a geometric line and which can not be traced entire by a certain mathematical motion. But when the formula is very complex, that which conforms to it passes for irregular. Thus we may say that in whatever manner God might have created the world, it would always have been regular and in a certain order. God, however, has chosen the most perfect, that is to say the one which is at the same time the simplest in hypotheses and the richest in phenomena, as might be the case with a geometric line, whose construction was easy, but whose properties and effects were extremely remarkable and of great significance. I use these comparisons to picture a certain imperfect resemblance to the divine wisdom, and to point out that which may at least raise our minds to conceive in some sort what cannot otherwise be expressed. I do not pretend at all to explain thus the great mystery upon which depends the whole universe.

VII. That miracles conform to the regular order although they go against the subordinate regulations; concerning that which God desires or permits and concerning general and particular intentions.

Now since nothing is done which is not orderly, we may say that miracles are quite within the order of natural operations. We use the term natural of these operations because they conform to certain subordinate regulations which we call the nature of things. For it can be said that this nature is only a custom of God's which he can change on the occasion of a stronger reason than that which moved him to use these regulations. As regards general and particular intentions, according to the way in which we understand the matter, it may be said on the one hand that everything is in accordance with his most general intention, or that which best conforms to the most perfect order he has chosen; on the other hand, however, it is also possible to say that he has particular intentions which are exceptions to the subordinate regulations above mentioned. Of God's laws, however, the most universal, i.e., that which rules the whole course of the universe, is without exceptions.

It is possible to say that God desires everything which is an object of his particular intention. When we consider the objects of his general intentions, however, such as are the modes of activities of created things and especially of the reasoning creatures with whom God wishes to co-operate, we must make a distinction; for if the action is good in itself, we may say that God wishes it and at times commands it, even though it does not take place; but if it is bad in itself and becomes good only by accident through the course of events and especially after chastisement and satisfaction have corrected its malignity and rewarded the ill with interest in such a way that more perfection results in the whole train of circumstances than would have come if that ill had not occurred, – if all this takes place we must say that God permits the evil, and not that he desired it, although he has co-operated by means of the laws of nature which he has established. He knows how to produce the greatest good from them.

VIII. In order to distinguish between the activities of God and the activities of created things we must explain the conception of an individual substance.

It is quite difficult to distinguish God's actions from those of his creatures. Some think that God does everything; others imagine that he only conserves the force that he has given to created things. How far can we say either of these opinions is right?

In the first place since activity and passivity pertain properly to individual substances (*actiones sunt suppositorum*) it will be necessary to explain what such a substance is. It is indeed true that when several predicates are attributes of a single subject and this subject is not an attribute of another, we speak of it as an individual substance, but this is not enough, and such an explanation is merely nominal. We must therefore inquire what it is to be an attribute in reality of a certain subject. Now it is evident that every true predication has some basis in the nature of things, and even when a proposition is not identical, that is, when the predicate is not expressly contained in the subject, it is still necessary that it be virtually contained in it, and this is what the philosophers call *in-esse*, saying thereby that the predicate is in the subject. Thus the content of the subject must always include that of the predicate in such a way that if one understands perfectly the concept of the subject, he will know that the predicate appertains to it also. This being so, we are able to say that this is the nature of an individual substance or of a complete being, namely, to afford a conception so complete that the concept shall be sufficient for the understanding of it and for the deduction of all the predicates of which the substance is or may become the subject. Thus the quality of king, which belonged to Alexander the Great, an abstraction from the subject, is not sufficiently determined to constitute an individual, and does not contain the other qualities of the same subject, nor everything which the idea of this prince includes. God, however, seeing the individual concept, or hæcceity, of Alexander, sees there at the same time the basis and the reason of all the predicates which can be truly uttered regarding him; for instance that he will conquer Darius and Porus, even to the point of knowing *a priori* (and not by experience) whether he died a natural death or by poison, – facts which we can learn only through history. When we carefully consider the connection of things we see also the possibility of saying that there was always in the soul of Alexander marks of all that had happened to him and evidences of all that would happen to him and traces even of everything which occurs in the universe, although God alone could recognize them all.

IX. That every individual substance expresses the whole universe in its own manner and that in its full concept is included all its experiences together with all the attendent circumstances and the whole sequence of exterior events.

There follow from these considerations several noticeable paradoxes; among others that it is not true that two substances may be exactly alike and differ only numerically, *solo numero*, and that what St. Thomas says on this point regarding angels and intelligences (*quod ibi omne individuum sit species infima*) is true of all substances, provided that the specific difference is understood as Geometers understand it in the case of figures; again that a substance will be able to commence only through creation and perish only through annihilation; that a substance cannot be divided into two nor can one be made out of two, and that thus the number of substances neither augments nor diminishes through natural means, although they are frequently transformed. Furthermore every substance is like an entire world and like a mirror of God, or indeed of the whole world which it portrays, each one in its own fashion; almost as the same city is variously represented according to the various situations of him who is regarding it. Thus the universe is multiplied in some sort as many times as there are substances, and the glory of God is multiplied in the same way by as many wholly different representations of his works. It can indeed be said that every substance bears in some sort the character of God's infinite wisdom and omnipotence, and imitates him as much as it is able to; for it expresses, although confusedly, all that happens in the universe, past, present and future, deriving thus a certain resemblance to an infinite perception or power of knowing. And since all other substances express this particular substance and accommodate themselves to it, we can say that it exerts its power upon all the others in imitation of the omnipotence of the creator.

X. That the belief in substantial forms has a certain basis in fact, but that these forms effect no changes in the phenomena and must not be employed for the explanation of particular events.

It seems that the ancients, able men, who were accustomed to profound meditations and taught theology and philosophy for several centuries and some of whom recommend themselves to us on account of their piety, had some knowledge of that which we have just said and this is why they introduced and maintained the substantial forms so much decried to-day. But they were not so far from the truth nor so open to ridicule as the common run of our new philosophers imagine. I grant that the consideration of these forms is of no service in the details of physics and ought not to be employed in the explanation of particular phenomena. In regard to this last point, the schoolmen were at fault, as were also the physicians of times past who followed their example, thinking they had given the reason for the properties of a body in mentioning the forms and qualities without going to the trouble of examining the manner of operation; as if one should be content to say that a clock had a certain amount of clockness derived from its form, and should not inquire in what that clockness consisted. This is indeed enough for the man who buys it, provided he surrenders the care of it to someone else. The fact, however, that there was this misunderstanding and misuse of the substantial forms should not bring us to throw away something whose recognition is so necessary in metaphysics. Since without these we will not be able, I hold, to know the ultimate principles nor to lift our minds to the knowledge of the incorporeal natures and of the marvels of God. Yet as the geometer does not need to encumber his mind with the famous puzzle of the composition of the continuum, and as no moralist, and still less a jurist or a statesman has need to trouble himself with the great difficulties which arise in conciliating free will with the providential activity of God, (since the geometer is able to make all his demonstrations and the statesman can complete all his deliberations without entering into these discussion which are so necessary and important in Philosophy and Theology), so in the same way the physicist can explain his experiments, now using simpler experiments already made, now employing geometrical and mechanical demonstrations without any need of the general considerations which belong to another sphere, and if he employs the co-operation of God, or perhaps of some soul or animating force, or something else of a similar nature, he goes out of his path quite as much as that man who, when facing an important practical question would wish to enter into profound argumentations regarding the nature of destiny and of our liberty; a fault which men quite frequently commit without realizing it when they cumber their minds with considerations regarding fate, and thus they are even sometimes turned from a good resolution or from some necessary provision.

XI. That the opinions of the theologians and of the so-called scholastic philosophers are not to be wholly despised.

I know that I am advancing a great paradox in pretending to resuscitate in some sort the ancient philosophy, and to recall *postliminio* the substantial forms almost banished from our modern thought. But perhaps I will not be condemned lightly when it is known that I have long meditated over the modern philosophy and that I have devoted much time to experiments in physics and to the demonstrations of geometry and that I, too, for a long time was persuaded of the baselessness of those "beings" which, however, I was finally obliged to take up again in spite of myself and as though by force. The many investigations which I carried on compelled me to recognize that our moderns do not do sufficient justice to Saint Thomas and to the other great men of that period and that there is in the theories of the scholastic philosophers and theologians far more solidity than is imagined, provided that these theories are employed *à propos* and in their place. I am persuaded that if some careful and meditative mind were to take the trouble to clarify and direct their thoughts in the manner of analytic geometers, he would find a great treasure of very important truths, wholly demonstrable.

XII. That the conception of the extension of a body is in a way imaginary and does not constitute the substance of the body.

But to resume the thread of our discussion, I believe that he who will meditate upon the nature of substance, as I have explained it above, will find that the whole nature of bodies is not exhausted in their extension, that is to say, in their size, figure and motion, but that we must recognize something which corresponds to soul, something which is commonly called substantial form, although these forms effect no change in the phenomena, any more than do the souls of beasts, that is if they have souls. It is even possible to demonstrate that the ideas of size, figure and motion are not so distinctive as is imagined, and that they stand for something imaginary relative to our preceptions as do, although to a greater extent, the ideas of color, heat, and the other similar qualities in regard to which we may doubt whether they are actually to be found in the nature of the things outside of us. This is why these latter qualities are unable to constitute "substance" and if there is no other principle of identity in bodies than that which has just been referred to a body would not subsist more than for a moment.

The souls and the substance-forms of other bodies are entirely different from intelligent souls which alone know their actions, and not only do not perish through natural means but indeed always retain the knowledge of what they are; a fact which makes them alone open to chastisement or recompense, and makes them citizens of the republic of the universe whose monarch is God. Hence it follows that all the other creatures should serve them, a point which we shall discuss more amply later.

XIII. As the individual concept of each person includes once for all everything which can ever happen to him, in it can be seen, *a priori* the evidences or the reasons for the reality of each event, and why one happened sooner than the other. But these events, however certain, are nevertheless contingent, being based on the free choice of God and of his creatures. It is true that their choices always have their reasons, but they incline to the choices under no compulsion of necessity.

But before going further it is necessary to meet a difficulty which may arise regarding the principles which we have set forth in the preceding. We have said that the concept of an individual substance includes once for all everything which can ever happen to it and that in considering this concept one will be able to see everything which can truly be said concerning the individual, just as we are able to see in the nature of a circle all the properties which can be derived from it. But does it not seem that in this way the difference between contingent and necessary truths will be destroyed, that there will be no place for human liberty, and that an absolute fatality will rule as well over all our actions as over all the rest of the events of the world? To this I reply that a distinction must be made between that which is certain and that which is necessary. Every one grants that future contingencies are assured since God foresees them, but we do not say just because of that that they are necessary. But it will be objected, that if any conclusion can be deduced infallibly from some definition or concept, it is necessary; and now since we have maintained that everything which is to happen to anyone is already virtually included in his nature or concept, as all the properties are contained in the definition of a circle, therefore, the difficulty still remains. In order to meet the objection completely, I say that the connection or sequence is of two kinds; the one, absolutely necessary, whose contrary implies contradiction, occurs in the eternal verities like the truths of geometry; the other is necessary only *ex hypothesi*, and so to speak by accident, and in itself it is contingent since the contrary is not implied. This latter sequence is not founded upon ideas wholly pure and upon the pure understanding of God, but upon his free decrees and upon the processes of the universe. Let us give an example. Since Julius Caesar will become perpetual Dictator and master of the Republic and will overthrow the liberty, of Rome, this action is contained in his concept, for we have supposed that it is the nature of such a perfect concept of a subject to involve everything, in fact so that the predicate may be included in the subject *ut possit inesse subjecto*. We may say that it is not in virtue of this concept or idea that he is obliged to perform this action, since it pertains to him only because God knows everything. But it will be insisted in reply that his nature or form responds to this concept, and since God imposes upon him this personality, he is compelled henceforth to live up to it. I could reply by instancing the similar case of the future contingencies which as yet have no reality save in the understanding and will of God, and which, because God has given them in advance this form, must needs correspond to it. But I prefer to overcome a difficulty rather than to excuse it by instancing other difficulties, and what I am about to say will serve to clear up the one as well as the other. It is here that must be applied the distinction in the kind of relation, and I say that that which happens conformably to these decrees is assured, but that it is not therefore necessary, and if anyone did the contrary, he would do nothing impossible in itself, although it is impossible *ex hypothesi* that that other happen. For if anyone were capable of carrying out a complete demonstration by virtue of which he could prove this connection of the subject, which is Caesar, with the predicate, which is his successful enterprise, he would bring us to see in fact that the future dictatorship of Caesar had its basis in his concept or nature, so that one would see there a reason why he resolved to cross the Rubicon rather than to stop, and why he gained instead of losing the day at Pharsalus, and that it was reasonable and by consequence assured that this would occur, but one would not prove that it was necessary in itself, nor that the contrary implied a contradiction, almost in the same way in which it is reasonable and assured that God will always do what is best although that which is less perfect is not thereby implied. For it would be found that this demonstration of this predicate as belonging to Caesar is not as absolute as are those of numbers or of geometry, but that this predicate supposes a sequence of things which God has shown by his free will. This sequence is based on the first free decree of God which was to do always that which is the most perfect and upon the decree which God made following the first one, regarding human nature, which is that men should always do, although freely, that which appears to be the best. Now every truth which is founded upon this kind of decree is contingent, although certain, for the decrees of God do not change the possibilities of things and, as I have already said, although God assuredly chooses the best, this does not prevent that which is less perfect from being possible in itelf. Although it will never happen, it is not its impossibility but its imperfection which causes him to reject it. Now nothing is necessitated whose opposite is possible. One will then be in a position to satisfy these kinds of difficulties, however great they may appear (and in fact they have not been less vexing to all other thinkers who have ever treated this matter), provided that he considers well that all contingent propositions have reasons why they are thus, rather than otherwise, or indeed (what is the same thing) that they have proof *a priori* of their truth, which render them certain and show that the connection of the subject and predicate in these propositions has its basis in the nature of the one and of the other, but he must further remember that such contingent propositions have not the demonstrations of necessity, since their reasons are founded only on the principle of contingency or of the existence of things, that is to say, upon that which is, or which appears to be the best among several things equally possible. Necessary truths, on the other hand, are founded upon the principle of contradiction, and upon the possibility or impossibility of the essences themselves, without regard here to the free will of God or of creatures.

XIV. God produces different substances according to the different views which he has of the world, and by the intervention of God, the appropriate nature of each substance brings it about that what happens to one corresponds to what happens to all the others, without, however, their acting upon one another directly.

After having seen, to a certain extent, in what the nature of substances consists, we must try to explain the dependence they have upon one another and their actions and passions. Now it is first of all very evident that created substances depend upon God who preserves them and can produce them continually by a kind of emanation just as we produce our thoughts, for when God turns, so to say, on all sides and in all fashions, the general system of phenomena which he finds it good to produce for the sake of manifesting his glory, and when he regards all the aspects of the world in all possible manners, since there is no relation which escapes his omniscience, the result of each view of the universe as seen from a different position is a substance which expresses the universe conformably to this view, provided God sees fit to render his thought effective and to produce the substance, and since God's vision is always true, our perceptions are always true and that which deceives us are our judgments, which are of us. Now we have said before, and it follows from what we have just said that each substance is a world by itself, independent of everything else excepting God; therefore, all our phenomena that is all things which are ever able to happen to us, are only consequences of our being. Now as the phenomena maintain a certain order conformably to our nature, or so to speak to the world which is in us (from whence it follows that we can, for the regulation of our conduct, make useful observations which are justified by the outcome of the future phenomena) and as we are thus able often to judge the future by the past without deceiving ourselves, we have sufficient grounds for saying that these phenomena are true and we will not be put to the task of inquiring whether they are outside of us, and whether others perceive them also.

Nevertheless it is most true that the perceptions and expressions of all substances intercorrespond, so that each one following independently certain reasons or laws which he has noticed meets others which are doing the same, as when several have agreed to meet together in a certain place on a set day, they are able to carry out the plan if they wish. Now although all express the same phenomena, this does not bring it about that their expressions are exactly alike. It is sufficient if they are proportional. As when several spectators think they see the same thing and are agreed about it, although each one sees or speaks according to the measure of his vision. It is God alone, (from whom all individuals emanate continually, and who sees the universe not only as they see it, but besides in a very different way from them) who is the cause of this correspondence in their phenomena and who brings it about that that which is particular to one, is also common to all, otherwise there would be no relation. In a way, then, we might properly say, although it seems strange, that a particular substance never acts upon another particular substance nor is it acted upon by it. That which happens to each one is only the consequence of its complete idea or concept, since this idea already includes all the predicates and expresses the whole universe. In fact nothing can happen to us except thoughts and perceptions, and all our thoughts and perceptions are but the consequence, contingent it is true, of our precedent thoughts and perceptions, in such a way that were I able to consider directly all that happens or appears to me at the present time, I should be able to see all that will happen to me or that will ever appear to me. This future will not fail me, and will surely appear to me even if all that which is outside of me were destroyed, save only that God and myself were left.

Since, however, we ordinarily attribute to other things an action upon us which brings us to perceive things in a certain manner, it is necessary to consider the basis of this judgment and to inquire what there is of truth in it.

XV. The action of one finite substance upon another consists only in the increase in the degrees of the expression of the first combined with a decrease in that of the second, in so far as God has in advance fashioned them so that they shall act in accord.

Without entering into a long discussion it is sufficient for reconciling the language of metaphysics with that of practical life to remark that we preferably attribute to ourselves, and with reason, the phenomena which we express the most perfectly, and that we attribute to other substances those phenomena which each one expresses the best. Thus a substance, which is of an infinite extension in so far as it expresses all, becomes limited in proportion to its more or less perfect manner of expression. It is thus then that we may conceive of substances as interfering with and limiting one another, and hence we are able to say that in this sense they act upon one another, and that they, so to speak, accommodate themselves to one another. For it can happen that a single change which augments the expression of the one may diminish that of the other. Now the virtue of a particular substance is to express well the glory of God, and the better it expresses it, the less is it limited. Everything when it expresses its virtue or power, that is to say, when it acts, changes to better, and expands just in so far as it acts. When therefore a change occurs by which several substances are affected (in fact every change affects them all) I think we may say that those substances, which by this change pass immediately to a greater degree of perfection, or to a more perfect expression, exert power and act, while those which pass to a lesser degree disclose their weakness and suffer. I also hold that every activity of a substance which has perception implies some pleasure, and every passion some pain, except that it may very well happen that a present advantage will be eventually destroyed by a greater evil, whence it comes that one may sin in acting or exerting his power and in finding pleasure.

XVI. The extraordinary intervention of God is not excluded in that which our particular essences express, because their expression includes everything. Such intervention, however, goes beyond the power of our natural being or of our distinct expression, because these are finite, and follow certain subordinate regulations.

There remains for us at present only to explain how it is possible that God has influence at times upon men or upon other substances by an extraordinary or miraculous intervention, since it seems that nothing is able to happen which is extraordinary or supernatural in as much as all the events which occur to the other substances are only the consequences of their natures. We must recall what was said above in regard to the miracles in the universe. These always conform to the universal law of the general order, although they may contravene the subordinate regulations, and since every person or substance is like a little world which expresses the great world, we can say that this extraordinary action of God upon this substance is nevertheless miraculous, although it is comprised in the general order of the universe in so far as it is expressed by the individual essence or concept of this substance. This is why, if we understand in our natures all that they express, nothing is supernatural in them, because they reach out to everything, an effect always expressing its cause, and God being the veritable cause of the substances. But as that which our natures express the most perfectly pertains to them in a particular manner, that being their special power, and since they are limited, as I have just explained, many things there are which surpass the powers of our natures and even of all limited natures. As a consequence, to speak more clearly, I say that the miracles and the extraordinary interventions of God have this peculiarity that they cannot be foreseen by any created mind however enlightened. This is because the distinct comprehension of the fundamental order surpasses them all, while on the other hand, that which is called natural depends upon less fundamental regulations which the creatures are able to understand. In order then that my words may be as irreprehensible as the meaning I am trying to convey, it will be well to associate certain words with certain significations. We may call that which includes everything that we express and which expresses our union with God himself, nothing going beyond it, our essence. But that which is limited in us may be designated as our nature or our power and in accordance with this terminology that which goes beyond the natures of all created substances is supernatural.

XVII. An example of a subordinate regulation in the law of nature which demonstrates that God always preserves the same amount of force but not the same quantity of motion: – against the Cartesians and many others.

I have frequently spoken of subordinate regulations, or of the laws of nature, and it seems that it will be well to give an example. Our new philosophers are unanimous in employing that famous law that God always preserves the same amount of motion in the universe. In fact it is a very plausible law, and in times past I held it for indubitable. But since then I have learned in what its fault consists. Monsieur Descartes and many other clever mathematicians have thought that the quantity of motion, that is to say the velocity multiplied by the mass* of the moving body, is exactly equivalent to the moving force, or to speak in mathematical terms that the force varies as the velocity multiplied by the mass. Now it is reasonable that the same force is always preserved in the universe. So also, looking to phenomena, it will be readily seen that a mechanical perpetual motion is impossible, because the force in such a machine, being always diminished a little by friction and so ultimately destined to be entirely spent, would necessarily have to recoup its losses, and consequently would keep on increasing of itself without any new impulsion from without; and we see furthermore that the force of a body is diminished only in proportion as it gives up force, either to a contiguous body or to its own parts, in so far as they have a separate movement. The mathematicians

* This term is employed here for the sake of clearness. Leibniz did not possess the concept "mass," which was enunciated by Newton in the same year in which the present treatise was written, 1686. Leibniz uses the terms "body," "magnitude of body," etc. The technical expression "mass" occurs once only in the writings of Leibniz (in a treatise published in 1695), and was there doubtless borrowed from Newton. For the history of the controversy concerning the Cartesian and Leibnizian measure of force, see Mach's *Science of Mechanics*, Chicago, 1893, pp. 272 et seq. [original translator's note]

to whom I have referred think that what can be said of force can be said of the quantity of motion. In order, however, to show the difference I make two suppositions: in the first place, that a body falling from a certain height acquires a force enabling it to remount to the same height, provided that its direction is turned that way, or provided that there are no hindrances. For instance, a pendulum will rise exactly to the height from which it has fallen, provided the resistance of the air and of certain other small particles do not diminish a little its acquired force.

I suppose in the second place that it will take as much force to lift a body A weighing one pound to the height CD, four feet, as to raise a body B weighing four pounds to the height EF, one foot. These two suppositions are granted by our new philosophers. It is therefore manifest that the body A falling from the height CD acquires exactly as much force as the body B falling from the height EF, for the body B at F, having by the first supposition sufficient force to return to E, has therefore the force to carry a body of four pounds to the distance of one foot, EF. And likewise the body A at D, having the force to return to C, has also the force required to carry a body weighing one pound, its own weight, back to C, a distance of four feet. Now by the second supposition the force of these two bodies is equal. Let us now see if the quantity of motion is the same in each case. It is here that we will be surprised to find a very great difference, for it has been proved by Galileo that the velocity acquired by the fall CD is double the velocity acquired by the fall EF, although the height is four times as great. Multiplying, therefore, the body A, whose mass is 1, by its velocity, which is 2, the product or the quantity of movement will be 2, and on the other hand, if we multiply the body B, whose mass is 4, by its velocity, which is 1, the product or quantity of motion will be 4. Hence the quantity of the motion of the body A at the point D is half the quantity of motion of the body B at the point F, yet their forces are equal, and there is therefore a great difference between the quantity of motion and the force. This is what we set out to show. We can see therefore how the force ought to be estimated by the quantity of the effect which it is able to produce, for example by the height to which a body of certain weight can be raised. This is a very different thing from the velocity which can be imparted to it, and in order to impart to it double the velocity we must have double the force. Nothing is simpler than this proof and Monsieur Descartes has fallen into error here, only because he trusted too much to his thoughts even when they had not been ripened by reflection. But it astonishes me that his disciples have not noticed this error, and I am afraid that they are beginning to imitate little by little certain Peripatetics whom they ridicule, and that they are accustoming themselves to consult rather the books of their master, than reason or nature.

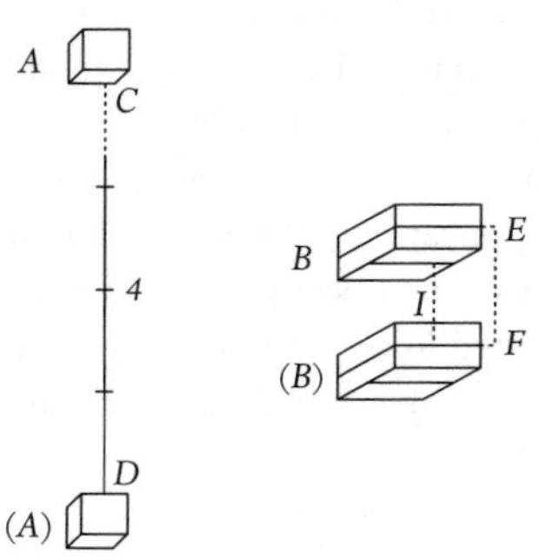

XVIII. The distinction between force and the quantity of motion is, among other reasons, important as showing that we must have recourse to metaphysical considerations in addition to discussions of extension if we wish to explain the phenomena of matter.

This consideration of the force, distinguished from the quantity of motion, is of importance, not only in physics and mechanics for finding the real laws of nature and the principles of motion, and even for correcting many practical errors which have crept into the writings of certain able mathematicians, but also in metaphysics it is of importance for the better understanding of principles. Because motion, if we regard only its exact and formal meaning, that is, change of place, is not something entirely real, and when several bodies change their places reciprocally, it is not possible to determine by considering the bodies alone to which among them movement or repose is to be attributed, as I could demonstrate geometrically, if I wished to stop for it now. But the force, or the proximate cause of these changes is something more real, and there are sufficient grounds for attributing it to one body rather than to another, and it is only through this latter investigation that we can determine to which one the movement must appertain. Now this force is something different from size, from form or from motion, and it can be seen from this consideration that the whole meaning of a body is not exhausted in its extension together with its modifications as our moderns persuade themselves. We are therefore obliged to restore certain beings or forms which they have banished. It appears more and more clear that although all the particular phenomena of nature can be explained mathematically or mechanically by those who understand them, yet nevertheless, the general principles of corporeal nature and even of mechanics are metaphysical rather than geometric, and belong rather to certain indivisible forms or natures as the causes of the appearances, than to the corporeal mass or to extension. This reflection is able to reconcile the mechanical philosophy of the moderns with the circumspection of those intelligent and well-meaning persons who, with a certain justice, fear that we are becoming too far removed from immaterial beings and that we are thus prejudicing piety.

XIX. The utility of final causes in Physics.

As I do not wish to judge people in ill part I bring no accusation against our new philosophers who pretend to banish final causes from physics, but I am nevertheless obliged to avow that the consequences of such a banishment appear to me dangerous, especially when joined to that position which I refuted at the beginning of this treatise. That position seemed to go the length of discarding final causes entirely as though God proposed no end and no good in his activity, or as if good were not to be the object of his will. I hold on the contrary that it is just in this that the principle of all existences and of the laws of nature must be sought, hence God always proposes the best and most perfect. I am quite willing to grant that we are liable to err when we wish to determine the purposes or councils of God, but this is the case only when we try to limit them to some particular design, thinking that he has had in view only a single thing, while in fact he regards everything at once. As for instance, if we think that God has made the world only for us, it is a great blunder, although it may be quite true that he has made it entirely for us, and that there is nothing in the universe which does not touch us and which does not accommodate itself to the regard which he has for us according to the principle laid down above. Therefore when we see some good effect or some perfection which happens or which follows from the works of God we are able to say assuredly that God has purposed it, for he does nothing by chance, and is not like us who sometimes fail to do well. Therefore, far from being able to fall into error in this respect as do the extreme statesmen who postulate too much foresight in the designs of Princes, or as do commentators who seek for too much erudition in their authors, it will be impossible to attribute too much reflection to God's infinite wisdom, and there is no matter in which error is less to be feared provided we confine ourselves to affirmations and provided we avoid negative statements which limit the designs of God. All those who see the admirable structure of animals find themselves led to recognize the wisdom of the author of things and I advise those who have any sentiment of piety and indeed of true philosophy to hold aloof from the expressions of certain pretentious minds who instead of saying that eyes were made for seeing, say that we see because we find ourselves having eyes. When one seriously holds such opinions which hand everything over to material necessity or to a kind of chance (although either alternative ought to appear ridiculous to those who understand what we have explained above) it is difficult to recognize an intelligent author of nature. The effect should correspond to its cause and indeed it is best known through the recognition of its cause, so that it is reasonable to introduce a sovereign intelligence ordering things, and in place of making use of the wisdom of this sovereign being, to employ only the properties of matter to explain phenomena. As if in order to account for the capture of an important place by a prince, the historian should say it was because the particles of powder in the cannon having been touched by a spark of fire expanded with a rapidity capable of pushing a hard solid body against the walls of the place, while the little particles which composed the brass of the cannon were so well interlaced that they did not separate under this impact, – as if he should account for it in this way instead of making us see how the foresight of the conqueror brought him to choose the time and the proper means and how his ability surmounted all obstacles.

XX. A noteworthy disquisition in Plato's Phaedo against the philosophers who were too materialistic.

This reminds me of a fine disquisition by Socrates in Plato's Phaedo, which agrees perfectly with my opinion on this subject and seems to have been uttered expressly for our too materialistic philosophers. This agreement has led me to a desire to translate it although it is a little long. Perhaps this example will give some of us an incentive to share in many of the other beautiful and well balanced thoughts which are found in the writings of this famous author.*

XXI. If the mechanical laws depended upon Geometry alone without metaphysical influences, the phenomena would be very different from what they are.

Now since the wisdom of God has always been recognized in the detail of the mechanical structures of certain particular bodies, it should also be shown in the general economy of the world and in the constitution of the laws of nature. This is so true that even in the laws of motion in general, the plans of this wisdom have been noticed. For if bodies were only extended masses, and motion were only a change of place, and if everything ought to be and could be deduced by geometric necessity from these two definitions alone, it would follow, as I have shown elsewhere, that the smallest body on contact with a very large one at rest would impart to it its own velocity, yet without losing any of the velocity that it had. A quantity of other rules wholly contrary to the formation of a system would also have to be admitted. But the decree of the divine wisdom in preserving always the same force and the same total direction has provided for a system. I find indeed that many of the effects of nature can be accounted for in a twofold way, that is to say by a consideration of efficient causes,

* There is a gap here in the MS., intended for the passage from Plato, the translation of which Leibniz did not supply. [translator's note]

and again independently by a consideration of final causes. An example of the latter is God's decree to always carry out his plan by the easiest and most determined way. I have shown this elsewhere in accounting for the catoptric and dioptric laws, and I will speak more at length about it in what follows.

XXII. Reconciliation of the two methods of explanation, the one using final causes, and the other efficient causes, thus satisfying both those who explain nature mechanically and those who have recourse to incorporeal natures.

It is worth while to make the preceding remark in order to reconcile those who hope to explain mechanically the formation of the first tissue of an animal and all the interrelation of the parts, with those who account for the same structure by referring to final causes. Both explanations are good; both are useful not only for the admiring of the work of a great artificer, but also for the discovery of useful facts in physics and medicine. And writers who take these diverse routes should not speak ill of each other. For I see that those who attempt to explain beauty by the divine anatomy ridicule those who imagine that the apparently fortuitous flow of certain liquids has been able to produce such a beautiful variety and that they regard them as overbold and irreverent. These others on the contrary treat the former as simple and superstitious, and compare them to those ancients who regarded the physicists as impious when they maintained that not Jupiter thundered but some material which is found in the clouds. The best plan would be to join the two ways of thinking. To use a practical comparison, we recognize and praise the ability of a workman not only when we show what designs he had in making the parts of his machine, but also when we explain the instruments which he employed in making each part, above all if these instruments are simple and ingeniously contrived. God is also a workman able enough to produce a machine still a thousand times more ingenious than is our body, by employing only certain quite simple liquids purposely composed in such a way that ordinary laws of nature alone are required to develop them so as to produce such a marvellous effect. But it is also true that this development would not take place if God were not the author of nature. Yet I find that the method of efficient causes, which goes much deeper and is in a measure more immediate and *a priori*, is also more difficult when we come to details, and I think that our philosophers are still very frequently far removed from making the most of this method. The method of final causes, however, is easier and can be frequently employed to find out important and useful truths which we should have to seek for a long time, if we were confined to that other more physical method of which anatomy is able to furnish many examples. It seems to me that Snellius, who was the first discoverer of the laws of refraction would have waited a long time before finding them if he had wished to seek out first how light was formed. But he apparently followed that method which the ancients employed for Catoptrics, that is, the method of final causes. Because, while seeking for the easiest way in which to conduct a ray of light from one given point to another given point by reflection from a given plane (supposing that that was the design of nature) they discovered the equality of the angles of incidence and reflection, as can be seen from a little treatise by Heliodorus of Larissa and also elsewhere. This principle Mons. Snellius, I believe, and afterwards independently of him, M. Fermat, applied most ingeniously to refraction. For since the rays while in the same media always maintain the same proportion of sines, which in turn corresponds to the resistance of the media, it appears that they follow the easiest way, or at least that way which is the most determinate for passing from a given point in one medium to a given point in another medium. That demonstration of this same theorem which M. Descartes has given, using efficient causes, is much less satisfactory. At least we have grounds to think that he would never have found the principle by that means if he had not learned in Holland of the discovery of Snellius.

XXIII. Returning to immaterial substances we explain how God acts upon the understanding of spirits and ask whether one always keeps the idea of what he thinks about.

I have thought it well to insist a little upon final causes, upon incorporeal natures and upon an intelligent cause with respect to bodies so as to show the use of these conceptions in physics and in mathematics. This for two reasons, first to purge from mechanical philosophy the impiety that is imputed to it, second, to elevate to nobler lines of thought the thinking of our philosophers who incline to materialistic considerations alone. Now, however, it will be well to return from corporeal substances to the consideration of immaterial natures and particularly of spirits, and to speak of the methods which God uses to enlighten them and to act upon them. Although we must not forget that there are here at the same time certain laws of nature in regard to which I can speak more amply elsewhere. It will be enough for now to touch upon ideas and to inquire if we see everything in God and how God is our light. First of all it will be in place to remark that the wrong use of ideas occasions many errors. For when one reasons in regard to anything, he imagines that he has an idea of it and this is the foundation upon which certain philosophers, ancient and modern, have constructed a demonstration of God that is extremely imperfect. It must be, they say, that I have an idea of God, or of a perfect being, since I think of him and we cannot think without having ideas; now the idea of this being includes all perfections and since existence is one of these perfections, it follows that he exists. But I reply, inasmuch as we often think of impossible chimeras, for example of the highest degree of swiftness, of the greatest number, of the meeting of the conchoid with its base or determinant, such reasoning is not sufficient. It is therefore in this sense that we can say that there are true and false ideas according as the thing which is in question is possible or not. And it is when he is assured of the possibility of a thing, that one can boast of having an idea of it. Therefore, the aforesaid argument proves that God exists, if he is possible. This is in fact an excellent privilege of the divine nature, to have need only of a possibility or an essence in order to actually exist, and it is just this which is called *ens a se*.

XXIV. What clear and obscure, distinct and confused, adequate and inadequate, intuitive and assumed knowledge is, and the definition of nominal, real, causal and essential.

In order to understand better the nature of ideas it is necessary to touch somewhat upon the various kinds of knowledge. When I am able to recognize a thing among others, without being able to say in what its differences or characteristics consist, the knowledge is confused. Sometimes indeed we may know clearly, that is without being in the slightest doubt, that a poem or a picture is well or badly done because there is in it an "I know not what" which satisfies or shocks us. Such knowledge is not yet distinct. It is when I am able to explain the peculiarities which a thing has, that the knowledge is called distinct. Such is the knowledge of an assayer who discerns the true gold from the false by means of certain proofs or marks which make up the definition of gold. But distinct knowledge has degrees, because ordinarily the conceptions which enter into the definitions will themselves have need of definition, and are only known confusedly. When at length everything which enters into a definition or into distinct knowledge is known distinctly, even back to the primitive conception, I call that knowledge adequate. When my mind understands at once and distinctly all the primitive ingredients of a conception, then we have intuitive knowledge. This is extremely rare as most human knowledge is only confused or indeed assumed. It is well also to distinguish nominal from real definition. I call a definition nominal when there is doubt whether an exact conception of it is possible; as for instance, when I say that an endless screw is a line in three dimensional space whose parts are congruent or fall one upon another. Now although this is one of the reciprocal properties of an endless screw, he who did not know from elsewhere what an endless screw was could doubt if such a line were possible, because the other lines whose ends are congruent (there are only two: the circumference of a circle and the straight line) are plane figures, that is to say they can be described *in plano*. This instance enables us to see that any reciprocal property can serve as a nominal definition, but when the property brings us to see the possibility of a thing it makes the definition real, and as long as one has only a nominal definition he cannot be sure of the consequences which he draws, because if it conceals a contradiction or an impossibility he would be able to draw the opposite conclusions. That is why truths do not depend upon names and are not arbitrary, as some of our new philosophers think. There is also a considerable difference among real definitions, for when the possibility proves itself only by experience, as in the definition of quicksilver, whose possibility we know because such a body, which is both an extremely heavy fluid and quite volatile, actually exists, the definition is merely real and nothing more. If, however, the proof of the possibility is *a priori*, the definition is not only real but also causal as for instance when it contains the possible generation of a thing. Finally when the definition, without assuming anything which requires a proof *a priori* of its possibility, carries the analysis clear to the primitive conception, the definition is perfect or essential.

XXV. In what cases knowledge is added to mere contemplation of the idea.

Now it is manifest that we have no idea of a conception when it is impossible. And in case the knowledge, where we have the idea of it, is only assumed, we do not visualize it because such a conception is known only in like manner as conceptions internally impossible. And if it be in fact possible, it is not by this kind of knowledge that we learn its possibility. For instance, when I am thinking of a thousand or of a chiliagon, I frequently do it without contemplating the idea. Even if I say a thousand is ten times a hundred, I frequently do not trouble to think what ten and a hundred are, because I assume that I know, and I do not consider it necessary to stop just at present to conceive of them. Therefore it may well happen, as it in fact does happen often enough, that I am mistaken in regard to a conception which I assume that I understand, although it is an impossible truth or at least is incompatible with others with which I join it, and whether I am mistaken or not, this way of assuming our knowledge remains the same. It is, then, only when our knowledge is clear in regard to confused conceptions, and when it is intuitive in regard to those which are distinct, that we see its entire idea.

XXVI. Ideas are all stored up within us. Plato's doctrine of reminiscence.

In order to see clearly what an idea is, we must guard ourselves against a misunderstanding. Many regard the idea as the form or the differentiation of our thinking, and according to this opinion we have the idea in our mind, in so far as we are thinking of it, and each separate time that we think of it anew we have another idea although similar to the preceding one. Some, however, take the idea as the immediate object of thought, or as a permanent form which remains even when we are no longer contemplating it. As a matter of fact our soul has the power of representing to itself any form or nature whenever the occasion comes for thinking about it, and I think that this activity of our soul is, so far as it expresses some nature, form or essence, properly the idea of the thing. This is in us, and is always in us, whether we are thinking of it or no. (Our soul expresses God and the universe and all essences as well as all existences.) This position is in accord with my principles that naturally nothing enters into our minds from outside.

It is a bad habit we have of thinking as though our minds receive certain messengers, as it were, or as if they had doors or windows. We have in our minds all those forms for all periods of time because the mind at every moment expresses all its future thoughts and already thinks confusedly of all that of which it will ever think distinctly. Nothing can be taught us of which we have not already in our minds the idea. This idea is as it were the material out of which the thought will form itself. This is what Plato has excellently brought out in his doctrine of reminiscence, a doctrine which contains a great deal of truth, provided that it is properly understood and purged of the error of pre-existence, and provided that one does not conceive of the soul as having already known and thought at some other time what it learns and thinks now. Plato has also confirmed his position by a beautiful experiment. He introduces a small boy, whom he leads by short steps, to extremely difficult truths of geometry bearing on incommensurables, all this without teaching the boy anything, merely drawing out replies by a well arranged series of questions. This shows that the soul virtually knows those things, and needs only to be reminded (animadverted) to recognize the truths. Consequently it possesses at least the idea upon which those truths depend. We may say even that it already possesses those truths, if we consider them as the relations of the ideas.

XXVII. In what respect our souls can be compared to blank tablets and how conceptions are derived from the senses.

Aristotle preferred to compare our souls to blank tablets prepared for writing, and he maintained that nothing is in the understanding which does not come through the senses. This position is in accord with the popular conceptions as Aristotle's positions usually are. Plato thinks more profoundly. Such tenets or practicologies are nevertheless allowable in ordinary use somewhat in the same way as those who accept the Copernican theory still continue to speak of the rising and setting of the sun. I find indeed that these usages can be given a real meaning containing no error, quite in the same way as I have already pointed out that we may truly say particular substances act upon one another. In this same sense we may say that knowledge is received from without through the medium of the senses because certain exterior things contain or express more particularly the causes which determine us to certain thoughts. Because in the ordinary uses of life we attribute to the soul only that which belongs to it most manifestly and particularly, and there is no advantage in going further.

When, however, we are dealing with the exactness of metaphysical truths, it is important to recognize the powers and independence of the soul which extend infinitely further than is commonly supposed. In order, therefore, to avoid misunderstandings it would be well to choose separate terms for the two. These expressions which are in the soul whether one is conceiving of them or not may be called ideas, while those which one conceives of or constructs may be called conceptions, *conceptus*. But whatever terms are used, it is always false to say that all our conceptions come from the so-called external senses, because those conceptions which I have of myself and of my thoughts, and consequently of being, of substance, of action, of identity, and of many others came from an inner experience.

XXVIII. The only immediate object of our perceptions which exists outside of us is God, and in him alone is our light.

In the strictly metaphysical sense no external cause acts upon us excepting God alone, and he is in immediate relation with us only by virtue of our continual dependence upon him. Whence it follows that there is absolutely no other external object which comes into contact with our souls and directly excites perceptions in us. We have in our souls ideas of everything, only because of the continual action of God upon us, that is to say, because every effect expresses its cause and therefore the essences of our souls are certain expressions, imitations or images of the divine essence, divine thought and divine will, including all the ideas which are there contained. We may say, therefore, that God is for us the only immediate external object, and that we see things through him. For example, when we see the sun or the stars, it is God who gives to us and preserves in us the ideas and whenever our senses are affected according to his own laws in a certain manner, it is he, who by his continual concurrence, determines our thinking. God is the sun and the light of souls, *lumen illuminans omnem hominem venientem in hunc mundum*, although this is not the current conception. I think I have already remarked that during the scholastic period many believed God to be the light of the soul, *intellectus agens animae rationalis*, following in this the Holy Scriptures and the fathers who were always more Platonic than Aristotelian in their mode of thinking. The Averroists misused this conception, but others, among whom were several mystic theologians, and William of Saint Amour, also I think, understood this conception in a manner which assured the dignity of God and was able to raise the soul to a knowledge of its welfare.

XXIX. Yet we think directly by means of our own ideas and not through God's.

Nevertheless I cannot approve of the position of certain able philosophers who seem to hold that our ideas themselves are in God and not at all in us. I think that in taking this position they have neither sufficiently considered the nature of substance, which we have just explained, nor the entire extension and independence of the soul which includes all that happens to it, and expresses God, and with him all possible and actual beings in the same way that an effect expresses its cause. It is indeed inconceivable that the soul should think using the ideas of something else. The soul when it thinks of anything must be affected effectively in a certain manner, and it must needs have in itself in advance not only the passive capacity of being thus affected, a capacity already wholly determined, but it must have besides an active power by virtue of which it has always had in its nature the marks of the future production of this thought, and the disposition to produce it at its proper time.

All of this shows that the soul already includes the idea which is comprised in any particular thought.

XXX. How God inclines our souls without necessitating them; that there are no grounds for complaint; that we must not ask why Judas sinned because this free act is contained in his concept, the only question being why Judas the sinner is admitted to existence, preferably to other possible persons; concerning the original imperfection or limitation before the fall and concerning the different degrees of grace.

Regarding the action of God upon the human will there are many quite different considerations which it would take too long to investigate here. Nevertheless the following is what can be said in general. God in co-operating with ordinary actions only follows the laws which he has established, that is to say, he continually preserves and produces our being so that the ideas come to us spontaneously or with freedom in that order which the concept of our individual substance carries with itself. In this concept they can be foreseen for all eternity. Furthermore, by virtue of the decree which God has made that the will shall always seek the apparent good in certain particular respects (in regard to which this apparent good always has in it something of reality expressing or imitating God's will), he, without at all necessitating our choice, determines it by that which appears most desirable. For absolutely speaking, our will as contrasted with necessity, is in a state of indifference, being able to act otherwise, or wholly to suspend its action, either alternative being and remaining possible. It therefore devolves upon the soul to be on guard against appearances, by means of a firm will, to reflect and to refuse to act or decide in certain circumstances, except after mature deliberation. It is, however, true and has been assured from all eternity that certain souls will not employ their power upon certain occasions.

But who could do more than God has done, and can such a soul complain of anything except itself? All these complaints after the deed are unjust, inasmuch as they would have been unjust before the deed. Would this soul a little before committing the sin have had the right to complain of God as though he had determined the sin. Since the determinations of God in these matters cannot be foreseen, how would the soul know that it was preordained to sin unless it had already committed the sin? It is merely a question of wishing to or not wishing to, and God could not have set an easier or juster condition. Therefore all judges without asking the reasons which have disposed a man to have an evil will, consider only how far this will is wrong. But, you object, perhaps it is ordained from all eternity that I will sin. Find your own answer. Perhaps it has not been. Now then, without asking for what you are unable to know and in regard to which you can have no light, act according to your duty and your knowledge. But, some one will object; whence comes it then that this man will assuredly do this sin? The reply is easy. It is that otherwise he would not be a man. For God foresees from all time that there will be a certain Judas, and in the concept or idea of him which God has, is contained this future free act. The only question, therefore, which remains is why this certain Judas, the betrayer who is possible only because of the idea of God, actually exists. To this question, however, we can expect no answer here on earth excepting to say in general that it is because God has found it good that he should exist notwithstanding that sin which he foresaw. This evil will be more than overbalanced. God will derive a greater good from it, and it will finally turn out that this series of events in which is included the existence of this sinner, is the most perfect among all the possible series of events. An explanation in every case of the admirable economy of this choice cannot be given while we are sojourners on earth. It is enough to know the excellence without understanding it. It is here that must be recognized *altitudinem divitiarum*, the unfathomable depth of the divine wisdom, without hesitating at a detail which involves an infinite number of considerations. It is clear, however, that God is not the cause of ill. For not only after the loss of innocence by men, has original sin possessed the soul, but even before that there was an original limitation or imperfection in the very nature of all creatures, which rendered them open to sin and able to fall. There is, therefore, no more difficulty in the supralapsarian view than there is in the other views of sin. To this also, it seems to me can be reduced the opinion of Saint Augustine and of other authors: that the root of evil is in the negativity, that is to say, in the lack or limitation of creatures which God graciously remedies by whatever degree of perfection it pleases him to give. This grace of God, whether ordinary or extraordinary, has its degrees and its measures. It is always efficacious in itself to produce a certain proportionate effect and furthermore it is always sufficient not only to keep one from sin but even to effect his salvation, provided that the man co-operates with that which is in him. It has not always, however, sufficient power to overcome the inclination, for, if it did, it would no longer be limited in any way, and this superiority to limitations is reserved to that unique grace which is absolutely efficacious. This grace is always victorious whether through its own self or through the congruity of circumstances.

XXXI. Concerning the motives of election; concerning faith foreseen and the absolute decree and that it all reduces to the question why God has chosen and resolved to admit to existence just such a possible person, whose concept includes just such a sequence of free acts and of free gifts of grace. This at once puts an end to all difficulties.

Finally, the grace of God is wholly unprejudiced and creatures have no claim upon it. Just as it is not sufficient in accounting for God's choice in his dispensations of grace to refer to his absolute or conditional prevision of men's future actions, so it is also wrong to imagine his decrees as absolute with no reasonable motive. As concerns foreseen faith and good works, it is very true that God has elected none but those whose faith and charity he foresees, *quos se fide donaturum praescivit*. The same question, however, arises again as to why God gives to some rather than to others the grace of faith or of good works. As concerns God's ability to foresee not only the faith and good deeds, but also their material and predisposition, or that which a man on his part contributes to them (since there are as truly diversities on the part of men as on the part of grace, and a man although he needs to be aroused to good and needs to become converted, yet acts in accordance with his temperament), – as regards his ability to foresee there are many who say that God, knowing what a particular man will do without grace, that is without his extraordinary assistance, or knowing at least what will be the human contribution, resolves to give grace to those whose natural dispositions are the best, or at any rate are the least imperfect and evil. But if this were the case then the natural dispositions in so far as they were good would be like gifts of grace, since God would have given advantages to some over others; and therefore, since he would well know that the natural advantages which he had given would serve as motives for his grace or for his extraordinary assistance, would not everything be reduced to his mercy? I think, therefore, that since we do not know how much and in what way God regards natural dispositions in the dispensations of his grace, it would be safest and most exact to say, in accordance with our principles and as I have already remarked, that there must needs be among possible beings the person Peter or John whose concept or idea contains all that particular sequence of ordinary and extraordinary manifestations of grace together with the rest of the accompanying events and circumstances, and that it has pleased God to choose him among an infinite number of persons equally possible for actual existence. When we have said this there seems nothing left to ask, and all difficulties vanish. For in regard to that great and ultimate question why it has pleased God to choose him among so great a number of possible persons, it is surely unreasonable to demand more than the general reasons which we have given. The reasons in detail surpass our ken. Therefore, instead of postulating an absolute decree, which being without reason would be unreasonable, and instead of postulating reasons which do not succeed in solving the difficulties and in turn have need themselves of reasons, it will be best to say with St. Paul that there are for God's choice certain great reasons of wisdom and congruity which he follows, which reasons, however, are unknown to mortals and are founded upon the general order, whose goal is the greatest perfection of the world. This is what is meant when the motives of God's glory and of the manifestation of his justice are spoken of, as well as when men speak of his mercy, and his perfection in general; that immense vastness of wealth, in fine, with which the soul of the same St. Paul was to thrilled.

XXXII. Usefulness of these principles in matters of piety and of religion.

In addition it seems that the thoughts which we have just explained and particularly the great principle of the perfection of God's operations and the concept of substance which includes all its changes with all its accompanying circumstances, far from injuring, serve rather to confirm religion, serve to dissipate great difficulties, to inflame souls with a divine love and to raise the mind to a knowledge of incorporeal substances much more than the present-day hypotheses. For it appears clearly that all other substances depend upon God just as our thoughts emanate from our own substances; that God is all in all and that he is intimately united to all created things, in proportion however to their perfection; that it is he alone who determines them from without by his influence, and if to act is to determine directly, it may be said in metaphysical language that God alone acts upon me and he alone causes me to do good or ill, other substances contributing only because of his determinations; because God, who takes all things into consideration, distributes his bounties and compels created beings to accommodate themselves to one another. Thus God alone constitutes the relation or communication between substances. It is through him that the phenomena of the one meet and accord with the phenomena of the others, so that there may be a reality in our perceptions. In common parlance, however, an action is attributed to particular causes in the sense that I have explained above because it is not necessary to make continual mention of the universal cause when speaking of particular cases. It can be seen also that every substance has a perfect spontaneity (which becomes liberty with intelligent substances). Everything which happens to it is a consequence of its idea or its being and nothing determines it except God only. It is for this reason that a person of exalted mind and revered saintliness may say that the soul ought often to think as if there were only God and itself in the world. Nothing can make us hold to immortality more firmly than this independence and vastness of the soul which protects it completely against exterior things, since it alone constitutes our universe and together with God is sufficient for itself. It is as impossible for it to perish save through annihilation as it is impossible for the universe to destroy itself, the universe whose animate and perpetual expression it is. Furthermore, the changes in this extended mass which is called our body cannot possibly affect the soul nor can the dissipation of the body destroy that which is indivisible.

XXXIII. Explanation of the relation between the soul and the body, a matter which has been regarded as inexplicable or else as miraculous; concerning the origin of confused perceptions.

We can also see the explanation of that great mystery "the union of the soul and the body," that is to say how it comes about that the passions and actions of the one are accompanied by the actions and passions or else the appropriate phenomena of the other. For it is not possible to conceive how one can have an influence upon the other and it is unreasonable to have recourse at once to the extraordinary intervention of the universal cause in an ordinary and particular case. The following, however, is the true explanation. We have said that everything which happens to a soul or to any substance is a consequence of its concept; hence the idea itself or the essence of the soul brings it about that all of its appearances or perceptions should be born out of its nature and precisely in such a way that they correspond of themselves to that which happens in the universe at large, but more particularly and more perfectly to that which happens in the body associated with it, because it is in a particular way and only for a certain time according to the relation of other bodies to its own body that the soul expresses the state of the universe. This last fact enables us to see how our body belongs to us, without, however, being attached to our essence. I believe that those who are careful thinkers will decide favorably for our principles because of this single reason, viz., that they are able to see in what consists the relation between the soul and the body, a parallelism which appears inexplicable in any other way. We can also see that the perceptions of our senses even when they are clear must necessarily contain certain confused elements, for as all the bodies in the universe are in sympathy, ours receives the impressions of all the others, and while our senses respond to everything, our soul cannot pay attention to every particular. That is why our confused sensations are the result of a variety of perceptions. This variety is infinite. It is almost like the confused murmuring which is heard by those who approach the shore of a sea. It comes from the continual beatings of innumerable waves. If now, out of many perceptions which do not at all fit together to make one, no particular one perception surpasses the others, and if they make impressions about equally strong or equally capable of holding the attention of the soul, they can be perceived only confusedly.

XXXIV. Concerning the difference between spirits and other substances, souls or substantial forms; that the immortality which men desire includes memory.

Supposing that the bodies which constitute a *unum per se*, as human bodies, are substances, and have substantial forms, and supposing that animals have souls, we are obliged to grant that these souls and these substantial forms cannot entirely perish, any more than can the atoms or the ultimate elements of matter, according to the position of other philosophers; for no substance perishes, although it may become very different. Such substances also express the whole universe, although more imperfectly than do spirits. The principal difference, however, is that they do not know that they are, nor what they are. Consequently, not being able to reason, they are unable to discover necessary and universal truths. It is also because they do not reflect regarding themselves that they have no moral qualities, whence it follows that undergoing a thousand transformations, as we see a caterpillar change into a butterfly, the result from a moral or practical standpoint is the same as if we said that they perished in each case, and we can indeed say it from the physical standpoint in the same way that we say bodies perish in their dissolution. But the intelligent soul, knowing that it is and having the ability to say that word "I" so full of meaning, not only continues and exists, metaphysically far more certainly than do the others, but it remains the same from the moral standpoint, and constitutes the same personality, for it is its memory or knowledge of this ego which renders it open to punishment and reward. Also the immortality which is required in morals and in religion does not consist merely in this perpetual existence, which pertains to all substances, for if in addition there were no remembrance of what one had been, immortality would not be at all desirable. Suppose that some individual could suddenly become King of China on condition, however, of forgetting what he had been, as though being born again, would it not amount to the same practically, or as far as the effects could be perceived, as if the individual were annihilated, and a king of China were the same instant created in his place? The individual would have no reason to desire this.

XXXV. The excellence of spirits; that God considers them preferable to other creatures; that the spirits express God rather than the world, while other simple substances express the world rather than God.

In order, however, to prove by natural reasons that God will preserve forever not only our substance, but also our personality, that is to say the recollection and knowledge of what we are (although the distinct knowledge is sometimes suspended during sleep and in swoons) it is necessary to join to metaphysics moral considerations. God must be considered not only as the principle and the cause of all substances and of all existing things, but also as the chief of all persons or intelligent substances, as the absolute monarch of the most perfect city or republic, such as is constituted by all the spirits together in the universe, God being the most complete of all spirits at the same time that he is greatest of all beings. For assuredly the spirits are the most perfect of substances and best express the divinity. Since all the nature, purpose, virtue and function of substances is, as has been sufficiently explained, to express God and the universe, there is no room for doubting that those substances which give the expression, knowing what they are doing and which are able to understand the great truths about God and the universe, do express God and the universe incomparably better than do those natures which are either brutish and incapable of recognizing truths, or are wholly destitute of sensation and knowledge. The difference between intelligent substances and those which are not intelligent is quite as great as between a mirror and one who sees. As God is himself the greatest and wisest of spirits it is easy to understand that the spirits with which he can, so to speak, enter into conversation and even into social relations by communicating to them in particular ways his feelings and his will so that they are able to know and love their benefactor, must be much nearer to him than the rest of created things which may be regarded as the instruments of spirits. In the same way we see that all wise persons consider far more the condition of a man than of anything else however precious it may be; and it seems that the greatest satisfaction which a soul, satisfied in other respects, can have is to see itself loved by others. However, with respect to God there is this difference that his glory and our worship can add nothing to his satisfaction, the recognition of creatures being nothing but a consequence of his sovereign and perfect felicity and being far from contributing to it or from causing it even in part. Nevertheless, that which is reasonable in finite spirits is found eminently in him and as we praise a king who prefers to preserve the life of a man before that of the most precious and rare of his animals, we should not doubt that the most enlightened and most just of all monarchs has the same preference.

XXXVI. God is the monarch of the most perfect republic composed of all the spirits, and the happiness of this city of God is his principal purpose.

Spirits are of all substances the most capable of perfection and their perfections are different in this that they interfere with one another the least, or rather they aid one another the most, for only the most virtuous can be the most perfect friends. Hence it follows that God who in all things has the greatest perfection will have the greatest care for spirits and will give not only to all of them in general, but even to each one in particular the highest perfection which the universal harmony will permit. We can even say that it is because he is a spirit that God is the originator of existences, for if he had lacked the power of will to choose what is best, there would have been no reason why one possible being should exist rather than any other. Therefore God's being a spirit himself dominates all the consideration which he may have toward created things. Spirits alone are made in his image, being as it were of his blood or as children in the family, since they alone are able to serve him of free will, and to act consciously imitating the divine nature. A single spirit is worth a whole world, because it not only expresses the whole world, but it also knows it and governs itself as does God. In this way we may say that though every substance expresses the whole universe, yet the other substances express the world rather than God, while spirits express God rather than the world. This nature of spirits, so noble that it enables them to approach divinity as much as is possible for created things, has as a result that God derives infinitely more glory from them than from the other beings, or rather the other beings furnish to spirits the material for glorifying him. This moral quality of God which constitutes him Lord and Monarch of spirits influences him so to speak personally and in a unique way. It is through this that he humanizes himself, that he is willing to suffer anthropologies, and that he enters into social relations with us and this consideration is so dear to him that the happy and prosperous condition of his empire which consists in the greatest possible felicity of its inhabitants, becomes supreme among his laws. Happiness is to persons what perfection is to beings. And if the dominant principle in the existence of the physical world is the decree to give it the greatest possible perfection, the primary purpose in the moral world or in the city of God which constitutes the noblest part of the universe ought to be to extend the greatest happiness possible. We must not therefore doubt that God has so ordained everything that spirits not only shall live forever, because this is unavoidable, but that they shall also preserve forever their moral quality, so that his city may never lose a person, quite in the same way that the world never loses a substance. Consequently they will always be conscious of their being, otherwise they would be open to neither reward nor punishment, a condition which is the essence of a republic, and above all of the most perfect republic where nothing can be neglected. In fine, God being at the same time the most just and the most debonnaire of monarchs, and requiring only a good will on the part of men, provided that it be sincere and intentional, his subjects cannot desire a better condition. To render them perfectly happy he desires only that they love him.

XXXVII. Jesus Christ has revealed to men the mystery and the admirable laws of the kingdom of heaven, and the greatness of the supreme happiness which God has prepared for those who love him.

The ancient philosophers knew very little of these important truths. Jesus Christ alone has expressed them divinely well, and in a way so clear and simple that the dullest minds have understood them. His gospel has entirely changed the face of human affairs. It has brought us to know the kingdom of heaven, or that perfect republic of spirits which deserves to be called the city of God. He it is who has discovered to us its wonderful laws. He alone has made us see how much God loves us and with what care everything that concerns us has been provided for; how God, inasmuch as he cares for the sparrows, will not neglect reasoning beings, who are infinitely more dear to him; how all the hairs of our heads are numbered; how heaven and earth may pass away but the word of God and that which belongs to the means of our salvation will not pass away; how God has more regard for the least one among intelligent souls than for the whole machinery of the world; how we ought not to fear those who are able to destroy the body but are unable to destroy the soul, since God alone can render the soul happy or unhappy; and how the souls of the righteous are protected by his hand against all the upheavals of the universe, since God alone is able to act upon them; how none of our acts are forgotten; how everything is to be accounted for; even careless words and even a spoonful of water which is well used; in fact how everything must result in the greatest welfare of the good, for then shall the righteous become like suns and neither our sense nor our minds have ever tasted of anything approaching the joys which God has laid up for those that love him.

17

G. W. F. Leibniz, *The Theodicy: Abridgement of the Argument*

The *Theodicy* is the only book that Leibniz published in his lifetime. A theodicy is a defense of God. Specifically, a theodicy explains how it is possible for God to be omniscient, omnipotent, and omnibenevolent and for innocent people to suffer. It seems that if someone knows that an innocent person is going to suffer and if that person has the power and knowledge needed to prevent that suffering, and if that person is good, then that person will prevent that suffering. But it appears to be a fact that innocent people do suffer, for example young children. This is often known as the problem of evil. One standard way of solving the problem of evil is to deny the premise that some people are innocent and to affirm that all people are sinners. Even newborn babies, who have not themselves committed a sin, are nevertheless born in a sinful state because the guilt of Adam and Eve is transmitted to every human being. This is the doctrine of original sin.

Even if this solution works, the problem of evil can be strengthened, that is, made more difficult to solve, by replacing the premise that all people are innocent with the premise that some people suffer disproportionately to their sins. Even if infants are sinners, they are not as morally bad as many adults who have lied, cheated, and physically and emotionally injured others. Yet, some infants suffer horribly for years and then die, while some bad adults live long, happy, and comfortable lives.

Leibniz's theodicy is supposed to be strong enough to solve even this stronger formulation of the problem of evil. His view is that, from the infinite number of possible worlds that God might have created, he created the one with the most good. Granted that there is much evil in this world, this evil is due to the fact that creatures, being finite, will always include corrupt beings. If a human being knew all of the possible worlds that could have been created, it would be obvious that God created the best one.

For Leibniz's biography, see the introduction to selection 16 above.

Some intelligent persons have desired that this supplement be made [to the Theodicy], and I have the more readily yielded to their wishes as in this way I have an opportunity again to remove certain difficulties and to make some observations which were not sufficiently emphasized in the work itself.

I. *Objection.* Whoever does not choose the best is lacking in power, or in knowledge, or in goodness.

God did not choose the best in creating this world.

Therefore, God has been lacking in power, or in knowledge, or in goodness.

Answer. I deny the minor, that is, the second premise of this syllogism; and our opponent proves it by this.

Prosyllogism. Whoever makes things in which there is evil, which could have been made without any evil, or the making of which could have been omitted, does not choose the best.

God has made a world in which there is evil; a world, I say, which could have been made without any evil, or the making of which could have been omitted altogether.

Therefore, God has not chosen the best.

Answer. I grant the minor of this prosyllogism; for it must be confessed that there is evil in this world which God has made, and that it was possible to make a world without evil, or even not to create a world at all, for its creation has depended on the free will of God; but I deny the major, that is, the first of the two premises of the prosyllogism, and I might content myself with simply demanding its proof; but in order to make the matter clearer, I have wished to justify this denial by showing that the best plan is not always that which seeks to avoid evil, since it may happen that *the evil is accompanied by a greater good*. For example, a general of an army will prefer a great victory with a slight wound to a condition without wound and without victory. We have proved this more fully in the large work by making it clear, by instances taken from mathematics and elsewhere, that an imperfection in the part may be required for a greater perfection in the whole. In this I have followed the opinion of St. Augustine, who has said a hundred times, that God has permitted evil in order to bring about good, that is, a greater good; and that of Thomas Aquinas (in libr. II. sent. dist. 32, qu. I, art. 1), that the permitting of evil tends to the good of the universe. I have shown that the ancients called Adam's fall *felix culpa*, a happy sin, because it had been retrieved with immense advantage by the incarnation of the Son of God, who has given to the universe something nobler than anything that ever would have been among creatures except for it. For the sake of a clearer understanding, I have added, following many good authors, that it was in accordance with order and the general good that God allowed to certain creatures the opportunity of exercising their liberty, even when he foresaw that they would turn to evil, but which he could so well rectify; because it was not fitting that, in order to hinder sin, God should always act in an extraordinary manner. To overthrow this objection, therefore, it is sufficient to show that a world with evil might be better than a world without evil; but I have gone even farther, in the work, and have even proved that this universe must be in reality better than every other possible universe.

II. *Objection.* If there is more evil than good in intelligent creatures, then there is more evil than good in the whole work of God.

Now, there is more evil than good in intelligent creatures.

Therefore, there is more evil than good in the whole work of God.

Answer. I deny the major and the minor of this conditional syllogism. As to the major, I do not admit it at all, because this pretended deduction from a part to the whole, from intelligent creatures to all creatures, supposes tacitly and without proof that creatures destitute of reason cannot enter into comparison nor into account with those which possess it. But why may it not be that the surplus of good in the non-intelligent creatures which fill the world, compensates for, and even incomparably surpasses, the surplus of evil in the rational creatures? It is true that the value of the latter is greater; but, in compensation, the others are beyond comparison the more numerous, and it may be that the proportion of number and quantity surpasses that of value and of quality.

As to the minor, that is no more to be admitted; that is, it is not at all to be admitted that there is more evil than good in the intelligent creatures. There is no need even of granting that there is more evil than good in the human race, because it is possible, and in fact very probable, that the glory and the perfection of the blessed are incomparably greater than the misery and the imperfection of the damned, and that here the excellence of the total good in the smaller number exceeds the total evil in the greater number. The blessed approach the Divinity, by means of a Divine Mediator, as near as may suit these creatures, and make such progress in good as is impossible for the damned to make in evil, approach as nearly as they may to the nature of demons. God is infinite, and the devil is limited; the good may and does go to infinity, while evil has its bounds. It is therefore possible, and is credible, that in the comparison of the blessed and the damned, the contrary of that which I have said might happen in the comparison of intelligent and non-intelligent creatures, takes place; namely, it is possible that in the comparison of the happy and the unhappy, the proportion of degree exceeds that of number, and that in the comparison of intelligent and non-intelligent creatures, the proportion of number is greater than that of value. I have the right to suppose that a thing is possible so long as its impossibility is not proved; and indeed that which I have here advanced is more than a supposition.

But in the second place, if I should admit that there is more evil than good in the human race, I have still good grounds for not admitting that there is more evil than good in all intelligent creatures. For there is an inconceivable number of genii, and perhaps of other rational creatures. And an opponent could not prove that in all the City of God, composed as well of genii as of rational animals without number and of an infinity of kinds, evil exceeds good. And although in order to answer an objection, there is no need of proving that a thing is, when its mere possibility suffices; yet, in this work, I have not omitted to show that it is a consequence of the supreme perfection of the Sovereign of the universe, that the kingdom of God is the most perfect of all possible states or governments, and that consequently the little evil there is, is required for the consummation of the immense good which is found there.

III. *Objection*. If it is always impossible not to sin, it is always unjust to punish.

Now, it is always impossible not to sin; or, in other words, every sin is necessary.

Therefore, it is always unjust to punish.

The minor of this is proved thus:

1. *Prosyllogism*. All that is predetermined is necessary.

Every event is predetermined.

Therefore, every event (and consequently sin also) is necessary.

Again this second minor is proved thus:

2. *Prosyllogism*. That which is future, that which is foreseen, that which is involved in the causes, is predetermined.

Every event is such.

Therefore, every event is predetermined.

Answer. I admit in a certain sense the conclusion of the second prosyllogism, which is the minor of the first; but I shall deny the major of the first prosyllogism, namely, that every thing predetermined is necessary; understanding by the *necessity* of sinning, for example, or by the impossibility of not sinning, or of not performing any action, the necessity with which we are here concerned, that is, that which is essential and absolute, and which destroys the morality of an action and the justice of punishments. For if anyone understood another necessity or impossibility, namely, a necessity which should be only moral, or which was only hypothetical (as will be explained shortly); it is clear that I should deny the major of the objection itself. I might content myself with this answer and demand the proof of the proposition denied; but I have again desired to explain my procedure in this work, in order to better elucidate the matter and to throw more light on the whole subject, by explaining the necessity which ought to be rejected and the determination which must take place. That *necessity* which is contrary to morality and which ought to be rejected, and which would render punishment unjust, is an insurmountable necessity which would make all opposition useless, even if we should wish with all our heart to avoid the necessary action, and should make all possible efforts to that end. Now, it is manifest that this is not applicable to voluntary actions, because we would not perform them if we did not choose to. Also their prevision and predetermination are not absolute, but presuppose the will: if it is certain that we shall perform them, it is not less certain that we shall choose to perform them. These voluntary actions and their consequences will not take place no matter what we do or whether we wish them or not; but, *through* that which we shall do and through that which we shall wish to do, which leads to them. And this is involved in prevision and in predetermination, and even constitutes their ground. And the necessity of such an event is called conditional or hypothetical, or the necessity of consequence, because it supposes the will, and the other *requisites*; whereas the necessity which destroys morality and renders punishment unjust and reward useless, exists in things which will be whatever we may do or whatever we may wish to do, and, in a word, is in that which is essential; and this is what is called an absolute necessity. Thus it is to no purpose, as regards what is absolutely necessary, to make prohibitions or commands, to propose penalties or prizes, to praise or to blame; it will be none the less. On the other hand, in voluntary actions and in that which depends upon them, precepts armed with power to punish and to recompense are very often of use and are included in the order of causes which make an action exist. And it is for this reason that not only cares and labors but also prayers are useful; God having had these prayers in view before he regulated things and having had that consideration for them which was proper. This is why the precept which says *ora et labora* (pray and work), holds altogether good; and not only those who (under the vain pretext of the necessity of events) pretend that the care which business demands may be neglected, but also those who reason against prayer, fall into what the ancients even then called the *lazy sophism*. Thus the predetermination of events by causes is just what contributes to morality instead of destroying it, and causes incline the will, without compelling it. This is why the *determination* in question is not a necessitation – it is certain (to him who knows all) that the effect will follow this inclination; but this effect does not follow by a necessary consequence, that is, one the contrary of which implies contradiction. It is also by an internal inclination such as this that the will is determined, without there being any necessity. Suppose that one has the greatest passion in the world (a great thirst, for example), you will admit to me that the soul can find some reason for resisting it, if it were only that of showing its power. Thus, although one may never be in a perfect indifference of equilibrium and there may be always a preponderance of inclination for the side taken, it, nevertheless, never renders the resolution taken absolutely necessary.

IV. *Objection*. Whoever can prevent the sin of another and does not do so, but rather contributes to it although he is well informed of it, is accessory to it.

God can prevent the sin of intelligent creatures; but he does not do so, and rather contributes to it by his concurrence and by the opportunities which he brings about, although he has a perfect knowledge of it.

Hence, etc.

Answer. I deny the major of this syllogism. For it is possible that one could prevent sin, but ought not, because he could not do it without himself committing a sin, or (when God is in question) without performing an unreasonable action. Examples have been given and the application to God himself has been made. It is possible also that we contribute to evil and that sometimes we even open the road to it, in doing things which we are obliged to do; and, when we do our duty or (in speaking of God) when, after thorough consideration, we do that which reason demands, we are not responsible for the results, even when we foresee them. We do not desire these evils; but we are willing to permit them for the sake of a greater good which we cannot reasonably help preferring to other considerations. And this is a *consequent* will, which results from *antecedent* wills by which we will the good. I know that some persons, in speaking of the antecedent and consequent will of God, have understood by the *antecedent* that which wills that all men should be saved; and by the *consequent*, that which wills, in consequence of persistent sin, that some should be damned. But these are merely illustrations of a more general idea, and it may be said for the same reason that God, by his antecedent will, wills that men should not sin; and by his consequent or final and decreeing will (that which is always followed by its effect), he wills to permit them to sin, this permission being the result of superior reasons. And we have the right to say in general that the antecedent will of God tends to the production of good and the prevention of evil, each taken in itself and as if alone (*particulariter et secundum quid*, Thom. I, qu. 19, art. 6), according to the measure of the degree of each good and of each evil; but that the divine consequent or final or total will tends toward the production of as many goods as may be put together, the combination of which becomes in this way determined, and includes also the permission of some evils and the exclusion of some goods, as the best possible plan for the universe demands.

[. . .]

V. *Objection.* Whoever produces all that is real in a thing, is its cause.
God produces all that is real in sin.
Hence, God is the cause of sin.

Answer. I might content myself with denying the major or the minor, since the term *real* admits of interpretations which would render these propositions false. But in order to explain more clearly, I will make a distinction. *Real* signifies either that which is positive only, or, it includes also privative beings: in the first case, I deny the major and admit the minor; in the second case, I do the contrary. I might have limited myself to this, but I have chosen to proceed still farther and give the reason for this distinction. I have been very glad therefore to draw attention to the fact that every reality purely positive or absolute is a perfection; and that imperfection comes from limitation, that is, from the privative: for to limit is to refuse progress, or the greatest possible progress. Now God is the cause of all perfections and consequently of all realities considered as purely positive. But limitations or privations result from the original imperfection of creatures, which limits their receptivity. And it is with them as with a loaded vessel, which the river causes to move more or less slowly according to the weight which it carries: thus its speed depends upon the river, but the retardation which limits this speed comes from the load. [. . .] And the original limitation or imperfection of creatures requires that even the best plan of the universe could not receive more good, and could not be exempt from certain evils, which, however, are to result in a greater good. There are certain disorders in the parts which marvellously enhance the beauty of the whole; just as certain dissonances, when properly used, render harmony more beautiful. But this depends on what has already been said in answer to the first objection.

VI. *Objection*. Whoever punishes those who have done as well as it was in their power to do, is unjust.

God does so.

Hence, etc.

Answer. I deny the minor of this argument. And I believe that God always gives sufficient aid and grace to those who have a good will, that is, to those who do not reject this grace by new sin. Thus I do not admit the damnation of infants who have died without baptism or outside of the church; nor the damnation of adults who have acted according to the light which God has given them. And I believe that if *any one has followed the light which has been given him*, he will undoubtedly receive greater light when he has need of it, as the late M. Hulseman, a profound and celebrated theologian at Leipsig, has somewhere remarked; and if such a man has failed to receive it during his lifetime he will at least receive it when at the point of death.

VII. *Objection*. Whoever gives only to some, and not to all, the means which produces in them effectively a good will and salutary final faith, has not sufficient goodness.

God does this.

Hence, etc.

Answer. I deny the major of this. It is true that God could overcome the greatest resistance of the human heart; and does it, too, sometimes, either by internal grace, or by external circumstances which have a great effect on souls; but he does not always do this. Whence comes this distinction? it may be asked, and why does his goodness seem limited? It is because, as I have already said in answering the first objection, it would not have been in order always to act in an extraordinary manner, and to reverse the connection of things. The reasons of this connection, by means of which one is placed in more favorable circumstances than another, are hidden in the depths of the wisdom of God: they depend upon the universal harmony. The best plan of the universe, which God could not fail to choose, made it so. We judge from the event itself; since God has made it, it was not possible to do better. Far from being true that this conduct is contrary to goodness, it is supreme goodness which led him to it. This objection with its solution might have been drawn from what was said in regard to the first objection; but it seemed useful to touch upon it separately.

VIII. *Objection*. Whoever cannot fail to choose the best, is not free.

God cannot fail to choose the best.

Hence, God is not free.

Answer. I deny the major of this argument; it is rather true liberty, and the most perfect, to be able to use one's free will for the best, and to always exercise this power, without ever being turned aside either by external force or by internal passions, the first of which causes slavery of the body, the second, slavery of the soul. There is nothing less servile, and nothing more in accordance with the highest degree of freedom, than to be always led toward the good, and always by one's own inclination, without any constraint and without any displeasure. And to object therefore that God had need of external things, is only a sophism. He created them freely; but having proposed to himself an end, which is to exercise his goodness, wisdom has determined him to choose the means best fitted to attain this end. To call this a *need*, is to take that term in an unusual sense which frees it from all imperfection, just as when we speak of the wrath of God.

18

G. W. F. Leibniz, *The Monadology*

The doctrine of the *Monadology* is the one most closely associated with Leibniz. A monad is a simple substance that is a component of composite substances. There have to be monads because there are complex objects, and the division of objects into parts cannot go on infinitely. The monads are not extended, because anything that is extended can be divided and hence is not simple. Monads are active, but not self-sufficient. God creates and conserves them.

No monad acts on any other. Each monad reflects the entire world from its own unique perspective.

Each monad perceives every other monad.

But these perceptions were preprogrammed by God and are not caused by the other monads.

The obvious question to ask is: "Why should anyone believe this doctrine of monads is true?" One answer is that it should be considered a metaphysical hypothesis analogous to a hypothesis in physics. The doctrine of monads will be rationally acceptable if it succeeds in explaining reality.

1. The Monad, of which we will speak here, is nothing else than a simple substance, which goes to make up composites; by simple, we mean without parts.

2. There must be simple substances because there are composites; for a composite is nothing else than a collection or *aggregatum* of simple substances.

3. Now, where there are no constituent parts there is possible neither extension, nor form, nor divisibility. These Monads are the true atoms of nature, and, in fact, the Elements of things.

4. Their dissolution, therefore, is not to be feared and there is no way conceivable by which a simple substance can perish through natural means.

5. For the same reason there is no way conceivable by which a simple substance might, through natural means, come into existence, since it can not be formed by composition.

6. We may say then, that the existence of Monads can begin or end only all at once, that is to say, the Monad can begin only through creation and end only through annihilation. Composites, however, begin or end gradually.

7. There is also no way of explaining how a Monad can be altered or changed in its inner being by any other created thing, since there is no possibility of transposition within it, nor can we conceive of any internal movement which can be produced, directed, increased or diminished there within the substance, such as can take place in the case of composites where a change can occur among the parts. The Monads have no windows through which anything may come in or go out. The Attributes are not liable to detach themselves and make an excursion outside the substance, as could *sensible species* of the Schoolmen. In the same way neither substance nor attribute can enter from without into a Monad.

8. Still Monads must needs have some qualities, otherwise they would not even be existences. And if simple substances did not differ at all in their qualities, there would be no means of perceiving any change in things. Whatever is in a composite can come into it only through its simple elements and the Monads, if they were without qualities, since they do not differ at all in quantity, would be indistinguishable one from another. For instance, if we imagine *a plenum* or completely filled space, where each part receives only the equivalent of its own previous motion, one state of things would not be distinguishable from another.

9. Each Monad, indeed, must be different from every other. For there are never in nature two beings which are exactly alike, and in which it is not possible to find a difference either internal or based on an intrinsic property.

10. I assume it as admitted that every created being, and consequently the created Monad, is subject to change, and indeed that this change is continuous in each.

11. It follows from what has just been said, that the natural changes of the Monad come from an internal principle, because an external cause can have no influence upon its inner being.

12. Now besides this principle of change there must also be in the Monad a manifoldness which changes. This manifoldness constitutes, so to speak, the specific nature and the variety of the simple substances.

13. This manifoldness must involve a multiplicity in the unity or in that which is simple. For since every natural change takes place by degrees, there must be something which changes and something which remains unchanged, and consequently there must be in the simple substance a plurality of conditions and relations, even though it has no parts.

14. The passing condition which involves and represents a multiplicity in the unity, or in the simple substance, is nothing else than what is called Perception. This should be carefully distinguished from Apperception or Consciousness, as will appear in what follows. In this matter the Cartesians have fallen into a serious error, in that they treat as nonexistent those perceptions of which we are not conscious. It is this also which has led them to believe that spirits alone are Monads and that there are no souls of animals or other Entelechies, and it has led them to make the common confusion between a protracted period of unconsciousness and actual death. They have thus adopted the Scholastic error that souls can exist entirely separated from bodies, and have even confirmed ill-balanced minds in the belief that souls are mortal.

15. The action of the internal principle which brings about the change or the passing from one perception to another may be called Appetition. It is true that the desire (*l'appetit*) is not always able to attain to the whole of the perception which it strives for, but it always attains a portion of it and reaches new perceptions.

16. We, ourselves, experience a multiplicity in a simple substance, when we find that the most trifling thought of which we are conscious involves a variety in the object. Therefore all those who acknowledge that the soul is a simple substance ought to grant this multiplicity

in the Monad, and Monsieur Bayle should have found no difficulty in it, as he has done in his *Dictionary*, article "Rorarius."

17. It must be confessed, however, that Perception, and that which depends upon it, are inexplicable by mechanical causes, that is to say, by figures and motions. Supposing that there were a machine whose structure produced thought, sensation, and perception, we could conceive of it as increased in size with the same proportions until one was able to enter into its interior, as he would into a mill. Now, on going into it he would find only pieces working upon one another, but never would he find anything to explain Perception. It is accordingly in the simple substance, and not in the composite nor in a machine that the Perception is to be sought. Furthermore, there is nothing besides perceptions and their changes to be found in the simple substance. And it is in these alone that all the internal activities of the simple substance can consist.

18. All simple substances or created Monads may be called Entelechies, because they have in themselves a certain perfection (ἔχουσι τὸ ἐντελές). There is in them a sufficiency (αὐτάρκεια) which makes them the source of their internal activities, and renders them, so to speak, incorporeal Automatons.

19. If we wish to designate as soul everything which has perceptions and desires in the general sense that I have just explained, all simple substances or created Monads could be called souls. But since feeling is something more than a mere perception I think that the general name of Monad or Entelechy should suffice for simple substances which have only perception, while we may reserve the term Soul for those whose perception is more distinct and is accompanied by memory.

20. We experience in ourselves a state where we remember nothing and where we have no distinct perception, as in periods of fainting, or when we are overcome by a profound, dreamless sleep. In such a state the soul does not sensibly differ at all from a simple Monad. As this state, however, is not permanent and the soul can recover from it, the soul is something more.

21. Nevertheless it does not follow at all that the simple substance is in such a state without perception. This is so because of the reasons given above; for it cannot perish, nor on the other hand would it exist without some affection and the affection is nothing else than its perception. When, however, there are a great number of weak perceptions where nothing stands out distinctively, we are stunned; as when one turns around and around in the same direction, a dizziness comes on, which makes him swoon and makes him able to distinguish nothing. Among animals, death can occasion this state for quite a period.

22. Every present state of a simple substance is a natural consequence of its preceding state, in such a way that its present is big with its future.

23. Therefore, since on awakening after a period of unconsciousness we become conscious of our perceptions, we must, without having been conscious of them, have had perceptions immediately before; for one perception can come in a natural way only from another perception, just as a motion can come in a natural way only from a motion.

24. It is evident from this that if we were to have nothing distinctive, or so to speak prominent, and of a higher flavor in our perceptions, we should be in a continual state of stupor. This is the condition of Monads which are wholly bare.

25. We see that nature has given to animals heightened perceptions, having provided them with organs which collect numerous rays of light or numerous waves of air and thus make them more effective in their combination. Something similar to this takes place in the case of smell, in that of taste and of touch, and perhaps in many other senses which are unknown

to us. I shall have occasion very soon to explain how that which occurs in the soul represents that which goes on in the sense-organs.

26. The memory furnishes a sort of consecutiveness which imitates reason but is to be distinguished from it. We see that animals when they have the perception of something which they notice and of which they have had a similar previous perception, are led by the representation of their memory to expect that which was associated in the preceding perception, and they come to have feelings like those which they had before. For instance, if a stick be shown to a dog, he remembers the pain which it has caused him and he whines or runs away.

27. The vividness of the picture, which comes to him or moves him, is derived either from the magnitude or from the number of the previous perceptions. For, oftentimes, a strong impression brings about, all at once, the same effect as a long-continued habit or as a great many re-iterated, moderate perceptions.

28. Men act in like manner as animals, in so far as the sequence of their perceptions is determined only by the law of memory, resembling the *empirical physicians* who practice simply, without any theory, and we are empiricists in three-fourths of our actions. For instance, when we expect that there will be day-light to-morrow, we do so empirically, because it has always happened so up to the present time. It is only the astronomer who uses his reason in making such an affirmation.

29. But the knowledge of eternal and necessary truths is that which distinguishes us from mere animals and gives us reason and the sciences, thus raising us to a knowledge of ourselves and of God. This is what is called in us the Rational Soul or the Mind.

30. It is also through the knowledge of necessary truths and through abstractions from them that we come to perform Reflective Acts, which cause us to think of what is called the I, and to decide that this or that is within us. It is thus, that in thinking upon ourselves we think of *being*, of *substance*, of the *simple* and *composite*, of a *material* thing and of *God* himself, conceiving that what is limited in us is in him without limits. These Reflective Acts furnish the principal objects of our reasonings.

31. Our reasoning is based upon two great principles: first, that of Contradiction, by means of which we decide that to be false which involves contradiction and that to be true which contradicts or is opposed to the false.

32. And second, the principle of Sufficient Reason, in virtue of which we believe that no fact can be real or existing and no statement true unless it has a sufficient reason why it should be thus and not otherwise. Most frequently, however, these reasons cannot be known by us.

33. There are also two kinds of Truths: those of Reasoning and those of Fact. The Truths of Reasoning are necessary, and their opposite is impossible. Those of Fact, however, are contingent, and their opposite is possible. When a truth is necessary, the reason can be found by analysis in resolving it into simpler ideas and into simpler truths until we reach those which are primary.

34. It is thus that with mathematicians the Speculative Theorems and the practical Canons are reduced by analysis to Definitions, Axioms, and Postulates.

35. There are finally simple ideas of which no definition can be given. There are also the Axioms and Postulates or, in a word, the primary principles which cannot be proved and, indeed, have no need of proof. These are identical propositions whose opposites involve express contradictions.

36. But there must be also a sufficient reason for contingent truths or truths of fact; that is to say, for the sequence of the things which extend throughout the universe of created

beings, where the analysis into more particular reasons can be continued into greater detail without limit because of the immense variety of the things in nature and because of the infinite division of bodies. There is an infinity of figures and of movements, present and past, which enter into the efficient cause of my present writing, and in its final cause there are an infinity of slight tendencies and dispositions of my soul, present and past.

37. And as all this detail again involves other and more detailed contingencies, each of which again has need of a similar analysis in order to find its explanation, no real advance has been made. Therefore, the sufficient or ultimate reason must needs be outside of the sequence or series of these details of contingencies, however infinite they may be.

38. It is thus that the ultimate reason for things must be a necessary substance, in which the detail of the changes shall be present merely potentially, as in the fountain-head, and this substance we call God.

39. Now, since this substance is a sufficient reason for all the above mentioned details, which are linked together throughout, *there is but one God, and this God is sufficient*.

40. We may hold that the supreme substance, which is unique, universal and necessary with nothing independent outside of it, which is further a pure sequence of possible being, must be incapable of limitation and must contain as much reality as possible.

41. Whence it follows that God is absolutely perfect, perfection being understood as the magnitude of positive reality in the strict sense, when the limitations or the bounds of those things which have them are removed. There where there are no limits, that is to say, in God, perfection is absolutely infinite.

42. It follows also that created things derive their perfections through the influence of God, but their imperfections come from their own natures, which cannot exist without limits. It is in this latter that they are distinguished from God. An example of this original imperfection of created things is to be found in the natural inertia of bodies.

43. It is true, furthermore, that in God is found not only the source of existences, but also that of essences, in so far as they are real. In other words, he is the source of whatever there is real in the possible. This is because the Understanding of God is in the region of eternal truths or of the ideas upon which they depend, and because without him there would be nothing real in the possibilities of things, and not only would nothing be existent, nothing would be even possible.

44. For it must needs be that if there is a reality in essences or in possibilities or indeed in the eternal truths, this reality is based upon something existent and actual, and, consequently, in the existence of the necessary Being in whom essence includes existence or in whom possibility is sufficient to produce actuality.

45. Therefore God alone (or the Necessary Being) has this prerogative that if he be possible he must necessarily exist, and, as nothing is able to prevent the possibility of that which involves no bounds, no negation, and consequently, no contradiction, this alone is sufficient to establish *a priori* his existence. We have, therefore, proved his existence through the reality of eternal truths. But a little while ago we also proved it *a posteriori*, because contingent beings exist, which can have their ultimate and sufficient reason only in the necessary being which, in turn, has the reason for existence in itself.

46. Yet we must not think that the eternal truths being dependent upon God are therefore arbitrary and depend upon his will, as Descartes seems to have held, and after him Monsieur Poiret. This is the case only with contingent truths which depend upon fitness or the choice of the greatest good; necessary truths on the other hand depend solely upon his understanding and are the inner objects of it.

47. God alone is the ultimate unity or the original simple substance, of which all created or derivative Monads are the products, and arise, so to speak, through the continual outflashings of the divinity from moment to moment, limited by the receptivity of the creature to whom limitation is an essential.

48. In God are present: Power, which is the source of everything; Knowledge, which contains the details of the ideas; and, finally, Will, which produces or effects changes in accordance with the principle of the greatest good. To these correspond in the created Monad, the subject or the basis of the faculty of perception and the faculty of appetition. In God these attributes are absolutely infinite or perfect, while in the created Monads or in the entelechies (*perfectihabies*, as Hermolaus Barbarus translates this word), they are imitations approaching him in proportion to their perfection.

49. A created thing is said to act outwardly in so far as it has perfection, and to Suffer from another in so far as it is imperfect. Thus action is attributed to the Monad in so far as it has distinct perceptions, and passion or passivity is attributed in so far as it has confused perceptions.

50. One created thing is more perfect than another when we find in the first that which gives an *a priori* reason for what occurs in the second. This is why we say that one acts upon the other.

51. In the case of simple substances, the influence which one Monad has upon another is only ideal. It can have its effect only through the mediation of God, in so far as in the Ideas of God each Monad can rightly demand that God, in regulating the others from the beginning of things, should have regarded it also. For, since one created Monad cannot have a physical influence upon the inner being of another, it is only through this primal regulation that one can have dependence upon another.

52. It is thus that among created things action and passion are reciprocal. For God, in comparing two simple substances, finds in each one reasons obliging him to adapt the other to it; and consequently that which is active in certain respects is passive from another point of view, – active in so far as that which we distinctly know in it serves to give a reason for that which occurs in another, and passive in so far as the reason for what transpires in it is found in that which is distinctly known in another.

53. Now as there are an infinity of possible universes in the Ideas of God, and but one of them can exist, there must be a sufficient reason for the choice of God which determines him to select one rather than another.

54. And this reason is to be found only in the fitness or in the degree of perfection which these worlds possess, each possible thing having the right to claim existence in proportion to the perfection which it involves.

55. This is the cause for the existence of the greatest good; namely, that the wisdom of God permits him to know it, his goodness causes him to choose it and his power enables him to produce it.

56. Now, this interconnection, relationship, or this adaptation of all things to each particular one, and of each one to all the rest, brings it about that every simple substance has relations which express all the others and that it is consequently a perpetual living mirror of the universe.

57. And as the same city regarded from different sides appears entirely different, and is, as it were, multiplied perspectively, so, because of the infinite number of simple substances, there are a similar infinite number of universes which are, nevertheless, only the aspects of a single one, as seen from the special point of view of each Monad.

58. Through this means has been obtained the greatest possible variety, together with the greatest order that may be; that is to say, through this means has been obtained the greatest possible perfection.

59. This hypothesis, moreover, which I venture to call demonstrated, is the only one which fittingly gives proper prominence to the greatness of God. Monsieur Bayle recognized this when in his *Dictionary* (article "Rorarius"), he raised objections to it; indeed, he was inclined to believe that I attributed too much to God, and more than should be attributed. But he was unable to bring forward any reason why this universal harmony, which causes every substance to express exactly all others, through the relation which it has with them, is impossible.

60. Besides, in what has just been said, can be seen the *a priori* reasons why things cannot be otherwise than they are. It is because God, in ordering the whole, has had regard to every part and in particular to each Monad whose nature it is to represent. Therefore, nothing can limit it to represent merely a part of the things. It is nevertheless true, that this representation is, as regards the details of the whole universe, only a confused representation, and is distinct only as regards a small part of them, that is to say, as regards those things which are nearest or most in relation to each Monad. If the representation were distinct as to the details of the entire universe, each Monad would be a Deity. It is not in the object represented that the Monads are limited, but in the modifications of their knowledge of the object. In a confused way they reach out to infinity or to the whole, but are limited and differentiated in the degree of their distinct perceptions.

61. In this respect composites are like simple substances. For all space is filled up; therefore, all matter is connected; and in a plenum or filled space every movement has an effect upon bodies in proportion to their distance, so that not only is every body affected by those which are in contact with it, and responds in some way to whatever happens to them, but also by means of them the body responds to those bodies adjoining them, and their intercommunication can be continued to any distance at will. Consequently every body responds to all that happens in the universe, so that he who saw all, could read in each one what is happening everywhere, and even what has happened and what will happen. He can discover in the present what is distant both as regards space and as regards time; *σύμπνοια πάντα*, as Hippocrates said. A soul can, however, read in itself only what is there represented distinctly. It cannot all at once open up all its folds, because they extend to infinity.

62. Thus although each created Monad represents the whole universe, it represents more distinctly the body which specially pertains to it, and of which it constitutes the entelechy. And as the body expresses all the universe through the interconnection of all matter in the plenum, the soul also represents the whole universe in representing this body, which belongs to it in a particular way.

63. The body belonging to a Monad, which is its entelechy or soul, constitutes together with the entelechy what may be called a *living being*, and with a soul what is called an *animal*. Now, this body of a living being or of an animal is always organic, because every Monad is a mirror of the universe according to its own fashion, and, since the universe is regulated with perfect order, there must needs be order also in the representative, that is to say, in the perceptions of the soul and consequently in the body through which the universe is represented in the soul.

64. Therefore, every organic body of a living being is a kind of divine machine, or natural automaton, infinitely surpassing all artificial automatons. Because a machine constructed by man's skill is not a machine in each of its parts; for instance, the teeth of a brass wheel have parts or bits which to us are not artificial products and contain nothing in themselves to show

the use to which the wheel was destined in the machine. The machines of nature, however, that is to say, living bodies, are still machines in their smallest parts *ad infinitum*. Such is the difference between nature and art, that is to say, between Divine art and ours.

65. The author of nature has been able to employ this divine and infinitely marvellous artifice, because each portion of matter is not only, as the ancients recognized, infinitely divisible, but also because it is really divided without end, every part into other parts, each one of which has its own proper motion. Otherwise it would be impossible for each portion of matter to express all the universe.

66. Whence we see that there is a world of created things, of living beings, of animals, of entelechies, of souls, in the minutest particle of matter.

67. Every portion of matter may be conceived as like a garden full of plants, and like a pond full of fish. But every branch of a plant, every member of an animal, and every drop of the fluids within it, is also such a garden or such a pond.

68. And although the ground and the air which lies between the plants of the garden, and the water which is between the fish in the pond, are not themselves plant or fish, yet they nevertheless contain these, usually so small, however, as to be imperceptible to us.

69. There is, therefore, nothing uncultivated, or sterile or dead in the universe, no chaos, no confusion, save in appearance; somewhat as a pond would appear at a distance when we could see in it a confused movement, and so to speak, a swarming of the fish, without, however, discerning the fish themselves.

70. It is evident, then, that every living body has a dominating entelechy, which in animals is the soul. The parts, however, of this living body are full of other living beings, plants and animals, which, in turn, have each one its entelechy or dominating soul.

71. This does not mean, as some who have misunderstood my thought have imagined, that each soul has a quantity or portion of matter appropriated to it or attached to itself for ever, and that it consequently owns other inferior living beings destined to serve it always; because all bodies are in a state of perpetual flux like rivers, and the parts are continually entering in and passing out.

72. The soul, therefore, changes its body only gradually and by degrees, so that it is never deprived all at once of all its organs. There is frequently a metamorphosis in animals, but never metempsychosis or a transmigration of souls. Neither are there souls wholly separate from bodies, nor bodiless spirits. God alone is without body.

73. This is also why there is never absolute generation or perfect death in the strict sense, consisting in the separation of the soul from the body. That which we call generation is development and growth, and that which we call death is envelopment and diminution.

74. Philosophers have been much perplexed in accounting for the origin of forms, entelechies, or souls. To-day, however, when it has been learned through careful investigations made in plant, insect, and animal life, that the organic bodies of nature are never the product of chaos or putrefaction, but always come from seeds in which there was without doubt some *preformation*, it has been decided that not only is the organic body already present before conception, but also that a soul, in a word, the animal itself, is also in this body; and it has been decided that, by means of conception the animal is disposed for a great transformation, so as to become an animal of another species. We can see cases somewhat similar outside of generation when grubs become flies and caterpillars become butterflies.

75. These little animals, some of which, by conception, become large animals, may be called spermatic. Those among them which remain in their species, that is to say, the greater

part, are born, multiply, and are destroyed, like the larger animals. There are only a few chosen ones which come out upon a greater stage.

76. This, however, is only half the truth. I believe, therefore, that if the animal never actually commences in nature, no more does it by natural means come to an end. Not only is there no generation, but also there is no entire destruction or absolute death. These reasonings, carried on *a posteriori*, and drawn from experience, accord perfectly with the principles which I have above deduced *a priori*.

77. Therefore, we may say, that not only the soul (the mirror of an indestructible universe) is indestructible, but also the animal itself is, although its mechanism is frequently destroyed in parts and although it puts off and takes on organic coatings.

78. These principles have furnished me the means of explaining on natural grounds the union, or, rather the conformity between the soul and the organic body. The soul follows its own laws, and the body has its laws. They are fitted to each other in virtue of the pre-established harmony between all substances, since they are all representations of one and the same universe.

79. Souls act in accordance with the laws of final causes through their desires, purposes and means. Bodies act in accordance with the laws of efficient causes or of motion. The two realms, that of efficient causes and that of final causes, are in harmony, each with the other.

80. Descartes saw that souls cannot at all impart force to bodies, because there is always the same quantity of force in matter. Yet, he thought that the soul could change the direction of bodies. This was, however, because at that time the law of nature, which affirms also the conservation of the same total direction in the motion of matter, was not known. If he had known that law, he would have fallen upon my system of Pre-established Harmony.

81. According to this system bodies act as if (to suppose the impossible) there were no souls at all, and souls act as if there were no bodies, and yet both body and soul act as if the one were influencing the other.

82. Although I find that essentially the same thing is true of all living things and animals, which we have just said, namely, that animals and souls begin from the very commencement of the world and that they come to an end no more than does the world, there is, as far as minds or rational souls are concerned nevertheless, this thing peculiar, that their little spermatic progenitors, as long as they remain such, have only ordinary or sensuous souls, but those of them which are, so to speak, elevated, attain by actual conception to human nature, and their sensuous souls are raised to the rank of reason and to the prerogative of minds.

83. Among the differences that there are between ordinary souls and spirits, some of which I have already instanced, there is also this that, while souls in general are living mirrors or images of the universe of created things, minds are also images of the Deity himself or of the author of nature. They are capable of knowing the system of the universe, and to imitate it somewhat by means of architectonic patterns, each mind being like a small divinity in its sphere.

84. Therefore, spirits are able to enter into a sort of social relationship with God, and with respect to them he is not only what an inventor is to his machine (as is his relation to the other created things), but he is also what a prince is to his subjects, and even what a father is to his children.

85. Whence it is easy to conclude that the totality of all the spirits must compose the city of God, that is to say, the most perfect state that is possible under the most perfect monarch.

86. This city of God, this truly universal monarchy, is a moral world within the natural world. It is what is noblest and most divine among the works of God. And in it consists in reality the glory of God, because he would have no glory were not his greatness and goodness known and wondered at by spirits. It is also in relation to this divine city that God properly has goodness. His wisdom and his power are shown everywhere.

87. As we established above that there is a perfect harmony between the two natural realms of efficient and final causes, it will be in place here to point out another harmony which appears between the physical realm of nature and the moral realm of grace, that is to say, between God, considered as the architect of the mechanism of the world and God considered as the Monarch of the divine city of spirits.

88. This harmony brings it about that things progress of themselves toward grace along natural lines, and that this earth, for example, must be destroyed and restored by natural means at those times when the proper government of spirits demands it, for chastisement in the one case and for a reward in the other.

89. We can say also that God, the Architect, satisfies in all respects God the Law-Giver, that therefore sins will bring their own penalty with them through the order of nature, and because of the very mechanical structure of things. And in the same way the good actions will attain their rewards in mechanical ways through their relation to bodies, although this cannot, and ought not, always to take place without delay.

90. Finally, under this perfect government, there will be no good action unrewarded and no evil action unpunished; everything should turn out for the well-being of the good; that is to say, of those who are not disaffected in this great state, who, after having done their duty, trust in Providence and who love and imitate, as is meet, the Author of all Good, delighting in the contemplation of his perfections according to the nature of that genuine, pure love which finds pleasure in the happiness of those who are loved. It is for this reason that wise and virtuous persons work in behalf of everything which seems conformable to the presumptive or antecedent will, and are, nevertheless, content with what God actually brings to pass through his secret, consequent and determining will, recognizing that if we were able to understand sufficiently well the order of the universe, we should find that it goes beyond all the desires of the wisest of us, and that it is impossible to have it better than it is, not only for all in general, but also for each one of us in particular, provided that we cleave as we should to the Author of all. For he is not only the Architect and the efficient cause of our being, but he is also our Lord and the Final Cause, who ought to be the whole goal of our will, and who, alone, can make our happiness.

Part IV

Political Philosophy

Introduction

Political philosophy may be defined as the study of the basic concepts and propositions of government. The concepts include sovereignty and law. The propositions include whether government is (or is not) natural to human beings, and whether government is justified because it is necessary for human flourishing or because people agree to be subject to a government or because God commanded it.

These concepts and propositions are fairly abstract or theoretical, and both Thomas Hobbes and Samuel Pufendorf embraced political philosophy as an abstract discipline. They wanted it to be as rigorous and precise as geometry or any natural science.

Not all of the great political theorists of the early modern period aimed at such rigor or had such scientific pretensions. Niccolò Machiavelli, for example, was not theoretical at all. On the basis of his observations of the behavior of princes and subjects and the study of history, such as the history of Rome and Florence, he formulated practical principles of governance. Because of the generality of these principles and their influence on the more theoretical philosophers, he deserves a place in political philosophy.

One characteristic shared by the three political philosophers represented in this part is that they were politically involved. Machiavelli served in the government of Florence. Hobbes advised the earl of Newcastle and unsuccessfully stood for parliament, in addition to writing books of political philosophy that directly related to the politics of his time. Pufendorf held various posts for Protestant leaders. Two other notable political philosophers who were politically involved were Hugo Grotius (1583–1645), author of *De jure belli ac pacis* (*On the Law of War and Peace*; 1625) and John Locke (1632–1704), author of *Two Treatises of Government*, which is excerpted in volume 4 of this series. Theory and practice were much closer in the modern period than they are now.

Religion was an important element in politics for Machiavelli, Hobbes, and Pufendorf. This is most explicit in Pufendorf, who wrote long treatises explaining and justifying the appropriate subordination of religion to the secular government. But thè relation between church and state was important to Hobbes also, as evidenced by the third and fourth parts of *Leviathan*, "Of the Christian Commonwealth," and "Of the Kingdom of Darkness." For Hobbes, religious and secular authority were united in one person. For Machiavelli, religion primarily had an instrumental role. It could and should be used by the prince to keep his subjects obedient.

Political philosophy in the seventeenth century was to a large extent an attempt to find the proper theoretical and working relationship between secular and religious authority. For a theory to enjoy widespread success, it could not favor any one Christian denomination over any other, because Europe was religiously too diverse. The Peace of Westphalia, which ended the Thirty Years War, supported the right of any Roman Catholic, Lutheran, or Calvinist ruler to be supreme in his territory. This negotiated toleration contributed to the drift toward greater secular authority and a diminishing role for religion in public life. It was an important part of the long process of secularization of western Europe, and later North America, a process that started in the sixteenth century.

19

Niccolò Machiavelli, *The Prince*

Niccolò Machiavelli (1469–1527) was a Renaissance Italian statesman, as well as a political philosopher. He worked in the government of the Florentine republic until 1512. As defense minister, he replaced the mercenary army with a citizens' militia. In his political works he argued for the superiority of citizen armies over militias. When the Medici regained control of Florence's government, Machiavelli was dismissed. In 1513 he was imprisoned and tortured for his alleged role in a conspiracy against the Medici. *The Prince* was written the same year but not published until 1532. Upon his release from prison he retired to the country to write. He unsuccessfully tried to ingratiate himself with the Medici to gain appointment to the government. When the republic was re-established, he was viewed with suspicion for courting the Medici. He died a bitter man.

His *Discourses on the First Ten Books of Livy* (published in 1531, written between 1513 and 1519), probably his greatest work, is in part a defense of republicanism, the view that citizens must participate in their government in order to remain free. He also wrote poems and plays, of which the most famous is *La Mandrangola* (*The Mandrake*), a comedy.

His most famous work, *The Prince* (1532), dedicated to Lorenzo de' Medici, is excerpted here. Interpretations of this book vary widely. Some think it is a defense of immorality in politics, others that it is a defense of the amorality of, or irrelevance of morality to, politics, and still others that it is a satire on politics. A moderate view, adopted here, is that Machiavelli is instructing a ruler on the most effective means for preserving political power. One of those means is to govern well: "The chief foundations of all states whether new, old, or mixed, are good laws." But this is only one. The other chief foundation of states is "good arms." That is why he says that a prince should make "war and its organization and discipline" his only aim.

Concerning the way a prince should govern, Machiavelli says that he will talk about the way things really are and not as they are imagined to be. The first of these hard truths is that a person who tries to be good will "come to grief." A prince must "learn how not to be good." Often this means appearing to be one thing but being another. It is good to appear to be generous ("liberal"), but not to be generous, since this impoverishes a person.

A prince should appear to be "merciful and not cruel." Since short-term mercy is often long-term cruelty, a prince must be willing to be accused of cruelty if it is necessary to keep "his subjects united and faithful." So the ruthless extermination of enemies may be the right action for a ruler. Such ruthlessness may earn the prince the reputation of being feared. So be it. If a choice needs to be made between being feared and being loved, it is better to be feared. In short, a prince should "seem to be all mercy, faith, integrity, humanity, and religion."

Although fortune plays a significant role in life, its effect should not be exaggerated. Machiavelli says: "fortune is a woman, and it is necessary, if you wish to master her, to conquer her by force; and it can be seen that she lets herself be overcome by the bold rather than by those who proceed by folly."[1]

Chapter XII
The Different Kinds of Militia and Mercenary Soldiers

[. . .] The chief foundations of all states, whether new, old, or mixed, are good laws and good arms. And as there cannot be good laws where there are not good arms, and where there are good arms there must be good laws, I will [. . .] now [. . .] speak of the arms.

[. . .]

Chapter XIV
The Duties of a Prince with Regard to the Militia

A prince should therefore have no other aim or thought, nor take up any other thing for his study, but war and its organisation and discipline, for that is the only art that is necessary to one who commands. [. . .] And one sees, on the other hand, that when princes think more of luxury than of arms, they lose their state. The chief cause of the loss of states, is the contempt of this art, and the way to acquire them is to be well versed in the same.

[. . .]

Because there is no comparison whatever between an armed and a disarmed man; it is not reasonable to suppose that one who is armed will obey willingly one who is unarmed; or that any unarmed man will remain safe among armed servants. [. . .]

He ought, therefore, never to let his thoughts stray from the exercise of war; and in peace he ought to practise it more than in war, which he can do in two ways: by action and by study. As to action, he must, besides keeping his men well disciplined and exercised, engage continually in hunting, and thus accustom his body to hardships; and meanwhile learn the nature of the land, how steep the mountains are, how the valleys debouch, where the plains lie, and understand the nature of rivers and swamps. To all this he should devote great attention.

[. . .]

1 I am just reporting Machiavelli's view, not endorsing it. Consider that, in addition to advancing scientifically, civilized people have advanced ethically in the last 500 years. However, one should not be complacent. It is all too easy to regress to barbarian values when appeals are made to individual or national self-interest.

Chapter XV
Of the Things for which Men, and Especially Princes, Are Praised or Blamed

It now remains to be seen what are the methods and rules for a prince as regards his subjects and friends. And [. . .] my intention being to write something of use to those who understand, it appears to me more proper to go to the real truth of the matter than to its imagination; and many have imagined republics and principalities which have never been seen or known to exist in reality; for how we live is so far removed from how we ought to live, that he who abandons what is done for what ought to be done, will rather learn to bring about his own ruin than his preservation. A man who wishes to make a profession of goodness in everything must necessarily come to grief among so many who are not good. Therefore it is necessary for a prince, who wishes to maintain himself, to learn how not to be good, and to use this knowledge and not use it, according to the necessity of the case.

Leaving on one side, then, those things which concern only an imaginary prince, and speaking of those that are real, I state that all men, and especially princes, who are placed at a greater height, are reputed for certain qualities which bring them either praise or blame. Thus one is considered liberal, another *misero* or miserly; [. . .] one a free giver, another rapacious; one cruel, another merciful; one a breaker of his word, another trustworthy; one effeminate and pusillanimous, another fierce and high-spirited; one humane, another haughty; one lascivious, another chaste; one frank, another astute; one hard, another easy; one serious, another frivolous; one religious, another an unbeliever, and so on. I know that every one will admit that it would be highly praiseworthy in a prince to possess all the above-named qualities that are reputed good, but as they cannot all be possessed or observed, human conditions not permitting of it, it is necessary that he should be prudent enough to avoid the scandal of those vices which would lose him the state, and guard himself if possible against those which will not lose it him, but if not able to, he can indulge them with less scruple. And yet he must not mind incurring the scandal of those vices, without which it would be difficult to save the state, for if one considers well, it will be found that some things which seem virtues would, if followed, lead to one's ruin, and some others which appear vices result in one's greater security and wellbeing.

Chapter XVI
Of Liberality and Niggardliness

Beginning now with the first qualities above named, I say that it would be well to be considered liberal; nevertheless liberality such as the world understands it will injure you, because if used virtuously and in the proper way, it will not be known, and you will incur the disgrace of the contrary vice. But one who wishes to obtain the reputation of liberality among men, must not omit every kind of sumptuous display, and to such an extent that a prince of this character will consume by such means all his resources, and will be at last compelled, if he wishes to maintain his name for liberality, to impose heavy taxes on his people, become extortionate, and do everything possible to obtain money. This will make his subjects begin to hate him, and he will be little esteemed being poor, so that having by this liberality injured many and benefited but few, he will feel the first little disturbance and be endangered by every peril. If he recognises this and wishes to change his system, he incurs at once the charge of niggardliness.

A prince, therefore, not being able to exercise this virtue of liberality without risk if it be known, must not, if he be prudent, object to be called miserly. In course of time he will be thought more liberal, when it is seen that by his parsimony his revenue is sufficient, that he can defend himself against those who make war on him, and undertake enterprises without burdening his people, so that he is really liberal to all those from whom he does not take, who are infinite in number, and niggardly to all to whom he does not give, who are few. [. . .]

For these reasons a prince must care little for the reputation of being a miser, if he wishes to avoid robbing his subjects, if he wishes to be able to defend himself, to avoid becoming poor and contemptible, and not to be forced to become rapacious; this niggardliness is one of those vices which enable him to reign. If it is said that Caesar attained the empire through liberality, and that many others have reached the highest positions through being liberal or being thought so, I would reply that you are either a prince already or else on the way to become one. In the first case, this liberality is harmful; in the second, it is certainly necessary to be considered liberal. Caesar was one of those who wished to attain the mastery over Rome, but if after attaining it he had lived and had not moderated his expenses, he would have destroyed that empire. [. . .] There is nothing which destroys itself so much as liberality, for by using it you lose the power of using it, and become either poor and despicable, or, to escape poverty, rapacious and hated. And of all things that a prince must guard against, the most important are being despicable or hated, and liberality will lead you to one or other of these conditions. It is, therefore, wiser to have the name of a miser, which produces disgrace without hatred, than to incur of necessity the name of being rapacious, which produces both disgrace and hatred.

Chapter XVII
Of Cruelty and Clemency, and Whether It Is Better to be Loved or Feared

Proceeding to the other qualities before named, I say that every prince must desire to be considered merciful and not cruel. He must, however, take care not to misuse this mercifulness. Cesare Borgia was considered cruel, but his cruelty had brought order to the Romagna, united it, and reduced it to peace and fealty. If this is considered well, it will be seen that he was really much more merciful than the Florentine people, who, to avoid the name of cruelty, allowed Pistoia to be destroyed. A prince, therefore, must not mind incurring the charge of cruelty for the purpose of keeping his subjects united and faithful; for, with a very few examples, he will be more merciful than those who, from excess of tenderness, allow disorders to arise, from whence spring bloodshed and rapine; for these as a rule injure the whole community, while the executions carried out by the prince injure only individuals. And of all princes, it is impossible for a new prince to escape the reputation of cruelty, new states being always full of dangers.

[. . .]

From this arises the question whether it is better to be loved more than feared, or feared more than loved. The reply is, that one ought to be both feared and loved, but as it is difficult for the two to go together, it is much safer to be feared than loved, if one of the two has to be wanting. For it may be said of men in general that they are ungrateful, voluble, dissemblers, anxious to avoid danger, and covetous of gain; as long as you benefit them, they are entirely yours; they offer you their blood, their goods, their life, and their children, as I have before said, when the necessity is remote; but when it approaches, they revolt. And the prince who has relied solely on their words, without making other preparations, is ruined; for the friendship which is gained by purchase and not through grandeur and nobility of spirit is bought but not secured, and at a pinch is not to be expended in your service. And men have less scruple in offending one who makes himself loved than one who makes himself feared; for love is held by a chain of obligation which, men being selfish, is broken whenever it serves their purpose; but fear is maintained by a dread of punishment which never fails.

Still, a prince should make himself feared in such a way that if he does not gain love, he at any rate avoids hatred; for fear and the absence of hatred may well go together, and will be always attained by one who abstains from interfering with the property of his citizens and subjects or with their women. And when he is obliged to take the life of any one, let him do so when there is a proper justification and manifest reason for it; but above all he must abstain from taking the property of others, for men forget more easily the death of their father than the loss of their patrimony. Then also pretexts for seizing property are never wanting, and one who begins to live by rapine will always find some reason for taking the goods of others, whereas causes for taking life are rarer and more fleeting.

But when the prince is with his army and has a large number of soldiers under his control, then it is extremely necessary that he should not mind being thought cruel; for without this reputation he could not keep an army united or disposed to any duty.

[. . .]

I conclude, therefore, with regard to being feared and loved, that men love at their own free will, but fear at the will of the prince, and that a wise prince must rely on what it in his power and not on what is in the power of others, and he must only contrive to avoid incurring hatred, a has been explained.

Chapter XVIII
In What Way Princes Must Keep Faith

How laudable it is for a prince to keep good faith and live with integrity, and not with astuteness, every one knows. Still the experience of our times shows those princes to have done great things who have had little regard for good faith, and have been able by astuteness to confuse men's brains, and who have ultimately overcome those who have made loyalty their foundation.

You must know, then, that there are two methods of fighting, the one by law, the other by force: the first method is that of men, the second of beasts; but as the first method is often insufficient, one must have recourse to the second. It is therefore necessary for a prince to know well how to use both the beast and the man. This was covertly taught to rulers by ancient writers, who relate how Achilles and many others of those ancient princes were given to Chiron the centaur to be brought up and educated under his discipline. The parable of this semi-animal, semi-human teacher is meant to indicate that a prince must know how to use both natures, and that the one without the other is not durable.

A prince being thus obliged to know well how to act as a beast must imitate the fox and the lion, for the lion cannot protect himself from traps, and the fox cannot defend himself from wolves. One must therefore be a fox to recognise traps, and a lion to frighten wolves. Those that wish to be only lions do not understand this. Therefore, a prudent ruler ought not to keep faith when by so doing it would be against his interest, and when the reasons which made him bind himself no longer exist. If men were all good, this precept would not be a good one; but as they are bad, and would not observe their faith with you, so you are not bound to keep faith with them. Nor have legitimate grounds ever failed a prince who wished to show colourable excuse for the non-fulfilment of his promise. Of this one could furnish an infinite number of modern examples, and show how many times peace has been broken, and how many promises rendered worthless, by the faithlessness of princes, and those that have been best able to imitate the fox have succeeded best. But it is necessary to be able to disguise this character well, and to be a great feigner and dissembler; and men are so simple and so ready to obey present necessities, that one who deceives will always find those who allow themselves to be deceived.

[. . .]

It is not, therefore, necessary for a prince to have all the above-named qualities, but it is very necessary to seem to have them. I would even be bold to say that to possess them and always to observe them is dangerous, but to appear to possess them is useful. Thus it is well to seem merciful, faithful, humane, sincere, religious, and also to be so; but you must have the mind so disposed that when it is needful to be otherwise you may be able to change to the opposite qualities. And it must be understood that a prince, and especially a new prince, cannot observe all those things which are considered good in men, being often obliged, in order to maintain the state, to act against faith, against charity, against humanity, and against religion. And, therefore, he must have a mind disposed to adapt itself according to the wind, and as the variations of fortune dictate, and, as I said before, not deviate from what is good, if possible, but be able to do evil if constrained.

A prince must take great care that nothing goes out of his mouth which is not full of the above-named five qualities, and, to see and hear him, he should seem to be all mercy, faith, integrity, humanity, and religion. And nothing is more necessary than to seem to have this last quality, for men in general judge more by the eyes than by the hands, for every one can see, but very few have to feel. Everybody sees what you appear to be, few feel what you are, and those few will not dare to oppose themselves to the many, who have the majesty of the state to defend them; and in the actions of men, and especially of princes, from which there is no appeal, the end justifies the means. Let a prince therefore aim at conquering and maintaining the state, and the means will always be judged honourable and praised by every one, for the vulgar is always taken by appearances and the issue of the event; and the world consists only of the vulgar, and the few who are not vulgar are isolated when the many have a rallying point in the prince. A certain prince of the present time, whom it is well not to name, never does anything but preach peace and good faith, but he is really a great enemy to both, and either of them, had he observed them, would have lost him state or reputation on many occasions.

Chapter XIX
That We Must Avoid Being Despised and Hated

[. . .]

For a prince must have two kinds of fear: one internal as regards his subjects, one external as regards foreign powers. From the latter he can defend himself with good arms and good friends, and he will always have good friends if he has good arms; and internal matters will always remain quiet, if they are not perturbed by conspiracy and there is no disturbance from without; and even if external powers sought to attack him, if he has ruled and lived as I have described, he will always if he stands firm, be able to sustain every shock.

[. . .]

Chapter XXV
How Much Fortune Can Do in Human Affairs and How It May Be Opposed

It is not unknown to me how many have been and are of opinion that worldly events are so governed by fortune and by God, that men cannot by their prudence change them, and that on the contrary there is no remedy whatever, and for this they may judge it to be useless to toil much about them, but let things be ruled by chance. This opinion has been more held in our day, from the great changes that have been seen, and are daily seen, beyond every human conjecture. When I think about them, at times I am partly inclined to share this opinion. Nevertheless, that our free-will may not be altogether extinguished, I think it may be true that fortune is the ruler of half our actions, but that she allows the other half or thereabouts to be governed by us. I would compare her to an impetuous river that, when turbulent, inundates the plains, casts down trees and buildings, removes earth from this side and places it on the other; every one flees before it, and everything yields to its fury without being able to oppose it; and yet though it is of such a kind, still when it is quiet, men can make provision against it by dykes and banks, so that when it rises it will either go into a canal or its rush will not be so wild and dangerous. So it is with fortune, which shows her power where no measures have been taken to resist her, and directs her fury where she knows that no dykes or barriers have been made to hold her. And if you regard Italy, which has been the seat of these changes, and who has given the impulse to them, you will see her to be a country without dykes or banks of any kind. If she had been protected by proper measures, like Germany, Spain, and France, this inundation would not have caused the great changes that it has, or would not have happened at all.

This must suffice as regards opposition to fortune in general. But limiting myself more to particular cases, I would point out how one sees a certain prince to-day fortunate and to-morrow ruined, without seeing that he has changed in character or otherwise. I believe this arises in the first place from the causes that we have already discussed at length; that is to say, because the prince who bases himself entirely on fortune is ruined when fortune changes. I also believe that he is happy whose mode of procedure accords with the needs of the times, and similarly he is unfortunate whose mode of procedure is opposed to the times. For one sees that men in those things which lead them to the aim that each one has in view, namely, glory and riches, proceed in various ways; one with circumspection, another with impetuosity, one by violence, another by cunning, one with patience, another with the reverse; and each by these diverse ways may arrive at his aim. One sees also two cautious men, one of whom succeeds in his designs, and the other not, and in the same way two men succeed equally by different methods, one being cautious, the other impetuous, which arises only from the nature of the times, which does or does not conform to their method of procedure. From this it results, as I have said, that two men, acting differently, attain the same effect, and of two others acting in the same way, one attains his goal and not the other. On this depend also the changes in prosperity, for if it happens that time and circumstances are favourable to one who acts with caution and prudence he will be successful, but if time and circumstances change he will be ruined, because he does not change his mode of procedure. No man is found so prudent as to be able to adapt himself to this, either because he cannot deviate from that to which his nature disposes him, or else because having always prospered by walking in one path, he cannot persuade himself that it is well to leave it; and therefore the cautious man, when it is time to act suddenly, does not know how to do so and is consequently ruined; for if one could change one's nature with time and circumstances, fortune would never change.

[. . .]

I conclude then that fortune varying and men remaining fixed in their ways, they are successful so long as these ways conform to circumstances, but when they are opposed then they are unsuccessful. I certainly think that it is better to be impetuous than cautious, for fortune is a woman, and it is necessary, if you wish to master her, to conquer her by force; and it can be seen that she lets herself be overcome by the bold rather than by those who proceed coldly. And therefore, like a woman, she is always a friend to the young, because they are less cautious, fiercer, and master her with greater audacity.

20

Thomas Hobbes, *Leviathan*

Thomas Hobbes (1588–1679) was born just outside of Malmesbury, a small town in Wiltshire. He attended Magdalen Hall, not to be confused with the more prestigious Magdalen College, Oxford. After college, he was employed by two branches of the wealthy Cavendish family in Derbyshire and Nottinghamshire, in the eastern part of the English Midlands. In his travels to Europe he visited Galileo, under house arrest at the time, and became a member of the intellectual circle organized by Marin Mersenne, which included Pierre Gassendi (1592–1655) and Descartes, although Descartes and Hobbes despised each other and met only once.

Later in 1640 Hobbes fled England because he feared for his life: he was opposed by enemies of the king, Charles I. Part of the enmity was due to his widely circulated manuscript, *The Elements of Law, Natural and Politic* (1640). He stayed in France, where his reputation as a mathematician and political philosopher grew. He spent a substantial amount of time with the exiled royal court, and for a time he tutored the future Charles II in mathematics. As we saw in part II, selection 9, he contributed the third set of objections to Descartes's *Meditations*. In 1642 and then in an expanded form in 1647, his book *De Cive* (*On the Citizen*) was published in France. After the English Civil War (1642–9), he began to think about returning to England, partly because some French Roman Catholic priests were opposed to him and partly because he wanted to return to his native country, even though it was in effect being ruled by the victorious rebels who had beheaded Charles I. In 1651 *Leviathan*, his greatest work, was published not long after his return. Living for the most part in London, he associated with many of the most prominent English intellectuals. When the monarchy was restored in 1660, Hobbes was both liked by Charles II and despised by the royalists, who had never acquiesced in the Commonwealth government. His enemies accused him of atheism, a charge he rebutted in several works.

During the 1660s and 1670s he engaged in disputes on a variety of topics with many scientists and mathematicians. The most rancorous of these was with John Wallis (1616–1703), a distinguished mathematician and the person who introduced the standard symbol for infinity, ∞. Hobbes's mathematical reputation plummeted because he could not acknowledge the defects in his proofs to square the circle. In his last years, he translated both the *Iliad* and the *Odyssey*. He died at the age of 91.

Hobbes, like many other seventeenth-century Englishmen, read Machiavelli's works. But unlike the Italian thinker, Hobbes wanted to make political philosophy a science in the same sense in which geometry was a science. In fact, geometry was his paradigmatic science. According to him, geometry studies the consequences of motion and determinate quantities. His philosophy, including his geometry, is thoroughly materialistic. A point is not something with no dimensions, but a body of which none of the actual dimensions is considered. A line is a body, of which only the length is considered. A plane is a body of which only the length and breadth are considered.

In theory, all the sciences are united. So, ideally political philosophy is derivable from physics or the science of natural human beings, although in fact Hobbes derives it from distinctively political concepts such as that of a law of nature.

The political part of *Leviathan* begins with a thought experiment in chapter XIII. Hobbes says that, if we consider human beings the way that nature makes them, all people are equal in intelligence and physical strength for practical purposes. No matter how much stronger or more intelligent one person is than anyone else, that person can be killed by any other person either alone or in concert with others, perhaps while the victim is asleep. (Hobbes must be thinking of human beings in a normal range, not those born with radical intellectual and physical impairments.) This natural condition is one without any laws at all. Human life in this natural condition, often called "the state of nature," is "solitary, poor, nasty, brutish and short." Although the state of nature is primarily a concept used in a thought experiment, and not a description of the historically earliest condition of human beings, Hobbes claims that it exists in three situations in real life: in international relations, during civil war, and where people are so primitive as to not have a government.

Because this initial state of nature contains no laws of any kind – for the sake of exposition let's call this "the primary state of nature" – nothing is forbidden. In other words, everyone has a right to everything, including the bodies of other people. Because (1) some people may need or think they need what other people have in order to live and because (2) some people want the glory of dominating other people, and because it is rational to think that everyone may fall into classes (1) or (2), everyone needs to be suspicious of everyone else, and if the opportunity presents itself, take pre-emptive action against them. Hence, human life is a war of all against all.

Since human beings desire to preserve their own life in relative comfort, they want to escape the state of nature, the condition of war. They cannot do this unless there are laws, not civil laws, because there is no government yet, but laws of nature by which they can generate a government to protect them. Let's call this condition, which consists of the natural condition of humans plus the laws of nature, "the secondary state of nature."

A law of nature is "a precept or general rule, found out by reason, by which a man is forbidden to do that which is destructive of his life, or taketh away the means of preserving the same, and to omit that by which he thinketh it may be best preserved." The first law of nature is that each person ought to try to make peace with his fellows. (Hobbes tacks on to this first law, "the sum of the right of nature," which is to figure out and use all the means that war provides. But the sum of the right of nature is no part of the first law of nature.) It is not clear how Hobbes actually proves the first law, but it is easily seen to follow by a *reductio ad absurdum* argument. If everyone does *not* seek peace, then they will destroy their lives. But, by the definition of the law of nature, they will not destroy their lives. Therefore, everyone seeks peace.

By a similar strategy, the second law, people should lay down their right to all things to the extent that others do, and the third, everyone should keep their covenants, and all the others are provable. These laws of nature allow people to transfer their rights[1] to either one person in order to create a monarchy, several people in order to create an oligarchy, or all the people jointly to create a democracy. In any of these cases, an artificial person, the sovereign, is created. This sovereign, according to Hobbes, is absolute: he has all the political power that there is and has the right to control any aspect of the behavior of citizens, including their religious behavior. (Each citizen's thoughts remain uncontrolled.) Absolute sovereignty should be contrasted with theories of limited sovereignty, according to which political power either is shared by more than one entity, for example by the federal and state governments in the US, or does not extend to every aspect of life.

Absolute sovereignty was no longer fashionable in England during the latter part of the seventeenth century, and thus Hobbes tried to moderate it in chapter 21 of *Leviathan* (not included here).

While the power of Hobbes's mind was acknowledged by all sides, his theory of the state of nature as a state of war, his defense of absolute sovereignty, and his uncompromising subordination of religion to the secular sovereign made him unpopular with many important people.

Part I

Chapter XIII
Of the Natural Condition of Mankind as Concerning their Felicity and Misery

1. Nature hath made men so equal in the faculties of body and mind, as that, though there be found one man sometimes manifestly stronger in body or of quicker mind than another; yet when all is reckoned together, the difference between man and man is not so considerable as that one man can thereupon claim to himself any benefit to which another may not pretend as well as he. For as to the strength of body, the weakest has strength enough to kill the strongest, either by secret machination or by confederacy with others that are in the same danger with himself.

2. And as to the faculties of the mind, setting aside the arts grounded upon words, and especially that skill of proceeding upon general and infallible rules, called science, which very few have and but in few things, as being not a native faculty born with us, nor attained, as prudence, while we look after somewhat else, I find yet a greater equality amongst men than that of strength. For prudence is but experience, which equal time equally bestows on all men in those things they equally apply themselves unto. That which may perhaps make such equality incredible is but a vain conceit of one's own wisdom, which almost all men think they have in a greater degree than the vulgar, that is, than all men but themselves and a few others, whom by fame or for concurring with themselves, they approve. For such is the nature of men that howsoever they may acknowledge many others to be more witty or more eloquent or more learned, they will hardly believe there be many so wise as themselves; for

1 Should people transfer some or all of their rights? Think of the consequences of each alternative in the light of what Hobbes says later about absolute sovereignty.

they see their own wit at hand and other men's at a distance. But this proveth rather that men are in that point equal, than unequal. For there is not ordinarily a greater sign of the equal distribution of anything than that every man is contented with his share.

3. From this equality of ability ariseth equality of hope in the attaining of our ends. And therefore if any two men desire the same thing, which nevertheless they cannot both enjoy, they become enemies; and in the way to their end (which is principally their own conservation, and sometimes their delectation only) endeavour to destroy or subdue one another. And from hence it comes to pass that where an invader hath no more to fear than another man's single power, if one plant, sow, build, or possess a convenient seat, others may probably be expected to come prepared with forces united to dispossess and deprive him, not only of the fruit of his labour, but also of his life or liberty. And the invader again is in the like danger of another.

4. And from this diffidence of one another, there is no way for any man to secure himself so reasonable as anticipation, that is, by force or wiles, to master the persons of all men he can so long till he see no other power great enough to endanger him; and this is no more than his own conservation requireth, and is generally allowed. Also, because there be some that, taking pleasure in contemplating their own power in the acts of conquest, which they pursue farther than their security requires, if others, that otherwise would be glad to be at ease within modest bounds, should not by invasion increase their power, they would not be able, long time, by standing only on their defence, to subsist. And by consequence, such augmentation of dominion over men being necessary to a man's conservation, it ought to be allowed him.

5. Again, men have no pleasure (but on the contrary a great deal of grief) in keeping company where there is no power able to overawe them all. For every man looketh that his companion should value him at the same rate he sets upon himself, and upon all signs of contempt or undervaluing naturally endeavours, as far as he dares (which amongst them that have no common power to keep them in quiet is far enough to make them destroy each other), to extort a greater value from his contemners, by damage; and from others, by the example.

6. So that in the nature of man, we find three principal causes of quarrel. First, competition; secondly diffidence; thirdly, glory.

7. The first maketh men invade for gain; the second, for safety; and the third, for reputation. The first use violence to make themselves masters of other men's persons, wives, children, and cattle; the second, to defend them; the third, for trifles, as a word, a smile, a different opinion, and any other sign of undervalue, either direct in their persons or by reflection in their kindred, their friends, their nation, their profession, or their name.

8. Hereby it is manifest that during the time men live without a common power to keep them all in awe, they are in that condition which is called war; and such a war as is of every man against every man. For WAR consisteth not in battle only, or the act of fighting, but in a tract of time, wherein the will to contend by battle is sufficiently known; and therefore the notion of *time* is to be considered in the nature of war, as it is in the nature of weather. For as the nature of foul weather lieth not in a shower or two of rain, but in an inclination thereto of many days together, so the nature of war consisteth not in actual fighting, but in the known disposition thereto during all the time there is no assurance to the contrary. All other time is PEACE.

9. Whatsoever therefore is consequent to a time of war, where every man is enemy to every man, the same consequent to the time wherein men live without other security than

what their own strength and their own invention shall furnish them withal. In such condition there is no place for industry, because the fruit thereof is uncertain; and consequently no culture of the earth; no navigation, nor use of the commodities that may be imported by sea; no commodious building; no instruments of moving and removing such things as require much force; no knowledge of the face of the earth; no account of time; no arts; no letters; no society; and which is worst of all, continual fear, and danger of violent death; and the life of man, solitary, poor, nasty; brutish, and short.

10. It may seem strange to some man that has not well weighed these things that nature should thus dissociate and render men apt to invade and destroy one another; and he may therefore, not trusting to this inference, made from the passions, desire perhaps to have the same confirmed by experience. Let him therefore consider with himself; when taking a journey, he arms himself and seeks to go well accompanied; when going to sleep, he locks his doors; when even in his house he locks his chests; and this when he knows there be laws and public officers, armed to revenge all injuries shall be done him; what opinion he has of his fellow subjects, when he rides armed; of his fellow citizens, when he locks his doors; and of his children, and servants, when he locks his chests. Does he not there as much accuse mankind by his actions as I do by my words? But neither of us accuse man's nature in it. The desires and other passions of man are in themselves no sin. No more are the actions that proceed from those passions till they know a law that forbids them; which, till laws be made, they cannot know; nor can any law be made till they have agreed upon the person that shall make it.

11. It may peradventure be thought there was never such a time nor condition of war as this; and I believe it was never generally so, over all the world, but there are many places where they live so now. For the savage people in many places of America, except the government of small families, the concord whereof dependeth on natural lust, have no government at all, and live at this day in that brutish manner, as I said before. Howsoever, it may be perceived what manner of life there would be, where there were no common power to fear, by the manner of life which men that have formerly lived under a peaceful government use to degenerate into a civil war.

12. But though there had never been any time wherein particular men were in a condition of war one against another; yet in all times kings and persons of sovereign authority, because of their independency, are in continual jealousies, and in the state and posture of gladiators, having their weapons pointing and their eyes fixed on one another, that is, their forts, garrisons, and guns upon the frontiers of their kingdoms, and continual spies upon their neighbours, which is a posture of war. But because they uphold thereby the industry of their subjects, there does not follow from it that misery which accompanies the liberty of particular men.

13. To this war of every man against every man, this also is consequent; that nothing can be unjust. The notions of right and wrong, justice and injustice, have there no place. Where there is no common power, there is no law; where no law, no injustice. Force and fraud are in war the two cardinal virtues. Justice and injustice are none of the faculties neither of the body nor mind. If they were, they might be in a man that were alone in the world, as well as his senses and passions. They are qualities that relate to men in society, not in solitude. It is consequent also to the same condition that there be no propriety, no dominion, no *mine* and *thine* distinct; but only that to be every man's that he can get, and for so long as he can keep it. And thus much for the ill condition which man by mere nature is actually placed in; though with a possibility to come out of it, consisting partly in the passions, partly in his reason.

14. The passions that incline men to peace are fear of death, desire of such things as are necessary to commodious living, and a hope by their industry to obtain them. And reason suggesteth convenient articles of peace upon which men may be drawn to agreement. These articles are they which otherwise are called the laws of nature, whereof I shall speak more particularly in the two following chapters.

Chapter XIV
Of the First and Second Natural Laws, and of Contracts

1. The right of nature, which writers commonly call *jus naturale*, is the liberty each man hath to use his own power as he will himself for the preservation of his own nature; that is to say, of his own life; and consequently, of doing anything which, in his own judgement and reason, he shall conceive to be the aptest means thereunto.

2. By Liberty is understood, according to the proper signification of the word, the absence of external impediments; which impediments may oft take away part of a man's power to do what he would, but cannot hinder him from using the power left him according as his judgement and reason shall dictate to him.

3. A Law of Nature (*lex naturalis*) is a precept or general rule, found out by reason, by which a man is forbidden to do that which is destructive of his life, or taketh away the means of preserving the same, and to omit that by which he thinketh it may be best preserved. For though they that speak of this subject use to confound *jus* and *lex, right* and *law*; yet they ought to be distinguished, because right consisteth in liberty to do or to forbear; whereas law determineth and bindeth to one of them; so that law and right differ as much as obligation and liberty, which in one and the same matter are inconsistent.

4. And because the condition of man (as hath been declared in the precedent chapter) is a condition of war of every one against every one, in which case every one is governed by his own reason, and there is nothing he can make use of that may not be a help unto him in preserving his life against his enemies; it followeth that in such a condition every man has a right to every thing, even to one another's body. And therefore, as long as this natural right of every man to every thing endureth, there can be no security to any man, how strong or wise soever he be, of living out the time which nature ordinarily alloweth men to live. And consequently it is a precept, or general rule of reason *that every man ought to endeavour peace, as far as he has hope of obtaining it; and when he cannot obtain it, that he may seek and use all helps and advantages of war*. The first branch of which rule containeth the first and fundamental law of nature, which is *to seek peace and follow it*. The second, the sum of the right of nature, which is *by all means we can to defend ourselves*.

5. From this fundamental law of nature, by which men are commanded to endeavour peace, is derived this second law: *that a man be willing, when others are so too, as far forth as for peace and defense of himself he shall think it necessary, to lay down this right to all things; and be contented with so much liberty against other men as he would allow other men against himself*. For as long as every man holdeth this right of doing anything he liketh, so long are all men in the condition of war. But if other men will not lay down their right, as well as he, then there is no reason for anyone to divest himself of his, for that were to expose himself to prey, which no man is bound to, rather than to dispose himself to peace. This is that law of the gospel: *Whatsoever you require that others should do to you, that do ye to them*. And that law of all men, *quod tibi fieri non vis, alteri ne feceris* [*What you do not want done to you, do not do to another*].

6. To *lay down* a man's *right* to anything is to *divest* himself of the *liberty* of hindering another of the benefit of his own right to the same. For he that renounceth or passeth away his right giveth not to any other man a right which he had not before, because there is nothing to which every man had not right by nature, but only standeth out of his way that he may enjoy his own original right without hindrance from him, not without hindrance from another. So that the effect which redoundeth to one man by another man's defect of right is but so much diminution of impediments to the use of his own right original.

7. Right is laid aside either by simply renouncing it or by transferring it to another. By *simply* RENOUNCING, when he cares not to whom the benefit thereof redoubeth. By TRANSFERRING, when he intendeth the benefit thereof to some certain person or persons. And when a man hath in either manner abandoned or granted away his right, then is he said to be OBLIGED or BOUND, not to hinder those to whom such right is granted, or abandoned, from the benefit of it; and that he *ought*, and it is DUTY, not to make void that voluntary act of his own; and that such hindrance is INJUSTICE and INJURY, as being *sine jure*; the right being before renounced or transferred. So that *injury* or *injustice*, in the controversies of the world, is somewhat like to that which in the disputations of scholars is called *absurdity*. For as it is there called an absurdity to contradict what one maintained in the beginning, so in the world it is called injustice and injury voluntarily to undo that which from the beginning he had voluntarily done. The way by which a man either simply renounceth or transferreth his right is a declaration or signification by some voluntary and sufficient sign or signs that he doth so renounce or transfer or hath so renounced or transferred the same to him that accepteth it. And these signs are either words only, or actions only; or, as it happeneth most often, both words and actions. And the same are the BONDS, by which men are bound and obliged, bonds that have their strength, not from their own nature (for nothing is more easily broken than a man's word), but from fear of some evil consequence upon the rupture.

8. Whensoever a man transferreth his right, or renounceth it, it is either in consideration of some right reciprocally transferred to himself, or for some other good he hopeth for thereby. For it is a voluntary act; and of the voluntary acts of every man, the object is some *good to himself*. And therefore there be some rights which no man can be understood by any words, or other signs, to have abandoned or transferred. As first a man cannot lay down the right of resisting them that assault him by force to take away his life, because he cannot be understood to aim thereby at any good to himself. The same may be said of wounds, and chains, and imprisonment, both because there is no benefit consequent to such patience, as there is to the patience of suffering another to be wounded or imprisoned, as also because a man cannot tell when he seeth men proceed against him by violence whether they intend his death or not. And lastly the motive and end for which this renouncing and transferring of right is introduced is nothing else but the security of a man's person in his life, and in the means of so preserving life as not to be weary of it. And therefore if a man by words, or other signs, seem to despoil himself of the end for which those signs were intended, he is not to be understood as if he meant it, or that it was his will, but that he was ignorant of how such words and actions were to be interpreted.

9. The mutual transferring of right is that which men call CONTRACT.

10. There is difference between transferring of right to the thing, and transferring or tradition, that is, delivery of the thing itself. For the thing may be delivered together with the translation of the right, as in buying and selling with ready money, or exchange of goods or lands; and it may be delivered some time after.

11. Again, one of the contractors may deliver the thing contracted for on his part, and leave the other to perform his part at some determinate time after, and in the meantime be trusted; and then the contract on his part is called PACT or COVENANT; or both parts may contract now to perform hereafter, in which cases he that is to perform in time to come, being trusted, his performance is called *keeping of promise*, or faith, and the failing of performance, if it be voluntary, *violation of faith*.

12. When the transferring of right is not mutual, but one of the parties transferreth in hope to gain thereby friendship or service from another or from his friends; or in hope to gain the reputation of charity or magnanimity; or to deliver his mind from the pain of compassion; or in hope of reward in heaven; this is not contract, but GIFT, FREE GIFT, GRACE; which words signify one and the same thing.

13. Signs of contract are either *express* or *by inference*. Express are words spoken with understanding of what they signify; and such words are either of the time *present* or *past*, as, *I give, I grant, I have given, I have granted, I will that this be yours*; or of the future, as, *I will give, I will grant*, which words of the future are called PROMISE.

14. Signs by inference are sometimes the consequence of words, sometimes the consequence of silence, sometimes the consequence of actions, sometimes the consequence of forbearing an action, and generally a sign by inference, of any contract, is whatsoever sufficiently argues the will of the contractor.

15. Words alone, if they be of the time to come, and contain a bare promise, are an insufficient sign of a free gift and therefore not obligatory. For if they be of the time to come, as, *tomorrow I will give*, they are a sign I have not given yet, and consequently that my right is not transferred, but remaineth till I transfer it by some other act. But if the words be of the time present or past, as, *I have given*, or *do give to be delivered tomorrow*, then is my tomorrow's right given away today; and that by the virtue of the words, though there were no other argument of my will. And there is a great difference in the signification of these words, *volo hoc tuum esse cras*, and *cras dabo*; that is, between *I will that this be thine tomorrow*, and, *I will give it thee tomorrow*, for the word *I will*, in the former manner of speech, signifies an act of the will present; but in the latter, it signifies a promise of an act of the will to come; and therefore the former words, being of the present, transfer a future right; the latter, that be of the future, transfer nothing. But if there be other signs of the will to transfer a right besides words, then, though the gift be free, yet may the right be understood to pass by words of the future, as if a man propound a prize to him that comes first to the end of a race, the gift is free; and though the words be of the future, yet the right passeth, for if he would not have his words so be understood, he should not have let them run.

16. In contracts the right passeth, not only where the words are of the time present or past, but also where they are of the future, because all contract is mutual translation or change of right; and therefore he that promiseth only, because he hath already received the benefit for which he promiseth, is to be understood as if he intended the right should pass, for unless he had been content to have his words so understood, the other would not have performed his part first. And for that cause, in buying and selling, and other acts of contract, a promise is equivalent to a covenant, and therefore obligatory.

17. He that performeth first in the case of a contract is said to MERIT that which he is to receive by the performance of the other, and he hath it as *due*. Also when a prize is propounded to many, which is to be given to him only that winneth, or money is thrown amongst many to be enjoyed by them that catch it, though this be a free gift; yet so to win or so to catch is to *merit*, and to have it as DUE. For the right is transferred in the propounding of

the prize and in throwing down the money, though it be not determined to whom, but by the event of the contention. But there is between these two sorts of merit this difference, that in contract I merit by virtue of my own power and the contractor's need, but in this case of free gift I am enabled to merit only by the benignity of the giver; in contract I merit at the contractor's hand that he should depart with his right; in this case of gift, I merit not that the giver should part with his right, but that when he has parted with it, it should be mine rather than another's. And this I think to be the meaning of that distinction of the Schools between *meritum congrui* and *meritum condigni*. For God Almighty, having promised paradise to those men, hoodwinked with carnal desires, that can walk through this world according to the precepts and limits prescribed by him, they say he that shall so walk shall merit paradise *ex congruo* [*from its appropriateness*]. But because no man can demand a right to it by his own righteousness, or any other power in himself, but by the free grace of God only, they say no man can merit paradise *ex condigno* [*from being deserved*]. This, I say, I think is the meaning of that distinction; but because disputers do not agree upon the signification of their own terms of art longer than it serves their turn, I will not affirm anything of their meaning; only this I say; when a gift is given indefinitely, as a prize to be contended for, he that winneth meriteth, and may claim the prize as due.

18. If a covenant be made wherein neither of the parties perform presently, but trust one another, in the condition of mere nature (which is a condition of war of every man against every man) upon any reasonable suspicion, it is void; but if there be a common power set over them both, with right and force sufficient to compel performance, it is not void. For he that performeth first has no assurance the other will perform after, because the bonds of words are too weak to bridle men's ambition, avarice, anger, and other passions, without the fear of some coercive power; which in the condition of mere nature, where all men are equal, and judges of the justness of their own fears, cannot possibly be supposed. And therefore he which performeth first does but betray himself to his enemy, contrary to the right he can never abandon of defending his life and means of living.

19. But in a civil estate, where there is a power set up to constrain those that would otherwise violate their faith, that fear is no more reasonable; and for that cause, he which by the covenant is to perform first is obliged so to do.

20. The cause of fear, which maketh such a covenant invalid, must be always something arising after the covenant made, as some new fact or other sign of the will not to perform, else it cannot make the covenant void. For that which could not hinder a man from promising ought not to be admitted as a hindrance of performing.

21. He that transferreth any right transferreth the means of enjoying it, as far as lieth in his power. As he that selleth land is understood to transfer the herbage and whatsoever grows upon it; nor can he that sells a mill turn away the stream that drives it. And they that give to a man the right of government in sovereignty are understood to give him the right of levying money to maintain soldiers, and of appointing magistrates for the administration of justice.

22. To make covenants with brute beasts is impossible, because not understanding our speech, they understand not, nor accept of any translation of right, nor can translate any right to another; and without mutual acceptation, there is no covenant.

23. To make covenant with God is impossible but by mediation of such as God speaketh to either by revelation supernatural or by his lieutenants that govern under him and in his name; for otherwise we know not whether our covenants be accepted or not. And therefore they that vow anything contrary to any law of nature, vow in vain, as being a thing

unjust to pay such vow. And if it be a thing commanded by the law of nature, it is not the vow, but the law that binds them.

24. The matter or subject of a covenant is always something that falleth under deliberation; for to covenant is in act of the will, that is to say, an act, and the last act, of deliberation, and is therefore always understood to be something to come, and which judged possible for him that covenanteth to perform.

25. And therefore, to promise that which is known to be impossible is no covenant. But if that prove impossible afterwards, which before was thought possible, the covenant is valid and bindeth, though not to the thing itself, yet to the value; or, if that also be impossible, to the unfeigned endeavour of performing as much as is possible, for to more no man can be obliged.

26. Men are freed of their covenants two ways, by performing or by being forgiven. For performance is the natural end of obligation, and forgiveness the restitution of liberty, as being a retransferring of that right in which the obligation consisted.

27. Covenants entered into by fear, in the condition of mere nature, are obligatory. For example, if I covenant to pay a ransom or service for my life to an enemy, I am bound by it. For it is a contract, wherein one receiveth the benefit of life, the other is to receive money or service for it; and consequently, where no other law (as in the condition of mere nature) forbiddeth the performance, the covenant is valid. Therefore prisoners of war, if trusted with the payment of their ransom, are obliged to pay it; and if a weaker prince make a disadvantageous peace with a stronger, for fear, he is bound to keep it, unless (as hath been said before) there ariseth some new and just cause of fear to renew the war. And even in commonwealths, if I be forced to redeem myself from a thief by promising him money, I am bound to pay it, till the civil law discharge me. For whatsoever I may lawfully do without obligation, the same I may lawfully covenant to do through fear; and what I lawfully covenant, I cannot lawfully break.

28. A former covenant makes void a later. For a man that hath passed away his right to one man today hath it not to pass tomorrow to another; and therefore the later promise passeth no right, but is null.

29. A covenant not to defend myself from force, by force, is always void. For (as I have shown before) no man can transfer or lay down his right to save himself from death, wounds, and imprisonment, the avoiding whereof is the only end of laying down any right; and therefore the promise of not resisting force, in no covenant transferreth any right, nor is obliging. For though a man may covenant thus, *unless I do so, or so, kill me*; he cannot covenant thus, *unless I do so, or so, I will not resist you when you come to kill me*. For man by nature chooseth the lesser evil, which is danger of death in resisting, rather than the greater, which is certain and present death in not resisting. And this is granted to be true by all men in that they lead criminals to execution and prison with armed men, notwithstanding that such criminals have consented to the law by which they are condemned.

30. A covenant to accuse oneself, without assurance of pardon, is likewise invalid. For in the condition of nature where every man is judge, there is no place for accusation; and in the civil state the accusation is followed with punishment, which, being force, a man is not obliged not to resist. The same is also true of the accusation of those by whose condemnation a man falls into misery, as of a father, wife, or benefactor. For the testimony of such an accuser, if it be not willingly given, is presumed to be corrupted by nature, and therefore not to be received; and where a man's testimony is not to be credited, he is not bound to give it. Also accusations upon torture are not to be reputed as testimonies. For torture is to

be used but as means of conjecture and light in the further examination and search of truth; and what is in that case confessed tendeth to the ease of him that is tortured, not to the informing of the torturers, and therefore ought not to have the credit of a sufficient testimony, for whether he deliver himself by true or false accusation, he does it by the right of preserving his own life.

31. The force of words being (as I have formerly noted) too weak to hold men to the performance of their covenants, there are in man's nature but two imaginable helps to strengthen it. And those are either a fear of the consequence of breaking their word or a glory or pride in appearing not to need to break it. This latter is a generosity too rarely found to be presumed on, especially in the pursuers of wealth, command, or sensual pleasure, which are the greatest part of mankind. The passion to be reckoned upon is fear; whereof there be two very general objects: one, the power of spirits invisible; the other, the power of those men they shall therein offend. Of these two, though the former be the greater power; yet the fear of the latter is commonly the greater fear. The fear of the former is in every man his own religion, which hath place in the nature of man before civil society. The latter hath not so, at least not place enough to keep men to their promises, because in the condition of mere nature, the inequality of power is not discerned, but by the event of battle. So that before the time of civil society, or in the interruption thereof by war, there is nothing can strengthen a covenant of peace agreed on against the temptations of avarice, ambition, lust, or other strong desire, but the fear of that invisible power which they every one worship as God, and fear as a revenger of their perfidy. All therefore that can be done between two men not subject to civil power is to put one another to swear by the God he feareth; which *swearing*, or OATH, is a *form of speech, added to a promise, by which he that promiseth signifieth that unless he perform he renounceth the mercy of his God, or calleth to him for vengeance on himself.* Such was the heathen form, *Let Jupiter kill me else, as I kill this beast*. So is our form, *I shall do thus, and thus, so help me God*. And this, with the rites and ceremonies which every one useth in his own religion, that the fear of breaking faith might be the greater.

32. By this it appears that an oath taken according to any other form or rite than his that sweareth is in vain and no oath; and that there is no swearing by anything which the swearer thinks not God. For though men have sometimes used to swear by their kings, for fear, or flattery; yet they would have it thereby understood they attributed to them divine honour. And that swearing unnecessarily by God is but profaning of his name; and swearing by other things, as men do in common discourse, is not swearing, but an impious custom, gotten by too much vehemence of talking.

33. It appears also that the oath adds nothing to the obligation. For a covenant, if lawful, binds in the sight of God, without the oath, as much as with it; if unlawful, bindeth not at all, though it be confirmed with an oath.

Chapter XV
Of Other Laws of Nature

1. From that law of nature by which we are obliged to transfer to another such rights as, being retained, hinder the peace of mankind, there followeth a third, which is this; *that men perform their covenants made*; without which, covenants are in vain and but empty words; and the right of all men to all things remaining, we are still in the condition of war.

2. And in this law of nature consisteth the fountain and original of JUSTICE. For where no covenant hath preceded, there hath no right been transferred; and every man has right to

everything; and consequently, no action can be unjust. But when a covenant is made, then to break it is *unjust* and the definition of INJUSTICE is no other than *the not performance of covenant*. And whatsoever is not unjust is *just*.

3. But because covenants of mutual trust, where there is a fear of not performance on either part (as hath been said in the former chapter), are invalid, though the original of justice be the making of covenants; yet injustice actually there can be none till the cause of such fear be taken away; which, while men are in the natural condition of war, cannot be done. Therefore before the names of *just* and *unjust* can have place, there must be some coercive power to compel men equally to the performance of their covenants by the terror of some punishment greater than the benefit they expect by the breach of their covenant, and to make good that propriety which by mutual contract men acquire in recompense of the universal right they abandon; and such power there is none before the erection of a commonwealth. And this is also to be gathered out of the ordinary definition of justice in the Schools, for they say that *justice is the constant will of giving to every man his own*. And therefore where there is no *own*, that is, no propriety [property], there is no injustice; and where there is no coercive power erected, that is, where there is no commonwealth, there is no propriety, all men having right to all things; therefore where there is no commonwealth, there nothing is unjust. So that the nature of justice consisteth in keeping of valid covenants; but the validity of covenants begins not but with the constitution of a civil power sufficient to compel men to keep them; and then it is also that propriety begins.

4. The fool hath said in his heart, there is no such thing as justice; and sometimes also with his tongue, seriously alleging that every man's conservation and contentment being committed to his own care, there could be no reason why every man might not do what he thought conduced thereunto; and therefore also to make or not make, keep or not keep covenants was not against reason when it conduced to one's benefit. He does not therein deny that there be covenants; and that they are sometimes broken, sometimes kept; and that such breach of them may be called injustice, and the observance of them justice; but he questioneth whether injustice, taking away the fear of God (for the same fool hath said in his heart there is no God), not sometimes stand with that reason which dictateth to every man his own good; and particularly then, when it conduceth to such a benefit as shall put a man in a condition to neglect not only the dispraise and revilings, but also the power of other men. The kingdom of God is gotten by violence; but what if it could be gotten by unjust violence? Were it against reason so to get it, when it is impossible to receive hurt by it? And if it be not against reason, it is not against justice; or else justice is not to be approved for good. From such reasoning as this, successful wickedness hath obtained the name of virtue; and some that in all other things have disallowed the violation of faith, yet have allowed it when it is for the getting of a kingdom. And the heathen that believed that Saturn was deposed by his son Jupiter believed nevertheless the same Jupiter to be the avenger of injustice, somewhat like to a piece of law in Coke's *Commentaries on Littleton*, where he says, if the right heir of the crown be attainted of treason, yet the crown shall descend to him, and *eo instante* the attainder be void; from which instances a man will be very prone to infer that when the heir apparent of a kingdom shall kill him that is in possession, though his father, you may call it injustice or by what other name you will; yet it can never be against reason, seeing all the voluntary actions of men tend to the benefit of themselves; and those actions are most reasonable that conduce most to their ends. This specious reasoning is nevertheless false.

5. For the question is not of promises mutual, where there is no security of performance on either side, as when there is no civil power erected over the parties promising, for such

promises are no covenants; but either where one of the parties has performed already or where there is a power to make him perform, there is the question whether it be against reason, that is, against the benefit of the other to perform or not. And I say it is not against reason. For the manifestation whereof we are to consider, first, that when a man doth a thing, which notwithstanding anything can be foreseen and reckoned on tendeth to his own destruction, howsoever some accident, which he could not expect, arriving may turn it to his benefit; yet such events do not make it reasonably or wisely done. Secondly, that in a condition of war, wherein every man to every man, for want of a common power to keep them all in awe, is an enemy, there is no man can hope by his own strength or wit to himself from destruction without the help of confederates, where every one expects the same defence by the confederation that any one else does; and therefore he which declares he thinks it reason to deceive those that help him can in reason expect no other means of safety than what can be had from his own single power. He, therefore, that breaketh his covenant and consequently declareth that he thinks he may with reason do so, cannot be received into any society that unite themselves for peace and defence but by the error of them that receive him; nor when he is received be retained in it without seeing the danger of their error; which errors a man cannot reasonably reckon upon as the means of his security; and therefore if he be left or cast out of society, he perisheth; and if he live in society, it is by the errors of other men, which he could not foresee nor reckon upon, and consequently against the reason of his preservation; and so, as all men that contribute not to his destruction forbear him only out of ignorance of what is good for themselves.

6. As for the instance of gaining the secure and perpetual felicity of heaven by any way, it is frivolous; there being but one way imaginable, and that is not breaking, but keeping of covenant.

7. And for the other instance of attaining sovereignty by rebellion, it is manifest that, though the event follow; yet because it cannot reasonably be expected, but rather the contrary, and because, by gaining it so, others are taught to gain the same in like manner, the attempt thereof is against reason. Justice therefore, that is to say, keeping of covenant, is a rule of reason by which we are forbidden to do anything destructive to our life, and consequently a law of nature.

8. There be some that proceed further and will not have the law of nature to be those rules which conduce to the preservation of man's life on earth, but to the attaining of an eternal felicity after death, to which [felicity] they think the breach of covenant may conduce and consequently be just and reasonable; such are they that think it a work of merit to kill or depose or rebel against the sovereign power constituted over them by their own consent. But because there is no natural knowledge of man's estate after death, much less of the reward that is then to be given to breach of faith, but only a belief grounded upon other men's saying that they know it supernaturally or that they know those that knew them that knew others that knew it supernaturally, breach of faith cannot be called a precept of reason or nature.

9. Others, that allow for a law of nature the keeping of faith, do nevertheless make exception of certain persons, as heretics, and such as use not to perform their covenant to others; and this also is against reason. For if any fault of a man be sufficient to discharge our covenant made, the same ought in reason to have been sufficient to have hindered the making of it.

10. The names of *just* and *unjust*, when they are attributed to men, signify one thing, and, when they are attributed to actions, another. When they are attributed to men, they signify

conformity or inconformity of manners to reason. But when they are attributed to action they signify the conformity or inconformity to reason, not of manners, or manner of life, but of particular actions. A just man therefore is he that taketh all the care he can that his actions may be all just; and an unjust man is he that neglecteth it. And such men are more often in our language styled by the names of righteous and unrighteous than just and unjust though the meaning be the same. Therefore a righteous man does not lose that title by one or a few unjust actions that proceed from sudden passion or mistake of things or persons; nor does an unrighteous man lose his character for such actions as he does or forbears to do for fear, because his will is not framed by the justice, but by the apparent benefit of what he is to do. That which gives to human actions the relish of justice is a certain nobleness or gallantness of courage, rarely found, by which a man scorns to be beholding for the contentment of his life to fraud or breach of promise. This justice of the manners is that which is meant where justice is called a virtue; and injustice, a vice.

11. But the justice of actions denominates men, not just, but *guiltless*; and the injustice of the same (which is also called injury) gives them but the name of *guilty*.

12. Again, the injustice of manners is the disposition or aptitude to do injury, and is injustice before it proceed to act and without supposing any individual person injured. But the injustice of an action (that is to say, injury) supposeth an individual person injured; namely him to whom the covenant was made; and therefore many times the injury is received by one man when the damage redoundeth to another. As when the master commandeth his servant to give money to a stranger; if it be not done, the injury is done to the master, whom he had before covenanted to obey; but the damage redoundeth to the stranger, to whom he had no obligation, and therefore could not injure him. And so also in commonwealths private men may remit to one another their debts, but not robberies or other violences, whereby they are endamaged, because the detaining of debt is an injury to themselves; but robbery and violence are injuries to the person of the commonwealth.

13. Whatsoever is done to a man, conformable to his own will signified to the doer, is not injury to him. For if he that doeth it hath not passed away his original right to do what he please by some antecedent covenant, there is no breach of covenant, and therefore no injury done him. And if he have, then his will to have it done, being signified, is a release of that covenant, and so again there is no injury done him.

14. Justice of actions is by writers divided into *commutative* and *distributive*; and the former they say consisteth in proportion arithmetical; the latter in proportion geometrical. Commutative, therefore, they place in the equality of value of the things contracted for; and distributive, in the distribution of equal benefit to men of equal merit. As if it were injustice to sell dearer than we buy, or to give more to a man than he merits. The value of all things contracted for is measured by the appetite of the contractors, and therefore the just value is that which they be contented to give. And merit (besides that which is by covenant, where the performance on one part meriteth the performance of the other part, and falls under justice commutative, not distributive) is not due by justice, but is rewarded of grace only. And therefore this distinction, in the sense wherein it useth to be expounded, is not right. To speak properly, commutative justice is the justice of a contractor; that is, a performance of covenant in buying and selling, hiring and letting to hire, lending and borrowing, exchanging, bartering, and other acts of contract.

15. And distributive justice [is] the justice of an arbitrator, that is to say, the act of defining what is just. Wherein, being trusted by them that make him arbitrator, if he perform his trust, he is said to distribute to every man his own; and this is indeed just distribution, and

may be called, though improperly, distributive justice, but more properly equity, which also is a law of nature, as shall be shown in due place.

16. As justice dependeth on antecedent covenant, so does Gratitude depend on antecedent grace, that is to say, antecedent free gift, and is the fourth law of nature, which may be conceived in this form: *that a man which receiveth benefit from another of mere grace endeavour that he which giveth it have no reasonable cause to repent him of his good will.* For no man giveth but with intention of good to himself, because gift is voluntary; and of all voluntary acts, the object is to every man his own good; of which, if men see [that] they shall be frustrated, there will be no beginning of benevolence or trust, nor consequently of mutual help, nor of reconciliation of one man to another; and therefore they are to remain still in the condition of *war*, which is contrary to the first and fundamental law of nature which commandeth men to *seek peace*. The breach of this law is called *ingratitude* and hath the same relation to grace that injustice hath to obligation by covenant.

17. A fifth law of nature is Complaisance; that is to say, *that every man strive to accommodate himself to the rest.* For the understanding whereof we may consider that there is in men's aptness to society a diversity of nature, rising from their diversity of affections, not unlike to that we see in stones brought together for building of an edifice. For as that stone which by the asperity and irregularity of figure takes more room from others than itself fills, and for hardness cannot be easily made plain, and thereby hindereth the building, is by the builders cast away as unprofitable and troublesome; so also, a man that by asperity of nature will strive to retain those things which to himself are superfluous and to others necessary, and for the stubbornness of his passions cannot be corrected, is to be left or cast out of society as cumbersome thereunto. For seeing every man, not only by right, but also by necessity of nature, is supposed to endeavour all he can to obtain that which is necessary for his conservation, he that shall oppose himself against it for things superfluous is guilty of the war that thereupon is to follow, and therefore doth that which is contrary to the fundamental law of nature, which commandeth *to seek peace*. The observers of this law may be called Sociable, (the Latins call them *commodi*); the contrary, *stubborn, insociable, forward, intractable*.

18. A sixth law of nature is this: *that upon caution of the future time, a man ought to pardon the offences past of them that, repenting, desire it.* For Pardon is nothing but granting of peace, which though granted to them that persevere in their hostility, be not peace, but fear; yet not granted to them that give caution of the future time is sign of an aversion to peace and therefore contrary to the law of nature.

19. A seventh is, *that in revenges* (that is, retribution of evil for evil), *men look not at the greatness of the evil past, but the greatness of the good to follow*. Whereby we are forbidden to inflict punishment with any other design than for correction of the offender or direction of others. For [. . .] to hurt without reason tendeth to the introduction of war, which is against the law of nature, and is commonly styled by the name of *cruelty*.

20. And because all signs of hatred or contempt provoke to fight, insomuch as most men choose rather to hazard their life than not to be revenged, we may in the eighth place, for a law of nature, set down this precept; *that no man by deed, word, countenance, or gesture, declare hatred or contempt of another*. The breach of which law is commonly called *contumely*.

21. The question who is the better man has no place in the condition of mere nature, where (as has been shown before) all men are equal. The inequality that now is has been introduced by the laws civil. [. . .] For there are very few so foolish that had not rather govern themselves than be governed by others; nor when the wise, in their own conceit,

contend by force with them who distrust their own wisdom, do they always, or often, or almost at any time, get the victory. If nature therefore have made men equal, that equality is to be acknowledged; or if nature have made men unequal, yet because men that think themselves equal will not enter into conditions of peace, but upon equal terms, such equality must be admitted. And therefore for the ninth law of nature, I put this, *that every man acknowledge another for his equal by nature*. The breach of this precept is *pride*.

22. On this law dependeth another, *that at the entrance into conditions of peace, no man require to reserve to himself any right which he is not content should be reserved to every one of the rest*. As it is necessary for all men that seek peace to lay down certain rights of nature, that is to say, not to have liberty to do all they list, so is it necessary for man's life to retain some, as right to govern their own bodies, enjoy air, water, motion, ways to go from place to place, and all things else without which a man cannot live or not live well. If in this case, at the making of peace, men require for themselves that which they would not have to be granted to others, they do contrary to the precedent law that commandeth the acknowledgement of natural equality, and therefore also against the law of nature. The observers of this law are those we call *modest*, and the breakers *arrogant* men. The Greeks call the violation of this law *pleonexia*, that is, a desire of more than their share.

23. Also, if *a man be trusted to judge between man and man*, it is a precept of the law of nature *that he deal equally between them*. For without that, the controversies of men cannot be determined but by war. He therefore that is partial in judgement doth what in him lies to deter men from the use of judges and arbitrators, and consequently (against the fundamental law of nature) is the cause of war.

24. The observance of this law, from the equal distribution to each man of that which in reason belonged to him, is called Equity, and (as I have said before) distributive justice; the violation, *acception of persons, prosopolepsia*.

25. And from this followeth another law: *that such things as cannot be divided be enjoyed in common, if it can be; and if the quantity of the thing permit, without stint; otherwise proportionably to the number of them that have right*. For otherwise the distribution is unequal, and contrary to equity.

26. But some things there be that can neither be divided nor enjoyed in common. Then, the law of nature which prescribeth equity requireth, *that the entire right, or else (making the use alternate) the first possession, be determined by lot*. For equal distribution is of the law of nature; and other means of equal distribution cannot be imagined.

[. . .]

28. And therefore those things which cannot be enjoyed in common, nor divided, ought to be adjudged to the first possessor; and in some cases to the first born, as acquired by lot.

29. It is also a law of nature, *that all men that mediate peace be allowed safe conduct*. For the law that commandeth peace, as the *end*, commandeth intercession, as the *means*; and to intercession the means is safe conduct.

30. And because, though men be never so willing to observe these laws, there may nevertheless arise questions concerning a man's action; [. . .] therefore unless the parties to the question covenant mutually to stand to the sentence of another, they are as far from peace as ever. This other, to whose sentence they submit, is called an Arbitrator. And therefore it is of the law of nature *that they that are at controversy submit their right to the judgement of an arbitrator*.

31. And seeing every man is presumed to do all things in order to his own benefit, no man is a fit arbitrator in his own cause. [. . .]

32. For the same reason no man in any cause ought to be received for arbitrator to whom greater profit or honour or pleasure apparently ariseth out of the victory of one party than of the other. [. . .]

33. And in a controversy of *fact*, the judge being to give no more credit to one than to the other, if there be no other arguments, must give credit to a third; or to a third and fourth; or more, for else the question is undecided, and left to force, contrary to the law of nature.

34. These are the laws of nature, dictating peace, for a means of the conservation of men in multitudes; and which only concern the doctrine of civil society. There be other things tending to the destruction of particular men, as drunkenness, and all other parts of intemperance, which may therefore also be reckoned amongst those things which the law of nature hath forbidden, but are not necessary to be mentioned, nor are pertinent enough to this place.

35. And though this may seem too subtle a deduction of the laws of nature to be taken notice of by all men, whereof the most part are too busy in getting food, and the rest too negligent to understand; yet to leave all men inexcusable, they have been contracted into one easy sum, intelligible even to the meanest capacity; and that is: *Do not that to another which thou wouldest not have done to thyself*; which showeth him that he has no more to do in learning the laws of nature but, when weighing the actions of other men with his own they seem too heavy, to put them into the other part of the balance, and his own into their place, that his own passions and self-love may add nothing to the weight; and then there is none of these laws of nature that will not appear unto him very reasonable.

36. The laws of nature oblige *in foro interno*, that is to say, they bind to a desire they should take place; but *in foro externo*; that is, to the putting them in act, not always. For he that should be modest and tractable, and perform all he promises in such time and place where no man else should do so, should but make himself a prey to others, and procure his own certain ruin, contrary to the ground of all laws of nature which tend to nature's preservation. And again, he that having sufficient security that others shall observe the same laws towards him, observes them not himself, seeketh not peace, but war, and consequently the destruction of his nature by violence.

37. And whatsoever laws bind *in foro interno* may be broken, not only by a fact contrary to the law, but also by a fact according to it, in case a man think it contrary. For though his action in this case be according to the law; yet his purpose was against the law; which, where the obligation is *in foro interno*, is a breach.

38. The laws of nature are immutable and eternal, for injustice, ingratitude, arrogance, pride, iniquity, acception of persons, and the rest can never be made lawful. For it can never be that war shall preserve life, and peace destroy it.

39. The same laws, because they oblige only to a desire and endeavour, mean an unfeigned and constant endeavour, are easy to be observed. For in that they require nothing but endeavour, he that endeavoureth their performance fulfilleth them; and he that fulfilleth the law is just.

40. And the science of them is the true and only moral philosophy. For moral philosophy is nothing else but the science of what is *good* and *evil* in the conversation [interactions] and society of mankind. *Good* and *evil* are names that signify our appetites and aversions, which in different tempers, customs, and doctrines of men are different; and divers men differ not only in their judgement on the senses of what is pleasant and unpleasant to the taste, smell, hearing, touch, and sight; but also of what is conformable or disagreeable to reason in the

actions of common life. Nay, the same man, in divers times, differs from himself; and one time praiseth, that is, calleth *good*, what another time he dispraiseth, and calleth *evil*. From whence arise disputes, controversies, and at last war. And therefore so long a man is in the condition of mere nature (which is a condition of war), as private appetite is the measure of good and evil; and consequently all men agree on this, that peace is good, and therefore also the way or means of peace, which (as I have shown before) are *justice, gratitude, modesty, equity, mercy*, and the rest of the laws of nature, are good; that is to say, *moral virtues*; and their contrary *vices*, evil. Now the science of virtue and vice is moral philosophy; and therefore the true doctrine of the laws of nature is the true moral philosophy. But the writers of moral philosophy, though they acknowledge the same virtues and vices; yet, not seeing wherein consisted their goodness, nor that they come to be praised as the means of peaceable, sociable, and comfortable living, place them in a mediocrity of passions, as if not the cause, but the degree of daring, made fortitude, or not the cause, but the quantity of a gift, made liberality.

41. These dictates of reason men use to call by the name of laws, but improperly; for they are but conclusions or theorems concerning what conduceth to the conservation and defence of themselves; whereas law, properly, is the word of him that by right hath command over others. But yet if we consider the same theorems as delivered in the word of God that by right commandeth all things, then are they properly called *laws*.

Chapter XVI
Of Persons, Authors, and Things Personated

1. A person is he *whose words or actions are considered, either as his own, or as representing the words or actions of another man, or of any other thing to whom they are attributed, whether truly or by fiction*.

2. When they are considered as his own, then is he called a *natural person;* and when they are considered as representing the words and actions of another, then is he a *feigned* or *artificial* person.

[. . .]

4. Of persons artificial, some have their words and actions *owned* by those whom they represent. And then the person is the *actor*; and he that owneth his words and actions is the AUTHOR, in which case the actor acteth by authority. For that which in speaking of goods and possessions is called an *owner*, and in Latin *dominus* in Greek *kurios*; speaking of actions, is called author. And as the right of possession is called dominion, so the right of doing any action is called AUTHORITY and sometimes *warrant*. So that by authority is always understood a right of doing any act; and *done by authority*, done by commission or license from him whose right it is.

5. From hence it followeth that when the actor maketh a covenant by authority, he bindeth thereby the author no less than if he had made it himself, and no less subjecteth him to all the consequences of the same. And therefore all that hath been said formerly (Chapter 14) of the nature of covenants between man and man in their natural capacity is true also when they are made by their actors, representers, or procurators, that have authority from them, so far forth as is in their commission, but no further.

[. . .]

7. When the actor doth anything against the law of nature by command of the author, if he be obliged by former covenant to obey him, not he, but the author breaketh the law of nature, for though the action be against the law of nature, yet it is not his; but, contrarily, to refuse to do it is against the law of nature that forbiddeth breach of covenant.

[. . .]

9. There are few things that are incapable of being represented by fiction. Inanimate things, as a church, a hospital, a bridge, may be personated by a rector, master, or overseer. But things inanimate cannot be authors, nor therefore give authority to their actors. Yet the actors may have authority to procure their maintenance, given them by those that are owners or governors of those things. And therefore such things cannot be personated before there be some state of civil government.

10. Likewise children, fools, and madmen that have no use of reason may be personated by guardians or curators, but can be not authors. [. . .]

11. An idol or mere figment of the brain may be personated, as were the gods of the heathen, which, by such officers as the state appointed, were personated and held possessions and other goods and rights, which men from time to time dedicated and consecrated unto them. But idols cannot be authors; for an idol is nothing. The authority proceeded from the state; and therefore before introduction of civil government the gods of the heathen could not be personated.

12. The true God may be personated. As he was, first, by Moses, who governed the Israelites (that were not his, but God's people), not in his own name (with *hoc dicit Moses* [*thus Moses says*], but in God's name, with (*hoc dicit Dominus* [*thus the Lord says*]). Secondly, by the Son of Man, his own son, our blessed Saviour Jesus Christ, that came to reduce the Jews and induce all nations into the kingdom of his Father; not as of himself, but as sent from his Father. And thirdly, by the Holy Ghost or Comforter, speaking and working in the Apostles; which Holy Ghost was a Comforter that came not of himself, but was sent and proceeded from them both on the day of Pentecost.

13. A multitude of men are made *one* person when they are by one man, or one person, represented, so that it be done with the consent of every one of that multitude in particular. For it is the *unity* of the representer, not the *unity* of the represented, that maketh the person *one*. And it is the representer that beareth the person, and but one person; and *unity* cannot otherwise be understood in multitude.

[. . .]

Part II
Of Commonwealth

Chapter XVII
Of the Causes, Generation, and Definition of a Commonwealth

1. The final cause, end, or design of men (who naturally love liberty, and dominion over others) in the introduction of that restraint upon themselves (in which we see them live in commonwealths) is the foresight of their own preservation and of a more contented life thereby,

that is to say, of getting themselves out from that miserable condition of war which is necessarily consequent (as hath been shown) to the natural passions of men, when there is no visible power to keep them in awe and tie them by fear of punishment to the performance of their covenants and observation of those laws of nature set down in the fourteenth and fifteenth chapters.

2. For the laws of nature (as *justice, equity, modesty, mercy*, and, in sum, *doing to other as we would be done to*) of themselves, without the terror of some power to cause them to be observed, are contrary to our natural passions that carry us to partiality, pride, revenge, and the like. And covenants without the sword are but words and of no strength to secure a man at all. Therefore, notwithstanding the laws of nature (which every one hath then kept, when he has the will to keep them, when he can do it safely), if there be no power erected or not great enough for our security, every man will and may lawfully rely on his own strength and art for caution against all other men. And in all places, where men have lived by small families, to rob and spoil one another has been a trade, and so far from being reputed against the law of nature, that the greater spoils they gained, the greater was their honour; and men observed no other laws therein but the laws of honour, that is, to abstain from cruelty, leaving to men their lives and instruments of husbandry. And as small families did then, so now do cities and kingdoms, which are but greater families (for their own security), enlarge their dominions, upon all pretences of danger and fear of invasion or assistance that may be given to invaders, endeavour as much as they can to subdue or weaken their neighbours by open force and secret arts, for want of other caution, justly, and are remembered for it in after ages with honour.

[...]

5. Nor is it enough for the security which men desire should last all the time of their life, that they be governed and directed by one judgement for a limited time, as in one battle or one war. For though they obtain a victory by their unanimous endeavour against a foreign enemy; yet afterwards, when either they have no common enemy, or he that by one part is held for an enemy is by another part held for a friend, they must needs by the difference of their interests dissolve and fall again into a war amongst themselves.

[...]

13. The only way to erect such a common power as may be able to defend them from the invasion of foreigners and the injuries of one another, and thereby to secure them in such sort as that by their own industry and by the fruits of the earth they may nourish themselves and live contentedly, is to confer all their power and strength upon one man or upon one assembly of men, that may reduce all their wills by plurality of voices unto one will; which is as much as to say, to appoint one man or assembly of men to bear their person; and every one to own and acknowledge himself to be author of whatsoever he that so beareth their person shall act or cause to be acted in those things which concern the common peace and safety; and therein to submit their wills, every one to his will, and their judgements to his judgement. This is more than consent or concord; it is a real unity of them all in one and the same person, made by covenant of every man with every man in such manner as if every man should say to every man, *I authorize and give up my right of governing myself to this man, or to this assembly of men, on this condition: that thou give up thy right to him, and authorize all*

his actions in like manner. This done, the multitude so united in one person is called a COMMONWEALTH; in Latin, CIVITAS. This is the generation of that great LEVIATHAN, or rather, to speak more reverently, of that *mortal god* to which we owe, under the *immortal God*, our peace and defense. For by this authority, given him by every particular man in the commonwealth, he hath the use of so much power and strength conferred on him that, by terror thereof, he is enabled to conform the wills of them all to peace at home and mutual aid against their enemies abroad. And in him consisteth the essence of the commonwealth, which, to define it, is *one person, of whose acts a great multitude, by mutual covenants one with another, have made themselves every one the author, to the end he may use the strength and means of them all as he shall think expedient for their peace and common defense.*

14. And he that carryeth this person is called SOVEREIGN, and said to have *sovereign power*, and every one besides, his SUBJECT.

15. The attaining to this sovereign power is by two ways. One, by natural force, as when a man maketh his children to submit themselves and their children to his government, as being able to destroy them if they refuse, or by war subdueth his enemies to his will, giving them their lives on that condition. The other is when men agree amongst themselves to submit to some man, or assembly of men, voluntarily, on confidence to be protected by him against all others. This latter may be called a political commonwealth or commonwealth by *institution*, and the former [may be called] a commonwealth by *acquisition*. And first, I shall speak of a commonwealth by institution.

Chapter XVIII
Of the Rights of Sovereigns by Institution

1. A *commonwealth* is said to be *instituted* when a *multitude* of men do agree and *covenant, every one with every one*, that to whatsoever *man* or *assembly of men* shall be given by the major part the *right* to *present* the person of them all, that is to say, to be their *representative*, every one, as well he that *voted for it* as he that *voted against it*, shall *authorize* all the actions and judgements of that man, or assembly of men, in the same manner as if they were his own, to the end to live peaceably amongst themselves and be protected against other men.

2. From this institution of a commonwealth are derived all the *rights* and *faculties* of him or them, on whom the sovereign power is conferred by the consent of the people assembled.

3. First, because they covenant, it is to be understood they are not obliged by former covenant to anything repugnant hereunto. And consequently they that have already instituted a commonwealth, being thereby bound by covenant to own the actions and judgements of one, cannot lawfully make a new covenant amongst themselves to be obedient to any other, in anything whatsoever, without his permission. And therefore, they that are subjects to a monarch cannot without his leave cast off monarchy and return to the confusion of a disunited multitude nor transfer their person from him that beareth it to another man or other assembly of men, for they are bound, every man to every man, to own and be reputed author of all that he that already is their sovereign shall do and judge fit to be done; so that any one man dissenting, all the rest should break their covenant made to that man, which is injustice; and they have also every man given the sovereignty to him that beareth their person; and therefore if they depose him, they take from him that which is his own, and so again it is injustice. Besides, if he that attempteth to depose his sovereign be killed or punished by him for such attempt, he is author of his own punishment, as being, by the institution, author of all

his sovereign shall do; and because it is injustice for a man to do anything for which he may be punished by his own authority, he is also upon that title unjust. And whereas some men have pretended for their disobedience to their sovereign a new covenant, made, not with men but with God, this also is unjust; for there is no covenant with God but by mediation of somebody that representeth God's person, which none doth but God's lieutenant who hath the sovereignty under God. But this pretence of covenant with God is so evident a lie, even in the pretenders' own consciences, that it is not only an act of an unjust, but also of a vile and unmanly disposition.

4. Secondly, because the right of bearing the person of them all is given to him [whom] they make sovereign by covenant only of one to another and not of him to any of them, there can happen no breach of covenant on the part of the sovereign; and consequently none of his subjects, by any pretence of forfeiture, can be freed from his subjection. [. . .] The opinion that any monarch receiveth his power by covenant, that is to say, on condition, proceedeth from want of understanding this easy truth: that covenants being but words and breath, have no force to oblige, contain, constrain, or protect any man, but what it has from the public sword, that is, from the untied hands of that man or assembly of men that hath the sovereignty, and whose actions are avouched by them all, and performed by the strength of them all in him united. [. . .]

5. Thirdly, because the major part hath by consenting voices declared a sovereign, he that dissented must now consent with the rest, that is, be contented to avow all the actions he shall do, or else justly be destroyed by the rest. [. . .] And whether he be of the congregation or not and whether his consent be asked or not, he must either submit to their decrees or be left in the condition of war he was in before, wherein he might without injustice be destroyed by any man whatsoever.

6. Fourthly, because every subject is by this institution author of all the actions and judgements of the sovereign instituted, it follows that whatsoever he doth can be no injury to any of his subjects nor ought he to be by any of them accused of injustice. [. . .]

7. Fifthly, and consequently to that which was said last, no man that hath sovereign power can justly be put to death or otherwise in any manner by his subjects punished. For seeing every subject is author of the actions of his sovereign, he punisheth another for the actions committed by himself.

8. And because the end of this institution is the peace and defence of them all, and whosoever has right to the end has right to the means, it belongs of right to whatsoever man or assembly that hath the sovereignty to be judge both of the means of peace and defence and also of the hindrances and disturbances of the same; and to do whatsoever he shall think necessary to be done, both beforehand, for the preserving of peace and security, by prevention of discord at home, and hostility from abroad; and when peace and security are lost, for the recovery of the same. And therefore.

9. Sixthly, it is annexed to the sovereignty to be judge of what opinions and doctrines are averse, and what [opinions and doctrines are] conducing to peace; and consequently on what occasions, how far, and what men are to be trusted withal in speaking to multitudes of people, and who shall examine the doctrines of all books before they be published. [. . .] And though in matter of doctrine nothing ought to be regarded but the truth; yet this is not repugnant to regulating of the same by peace. For doctrine repugnant to peace can no more be true than peace and concord can be against the law of nature. [. . .] Yet the most sudden and rough bustling in of a new truth that can be does never break the peace, but only sometimes awakes the war. For those men that are so remissly governed that they dare take

up arms to defend or introduce an opinion are still in war; and their condition not peace, but only a cessation of arms for fear of one another; and they live, as it were, in the precincts of battle continually. It belongeth therefore to him that hath the sovereign power to be judge, or constitute all judges of opinions and doctrines, as a thing necessary to peace, thereby to prevent discord and civil war.

10. Seventhly, is annexed to the sovereignty the whole power of prescribing the rules whereby every man may know what goods he may enjoy and what actions he may do without being molested by any of his fellow subjects; and this is it men call *propriety* [*property*]. [. . .] These rules of propriety (or *meum* and *tuum*) and of *good, evil, lawful,* and *unlawful* in the actions of subjects are the civil laws, that is to say, the laws of each commonwealth in particular. [. . .]

11. Eighthly, is annexed to the sovereignty the right of judicature, that is to say, of hearing and deciding all controversies which may arise concerning law, either civil or natural, or concerning fact. [. . .]

12. Ninthly, is annexed to the sovereignty the right of making war and peace with other nations and commonwealths, that is to say, of judging when it is for the public good, and how great forces are to be assembled, armed, and paid for that end, and to levy money upon the subjects to defray the expenses thereof. [. . .]

13. Tenthly, is annexed to the sovereignty the choosing of all counsellors, ministers, magistrates, and officers, both in peace and war. [. . .]

14. Eleventhly, to the sovereign is committed the power of rewarding with riches or honour and of punishing with corporal or pecuniary punishment or with ignominy [disgrace], every subject according to the law he hath formerly made. [. . .]

[. . .]

Chapter XX
Of Dominion Paternal and Despotical

1. A commonwealth *by acquisition* is that where the sovereign power is acquired by force; and it is acquired by force when men singly, or many together by plurality of voices, for fear of death or bonds, do authorize all the actions of that man or assembly that hath their lives and liberty in his power.

2. And this kind of dominion or sovereignty differeth from sovereignty by institution only in this, that men who choose their sovereign do it for fear of one another and not of him whom they institute; but in this case, they subject themselves to him they are afraid of. In both cases they do it for fear; which is to be noted by them that hold all such covenants, as proceed from fear of death or violence, void; which, if it were true, no man in any kind of commonwealth could be obliged to obedience. It is true that in a commonwealth once instituted or acquired, promises proceeding from fear of death or violence are no covenants nor obliging when the thing promised is contrary to the laws; but the reason is not because it was made upon fear, but because he that promiseth hath no right in the thing promised. Also, when he may lawfully perform and doth not, it is not the invalidity of the covenant that absolveth him, but the sentence of the sovereign. Otherwise, whensoever a man lawfully promiseth, he unlawfully breaketh; but when the sovereign, who is the actor, acquitteth him, then he is acquitted by him that extorted the promise, as by the author of such absolution.

3. But the rights and consequences of sovereignty are the same in both. His power cannot without his consent be transferred to another; he cannot forfeit it; he cannot be accused by any of his subjects of injury; he cannot be punished by them; he is judge of what is necessary for peace and judge of doctrines; he is sole legislator and supreme judge of controversies and of the times and occasions of war and peace; to him it belongeth to choose magistrates, counselors, commanders, and all other officers and ministers, and to determine of rewards and punishments, honour and order. The reasons whereof are the same which are alleged in the precedent chapter for the same rights and consequences of sovereignty by institution.

21

Samuel Pufendorf, *On the Duty of Man and Citizen*

One of Hobbes's begrudging admirers was Baron Samuel Pufendorf (1632–94), who tried to domesticate Hobbes's view. Pufendorf, born in Saxony, studied at the University of Lund, in Sweden, and the University of Jena, where he received a master's degree in 1656. In 1658 he wrote his first treatise on natural law, *Elements of Universal Jurisprudence*, while in prison because of a war between Sweden and Denmark. (He was the tutor to the children of the Swedish ambassador to Denmark.) He began to teach law in the Faculty of Philosophy at the University of Heidelberg in 1661.

In 1670 he became Professor of Natural Law and International Law at the University of Lund. Two years later he published the magnificent *On the Law of Nature and Nations*. In the following year, he published an abridgment of it, *On the Duty of Man and Citizen*, which is excerpted in this section. In 1677 he was appointed privy councillor, secretary of state, and royal historian to Charles XI of Sweden. Important publications continued to flow from his pen: *Introduction to the History of the Principal Realms and States as They Currently Exist in Europe* (1682), *On the Nature of Religion in Relation to Civil Life* (1687), and *The Law of Covenants, or on the Consensus and Dissensus among Protestants* (1689).

In 1688 he became privy and judicial councillor to Frederick William I of Prussia, and later to Frederick III. In 1694 he was made baron by Charles X of Sweden; he died on the trip back to Prussia later that year.

In *On the Duty of Man and Citizen*, Pufendorf restricts human actions to those actions that distinguish humans from brute animals, in effect, those that depend on "the will." Because each person's actions are sometimes in conflict with each other, not to mention in conflict with those of other people, law is needed to achieve "order and decency." By law, Pufendorf means "a decree by which a superior obliges one who is subject to him to conform his actions to the superior prescript." Obligation is "a bond of right by which we are constrained." It places "a kind of bridle on our liberty." Humans are subject to obligations because they understand what is demanded of them, and can control their behavior by their will.

A complete law has two parts: a part that states what is to be done and a part that states the punishment for not obeying the law. Actions that accord with law are good and those that break the law are bad.

Pufendorf explains the misery of the natural condition of human beings as the result of their weakness. If a human being grew up without the help of other people, he would be "a more miserable animal, without speech presumably and naked." He calls this "the natural state of man." People need people in order to flourish. Unfortunately, humans have "a greater tendency to do harm than any of the beasts" and are susceptible to greed, avarice, envy, and rivalry. In order to be safe, people need to be sociable. These laws of sociality are the natural laws, and the "fundamental natural law" is that "every man ought to do as much as he can to cultivate sociality."

The natural state of man as it actually exists shows each man joined with others but having nothing in common with them and "having no duty to them." After humans multiplied, they "recognized the disadvantages of life apart" and began to form small states. Natural law teaches people to refrain from fighting, but it cannot guarantee security because some people who see a profit to be made or "who have confidence in their own strength or cunning" will violate it. Divine punishment works too slowly to be an effective deterrent. The only solution to the miseries of the natural state is for each person to "submit his will to the will of one man or one assembly," and to take the will of that person or assembly as the will of each and all of them in matters that concern common security. The civil state gets its power from the strength that each citizen contributes to the enforcement of its laws. The civil state, then, is "conceived as one person, and is separated and distinguished from all particular men by a unique name; and it has its own special rights and property."

This account of the civil state, Pufendorf insists, does not imply that civil authority is independent of God, for God wants all men to obey natural law, and the best way to get people to obey it is through the civil state. By the principle that whoever commands the end commands "the necessary means to that end," God is understood to have commanded the establishment of civil states.

Book I

1
On Human Action

1. By 'duty' [*officium*] here I mean human action in conformity with the commands of law on the ground of obligation. To explain this, one must first discuss the nature of human action and the nature of laws in general.
2. By 'human action' I do not mean any motion which has its origin in man's faculties [*facultas*] but only such as is begun and directed by the faculties which the great and good Creator has given to mankind above and beyond the animals. I mean motion initiated in the light of understanding and at the command of will.

[. . .]

2
On the Rule of Human Actions, or On Law in General

1. Human actions arise from the will. But the acts of will of an individual are not consistent in themselves; and the wills of different men tend in different directions. For mankind to have achieved order and decency therefore, there must have been some rule to which those

wills might conform. For otherwise if each man, amid so much liberty to will and such diversity of inclinations and desires, had done whatever came into his mind without reflective reference to a fixed rule, the result would inevitably have been great confusion among men.
2. This rule is called law [*lex*]. Law is a decree by which a superior obliges one who is subject to him to conform his actions to the superior's prescript [*praescriptum*].
3. To understand this definition better, one must answer these questions: what is obligation? what is its origin? who can incur obligation, and who can impose obligation on another?

Obligation is commonly defined as a bond of right by which we are constrained by the necessity of making some performance. That is, obligation places a kind of bridle on our liberty, so that, though the will can in fact take different directions it yet finds itself imbued by it with an internal sense (so to speak), so that it is compelled to recognize that it has not acted rightly if the subsequent action does not conform to the prescribed rule. Consequently, if anything bad happens to a man for that reason, he judges that he deserves it, since he could have avoided it by following the rule, as he should have done.
4. There are two reasons why man is fit to incur obligation: (1) he has a will capable of moving in various directions and so able to conform to the rule; and (2) he is not free from the authority of a superior. For there is no expectation of free action where an agent's powers are tied by nature to a uniform mode of behaviour; and it is pointless to prescribe a rule to one who can neither understand nor conform to it. It follows therefore that one is capable of obligation if he has a superior, if he can recognize a prescribed rule and if he has a will which is capable of taking different directions, yet (when a rule has been prescribed by a superior) is imbued with the sense that it may not rightly deviate from it. With such a nature, it is evident, man is endowed.
5. An obligation is introduced into a man's mind by a superior, by one who has not only the strength to inflict some injury on the recalcitrant, but also just cause to require us to curtail the liberty of our will at his discretion. When a person in this position has signified his will, fear tempered by respect [*reverentia*] must arise in a man's mind [*animus*] – fear from power, respect from reflection on the reasons which ought to induce one to accept his will even apart from fear. For anyone who can give no reason except mere strength why he will impose an obligation upon me against my will can indeed terrify me, so that I think it better [*satius*] to obey him for the time being to avoid a greater evil, but when the threat is gone, nothing any longer prevents me from acting at my discretion rather than his. On the other hand, if a person has reasons why I should obey him but lacks the strength to inflict injury on me, I can disregard his orders with impunity, unless one more powerful than he comes to assert the authority I have flouted.

The reasons which justify a person's claim to another's obedience are: if he has conferred exceptional benefits on him; if it is evident that he wishes the other well and can look out for him better than he can for himself; if at the same time he actually claims direction of him; and, finally, if the other party has voluntarily submitted to him and accepted his direction.
6. For the law to exert its force in the minds to whom it applies, there must be knowledge of who the legislator is and of what the law itself is. For no one will offer obedience not knowing whom he should obey or what he is obliged to do.

[. . .]

7. Every complete law has two parts: the one part in which what is to be done or not done is defined, and the other which declares the punishment prescribed for one who ignores a

precept or does what is forbidden. For because of the wickedness of human nature which loves to do what is forbidden, it is utterly useless to say 'Do this!' if no evil awaits him who does not, and similarly, it is absurd to say, 'You will be punished', without first specifying what deserves the punishment.

So then the whole force of the law consists in making known what the superior wants us to do or not to do, and the penalty set for violators. The power of creating an obligation, that is, of imposing an internal necessity, and the power to compel or to enforce observance of the laws by means of penalties, lie properly with the legislator and with him to whom the protection and execution of the laws is committed.

[. . .]

10. Equity [. . .] is a correction of the law where law is deficient through its universality; or a skilful interpretation of the law by which it is shown from natural reason that some particular case is not covered by a general law since an absurd situation would result if it were. Not all cases can be foreseen or expressly provided for because of their infinite variety. Hence judges, who have the task of applying the general provisions of a law to particular cases, must except from the law the sort of cases that the legislator would have excepted if he had been present or if he had foreseen such cases.

11. [. . .] Actions in accordance with law are called good [*bonus*]; contrary to law bad [*malus*]. For an action to be good, it must be totally in accordance with law; for an action to be bad, it need only be deficient at a single point.

12. Justice is sometimes an attribute of actions, sometimes of persons. When justice is ascribed to a person, it is usually defined as a constant and unremitting will to render to each his own. The just man is defined as one who delights in doing just actions or strives after justice or attempts in everything to do what is just. The unjust man, by contrast, is he who neglects to render each his own, or who thinks that the criterion should be not his duty but his own immediate advantage. Consequently some of a just man's actions may be unjust and vice versa. For the just man does justice because of the law's command and injustice only through weakness; whereas the unjust man does justice because of the penalty attached to the law and injustice through the wickedness of his heart.

13. Justice as an attribute of actions is simply the appropriate fitting of actions to persons. And a just action is one which is done to the person to whom it is appropriate to do it by deliberate choice or with knowledge and intention. Thus the major difference in the case of actions between justice and goodness is that goodness denotes merely conformity with the law whereas justice involves in addition a relationship to those in respect of whom the action is done. This is also the reason why justice is said to be a virtue in respect of another person.

[. . .]

3
On Natural Law

1. What is the character of natural law? What is its necessity? And in what precepts does it consist in the actual condition of mankind? These questions are most clearly answered by a close scrutiny of the nature and character of man. [. . .]

2. In common with all living things which have a sense of themselves, man holds nothing more dear than himself, he studies in every way to preserve himself, he strives to acquire what seems good to him and to repel what seems bad to him. This passion is usually so strong that all other passions give way before it. And if anyone attempts to attack a man's safety, he cannot fail to repel him, and to repel him so vigorously that hatred and desire for revenge usually last long after he has beaten off the attack.
3. On the other hand man now seems to be in a worse condition than the beasts in that scarcely any other animal is attended from birth with such weakness [*imbecillitas*]. [. . .] Let us imagine a man coming to adult years without any care and fostering from other men. He would have no knowledge except what has sprung by a kind of spontaneous generation from his own intelligence. He would be in solitude, destitute of all the help and company of others. Evidently, one will scarcely find a more miserable animal, without speech presumably and naked, who has no resource but to tear at grass and roots or to pick wild fruits, to slake his thirst at the spring or river or from the puddle in his path, to seek shelter in caves from the assaults of the storm or to protect his body as best he may with moss or grass. Time would pass most tediously with nothing to do; at every noise or approach of another animal he would start in terror; and would at last die of hunger or cold or in the jaws of a wild beast.

By contrast, all the advantages that attend human life today derive from men's mutual assistance. There is nothing in this world, save the great and good God Himself, from which greater advantage can come to man than from man himself.
4. But this animal which is so mutually helpful suffers from a number of vices and is endowed with a considerable capacity for harm. His vices render dealing with him risky and make great caution necessary to avoid receiving evil from him instead of good.

In the first place, he is seen to have a greater tendency to do harm than any of the beasts. [. . .] Nature has provided that the beasts should not need clothes; but man delights in being clothed for ostentation as well as from necessity. Many other passions and desires are found in the human race unknown to the beasts, as, greed for unnecessary possessions, avarice, desire of glory and of surpassing others, envy, rivalry and intellectual strife. It is indicative that many of the wars by which the human race is broken and bruised are waged for reasons unknown to the beasts. And all these things can and do incite men to inflict harm on each other. There is moreover in many men a kind of extraordinary petulance, a passion for insulting others, at which others cannot fail to be offended and to gird themselves to resist, however restrained their natural temper, in order to preserve and protect their persons and their liberty. Sometimes too men are incited to mutual injury by want and because their actual resources are not adequate to their desires or their need.
5. Men's capacity for mutual infliction of injury is also very powerful. [. . .] [T]heir mental ingenuity facilitates attack by cunning and stratagem where open assault is out of the question. And so it becomes very easy to inflict death, the worst of man's natural evils.

[. . .]

8. The laws of this sociality [*socialitas*], laws which teach one how to conduct oneself to become a useful [*commodum*] member of human society, are called natural laws.
9. On this basis it is evident that the fundamental natural law is: every man ought to do as much as he can to cultivate and preserve sociality.

[. . .]

Book II

1
On Men's Natural State

[. . .]

2. Men's state is either natural or adventitious. Natural state may be considered, in the light of reason alone, in three ways: in relation to God the Creator; or in the relation of each individual man to himself; or in relation to other men.
3. Considered from the first point of view, the natural state of man is the condition in which he was placed by his Creator with the intention that he be an animal excelling other animals. It follows from this state that man should recognize and worship his Creator, admire His works, and lead his life in a manner utterly different from that of the animals. Hence this state is in complete contrast with the life and condition of the animals.
4. From the second point of view, we may consider the natural state of man, by an imaginative effort, as the condition man would have been in if he had been left to himself alone, without any support from other men, given the condition of human nature as we now perceive it. It would have been, it seems, more miserable than that of any beast, if we reflect on the great weakness of man as he comes into this world, when he would straight away die without help from others, and on the primitive life he would lead if he had no other resources than he owes to his own strength and intelligence. One may put it more strongly: the fact that we have been able to grow out of such weakness, the fact that we now enjoy innumerable good things, the fact that we have cultivated our minds and bodies for our own and others' benefit – all this is the result of help from others. In this sense the natural state is opposed to life improved by human industry.
5. From the third point of view, we consider the natural state of man in terms of the relationship which men are understood to have with each other on the basis of the simple common kinship which results from similarity of nature and is antecedent to any agreement or human action by which particular obligations of one to another have arisen. In this sense men are said to live in a natural state with each other when they have no common master, when no one is subject to another and when they have no experience either of benefit or of injury from each other. In this sense the natural state is opposed to the civil state.
6. The character of the natural state, furthermore, may be considered either as it is represented by fiction or as it is in reality. It would be a fiction if we supposed that in the beginning there existed a multitude of men without any dependence on each other, as in the myth of the brothers of Cadmus, or if we imagined that the whole human race was so widely scattered that every man governed himself separately, and the only bond between them was likeness of nature. But the natural state which actually exists shows each man joined with a number of other men in a particular association, though having nothing in common with all the rest except the quality of being human and having no duty to them on any other ground. This is the condition [*status*] that now exists between different states [*civitas*] and between citizens of different countries [*respublica*], and which formerly obtained between heads of separate families.
7. Indeed it is obvious that the whole human race was never at one and the same time in the natural state. The children of our first parents, from whom the Holy Scriptures teach that all mortal men take their origin, were subject to the same paternal authority [*patria potestas*].

[. . .] and the special bond of kinship, and the affection that goes with it, gradually withered away leaving only that common element that results from similarity of nature. The human race then multiplied remarkably; men recognized the disadvantages of life apart; and gradually, those who lived close to each other drew together, at first in small states [*civitates*], then in larger states as the smaller coalesced, freely or by force. Among these states the natural state [*status*] still certainly exists; their only bond is their common humanity.
8. The principal law of those who live in the natural state is to be subject only to God and answerable to none but Him.

[. . .]

9. The state of nature may seem extraordinarily attractive in promising liberty and freedom from all subjection. But in fact before men submit to living in states, it is attended with a multitude of disadvantages, whether we imagine individuals existing in that state or consider the condition of separate heads of households. [. . .] [Y]ou will see a naked dumb animal, without resources, seeking to satisfy his hunger with roots and grasses and his thirst with whatever water he can find, to shelter himself from the inclemencies of the weather in caves, at the mercy of wild beasts, fearful of every chance encounter. Those who were members of scattered families may have enjoyed a somewhat more developed way of life but in no way comparable with civil life; and this not so much because of poverty, which the family (where desires are limited) seems capable of relieving, as because it can do little to ensure security. To put the matter in a few words, in the state of nature each is protected only by his own strength; in the state by the strength of all. There no one may be sure of the fruit of his industry; here all may be. There is the reign of the passions, there is war, fear, poverty, nastiness, solitude, barbarity, ignorance, savagery; here is the reign of reason, here there is peace, security, wealth, splendour, society, taste, knowledge, benevolence.
10. In the natural state, if one does not do for another what is due by agreement, or does him wrong, or if a dispute arises in other ways, there is no one who can by authority compel the offender to perform his part of the agreement or make restitution, as is possible in states, where one may implore the aid of a common judge. But as nature does not allow one to plunge into war on the slightest provocation, even when one is fully convinced of the justice of his cause, an attempt must first be made to settle the matter by gentler means, namely, by friendly discussion between the parties and an absolute (not conditional) mutual promise or by appeal to the decision of arbitrators.

[. . .]

5
On the Impulsive Cause of Constituting the State

We cannot therefore infer directly from man's sociality [*socialitas*] that his nature tends precisely to civil society.

[. . .]

[T]he true and principal cause why heads of households abandoned their natural liberty and had recourse to the constitution of states was to build protection around themselves against the evils that threaten man from man. For just as, after God, man may do more good for his fellow-man than anything else, so he may do most harm. And they judge rightly of the evil of men, and the remedy of that evil, who formulated the saying: 'Without courts of law, men would devour each other.'

[. . .]

8. The cause of the constitution of states will become still clearer if we reflect that no other means would have been adequate to restrain the evil in man.

Admittedly, natural law teaches that men should refrain from all infliction of injuries. But respect for that law cannot guarantee a life in natural liberty with fair security. There may indeed be men of such good character that they would not want to wrong others even with a guarantee of impunity, others too who would somehow repress their desires through fear of consequent evil. However, there are also a great many men to whom laws mean nothing in the face of an expectation of profit, and who have confidence in their own strength or cunning to repel or elude their victims' vengeance.

[. . .]

9. [. . .] Divine vengeance tends to proceed at a slow pace; and this gives opportunity to the wicked among mankind to ascribe the sufferings of the impious to other causes, especially as they often see them abundantly provided with those things by which the vulgar measure happiness. There is also the fact that the stings of conscience which precede a crime do not seem to be as strong as those which follow it, when what has been done no longer can be undone. Truly the effective remedy for suppressing evil desires, the remedy perfectly fitted to the nature of man, is found in states.

6
On the Internal Structure of States

[. . .]

3. [. . .] [T]hose who have once consented to peace and mutual help for the common good must be prohibited from dissenting thereafter, whenever their own private good seems to be in conflict with the public good.

[. . .]

5. The only means by which the wills of many may be united is that each submit his will to the will of one man or one assembly, in such a way that from that time on whatever that man or that assembly wills in what concerns the common security be taken as the will of all and everyone.

6. Similarly, such a power as all men may fear can only be constituted among a number of men if each and every one [*omnes & singuli*] obliges himself to use his force as he shall determine to whom all have resigned the direction of their forces.

Only when they have achieved a union of wills and forces is a multitude of men brought to life as a corporate body stronger than any other body, namely a state [*civitas*].

[. . .]

10. A state so constituted is conceived as one person [*persona*], and is separated and distinguished from all particular men by a unique name; and it has its own special rights and property, which no one man, no multitude of men, nor even all men together, may appropriate apart from him who holds the sovereign power or to whom the government of the state has been committed. Hence a state is defined as a composite moral person, whose will blended and combined from the agreement of many is taken as the will of all so that it may employ the forces and capacities of every individual for the common peace and security.
11. The will of the state as the principle of public actions expresses itself either through one man or through one assembly, according as supremacy has been conferred on the one or the other. When the government of the state is in the hands of one man, the state is understood to will whatever he has decided (assuming that he is sane) in anything within the purpose of a state.

[. . .]

14. This account of the origin of states does not imply that civil authority [*imperium civile*] is not rightly said to be of God. For God wills that all men practise natural law, but with the multiplication of mankind such a horrid life was likely to ensue for men that there would scarcely have been a place left for natural law. It is the institution of states which most favours the practice of natural law. And therefore (since he who commands the end is held also to command the necessary means to that end), God too, is understood to have given prior command to the human race, mediated through the dictates of reason, that when it had multiplied, states should be constituted, which are so to speak brought to life by sovereign power. In the Holy Scriptures too He expressly gives His approval to their order and assures the sanctity of that order by special laws and so demonstrates His particular concern for it.

7
On the Functions of the Sovereign Power

[. . .]

3. The over-riding purpose of states is that, by mutual cooperation and assistance, men may be safe from the losses and injuries which they may and often do inflict on each other.

Further Reading

A Note on Female Philosophers. The only female philosopher represented in the preceding selections is Princess Elizabeth of Bohemia. Two or three other women have some claim to be included. One is Margaret Cavendish. Another is Anne Conway. In the end, space would not permit including their work. Those who wish to learn more about them should read:

Cavendish, Margaret. 1994. *The Blazing World & Other Writings*, ed. Kate Lilley. London: Penguin Books.
Cavendish, Margaret. 2003. *Political Writings*, ed. Susan James. Cambridge: Cambridge University Press.
Conway, Anne. 1996. *Principles of the Most Ancient and Modern Philosophy*, tr. and ed. Allison Coudert. Cambridge: Cambridge University Press.
Kersey, Ethel, ed. 1989. *Woman Philosophers: A Bio-Critical Sourcebook*. New York: Greenwood Press.

SUGGESTED SECONDARY SOURCES

Note: The articles on individual seventeenth-century philosophers in the *Stanford Encyclopedia of Philosophy* <http://plato.stanford.edu/> are uniformly clear, comprehensive, and authoritative.

Cambridge University Press publishes an excellent series of books with titles of the form, *The Cambridge Companion to X*, where *X* is the name of a seventeenth-century philosopher. There are volumes for Descartes, Hobbes, Spinoza, Malebranche, and Leibniz. They are not included in the bibliography below.

GENERAL

Garber, Daniel, and Michael Ayers, eds. 1998. *The Cambridge Companion to Seventeenth-Century Philosophy*, 2 vols. Cambridge: Cambridge University Press.

PART I

Burtt, E. A. 1954. *The Metaphysical Foundations of Modern Science*. New York: Anchor Books.
Cohen, I. Bernard. 1985. *The Birth of a New Physics*. New York: W. W. Norton.
Force, James, and Richard Popkin. 1990. *Essays on the Context, Nature, and Influence of Isaac Newton's Theology*. Dordrecht: Kluwer Academic Publishers.
James, Susan. 1997. *Passion and Action: The Emotions in Seventeenth Century Philosophy*. Oxford: Clarendon Press.

Popkin, Richard. 2003. *The History of Scepticism: From Savonarola to Bayle*, revised and expanded edn. New York: Oxford University Press.

Sorell, Tom. 1986. *Hobbes*. London: Routledge.

Sorell, Tom, ed. 1993. *The Rise of Modern Philosophy*. Oxford: Clarendon Press.

PART II

Dicker, Georges. 1993. *Descartes: An Analytical and Historical Introduction*. New York: Oxford University Press.

Kenny, Anthony. 1968. *Descartes*. New York: Random House.

Williams, Bernard. 1990. *Descartes: The Project of Pure Inquiry*. London: Penguin Books.

Wilson, Margaret. 1978. *Descartes*. London: Routledge & Kegan Paul.

PART III

Curley, Edwin. 1988. *Behind the Geometrical Method: A Reading of Spinoza's Ethics*. Princeton: Princeton University Press.

Hooker, Michael. 1982. *Leibniz: Critical and Interpretive Essays*. Minneapolis: University of Minnesota Press.

Loeb, Louis. 1981. *From Descartes to Hume: Continental Metaphysics and the Development of Modern Philosophy*. Ithaca: Cornell University Press.

Mates, Benson. 1986. *The Philosophy of Leibniz: Metaphysics and Language*. New York: Oxford University Press.

Nadler, Stephen. 1999. *Spinoza: A Life*. Cambridge: Cambridge University Press.

Popkin, Richard. 2004. *Spinoza*. Oxford: Oneworld.

Von Leyden, W. 1968. *Seventeenth Century Metaphysics*. New York: Barnes & Noble.

Woolhouse, Roger. 1993. *The Concept of Substance in Seventeenth Century Metaphysics: Descartes, Spinoza, Leibniz*. London: Routledge.

PART IV

Martinich, A. P. 1995. *A Hobbes Dictionary*. Cambridge, MA: Blackwell.

Martinich, A. P. 1999. *Hobbes: A Biography*. Cambridge: Cambridge University Press.

Martinich, A. P. 2005. *Hobbes*. London: Routledge.

Skinner, Quentin. 1981. *Machiavelli*. New York: Oxford University Press.

Tarcov, Nathan, and Thomas Pangle. 1987. *History of Political Philosophy*, 3rd edn., ed. Leo Strauss and Joseph Cropsey. Chicago: University of Chicago Press, pp. 907–38.

Tuck, Richard. 1993. *Philosophy and Government, 1572–1651*. Cambridge: Cambridge University Press.

Index

Bold page numbers refer to complete selections.